M000216962

A NEW

VOCABULARY FOR

GLOBAL MODERNISM

Modernist Latitudes

Modernist Latitudes

Jessica Berman and Paul Saint-Amour, Editors

Modernist Latitudes aims to capture the energy and ferment of modernist studies by continuing to open up the range of forms, locations, temporalities, and theoretical approaches encompassed by the field. The series celebrates the growing latitude ("scope for freedom of action or thought") that this broadening affords scholars of modernism, whether they are investigating little-known works or revisiting canonical ones. Modernist Latitudes will pay particular attention to the texts and contexts of those latitudes (Africa, Latin America, Australia, Asia, Southern Europe, and even the rural United States) that have long been misrecognized as ancillary to the canonical modernisms of the global North.

Barry McCrea, *In the Company of Strangers: Family and Narrative in Dickens, Conan Doyle, Joyce, and Proust*, 2011

Jessica Berman, *Modernist Commitments: Ethics, Politics, and Transnational Modernism*, 2011

Jennifer Scappettone, *Killing the Moonlight: Modernism in Venice*, 2014

Nico Israel, *Spirals: The Whirled Image in Twentieth-Century Literature and Art*, 2015

Carrie Noland, *Voices of Negritude in Modernist Print: Aesthetic Subjectivity, Diaspora, and the Lyric Regime*, 2015

Susan Stanford Friedman, *Planetary Modernisms: Provocations on Modernity Across Time*, 2015

Steven S. Lee, *The Ethnic Avant-Garde: Minority Cultures and World Revolution*, 2015

Thomas S. Davis, *The Extinct Scene: Late Modernism and Everyday Life*, 2016

Carrie J. Preston, *Learning to Kneel: Noh, Modernism, and Journeys in Teaching*, 2016

Gayle Rogers, *Incomparable Empires: Modernism and the Translation of Spanish and American Literature*, 2016

Celia Marshik, *At the Mercy of Their Clothes: Modernism, the Middlebrow, and British Garment Culture*, 2016

Christopher Reed, *Bachelor Japanists: Japanese Aesthetics and Western Masculinities*, 2016

Donal Harris, *On Company Time: American Modernism in the Big Magazines*

Eric Bulson, *Little Magazine, World Form*, 2016

Aarthi Vadde, *Chimeras of Form: Modernist Internationalism Beyond Europe, 1914–2014*, 2016

A NEW

VOCABULARY FOR

GLOBAL MODERNISM

EDITED BY

ERIC HAYOT AND REBECCA L. WALKOWITZ

COLUMBIA UNIVERSITY PRESS

New York

COLUMBIA UNIVERSITY PRESS

Publishers Since 1893

NEW YORK   CHICHESTER, WEST SUSSEX

cup.columbia.edu

Copyright © 2016 Columbia University Press

All rights reserved

Library of Congress Cataloging-in-Publication Data

Names: Hayot, Eric, 1972– editor. | Walkowitz, Rebecca L., 1970– editor.

Title: A new vocabulary for global modernism / edited by Eric Hayot and Rebecca L. Walkowitz.

Description: New York : Columbia University Press, 2016. | Series: Modernist latitudes |
Includes bibliographical references and index.

Identifiers: LCCN 2016013382 (print) | LCCN 2016026280 (ebook) | ISBN 9780231165204
(cloth : alk. paper) | ISBN 9780231165211 (pbk. : alk. paper) | ISBN 9780231543064 (e-book)

Subjects: LCSH: Civilization, Modern—21st century. | Globalization—Social aspects. |
Modernism (Aesthetics)

Classification: LCC CB428 .N49 2016 (print) | LCC CB428 (ebook) | DDC 909—dc23

LC record available at https://lccn.loc.gov/2016013382

Columbia University Press books are printed on permanent and durable acid-free paper.

This book is printed on paper with recycled content.

Printed in the United States of America

COVER DESIGN: ARCHIE FERGUSON

CONTENTS

ACKNOWLEDGMENTS

We would like to thank all of our colleagues in the American Comparative Literature Association and the Modernist Studies Association, whose questions, ideas, and work have inspired this book. We're grateful to our contributors for so gamely entering into the project. *A New Vocabulary* would not have been possible without the intelligence and work of series editors Jessica Berman and Paul Saint-Amour and of Philip Leventhal at Columbia University Press. Eric says thank you to Lea; Rebecca says thank you to Henry.

A NEW

VOCABULARY FOR

GLOBAL MODERNISM

1. INTRODUCTION

ERIC HAYOT AND REBECCA L. WALKOWITZ

WHY THIS BOOK NOW?

A New Vocabulary for Global Modernism could not have been written ten years ago. It operates in the wake of the field's unprecedented expansion. Once focused exclusively on artworks produced in Europe and the United States, modernist studies now engages with aesthetic objects and expressive culture produced in spaces throughout the world. Hefty anthologies such as *The Oxford Handbook of Global Modernisms* and *The Oxford Handbook of Modernisms*, published in 2012 and 2010, respectively, introduce readers to the creativity of artists and intellectuals in Havana, Hanoi, and Helsinki as well as in London, Paris, and New York. *A New Vocabulary for Global Modernism* begins from the premise, established by these substantial reference works and by a series of ground-clearing essays that preceded them, that modernism was a world phenomenon.[1] Instead of describing more modernism, therefore, this collection shifts its attention to what we take to be a second but crucial labor. Our contributors ask what happens to the foundational concepts of modernism and to the methods we bring to modernist studies when we approach the field globally. *A New Vocabulary* brings together some of the most prominent critics thinking and writing at the intersection of world literature and modernist studies. Their essays open up the study of global modernism in two ways. The first way involves showing how the intellectual paradigms we've long associated with modernism—such as tradition, antiquity, style, classic, and translation—are transformed and how new paradigms—such as context, puppets, slum, copy, and pantomime—emerge when the archive extends beyond the European center. The second way explores how our methodologies change when we approach modernism comparatively and when we draw out modernism's own engagement with ideas of the world. This book thus adds to the archive of modernist works but also to the archive of works that imagine other worlds and other versions of the world.

A *New Vocabulary* is therefore not a reference but a user's manual. It is a set of instructions for entering into modernism from a global perspective and for entering into a global perspective from modernism. This difference, between sampling modernism and revising the organizing principles of modernism, has shaped the form of the object you have before you. Readers will notice, first of all, that the essays are organized by words rather than by geographies. A *New Vocabulary* does not accumulate distinctive national or regional traditions. It is not organized as a list or an atlas of located modernisms—modernism in Norway, modernism in India, modernism in Peru, and so on. Instead, each essay draws out connections across several geographies, often following an idea as it travels among various readers and writers and visual artists. So, for example, Judith Brown traces *style* as it moves from being an Orientalist term in European art criticism to a term deployed by "the Orient" itself and, thus, considers how Indian artists overtook and reshaped a concept that had implicitly excluded them. Martin Puchner lights on *puppets* to show that childhood, folklore, and cults—phenomena usually excluded from modernism—were at the heart of modernism's engagement with exoticism and images of the nonhuman. Puchner demonstrates that the European fascination with Asian puppetry was animated in part by a desire to diminish rather than extend human agency. Refining the usual claim that European artists used non-European devices to heighten their own sense of individualism while negating the individualism of others, Puchner argues that theater makers in the West turned to the East to imitate its models of antihumanism and that non-Western theater makers have used intercultural puppetry to generate novel forms of estrangement.

As these two essays intimate, the volume draws on the aesthetic practices of several continents, numerous languages, and many cultures. Readers will find discussions of novels, poetry, drama, performance, music, architecture, photography, film, and sculpture created throughout the world, including artworks that got their start in Argentina, Brazil, China, Egypt, France, Germany, India, Ireland, Japan, Kenya, Mexico, Russia, Senegal, South Africa, Turkey, the United Kingdom, and the United States. They will find analysis of materials produced originally in Arabic, Aramaic, Bengali, Chinese, English, Egyptian, French, German, Gikuyu, Greek, Hindi, Italian, Latin, Portuguese, Russian, Spanish, and Turkish. Yet, for all this diversity, the volume does not approach the global as a single or inert container. The essays describe the many different itineraries and rationales that have helped generate and distribute modernism. We've approached our project from the bottom up: *If you want to theorize modernism globally, you have to theorize modernism's ideas of the global.* The "global" is never some fixed center around which other ideas revolve (even when it is conceived that way); it is instead a shifting concept of fixity and centrality, a set of claims made about the world (another concept) and how it works, whose force depends in every case on the situation and context of its elaboration. Understanding the "global" in/and/of modernism thus means discovering the language of the global as it operates, sometimes only locally and sometimes variously in many locales, throughout well-known as well as newly visible modernist works. Readers may also notice that the language of the global goes well beyond English. Many of our contributors approach global modernism from the perspective of artworks that have operated, at least in part, in relatively local languages. Narrating modernism's global actors, origins, energies, and critical frameworks, these essays invite us to imagine new literary histories. *A New Vocabulary* is thus a companion to an emergent field. Contributors offer self-consciously revisionist interpretations that provide readers with an alternative way of thinking about what modernism was and is.

In addition to the absence of spatial markers, readers may notice among our collection of words the absence of contemporary critical markers such as race, class, gender, empire, sexuality, and disability. These frameworks, which have been crucial to the intellectual work of the past several decades and to the scholarship that helped make Europe one space among many, are certainly present in this book.[2] In particular, *A New Vocabulary* is indebted to the postcolonial critique of Eurocentrism (Europe as the self-generating origin of aesthetic innovation), diffusion (the idea that modernism began in the West and then moved to Rest), and parity (the world modeled as an abstract distribution of equivalent nations). The concepts gathered in this volume are made possible by that critique. However, our essays route their global approaches through the language of modernist practices, institutions, and aesthetic categories. Instead of thinking about the global through paradigms that have operated at the same worldly scale, the essays in this volume recalibrate older and flatter paradigms (those that have appeared to be universal to modernism) and fashion new paradigms from materials that have seemed unworldly because too small or too abstract or, indeed, too local. Highlighting formal or aesthetic properties, contributors are engaged in a process of defamiliarization: showing how concepts that seem generic to (all) modernism have global origins or implications and developing fresh concepts drawn from modernism's expanded archive.

Readers interested in contemporary frameworks can nevertheless use the volume to consider how global modernism alters or refines those terms. Monica Miller's treatment of *pantomime*, for example, shows how contemporary African and African American visual artists reflect on the geopolitical and aesthetic history of race by engaging with the modernist figure of the black-and-white harlequin/mime. Miller uses the global phenomenon of the *pantomime*—not only its ubiquity but also its divergent uses—to rethink the more typically regional history of masks and mimicry within U.S. literary and visual culture. Christopher Reed's essay on *alienation* approaches race and imperialism from the perspective of Japanism (the vogue for Japanese art and culture within Europe and the United States). Reed shows how *alienation* allowed artists marginalized by their sexuality to make new versions of home by cultivating the foreignness they imagined elsewhere. Reed's essay takes up what appears to be a structural or formal principle of modernism and shows how it was used to project and imagine specific ways of being in the world. In a similar way, Tsitsi Jaji argues that intellectuals of African heritage, such as the British–Sierra Leonean composer Samuel Coleridge-Taylor and the Batswana–South African linguist and writer Solomon Tshekisho Plaatje, made the concept of the *classic* into a "curatorial procedure." She shows how these artists standardized the vernacular and vernacularized the standard, putting virtuosity in service to black transnationalism. What we notice in each of these cases is the testing and refining of modernism's foundational concepts against new examples and archives and, at the same time, an effort to make those concepts newly useful for global approaches to the field. Earlier versions of concepts continue to function, but they no longer exhaust all possible meanings and uses: *pantomime, alienation,* and *classic,* to follow just the examples we have introduced thus far, operate in alternative ways once we look beyond the dominant spaces, languages, and actors in which we have known them. This is why modernism changes when we shift its geographic and linguistic ambit: because the concepts mean something new, because we need new concepts.

HOW TO USE THIS BOOK

Why a *vocabulary*? We considered alternatives. One was "keywords," a term made famous by Raymond Williams, whose analysis of the language of everyday life via terms like "culture," "society," and "class" revealed the vast icebergs of ideology that sustain ordinary discourse. But "keywords" are (to be a bit obvious about things) already "key," steeped in advance in the stuff of culture and so in need of unpacking and illumination. Many of the words in this new vocabulary are not so crucial or so established. They have never grounded a universal theory of the modernist, and we do not intend them to do so here. Instead, these words cut diagonally across the ways we have thought modernism until now, slicing the centers and the margins into new configurations.

We considered calling the book a "dictionary" of global modernism instead. But a dictionary is a report on language as it's used, a codification of existing practices. In the long run a dictionary functions, too, as a guide to future use. A dictionary aims for a completeness; it elaborates the whole of a language, performs a total circuit of a conceptual field (*The Dictionary of Obscure Sorrows*, for example). Neither of those goals—the codification of existing practice or the encirclement of an established whole—was the right one for this book.

A vocabulary, then. These words are new, emergent, unestablished, or old, odd, out of fashion. They ostentatiously do not belong to the general list of terms that govern the study of modernism today. Some of the terms are practically preconceptual. Words like *slum, puppets, animal,* or *obsolescence* have never had any currency in modernist scholarship: too small, too located in a specific set of examples, they seem unable to generate a theoretical approach to the field as a whole. Other words had currency once and lost it: *classic, tradition,* and *antiquity,* for instance, have conceptual inheritances decades or even centuries old. Having fallen out of common use, they indicate in contemporary use a mode of thought—"what is tradition?" "how can we know whether something is a classic?"—that functions mainly as the object of critical thinking and never as a ground. To reverse that polarity, to think of something like antiquity as a concept that modernism thinks not just about but through, is one of the tasks of this book.

Still other words here—*war, library, alienation, form*—have developed some contemporary critical value in the context of an earlier modernist studies. They feel somehow prior to, or made obsolete by, the recent shift toward the global, which renders them too narrow, too European, too enraptured by the aesthetic. Yet if we begin again from them, abandoning the sense that we already know what something like "form" means in the modernist context, we find, as Jahan Ramazani does here, that new meanings emerge. Passing through the diffusionist model of literary production emblematized by Franco Moretti's phrase "foreign form, local content," Ramazani finds in *form* not only a new (and more global) modernism but also a new (and less provincial) theory of literature's transnational production.

In this way, Ramazani's essay defamiliarizes the common use of *form* within modernist studies and defamiliarizes modernist studies in turn, thereby modeling the more general practice of the book. This shift from the word to the field, the former allowing for a new perspective on the latter, is what generates the newness of the vocabulary here, whether the words in question begin as "new" to us or not. In being used these ways the words reveal a new version of what we thought we knew all along, in a world in which what we "know" includes, always in advance, that we're using the right vocabulary for the job. These essays aim to destabilize that knowledge.

This explains, we think, some of the flatness or literalness of the choices our authors have made. Take *war* or *alienation*. "Everyone" knows that the old European modernism had something to do with both. But of course that knowledge is only partial because behind the usual use of a word like "war" (in relation to modernism) it will turn out that we have tended to mean mainly one war, the Great War—because we "knew" that modernism began in Europe—and not any of the other wars going on at roughly the same time, elsewhere in the world, which generated their own local responses. Or, for that matter, we might consider the responses in those other places to Europe's Great War, which was, as Mariano Siskind shows us, a "world" war before it was called a "world" war (two useful comparatives here include the Sino-Japanese War of 1894–1895 and the Russo-Japanese War a decade later). Likewise, *alienation*, as Christopher Reed demonstrates, goes quickly from being a matter of aesthetic concern to being fully imbricated with the geographic as soon as one is willing to take seriously the erotics of travel or the forms of mutual pleasure and affiliation that bind the "appropriating" culture to what it "appropriates" (the term, Reed shows, is too simply used). In neither case is it a question of showing how a "nonglobal" term becomes global in the right hands but rather of showing that if one simply begins from a fairly simple-minded reading of a word, in which "war" is not code for one particular war and "alienation" is not code for only one limited kind of alienation, one finds that the global was there (in modernism, everywhere) all along. This, too, is one of the larger arguments of the book: that the global in modernism is not something that one has to be smarter or cleverer than anyone else to seek out and identify, something that requires special tools or a kind of extra effort on top of the effort that "nonglobal" modernism demands. Rather, it is enough simply to relax one's focus for a moment, to be slightly less clever than we have been so far, in order to see that there is no "modernism" without the global in it and that a literal reading of many of modernism's major concepts (including, say, "style" or "form") will get you to a modernism about which one does not have to ask, anymore, whether it is global or not since the two concepts are so clearly intertwined from their mutually constitutive beginnings.

Why, then, do we need the phrase "global modernism" at all? If the global is there from the beginning—if it appears in the active practice of modernism as it translates, travels, and otherwise generates itself from the interaction between the local and the regional, the local and the foreign, the local and the global, or if, more theoretically, we think of modernism as a particular kind of response to a modernity defined as a novel experience of the globe as such—then why not just use the term "modernism," allow the global to be understood as always already present there, and be done with it? Actually, that's one of the endpoints of the project of this book, a project that we and our contributors have been engaged in together in a variety of ways for the last two decades. But we are not there yet. We're getting there, but we're not there yet. Hence, while we wait, but only for now, we will speak of *global* modernism to indicate that the force of the adjective is still needed as a contrast for some other more local or "normal" modernism imagined to be not so, or not at all, global. But for us the question is already decided. We are not asking, was modernism global? It was and is, in theory and in practice. The concepts that point us to this globalism are not, then, just spatial or linguistic terms like "planet" or "world" or even (to pick a term from this volume) "translation." Global concepts are also "copy" or "antiquity" or "puppets." It is not therefore simply a question of saying modernism happened all over the world. It did, but the point is that in local instances of modernism we will find the traces of world thinking and world imagining that both respond to specifically global pressures (colonialism, trade, war) and, taking up the important imaginative task of the aesthetic, *anticipate* into being the structures of feeling that will come to help make sense of and shape the world we live in. These versions of the global are, inevitably, different. Though they may overlap, the global that emerges through the lens of "animal" is not the one that emerges through the lens of "context." The global is multiply produced, multiply imagined, and these productions and imaginations take place not in a worldless vacuum but in a context that teems with varieties of large- and small-scale spatial and historical concepts that help generate ideas like the worldly or the global but also, dialectically and oppositionally, concepts like the partial or the local or the small.

More than one global, then. But still one modernism. Weakly defined, fluid, internally differentiated, this modernism is nonetheless singular, we claim, insofar as it corresponds to a set of historical circumstances that have not happened exactly this way before and that have carried in their wake a variety of social changes (capitalism, secularization, modernity) that, for now, seem to define a period and a state of affairs. We imagine modernism to be a reaction to the various points of intersection between that state of affairs and the local conditions of its production; the interaction between those conditions and the state, the small and the large, passes through a variety of other spatial and temporal scales—the year, the decade, the century, or the neighborhood, the city, the nation, the continent—on the way from its alpha to its omega. The omega—the "globe," the world considered as a coherent, interlocking, and fully transactable, crossable whole—helps define the system as such, but it does not do so alone and does not, cannot, do so definitively. Instead, the omega, the modern world-picture, is remade every time in relation to the moment, the text, or the work that imagines it. At least as much is made visible in this collection of essays, which gives us sixteen words but also sixteen relationships between the local and the global, the small and the large, each of which amounts to a partial view of some larger describable whole called modernism, which we are still only beginning, after a century and more, to understand.

WHAT'S NEXT

Categories operate through social activity. Use reifies them into abstractions, at which point they seem to emerge by themselves rather than from a series of linked practices. Looking at one specific form of social practice, the use of language, thus allows us to create a genealogy for the categories through which we think and reveals those categories as tools to be remade. Making or remaking vocabulary, then, shows us how categories work and invites us to open up those categories to new and future meanings.

If one does not want to claim a certain lexical completeness—and we don't—then one would be well advised to think of this collection of words as merely "vocabulary" and not "a vocabulary," as a set of words bound by no closing declaration or parenthesis. The words are not arbitrary or aren't so in any simple way: they're the best words we and the writers collected here could come up with, for now, given what we know and how we work. Other words fell, here and there, by the wayside. But only *this* wayside. Other writers, other readers, will make other roads, for which this book will function as one of many waysides, for which the slant ambition of this project, to remake modernism from a variety of sideways, will itself be slanted, detoured, or refracted or even—why not?—unreadable or ignored.

That possibility captures the slightly contradictory ambition of this book. On the one hand, we want to suggest that these concepts are part of a single whole, the project of ~~global~~ modernism, and that they are needed to help replace or extend existing vocabularies. On the other, we want to assert, despite the necessary finitude of *this* book, that the expanded lexicon we are imagining is not yet established and that it ought to be thought of as a future whole or, rather, a whole whose wholeness is infinitely deferred into a future that extends well beyond anything even imagined here. To contribute to that project, we have included at the end of this volume a partial list of "more vocabulary" to which we and our contributors imagine you adding. It's a partial list because we hope you'll extend it and because we know new words will emerge in the course of modernism's revision. We thus invite you to inhabit and to learn from our concepts but also to upend them, to alter them for your private use, and, most importantly, to change and perhaps someday (even someday soon) replace them with words of your own.

New York and State College, September 2015

NOTES

1. Chief among those essays are Susan Stanford Friedman, "Periodizing Modernism" and "Planetarity"; the essays collected in Caughie, *Disciplining Modernism*;

the essays collected in Doyle and Winkiel, eds., *Geomodernisms*; and the essays collected in a special issue on "Modernism and Transnationalisms" in *Modernism/modernity*, the flagship journal for the field of modernist studies.

2. The most well-known critique of the "diffusion" model, in which Europe was the source of modernity, is *Provincializing Europe*.

WORKS CITED

Brooker, Peter, Andrzej Gasiorek, Deborah Longworth, and Andrew Thacker, eds. *The Oxford Handbook of Modernisms*. Oxford: Oxford University Press, 2010.

Caughie, Pamela L. *Disciplining Modernism*. Basingstoke: Palgrave Macmillan, 2009.

Chakrabarty, Dipesh. *Provincializing Europe: Postcolonial Thought and Historical Difference*. Princeton, N.J.: Princeton University Press, 2000.

Doyle, Laura, and Laura Winkiel, eds. *Geomodernisms: Race, Modernism, Modernity*. Bloomington: Indiana University Press, 2005.

Friedman, Susan Stanford. "Periodizing Modernism: Postcolonial Modernities and the Space/Time Borders of Modernist Studies." *Modernism/modernity* 13, no. 3 (2006): 425–443.

Friedman, Susan Stanford. "Planetarity: Musing Modernist Studies." *Modernism/modernity* 17, no. 3 (2010): 471–499.

"Modernism and Transnationalisms." *Modernism/modernity* 13, no. 3 (2006).

Wolleager, Mark, ed., with Matt Eatough. *The Oxford Handbook of Global Modernisms*. New York: Oxford University Press, 2012.

2. ALIENATION

CHRISTOPHER REED

Far from a unique and heroic vanguard of individuals, the avant-garde, from this demystifying perspective, is recognized as participating within and among other collective forms of alienation that call for historical acknowledgment and structural analysis.

Lines often treated as boundaries that separate identities conceived as binaries might better be seen as cables linking various contingents as they trace the contours of religious conversion, class consciousness, environmental activism, gender politics, sexual orientation—all complex formations of alienation that have provoked dynamics of identification and appropriation around the globe.

Doing triple duty as a noun, an adjective, and (uncommonly) a verb, "alien" denotes, respectively, a foreigner, foreignness, and the act of estrangement. "Alienation" is thus central to the idea of the "global," a rubric defined by the juxtaposition of people and places conceived as alien to one another because of their different positions on the terrestrial globe and/or united on a planet made coherent by the imagined perspective of "aliens" from outer space. As deeply imbricated as conceptions of the alien and the global are, ideas of "alienation" may be even more embedded in definitions of modernity and modernism. A recent guide to "key concepts" in cultural theory defines alienation through Marx as "the estrangement of humanity from its society, and its essential or potential nature" because of "the division of labour under capitalism," and therefore as one among other unhappy affects (along with powerlessness, meaninglessness, and isolation) supposedly characteristic of modern life. This guide offers another "less precisely defined" use of the term associated with "the condition of modern society." Here alienation is said to invoke "the metaphorical association of being a foreigner, outsider or stranger in one's own land" with the result that "alienation may be readily associated with the experience of exile as in some sense paradigmatic of the experience of the twentieth century."[1]

If alienation—both the specific Marxist dynamic and the broader phenomenon it attempts to explain—is characteristic of modernity, it is central
to modernism. Renato Poggioli's canonic *Theory of the Avant-Garde* posited
"the state of alienation" as the fundamental condition of the avant-garde artist, whose alienation is so total it comprises antagonism toward the current
moment *and* toward tradition, toward the mass public *and* toward elite patrons, and toward any idea of ethics beyond "the negative and destructive
principle of art for art's sake."[2] For him, to be modernist was to be alienated.

More specifically, the Brechtian "alienation effect" (*Verfremdungseffekt*)
was closely linked to sensations evoked by strangers and foreignness (the
twinned meanings of *fremde*) through its similarities with Chinese theater,
which Brecht saw in Moscow and wrote about for an Anglophone audience.[3]
Refusing audiences the comforts of conventional forms of identification
with actors, characters, and the overall performance and by implication its
author(s), Brecht's formulation of theater as an encounter with the strange/
foreign offers a paradigm for avant-garde art in general. From romantic exoticism, through modernist primitivism, to the multiculturalism of today's
global art market, alienation is key to the aesthetics of an avant-garde that
casts its innovations as invocations of elsewhere.

Common explanations that modernist alienation "reflects" the alienation
of modern society fall short of acknowledging that the alienation of indus-
trialized labor and the forced migration of generations of laborers create the
conditions that allow such middle-class formations as the avant-garde and
academia to thrive. Anxieties about that dependence may explain the re-
luctance of artists and academics to acknowledge, let alone theorize, the
workings of alienation as a site of profit and pleasure in those settings. Academic affects that signify critical acumen by negativity register avant-garde
alienation as loss or as weary but necessary work, ignoring the substantial
rewards—emotional, intellectual, authoritative, sensual, and financial—that
make participation in and analysis of the avant-garde among the most cov-
eted and competitive professions in the global economy. The fact is that, although many moderns had (and have) migration thrust upon them, many
others—especially modernists—eagerly sought out geographic displacement,
from the provinces to the city, as from the hegemon to exotic elsewheres. The
myriad memoirs of the avant-garde in cities from Paris and London to New
York and Shanghai, or in pilgrimage points like St. Ives in Cornwall or Taos
in New Mexico, offer ample proof of the pleasures of this mode of alienation.
To be alien is, among other things, to be free from the constraints of one's

home culture and, because foreignness can serve as an alibi for many forms of deviance, free, too, from many of the constraints the host culture imposes on locals.

One salutary effect of the rubric "global modernism" is to disrupt the comfortable conventions of modernist discourse around aliens and alienation. In addition to raising the issues just introduced, the rubric challenges the imperialist dynamics built into common modernist vocabularies of an "avant-garde" and its "movements," two terms derived from military theory during an era when European armies were primarily engaged in imperial conquest and domination.[4] In this paradigm, the modernist European (later American) artist gains acclaim by pillaging elements from alien cultures, a mode of global engagement conceived from a Euro-American perspective and quite compatible with the basic bourgeois value of competitive, acquisitive individualism. This analysis goes a long way toward explaining the apparent conundrum of an avant-garde that supposedly provokes the bourgeoisie drawing its agents and audiences overwhelmingly from that class.[5] My first task in analyzing ideas of the alien, then, is to demystify claims for avant-garde alienation as a form of artistic individualism by examining its status as a convention that links the vanguard artist with his (and occasionally her) capitalist patrons. A second task is to tease out the importance of alienation where it has been less recognized in histories of modernism. Together, these projects, quickly sketched in this essay, complicate assumptions about the status of the alien and alienation in art and academia today.

Enactments of alienation are ubiquitous in both the canons of modernism and the lifestyles associated with modernity: Pablo Picasso's citations of African masks, Ezra Pound's use of Chinese and Japanese poetry, the innumerable movements associated with borderless spiritualisms from Madame Blavatsky to Baha'i, to name just a few. Not unique to visual culture, these conventions take on particular clarity and force in media for which the processes of cross-cultural identification and emulation commonly muddled under the term *influence* (which Michael Baxandall called the "curse of art criticism" for its "wrong-headed grammatical prejudice about who is the agent and who the patient")[6] play out without even the rudimentary disciplines of vocabulary and grammar associated with written or spoken languages, which require practice and engagement with knowledgeable interlocutors to translate. Audiences looking at artifacts from abroad or artists "borrowing" motifs (with no intention of returning them) experience a sense of understanding that is impossible when confronting words in an unknown language. Calling art the "*esperanto* of European hegemony," Donald Preziosi cites the "museographic practices" associated with vision and display as fundamental to creating the "imaginary space-time and a storied space" where modern ideas of history and subjecthood are constituted.[7]

As important as ubiquitous modernist practices of exhibition and encounter may be, their ideological underpinnings are paradoxical. The aestheticization of individualist alienation that defines the modernist artist is achieved by invoking one group—an "Other" culture—in order to claim a place in a second: the avant-garde. In modernism's heyday, this system guaranteed both the protean individualism of the avant-garde artist and the subindividual status of those whose aesthetics were invoked. The importance of this dynamic is registered in the energy poured into debates over who was the first *japoniste* or the first European artist to use African forms. In the illogical logic of modernism, to "discover" and draw from Japanese prints or African carvings is to be original; to discover and draw from other Western artists is to be derivative. The double standard by which modernists' citations of the Other signified both Western individualism and non-Western collectivity was notoriously epitomized by the blockbuster 1984 Museum of Modern Art exhibition *"Primitivism" in Twentieth Century Art*, where labels and catalog illustrations compared dated art by individual European and (nonnative) American artists with undated works identified by "tribe." As the anthropologist James Clifford noted, the exhibition was structured to present Picasso as the "hero, whose virtuoso work, an exhibit caption tells us, contains more affinities with the tribal than that of any other pioneer modernist."[8]

These modernist dynamics continue to structure the art market (and have their analogs in academia). To achieve gallery representation or space in textbook and museum surveys, artists identified as alien (a highly charged concept that, as debates over immigration in Europe and the United States show, need not mean foreign-born) are expected to perform those identities in ways that are legible to the global marketplace. Artists from the dominant culture who invoke marginalized identities and art forms, in contrast, must be careful not to appear "political," a common but largely untheorized category that, in practice, means appearing to speak for or with—rather than critically or ironically about—collective manifestations of alienation, be they ethnic, economic, or sexual. Art presented as collective (as distinct from art authorized by a single figure, even if produced by assistants or contractors) finds little purchase in the art market even as avant-garde accolades accrue to artists who perform critical or ironic alienation from collective social movements such as feminism.[9] Thus the art market continually reinscribes a hierarchy in which alienated individualism characterizes those in the dominant culture while politically engaged collectivity stigmatizes and subordinates.

One measure of the strength of these modernist tendencies is their persistence in the face of strenuous critique through an era that styles itself "postmodern." Incisive analyses of Orientalism and primitivism—the overlap of these concepts reflects the modernist construction of the Occident as comparatively advanced or civilized—have contested the dynamics by which the avant-garde invokes the Other in ways that claim the prerogatives of progress and civilization for itself. The deep ideological and financial investments of prominent art institutions in modernist practices of art making and collection, however, render the implications of these critiques unassimilable. The catalog of the Museum of Modern Art's 1984 *"Primitivism"* exhibition offers one example. Acknowledging that "the words Primitive and primitivism have been criticized by some commentators as ethnocentric and pejorative," the chief curator, introducing the catalog, defended his use of the term, which he asserted was "comparable" to *japonisme* with "implications that have been entirely affirmative."[10] Three decades later, in 2015, the opening wall text for the Metropolitan Museum of Art's exhibition *China: Through the Looking Glass* acknowledged that "the fashions in this exhibition . . . belong to the practice of Orientalism, which since the publication of Edward Said's seminal treatise on the subject in 1978 has taken on negative connotations of Western supremacy and segregation" before going on to explain:

> While neither discounting nor discrediting the issue of the representation of "subordinated otherness" outlined by Said, this exhibition attempts to propose a less politicized and more positivistic [*sic*] examination of Orientalism as a site of infinite and unbridled creativity. Through careful juxtapositions of Western fashions and Chinese costumes and decorative arts, it presents a rethinking of Orientalism as an appreciative cultural response by the West to its encounters with the East.[11]

Similar forms of evasion characterize art-historical writing. The entry for "Primitive" in the anthology *Critical Terms for Art History* (first published in 1996 and reissued in 2003) acknowledges the colonial power dynamics of primitivism but focuses on the "positive valances" of the category of the primitive "when Western culture itself was thought to be 'overly civilized' and thus in need of rejuvenation through contact with societies in an earlier

stage of development."[12] Readers are also assured that "primitivism among
. the modernists also sometimes expressed an artist's political concern with
the plight of exploited and oppressed native populations," citing Picasso and
Paul Gauguin as examples (229). Like the Met's vague allusions to "apprecia-
tive cultural response," the fuzziness of the formulation "political concern" in
relation to the ideologies and identifications of these highly canonic—and, in
their sociopolitical relationship to their non-European sources, highly problematic—avant-garde artists is matched by the vagueness of the scare-quoted
category "overly civilized" to allude to forms of alienation that sent modernists to seek extra-European conventions of thought and representation. These
evasions were matched by another. The first edition of *Critical Terms for Art
History*, as Jaś Elsner observed in the second, "studiously avoided" the word
"influence" (104). Rather than analyzing this ubiquitous term, both editions
of this authoritative guide simply replace "influence" with "appropriation" "so
as to emphasize personal agency" of "the maker or receiver" (162–163). But
by then focusing on intra-European "appropriation"—from ancient Greece
or within English pastoral art and literature—the analysis shies away from
issues of global interchange, offering as a rationale the observation that "the
full force of multiculturalism has yet to be felt in the broader areas of art history" (168).

If art history delayed feeling "multiculturalism," one explanation is that
still-sacrosanct equations of avant-garde alienation with individualism resist
analysis of aesthetics as collectively produced or experienced. Study of specific links between antipathy toward middle-class sex and gender norms and
attraction to non-Western cultures, for example, reveals the avant-garde as
one among many interrelated urban subcultures (including ethnic, political,
and sexual subcultures) that emerged in Western cities around the turn of the
twentieth century. Far from a unique and heroic vanguard of individuals, the
avant-garde, from this demystifying perspective, is recognized as participating within and among other collective forms of alienation that call for historical acknowledgment and structural analysis.

Productive inquiry along these lines has been discouraged, however, not
only by the ongoing dependence of scholarly discourse—for both financial
sustainability and cultural authority—on the individualist rhetorics of the
avant-garde but also by the terms in which critiques of Orientalism and primitivism were and are often articulated. These, too, often inhibit analysis of the
complex relationships between alienation and identification as between the
avant-garde and other constituencies. For examples, I return to two already-

cited essays proposing to guide critical thinking about art. The essay on "Appropriation" in *Critical Terms for Art History*, despite disavowing "multiculturalism," concludes by invoking postcolonial critique: "As Edward Said has long understood, in every cultural appropriation there are those who act and those who are acted upon, and for those whose memories and cultural identities are manipulated by . . . appropriations, the consequences can be disquieting or painful" (172). This oversimplified binary of actors versus acted-upons, whose options are limited to a choice between disquietude and pain, is further homogenized in Preziosi's *The Art of Art History* (first published in 1998 and reissued in 2009). Describing the ideological power of modernist "museographic practices," Preziosi asserts that "there is no 'artistic tradition' anywhere in the world which today is not fabricated through the historicism and essentialisms of European museology and museography, and (of course) in the very hands of the colonized themselves." He characterizes "the brilliance of this colonization" as "quite breathtaking" in the way it "makes colonial subjects of us all" (493). Such theorizations of postcolonialism lurch between an identity politics structured through simplistic binaries (exploited vs. exploiter, East vs. West, black vs. white, pained vs. empowered, etc.) and an equally reductive overgeneralization of "us all" as "colonial subjects." Both approaches forestall analysis of the complexities of identifications and alienations within and across cultures even as they seem to foreclose any kind of principled response in an era when Internet access and global travel for trade, tourism, and teaching push us constantly beyond the precincts of the local— itself a concept that requires for definition an internalized idea of the alien. Put another way, it is hard to imagine any cultural actor who has not made imaginative use of some exoticized—often self-exoticized—Other. Righteous condemnation and blasé resignation are both inadequate responses.

Correctives to such oversimplifications from within postcolonial studies have stressed the historical heterogeneity of Orientalisms—including "reverse-Orientalism"[13]—and offered models of what Mary Louise Pratt calls "transculturation" and Homi Bhabha calls "mimicry" as ways of registering agency among those Said cast as "acted upon." Ideas of alienation are central to these models of colonized subjects' hybridity, which have been theorized in a general way using Jacques Lacan's idea of the mirror stage, in which the self is constituted as an image that is at once I and not-I: an alienation invoked at the moment of the subject's constitution. But much remains unexplored about the dynamics of alienation and creativity for specific cultures and individuals, even—or especially—when these cases affect received histories of modernism and the historiographies through which modernists constituted their primitive/Oriental Others.

Scant attention is paid in art history or postcolonial studies, for instance, to Khalil Bey (Khalil Sherif Pasa, 1831–1879), an Ottoman diplomat, educated in Egypt and France, who was an important patron and collector in the Parisian avant-garde of the 1860s. Khalil cannily deployed Orientalist tropes to channel his hybridity into prestige. One Paris journal celebrated him as "a prince from an Oriental tale . . . who remained Turkish through his lavish generosity and taste for women and gambling, but became Parisian through his wit, his elegance, his love of the theatre and the arts." Although he collected a wide range of European paintings, journalists focused on his penchant for lesbian imagery and related claim to have a villa in Lesbos. When Khalil commissioned Gustave Courbet's famous *Le sommeil* (The sleepers), his second painting of sex between women, one paper reported, "No need to tell you that it is just as indecent as the first. After all it's for a Turk!" Khalil also owned a version of J. A. D. Ingres's famous *Turkish Bath*—an orgy of naked women—and, most notoriously, Courbet's *L'origine du monde*, an image of female genitalia, which was later acquired by Lacan. Both men kept the painting concealed—Khalil behind a curtain, Lacan behind a screen painted with an abstract version of the composition—allowing them to reveal it for maximum effect in performances of identity that figured them as ambassadors to an exotic elsewhere (the Orient, the psyche) figured by the sign of woman. Issues of sex and sexuality, complex in themselves, are further complicated in Khalil's case by national, geographical, and cultural dynamics of alienation. He is reputed to have met a French head of state's comment, "Mr. Ambassador, you must find things here very different from back at home," with the response: "Not at all, we are just as backward as you are."[14] Even if this anecdote is apocryphal, its attachment to Khalil reveals how his cosmopolitan hybridity could be forged as much through compounding alienations as through the multiple identifications emphasized in postcolonial theory.

Related issues are raised by the men who in Western accounts of the avant-garde incarnate Japanese exoticism. The *Book of Tea* by Okakura Kakuzo (also known as Okakura Tenshin, 1862–1913) was—and is—often seen as an articulation of Japanese authenticity. But it was written in Boston, in English, in 1906 by a man who, raised and educated among expatriates in Japan, was literate in English before he could read Japanese. Okakura's sense of Japanese identity incorporated the nostalgia of his Western mentors—Ernest Fenollosa, Edward Morse, and other Bostonians—for an "authentic" premodern Ja-

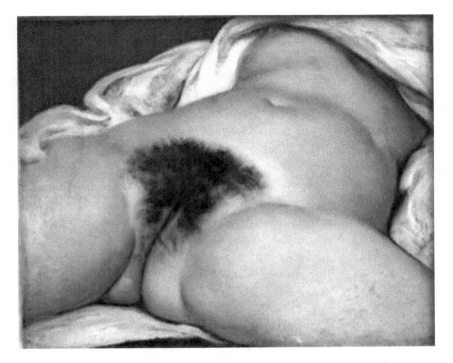

FIGURE 2.1 Gustave Courbet, *Origine du monde*, 1866, oil on canvas, Musée d'Orsay.

pan, so much so that when, with the advocacy of his Western patrons, he was appointed to head Japan's government-sponsored art academy he designed archaic uniforms for the students and faculty to wear. When competing contingents eager to embrace ideas of Japan's modernity ousted him from that position, his Boston patrons arranged for him to come to the Museum of Fine Arts. There his curatorial authority contributed substantially to newly gerrymandered canons of East Asian "art"—a Western concept awkwardly applied to global visual culture—that favored aristocratic antiques over the popular prints and modern pottery and textiles relished by the Victorians. Okakura's affirmation of what he cast as Japanese "tradition," long understood as a mode of identification *with* Japan, invites analysis as a manifestation of alienation *from* modern Japan.

Similar dynamics followed a different trajectory for the dancer and choreographer Michio Ito (1892–1961), who turns up in histories of the avant-garde that recount the development of W. B. Yeats's 1916 "play for dancers" *At the Hawk's Well*. There Ito figures as a personification of Japanese tradition: a samurai Noh dancer "discovered" by Ezra Pound poverty-stricken in a London garret.[15] In fact, they met in London's fashionable bars and salons, and Ito's dance training was in Delacrozian eurythmics, which he studied in Germany. By Ito's account, when Pound first asked for help, he responded that all he knew was "there's nothing more boring than Noh." When he nevertheless arranged for other expatriate Japanese to perform Noh steps for Pound and Yeats, however, Ito found himself astonished that "anything that good could come out of Japan!" His choreography and performance for *At the Hawk's Well*—the avant-garde accomplishment of which was entirely credited to Yeats—and subsequent long career as a modernist dancer and choreographer in the United States and Japan grew from this moment of surprised recognition born of the low expectations associated with his cosmopolitan alienation from Japan. For both Ito and Okakura, in sum, alienation as much as identification motivated their construction of Japanese tradition, with significant results for ideas of the Orient in both East and West.

To ignore the dynamics of alienation and identification among those the avant-garde cast as Other perpetuates definitions of the avant-garde as exclusively Euro-American and oversimplifies the positions of those outside the hegemon. Making East and West (or North and South) opposing monoliths obscures the varieties of interactions between them and overlooks cross-currents within those categories, including instances when those cast as exotic appropriate that designation or internalize that perspective on their home culture for profit, pleasure, or the related aesthetic effects recognized as modernist. Lines often treated as boundaries that separate identities conceived as binaries might better be seen as cables linking various contingents as they trace the contours of religious conversion, class consciousness, environmental activism, gender politics, sexual orientation—all complex formations of alienation that have provoked dynamics of identification and appropriation around the globe.

The power that Said's *Orientalism* gained by subsuming such complexities into binaries of East and West was purchased at the cost of overlooking such complexities. That cost was clear to those who approached his book from the perspective of visual culture. Reviewers noted the fissure between the argument of a text that makes no reference to art and the painting chosen for the book's cover (and maintained through its twenty-fifth anniversary edition): Jean-Léon Gérôme's *The Snake Charmer* (ca. 1879). The image shows the elderly "charmer" playing a flute that points directly at the genitals of a naked boy whose body is dangerously wrapped in a phallic snake. In the picture, an

FIGURE 2.2 Jean-Leon Gerome, *The Snake Charmer*, c. 1879, oil on canvas, Clark Art Institute.

audience of older men stares at the boy's frontal nudity while the audience of the picture is presented with his taut buttocks. Thus the painting seems to support the book's argument that the West created an idea of the Orient to buttress its own moral superiority as a way of justifying its domination. While this artwork, much reproduced today, may represent what colonialism is imagined to be *now* as the object (or target) of postcolonial studies, however, the history of its reception during the century after it was painted suggests that it served no such straightforwardly reassuring or empowering function for Western viewers. The painting steadily lost value as it moved from French to American owners until the son of its second American owners bought it as a souvenir of his childhood in 1942 for just five hundred dollars. This plummeting value is invariably explained by reference to the triumph of impressionism and subsequent modernist styles over academic painting. But this raises broader questions of why the Oriental *motifs* prevalent in eighteenth- and early-to-mid-nineteenth-century visual culture gave way to the appropriations of non-Western *styles* that constitute the story of modernism from the *japonisme* of the impressionists onward (a parallel case can be made for texts, as the romantics' evocations of the Near East gave way to Pound's "hokku" or Marcel Proust's *japoniste* effects). Disturbing paintings such as *The Snake Charmer* or Courbet's *L'origine du monde* still trouble—in much more obvious ways than debates over perspective and abstraction—Western consensuses around issues of religion, class, industrialization, gender, and sexuality, inviting debate over the kinds of issues arbiters of modernism avoided as "political."

The potential of *The Snake Charmer* to challenge Western consensus is related to its power to compel attention—a quality that no doubt motivated its selection to attract readers to Said's book. That power, originating as shock at the representation of what had seemed unrepresentable, engages varieties of alienation that cut across boundaries between East from West: alienation as disgust at the artist or milieu that created this image or, conversely, alienation as exhilaration at the flouting of rules that prohibit such representations. These reactions might be focused on the Eastern culture depicted, the Western artist doing the depicting, or—most likely—on the intersection of the two. Hence the ongoing fascination with the intersection marked by the terms "global" and "modernism." Similar dynamics undoubtedly attended the stylistic Orientalisms and primitivisms of the avant-garde in their original disruptive iterations, before the repetition and theorization of these works absorbed them into comfortable Western canons. But in academic art they play out much more clearly and for audiences that include those outside the bourgeois forums of museums and universities where repetition and theorization assimilate the output of the avant-garde into Western power structures.

If the habits of academic fields organized around the study of the avant-garde overlook the cross-cutting trajectories of alienation, so too do historiographies of Orientalism and primitivism conceived in binary terms. Scholars such as Billie Melman and Mary Roberts have challenged Said's inattention to gender and the difference it makes within and between categories of Orient and Occident. Others have questioned Said's erasure of sexual identity. "Many of the Orientalists Said takes up were homosexual, or rumored to be. But that is a circumstance that intrudes on Said's argument only at its edges," John Treat observes, before arguing that postcolonial scholars following Said, by denouncing what they present as Western "fantasies of illicit sexuality" set in the East, end up repeating the attitudes of "missionaries of a scandalized West."[16] If postcolonial theory has been reluctant to engage the alienation from Western gender and sexual norms that characterized many of those who were attracted to the East, it has altogether ignored the complementary dynamic, acknowledged in passing by a study of *ukiyo-e* imagery that observes that in Tokugawa Japan "the links between those who studied the West and those who favoured *nanshoku* [sex between boys and men] are oddly close."[17]

To take seriously the role of alienation from Western norms of gender, ethnicity, and religion in constructing knowledges of the East would mean rewriting the history of Orientalism and primitivism to account not only for how subalterns such as Okakura and Ito forged a modernism grounded in ambivalent alienation from their home culture but also for the ways Euro-Americans forged ideas of the East in response to their alienation from the West. From the expatriate American painter J. A. M. Whistler to the Parisian writer Edmond de Goncourt, alienated aesthetes pioneered the *japonisme* that became the signature of Aestheticism. Other Parisian *japonistes*, such as Henri Cernuschi and Hugues Krafft, both doubly alienated as bachelors from non-Gallic families, channeled their outsider status into scholarly interest in the Orient (the Musée Cernuschi remains today as the City of Paris's East Asian art museum, a legacy of this history). Other figures whose alienation significantly inflected Western understandings of the East include the Bosto-nians William Sturgis Bigelow and Percival Lowell, whose studies of Buddhist reincarnation and Shinto spirit possession respectively were fueled by fasci-nation with lineages of men that could serve as alternatives to bourgeois fam-ily structures. Bigelow's lavish patronage furnished Boston museums with the antiques that became exemplary of the canons of Japanese "art," and he encouraged the display of the Boston Museum of Fine Arts's Japanese collec-tion in galleries ranged around an ersatz Buddhist temple, establishing a par-adigm followed by other Western museums. Lafcadio Hearn, Oscar Wilde, Gary Snyder, Roland Barthes—the role of all these figures (and many more) in the Western construction of Japan might all be narrated as manifestations of alienation, the specifics of which helped shape modern ideas of Japan.

My point is not to mitigate or excuse the exploitations associated with Euro-American interactions around the globe. There is plenty to criticize in the history of re-presentations of non-Western culture in Western institu-tions. But it is time to move past the oversimplifications of the actor/acted-upon binary to acknowledge and analyze the dynamics of oppression and opportunity that characterize that history and continue to condition under-standings of East and West today. There is no reason to assume that contem-porary practices of global engagement are untouched by the heady mixtures of pleasure and coercion that characterized earlier episodes of global mo-dernity and modernism. At the very least, attention to alienation as a way of understanding crosscurrents of exploitation and empathy, expulsion and adoption, collusion and transgression, pain and pleasure may head off contemporary tendencies toward self-righteousness grounded in an exclusive focus on identity and identification, which all too often becomes an alibi for the replication of the dynamics of primitivism and Orientalism under other names. Ultimately alienation and identification are inseparable and complementary. Our historical understanding of global modernism and our ethical assessments of our positions in the world today require us to recognize and engage this complex dynamic.

NOTES

1. Andrew Edgar and Peter Sedgwick, *Cultural Theory: Key Concepts* (London: Routledge, 1999), 18–20.
2. Renato Poggioli, *The Theory of the Avant-Garde* (1962), trans. Gerald Fitzgerald (Cambridge, Mass.: Harvard University Press, 1968), 127.
3. Now commonly referenced as "Alienation Effects in Chinese Acting," Brecht's essay was originally published in a London journal as "The Fourth Wall of China: An Essay on the Effect of Disillusion in the Chinese Theatre," *Life and Letters* 15, no. 6 (1936): 116–123. Although Brecht wrote in German, his biographer describes the essay as "written for the English-speaking world where he increasingly saw his future. Stephen Parker, *Bertolt Brecht: A Literary Life* (London: Bloomsbury, 2014), 352.
4. Both terms came to English from French. The *Oxford English Dictionary* cites a first usage of "avant-garde" as an English word in 1910. According to the *OED*, the word "movement," rarely used before the eighteenth century, came into common parlance as military terminology (this is the *OED*'s second meaning, with a first citation from 1762 and a definition quoted from a military dictionary of 1876: "the regular and orderly motion of an army for some particular purpose"). The *OED*'s sixth meaning—after the "movements" of watches and so forth—is a "course or series of actions and endeavours on the part of a body of persons, moving or tending toward some special end." The example given is the "Oxford Movement." The *OED*, originally compiled in the second half of the nineteenth century, gives no examples of "movement" specifically applied to groups in the arts, which were referred to as "schools," a term with very different connotations. The first Anglophone uses of "movement" in relation to art I have found concern the Pre-Raphaelites. An article in *Tinsley's Magazine* 8 (1871): 392, mentions "the growing Preraphaelite movement"; an 1894 book is titled *Dante Rossetti and the Pre-Raphaelite Movement.* But

"Pre-Raphaelite school" was also common. By the twentieth century, "school" was rarely used to describe artistic contingents, and when it was it carried pejorative implications of pretentious or old-fashioned rule following.

5. My analysis is grounded in Raymond Williams's incisive explication of the avant-garde as a bourgeois "class fraction." Raymond Williams, "The Bloomsbury Fraction," in *Culture and Materialism: Selected Essays* (London: Verso, 1980), 148–169.

6. M. Baxandall, *Patterns of Intention: On the Historical Explanation of Pictures* (New Haven, Conn.: Yale University Press, 1985), 58–59.

7. Donald Preziosi, "The Art of Art History," in *The Art of Art History: A Critical Anthology*, 2nd ed., ed. Donald Preziosi (1998; Oxford: Oxford University Press, 2009), 489, 493.

8. James Clifford, "Stories of the Tribal and the Modern," in *The Predicament of Culture: Twentieth-Century Ethnography, Literature, and Art* (Cambridge, Mass.: Harvard University Press, 1988), 191.

9. See, for example, the discussion of Nicole Eisenman in Christopher Reed, *Art and Homosexuality: A History of Ideas* (New York: Oxford University Press, 2011), 242–243. The difference between the avant-garde and the counterculture is discussed by Elissa Auther and Adam Lerner in the introduction to the anthology *West of Center: Art and the Counterculture Experiment in America, 1965–1977* (Minneapolis: University of Minnesota Press, 1912), xvii–xxxvi.

10. This argument was sustained through a long and vitriolic public exchange between an editor at *Artforum* and the curators of the exhibition, reprinted in Bill Beckley, ed., *Uncontrollable Beauty: Toward a New Aesthetics* (New York: Allworth, 1998), 149–260.

11. The exhibition ran July 22–September 7, 2015. This wall text also appeared on the webpage for the exhibition. http://www.metmuseum.org/exhibitions/listings/2015/china-through-the-looking-glass/exhibition-galleries.

12. Robert S. Nelson and Richard Shiff, eds., *Critical Terms for Art History*, 2nd ed. (Chicago: University of Chicago Press, 2003), 219. Further references are cited in the text.

13. R. A. Miller defined "reverse Orientalism" in *Japan's Modern Myth: The Language and Beyond* (New York: Weatherhill, 1982) to describe "the ideology of sociolinguistic exclusiveness." Miller explains: "It is rather as if the Japanese were, in this instance at least, determined to do it to themselves and to their own culture before others can do it for and to them—the 'doing' in both instances being the creation of an image in terms of which other cultures or traditions will consist of something radically different—what Said calls establishing the Other" (209). Although Miller's focus is on the Japanese language after World War II, he traces

manifestations of "reverse Orientalism" to "the period of the Meiji Restoration when the spectacle of a prostrate China being picked to bits by the predatory Western powers was understandably a matter of concern" (210). His paradoxical conclusion is that this constructed authenticity is authentically Japanese: "something truly unique, a genuine innovation of Japanese society and culture" (211). Yuko Kikuchi uses "Reverse Orientalism" to analyze the presentation of Japanese crafts in the West after World War II. *Japanese Modernization and Mingei Theory* (London: Routledge Curzon, 2004), 197.

14. Francis Haskell, "A Turk and His Pictures in Nineteenth-Century Paris," *Oxford Art Journal* 5, no. 1 (Spring 1982): 46.

15. See, for example, Richard Ellman, *Yeats: The Man, the Masks* (New York, Macmillan, 1948), 212. This respected study has been much reissued, most recently in 1999. Descriptions of Ito as a Noh dancer who "performed the play" rather than as a modern choreographer who collaborated in creating the performance persist; see Karen E. Brown, *The Yeats Circle: Verbal and Visual Relations in Ireland, 1880–1939* (Farnham: Ashgate, 2011), 64.

16. John Whittier Treat, *Great Mirrors Shattered* (New York: Oxford University Press, 1999), 86, 199, 209.

17. Timon Screech, *Sex and the Floating World: Erotic Images in Japan, 1700–1820*, 2nd ed. (London: Reaktion, 2009), 287.

WORKS CITED

Auther, Elissa, and Adam Lerner, eds. *West of Center: Art and the Counterculture Experiment in America, 1965–1977*. Minneapolis: University of Minnesota Press, 1912.

Baxandall, M. *Patterns of Intention: On the Historical Explanation of Pictures*. New Haven, Conn.: Yale University Press, 1985.

Beckley, Bill, ed. *Uncontrollable Beauty: Toward a New Aesthetics*. New York: Allworth, 1998.

Bhabha, Homi. *The Location of Culture*. London: Routledge, 1994.

Brecht, Bertolt. "The Fourth Wall of China: An Essay on the Effect of Disillusion in the Chinese Theatre." *Life and Letters* 15, no. 6 (1936): 116–123.

Brown, Karen E. *The Yeats Circle: Verbal and Visual Relations in Ireland, 1880–1939*. Farnham: Ashgate, 2011.

Clifford, James. "Stories of the Tribal and the Modern." In *The Predicament of Culture: Twentieth-Century Ethnography, Literature, and Art*. Cambridge, Mass.: Harvard University Press, 1988.

Edgar, Andrew, and Peter Sedgwick. *Cultural Theory: Key Concepts*. London: Routledge, 1999.

Ellman, Richard. *Yeats: The Man, the Masks*. New York, Macmillan, 1948.

Guth, Christine. "Charles Longfellow and Okakura Kakuzo: Cultural Cross-Dressing in the Colonial Context." *positions* 8, no. 3 (Winter 2000): 605–636.

Haskell, Francis. "A Turk and His Pictures in Nineteenth-Century Paris." *Oxford Art Journal* 5, no. 1 (Spring 1982): 40–47.

Hokenson, Jan Walsh. *Japan, France, and East-West Aesthetics*. Madison, N.J.: Fairleigh Dickinson University Press, 2004.

Inankur, Zeynep, Reina Lewis, and Mary Roberts, eds. *The Poetics and Politics of Place: Ottoman Istanbul and British Orientalism*. Istanbul: Pera Museum, 2011.

Karatani Kōjin. "Japan as Museum: Okakura Tenshin and Ernest Fenollosa." Trans. Sabu Kohso. In *Japanese Art After 1945: Scream Against the Sky*, ed. Alexandra Munro, 33–39. New York: Harry N. Abrams, 1994.

Kikuchi, Yuko. *Japanese Modernization and Mingei Theory*. London: Routledge Curzon, 2004.

Lowe, Lisa. *Critical Terrains: French and British Orientalisms*. Ithaca, N.Y.: Cornell University Press, 1991.

Melman, Billie. *Women's Orients: English Women in the Middle East, 1718–1918*. Ann Arbor: University of Michigan Press, 1992.

Miller, R. A. *Japan's Modern Myth: The Language and Beyond*. New York: Weatherhill, 1982.

Nelson, Robert S., and Richard Shiff, eds. *Critical Terms for Art History*. 1st ed. Chicago: University of Chicago Press, 1996.

——. *Critical Terms for Art History*. 2nd ed. Chicago: University of Chicago Press, 2003.

Okakura Tenshin and the Museum of Fine Arts Boston. Nagoya: Nagokya/Bosuton Bijutuskan, 1999.

Parker, Stephen. *Bertolt Brecht: A Literary Life*. London: Bloomsbury, 2014.

Poggioli, Renato. *The Theory of the Avant-Garde*. 1962. Trans. Gerald Fitzgerald. Cambridge, Mass.: Harvard University Press, 1968.

Preziosi, Donald. "The Art of Art History." In *The Art of Art History: A Critical Anthology*, 2nd ed., ed. Donald Preziosi. Oxford: Oxford University Press, 2009.

Reed, Christopher. *Art and Homosexuality: A History of Ideas*. New York: Oxford University Press, 2011.

——. "Modernizing the Mikado: Japan, Japanism, and the Limitations of the Avant-Garde." *Visual Culture in Britain* 14, no. 1 (March 2013): 68–86.

Roberts, Mary. *Intimate Outsiders: The Harem and Orientalist Art and Travel Literature*. Durham, N.C.: Duke University Press, 2007.

Rubin, William, ed. *"Primitivism" in Twentieth-Century Art: Affinity of the Tribal and the Modern*. New York: Museum of Modern Art, 1984.

Screech, Timon. *Sex and the Floating World: Erotic Images in Japan, 1700–1820*. 2nd ed. London: Reaktion, 2009.

Treat, John Whittier. *Great Mirrors Shattered*. New York: Oxford University Press, 1999.

Williams, Raymond. "The Bloomsbury Fraction." In *Culture and Materialism: Selected Essays*, 148–149. London: Verso, 1980.

3. ANIMAL

EFTHYMIA RENTZOU

The animal as a modernist topos appears as an invitation to us humans to enter into a different relation with the world, a universalizing trope that aims to rethink the human globally.

If one seeks the other side of the human in modernist literature and art, the machine appears immediately as the obvious candidate. Modern machines changed perceptions of space and time, agency and productivity, subjectivity and the collective, but they also emerged as the great unifiers across cultures, nations, and languages, facilitating a tighter world through transportation and communication. Machines instigated the modern imaginary of a different human, a fantasy hybrid of the mechanical and the organic that at the same time threatened and broadened traditional understandings of humanity. As mechanical fantasy invaded modernist imagination it acted upon the concept of the human, offering both a counterpoint, and eventually a negative image, of what the human is or could be and the possibility of prostheses to existing faculties, proposing to extend the human itself.

In parallel with this salient mechanical trope, however, another entity cuts through the modernist imagination as an alternative pendant to the human: the animal. A perennial "other" for the human at least since Aristotle, the animal is both ubiquitous and invisible in the modernist imaginary. In critical readings of modernism, animals are eclipsed by the modernity of the machine, obscured and dismissed as traditional allegories or symbols, or tackled in organicist or natural paradigms often deemed regressive and incompatible with the heroic conception of modernism as ushering in a new era. The logic of exclusion underlying the preponderance of the human-machine pair has forcefully pushed the animal into the marginal zone of minor genres, lesser authors, or peripheral modernisms, normalizing its presence in Aimé Césaire or Julio Cortazar, for instance, but not knowing what to do with it in Virginia Woolf or even Franz Kafka. Yet animals have a pervasive presence in canonical and marginal modernist texts in both the European and non-European archive, creating a network of references and meanings that attests to modernism as a global operation of rethinking the human. Animals abound in modernism and break the dyadic system of human-machine, introducing a third pole for understanding the human that opens up the antithetical structures imposed by this system. Animals function as signifiers for the decentering of the human as a riddle of culture and nature, an operation that proves to be more deeply unsettling than the human-machine binary. If the latter, after all, leaves human's centrality in the world intact, what the modernist animals do is to offset the Western humanist tradition that posits the human as the sole and uncontestable subject in the world thanks to his capacity for *logos*. With a remarkable versatility that covers all kinds of species—insects, mammals, fish, and some imaginary ones—wild and domesticated, exotic and quaint, it is not an exaggeration to say that animals bridge local traditions with one global aspiration: modernism's sustained contestation of Western notions of humanism and, with that, of Western values as a whole. The animal as a modernist topos appears as an invitation to us humans to enter into a different relation with the world, a universalizing trope that aims to rethink the human globally.

The impact of Darwin and Darwinism on these new perceptions of the human cannot be overstated. Darwin's theory of evolution was one of the deep epistemological shifts that shattered many certainties in the Western humanist tradition and brought animals and humans much closer together not only from a biological point of view but also from a moral and metaphysical one. *On the Origin of Species* (1859) and *The Descent of Man* (1871) suggested only a difference of degree, not of kind, between human and animal. Indeed, Darwin was cautious about even the possibility of distinguishing between species. In Darwin's wake, the human's status as absolute difference from the rest of the natural world eroded, and this radical difference became gradation. Toppled from a central and fixed position of alterity and exception, the human is shaped by Darwin as a transitory and uncertain series of insensible differences, a porous entity open to the rest of organic life. Nature itself, the world, was likewise recast because Darwin's theory of evolution represented it not as the result of a mimesis, meaning as the image of God and God's plan, but rather as a self-referential and self-regulating object that obeys its own internal rules without reference to anything outside of it (Norris, *Beasts*, 26). Darwinian nature is like a self-reflexive text that has displaced God as the supreme narrator along with the human as the supreme subject.

Darwin's positivist empiricism was both a culmination of Enlightenment epistemology and a break with its philosophical tradition regarding the human. In this tradition a clear hierarchical order had placed the human at the top of creation, an order that hinged on the unique human capacity for *logos*. The dividing line between animals and humans could vary slightly, from reason, according to Descartes, who saw in the animal a machine or organic automaton, to imagination, as Jean-Jacques Rousseau suggested. However, the common denominator of all categorical and hierarchical distinctions between animals and humans remained language. Language, either as reason or imagination, marked a firm boundary that Darwin set out to cross, thus trespassing, armed with new biological arguments, upon a centuries-long philosophical discussion on ontology and metaphysics. Aspects of the human considered to be spiritual, such as reasoning, moral values, the love of beauty, and language itself, became objects of evolution as process—another series of imperceptible differences. When Darwin suggests that language might have developed from musical vocalizations similar to birdsong and other animal cries, he reverses the symbolic function of human language from an ultimate barrier between species to a possible glorious link.

Darwin's preoccupation with mental phenomena became even clearer in *The Expression of the Emotions in Man and Animals* (1872), in which evolution crosses over into psychology. The influence of Darwin on Sigmund Freud's conceptualization of human psychosexual development, which added an important element to modernist understandings of the human, is well documented. In Freud, ontogeny—the development of the human from fetus to adult—is often seen as a recapitulation of phylogeny—the evolution of the human species—locking together the evolution of the species with the development of the psyche. Moreover, Freud's association of the libido, of drives, and ultimately of the unconscious with an instinctual realm akin to animality offered a new dimension to the human/animal divide. The pair conscious/unconscious reproduces, to some degree, the human/animal dichotomy, with language again as the dividing line. Psychoanalysis is based upon the premise of making the unconscious speak in a way that is intelligible for the conscious, thus overcoming instinctual animality. For Freud, the demarcation line between human and animal is still speech, but he opens the possibility of some communication between the two. The unconscious, like the animal, is invisible because unintelligible, but what if we could make it (as well as the animal) speak? What if there were a bridging language between them, and, if so, what would it look like? Freud, after Darwin, posits language as the key to opening up the human, an opening that rests directly or indirectly on the animal. It is this association of language with animals no longer as a means of exclusion but rather as an unexpected realm of inclusion that is thematized in modernist elaborations of the human-animal articulation.

Animals, for the longest time in modernism's blind spot, work through different literary genres and in different parts of the world as a common code for pushing the limits of language. The modernist crisis of representation, constantly interrogating the relation between language and the world, finds one of its most potent ciphers in the body of the animal. Animals become pressure points for the concept of subjectivity, channeling experimentations with literary representation. The presence of animals in modernist texts thus goes beyond a thematic constant to become both a vector for questioning forms and modes of writing and a cornerstone for an ontological, ethical, and ultimately political reconsideration of the humanist human.

This kind of operation is prominently articulated in Franz Kafka's animal narratives. Gilles Deleuze and Félix Guattari underscore how Kafka's "becoming animal" in these stories combines radical modes of representation with radical philosophical and political positions. They consider the "becoming animal" as a way for a Czech Jew to escape from the hegemony of a major language (German) but also from any kind of symbolic order: the family and the father, capitalist social organization, or even the process of signification altogether. "Becoming animal" emphasizes a process—not unlike Darwin's processual thinking—that creates "nonsignifying signs" of "zones of liberated intensities" that hover between species (13). The result is a subjectivity that is deterritorialized and not recomposed as a coherent entity. "Becoming" as a driving force of the text is especially prominent in Kafka's most notorious story, *The Metamorphosis* (1915). Although Gregor Samsa wakes up already in the form of a vermin, the narrative that adopts his point of view is structured around the push and pull of his preexisting human consciousness and his newly emerging grasp of the world as an insect. At first, he thinks he can still speak, only to hear his boss declare: "That was the voice of an animal" (10). He soon discovers the pleasures of walking on the walls and hanging from the ceiling, but he is still attracted to music, which makes him wonder, "was he an animal if music could captivate him so?" The end result of this tension is the death of Gregor and the "metamorphosis" of his sister, Grete, from a submissive girl into a strong-willed woman. The narrative starts with the fait accompli of Gregor's transformation, complete with the details of his new insect body; it ends with the image of Grete stretching her young body in the fresh air. Ontogeny and (reverse) phylogeny are cleverly combined in this narration of becomings: from human to insect to death, from immature girl to woman to sexuality. The violence and unruliness of one transformation infers that of the other. Gregor's becoming animal finds its parallel in Grete's becoming autonomous adult. From a narrative viewpoint Kafka's venture into the realm of the fantastic turns on its head the basic structure of the *bildungsroman*, that of coming of age. The animal provides the hinge for the inversion.

A reverse becoming, from animal into human, is at the center of Kafka's short story "A Report to an Academy" (1917). An ape turned human with the name Rotpeter addresses an "academy": he is called to describe the life he had as an ape before his transformation. Rotpeter, though, cannot remember anything from his life as an animal and remarks in a very Darwinian manner: "Your life as apes, gentlemen, insofar as something of that kind lies behind you, cannot be further removed from you than mine is from me" (250). His becoming human and his acquisition of language have obliterated any memory of being animal. Thus he changes the topic of the report to describe how he became human through the imitation of his capturers. Apes ape; this is what Rotpeter did to become human. His detailed description of his mimicry—how he learned to use his mouth to spit, drink alcohol, smoke, and finally speak like a human—plants, however, a doubt in the reader's mind: is Rotpeter's report also some kind of imitation? Is he fake? Some eighty years later and from a different part of the world, John Coetzee will make this point through his heroine in *Elizabeth Costello* (2003). Costello, a writer, delivers a lecture on "Realism" before an academic public, with Kafka's story as her starting point. For her, "A Report to an Academy" exemplifies literature as uncertainty: we do not know for sure whether the narrator is truly an ape, or a human posing as an ape, or even whether the academy consists of humans or apes. Elizabeth Costello maintains that we cannot know what is going on in the narrative because Kafka wrote a literature that was no longer a faithful and trustworthy "word-mirror" in the manner of realism. But though we may not know what species are in the story, what we do know, Costello passionately asserts, is that whoever Rotpeter is, he is embedded deeply in his reality, and Kafka makes sure that we, as readers, feel this embedment, that we get a feeling for his subjective experience. The late modernist Coetzee points out that modernism shifted literature from being an illusionist's mirror of reality to offering an exploration of a subject's investment in reality and that this shift was operated through the uncertain space of becoming between animal and human.

Modernist tales of becoming animal permit on the one hand the creation of radically different subjects, deterritorializing precisely the notions of human subjectivity and agency, notions of self and world, that disturb the reader's certainties. On the other hand, such transformations exemplify modernism's rerouting of literature's referentiality from a phenomenological to an ethical perspective on the real, thanks to the animal as an extreme subject. The impossible task of faithfully representing an objective reality is superseded by the dominance of the hypersubjective. The animal, though, questions even this possibility, the representation of subjectivity, as in Virginia Woolf's *Flush: A Biography* (1933), the life story of the poet Elizabeth Barrett Browning's dog. With the title already Woolf displaces a discourse on the animal from "zoology" to "biography," from "zoe" as simple existence to "bios," a lived life, and from "logos" to "graphein," to writing. Woolf had already experimented with the biographical genre in *Orlando: A Biography*, in which fiction and biography were intertwined and where other barriers, such as gender, time, and space, were regularly transgressed. The biographical genre as a paradigm for narration goes even further with *Flush* and calls into question the possibility of biography altogether: can one write a life? What does it mean to narrate someone else's life without having the experience of it? How can one imagine the world through the eyes of another? And what if this other is of a different species?

An interesting variation on the animal as extreme subject is a peculiar work within Greek modernism, Yannis Skarimbas's novella *The Divine He-Goat* (1933). Exiled for decades at the fringes of canonical Greek modernism, Skarimbas's texts present a thick layering of discursive registers that outline extremely complex and at the same time fragmentary subjectivities. The main character of the novella, Yannis, is a cultivated bourgeois turned globetrotting bum who has placed himself completely outside the norms of society and its morals. Similar to Blaise Cendrars's Moravagine of the homonymous novel, Yannis is absolutely evil. The narrative—which follows Yannis's immersion in the married life of a woman he had once loved—adopts his perspective and his voice, which moves with ease from high literary references to regional-isms and argot and often to neologisms that break down language completely. The richness of this interior monologue is counterbalanced by the poverty of Yannis's actual utterances. His spoken words are minimal, he often repeats what others say in lieu of an answer, he stumbles and stutters on purpose, he deforms words, or he uses the voices of animals. Yannis barks, quacks, and bleats like the he-goat with whom he identifies. While his transforma-tion into an animal functions on the symbolic level to show his complete rebellion against societal norms, his animal voice in combination with the disintegration of human language brings back to the surface the association of the animal with language, speech, and their limits. In modernist narra-tives, speaking—and writing—*as* the animal bears the Freud-tinted ability to voice the deepest layers of the human psyche. But it also reiterates a thought that haunted modernists: the impossibility of human language to signify. In Kafka, Woolf, Coetzee, and Skaribas, the animals speak and thus materialize, in their sometimes unyielding carnality, a subjectivity that cannot be con-tained within human limits. But these "becoming animals" cannot be con-tained in traditional literary genres either. Interspecies metamorphosis allows us to reflect on the rules of literature, realism, the *bildungsroman*, biography, fantasy, and ultimately on literature's connection with the real. The voice of the animal stages literature not as a word-mirror but as a word deflector.[1]

This general quest to transcend language and its semantics and convey an unmediated experience of the world finds its most distilled version in mod-ernist poetry. Poetry, Stéphane Mallarmé said, is the redemption of language from its deficiencies, from its lack of perfection, through the creation of an idiom that is total in itself. The quest of perfection also passed sometimes through the mechanical paradigm—William Carlos Williams's dictum on the poem as a machine, small or large, made out of words is telling. Poetry conceived as machine entertains the possibility of a new language that could represent the new pace of modernity. One can think of the futurist poems imagined as perfect, powerful machines rhythmed by the syncopating ono-matopoeias of the new technology or of the Dadaist poems as the relics of dysfunctional machines from the Great War. However, poetry as machine projects the idea of a different language, which is still used in the same way as human language. The process of signification is not altered; only the signs are. On the contrary, the animal seems to foster both radical foreignness and splendid autonomy for modernist poetry in a way that short-circuits the pro-cess of poetic representation itself. This is what Georges Bataille points to in *Theory of Religion* (1948) when he remarks that we can only speak of the animal's point of view in a poetic way: "Nothing is more closed to us than this animal life from which we are descended" (20). Thus poetry is the only means of imagining what the animal sees because "poetry describes nothing that does not slip toward the unknowable" (21). Bataille brings together animal and poetry through their common hermeticism: the animal life is closed and unreachable for humans, and poetry is closed to human knowledge; it speaks what cannot be known. The syllogism is simple and gives to the animal's speechlessness a different dimension. Animals do not share everyday language with humans, but poetry is made to be a radically different language, one as foreign and as elliptic as the silence of beasts. This may well be the logic underlying the presence and centrality of numerous animals in modernist poetry as a conduit for the Mallarmean dream of a total language.

Indeed, it is this totality of the animal that Rainer Maria Rilke admires in the eighth of the *Duino Elegies* (1925). The animal is capable of seeing "the open," that is, a pure space of boundless existence, as opposed to the human gaze that is always oriented toward objects, a gaze always looking into things instead of out of things. The eyes of animals show humans what there really *is*, maintains Rilke, tweaking the standard trope of the poet as the one who sees what others cannot: "Forever turned toward objects, we see in them / the mere reflection of the realm of freedom, / which we have dimmed. Or when some animal / mutely, serenely, looks us through and through" (49). This densely theoretical poem, which will find philosophical elaboration in both Martin Heidegger and Giorgio Agamben, is not the first in which Rilke contemplates the animal's view. Two of his Parisian *New Poems* written around 1906, "The Panther" and "Black Cat," thematize the gaze of the feline. In both poems the eyes of the animal function as places where the world is arrested, suspended, and where it ultimately disappears. The panther in the zoo of the Jardin des Plantes cannot face the world because of the bars of his cage, but occasionally a glimpse of the world is captured like prey: "Only at times, the curtain of the pupils / lifts, quietly—. An image enters in, / rushes down through the tensed, arrested muscles, / plunges into the heart and is gone" (25). The domestic black cat, on the other hand, gazes back to the human, provoking a moment of suspension: "she turns her face to yours; / and with a shock, you see yourself, tiny, inside the golden amber of her eyeballs / suspended, like a prehistoric fly" (65). This is a moment of *anagnorisis* of self and world elaborated further by Rilke in the eighth of the *Duino Elegies*.

It opens the possibility of experiencing a complete moment of simply being in the world—like an animal. This experience of animal-being is necessarily extralinguistic, and as such it may only be inferred by poetry as an alternative to language and as a glimpse of an unmediated "real."

The animal as a vector of the unknowable and the unspeakable may also be seen behind numerous animal descriptions in modernist versions of the ancient genre of the bestiary. From Guillaume Apollinaire's deceptively naive 1911 *Bestiary or the Parade of Orpheus*, beautifully illustrated by Raoul Dufy's woodcuts, to Marianne Moore's sprawling animal kingdom throughout her nuanced and complex poetry, to Paul Eluard's *The Animals and Their Men, and the Men and Their Animals* (1920), modernist poets compile descriptions of animals, simple or cryptic, and with them deploy their poetics. But perhaps the close association of the animal body and the power of literature exemplified in poetry finds its most memorable incarnation in a different modernist bestiary. Jorge Luis Borges's *Book of Imaginary Beings* (1957) is a fantastic zoology, as the original title in Spanish explains, arranged through the encyclopedic convention of alphabetical order. Strictly speaking, this is not a poetic bestiary. Nonetheless, the book brings together and collates numerous traditions and literary references, combining anthological and encyclopedic features that create, as Borges says in the preface, a mythological zoo. This cultural zoo is meant to delight readers the way children are delighted when they discover animals in a zoological garden. Borges ponders the possibility of endlessly extending the list of these fantastic creatures since "a monster is no more than a combination of parts of real beings, and the possibilities of permutation border on the infinite." But the reality is different: "This, however, does not happen; our monsters would be stillborn" (14). The reason for this contrast between infinite combinatory possibilities and the limited number of attested fantastic animals is that only a few of these creatures can get a grip on human imagination. The structure reproduced here is the one operating in Borges's well-known story "The Library of Babel" (1941). The library contains a quasi-infinite number of books, each counting 410 pages, representing every possible ordering of twenty-five alphabetic characters, of which only a few are actually meaningful. The library contains every possible written combination in the form of a book, but which ones can we actually read? In *The Book of Imaginary Beings* the endless combinatory possibility of language and literature is transferred to the body of the animal, with the same conclusion: yes, we could imagine any possible creature, but which ones would we fear? The animal becomes a bodily materialization of the power of representation; rearranging the body of the animal and rearranging letters and words are part of the same process.

The animal leads Borges to create a kind of encyclopedia of human imagination, thus using the quintessential Enlightenment project of classification to illustrate something that cannot be classified, the monstrous. Another reversal of the Enlightenment trope is of course the Chinese encyclopedia that Borges mentions in his essay "The Analytical Language of John Wilkins" (1942). The only example given from this apocryphal Chinese encyclopedia is one of animal classification, divided into fourteen unexpected categories: animals belonging to the emperor, embalmed animals, the sirens, the fabulous animals, those who just broke the water pitcher, and so on. In both of Borges's lists the animal is fuel for dynamiting a certain kind of thought, the heritage of the Enlightenment's certainty of an absolute and universal order of things that cannot imagine any alternative. Classifications of animals are deployed as a way to stretch the Enlightenment straightjacket and with it the Western tradition's image of itself as universal truth. This is certainly the case in Oswald de Andrade's 1928 "Cannibalist Manifesto," a work that established the direction of Brazilian modernism and openly attacks the West— Europe—through the trope of animality. This manifesto is a declaration for a native Brazilian modernism, one that would not be a simple imitation of European modernism but a creation of an autonomous culture through the cannibalization and ingestion of Europe. *Antropofagia* as a creative principle obviously rides on and reverses both a colonial logic and a European perception of the primitive as animal. Andrade fully appropriates Western perceptions of savages as animals in order to switch the value of cannibalism from negative to positive. Brazil is not seen as the terrain of an animalized savage to be civilized but rather as the terrain of an animal-human that eats up the whole defunct Western culture: "But those who came here weren't crusaders. They were fugitives from a civilization we are eating, because we are strong and vindictive like the Jabuti [tortoises]" (41). Here the identification with the animal is meant openly as an aggressive resistance against the hegemony of the West.

Within modernism's increasingly self-conscious worldwide reach, the search for an idiom that would both partake in this global endeavor and express the locality of its inception pushes the Brazilians to adopt an animal paradigm. In doing so, they tap into a source that is as universal as the human but that uproots the fundamental assumptions of Western thought about the human. The undermining of the Western, universalist, humanist human via the animal is a generalized modernist operation, but it gains probably its full political, representational, and global potential in the works of surrealism. Surrealism, spurred by a devastating world war, contested from its beginnings the principles and values of the West and had as its horizon in its various generic, media, and national iterations a revolution of representation, of ethics, and of politics. Unique among the historical avant-garde movements in its global resonance, surrealism—for many non-Europeans—exemplified modernism as the expression of a heterogeneous but unified world. The deliberate universalism of surrealism, with its very distinct political components—antibourgeois, antinational, anticolonial—rested on a total liberation of the human from binding constraints, including that of anthropocentrism. Animals thus populate en masse the surrealist universe, creating persistent images that upset the human as cultural and natural entity. The examples are many; in the visual arts one has only to think of Max Ernst and his hybrid human-animal creatures (including his bird alter ego, Loplop), Remedios Varo's and Léonore Fini's cats and other animals, Victor Brauner's hybrid animal-object *Wolf-table*, Meret Oppenheim's use of animal fur for her tea cup *Object*, Wilfredo Lam's complex animals, not to mention Salvador Dalí's anamorphic animal-humans and many others. In literature animals crisscross languages and genres, for example in Leonora Carrington's stories written in English, French, or Spanish, offering haunting animal-human encounters, as in "The Debutante," in which a hyena wearing the face of a maid it just devoured replaces the narrator in her society debut.

But from a theoretical point of view, the most sustained treatment of the animal as a universalist and antihumanist trope within surrealism is to be found in the Parisian surrealist magazine *Minotaure* (1933–1939), which brought lesser-known writers and artists together with those that marked the modernist canon: André Breton, Marcel Duchamp, Pablo Picasso, René Magritte, Roger Caillois, Brassaï, Jacques Lacan, Diego Rivera, Roberto Matta, Hans Bellmer, Nicolas Calas, Gisèle Prassinos, Benjamin Péret, Wolfgan Paalen, and Man Ray, to name a few. As its editorials declared, this very luxurious magazine wished to express through its texts and its exquisite illustrations a new universality, that of a modern aesthetic. The title of the magazine, evoking the Greek monster and the Cretan mythological cycle already dear to such artists as Giorgio de Chirico and Picasso, seems at first to sit astride ancient Greece as a topos of the universalist common culture of humanism. However, the elaboration of the title *Minotaure* as the guiding principle of the magazine points to a debunking of the kind of humanism for which the classical was supposed to stand. The cover of each issue, created especially by an artist as a new representation of the mythic human-animal hybrid, gave the cue to a sustained dismantling of the human figure as a complete, coherent, and closed entity. In parallel, animals creep in throughout the pages of the magazine, in photographs and articles, creating a continuum with the human that destabilizes even further the latter's perceived autonomy, centrality, and exceptional status. The magazine, in staying true to its title, was a constant faceoff between human and animal that created a new vocabulary for understanding both. What *Minotaure* produced in its thirteen widely disseminated issues is a perception of the human open to the animal that aspires to break down dichotomies of culture and nature along with dichotomies of reason and the irrational, body and mind. The result is an intense mode of anthropological thinking—in the sense of an inquiry into the human—that decenters the *anthropos* by opening its realm to the animal. *Minotaure*, in its multiple, collective, and multimedia form, can thus be seen as a paradigm for the modernist animal in general as a signifier for a new humanism, one no less encompassing than its Renaissance and Enlightenment predecessors.

The humanism that modernism articulates through the animal is indeed a critique of the whole Western tradition, a critique coming from within and from without. The anticolonialist or postcolonialist logic of the latter, the non-Western global archive, joins with European critical stances of the West's hegemony in following the animal's trail. Reaching farther than the human-machine dyad, which tends to emphasize the divide between nature and culture and leads to a dualistic ontology that folds back into rather traditionalist understandings of the human, the animal upsets these divides and proposes an alternative universalism. This alternative universalism can be described as a nonanthropocentric humanism, with the oxymora and paradoxes that the term carries, one that pulls the rug out from under a Western humanism based on classical understandings of the human. This universalism surpasses the chronological limits of the industrial era imposed by the human-machine opposition and delves into the long history of the human-animal philosophical coupling.

No longer an "other," modernist animals gaze, speak, and exist as open possibilities for a different signification of the world as they are for a different human. Poems, manifestoes, magazines, biographies, narratives of transformation, taxonomies, and bestiaries rediscover animals as a common, universal denominator that upsets certainties: everyone knows animals, but no one really does. Entrenched in the textual intricacies of modernist grappling with the real, the animal emerges as a global encoding of experimental positionings. Animals incite to try out different possibilities for exploring subjectivity and voice and for reflecting on genres and their representational heft, and at the same time they incite to rethink the global political implications of the Western human as an uncontested authority. Lurking at the sidelines of twentieth-century antihumanism and debates on the "end of (hu)man" as a philosophical, normative, and political concept, the animal has stealthily radicalized the meaning of being human and has become a conduit for an alternative universality.

NOTE

1. The becoming animal (or human) takes different twists and turns in modernist writing across the globe. For example, Mikhail Bulgakov's *The Heart of a Dog* (1925) narrates the transformation of a dog into a human after a successful operation—recalling H. G. Wells's vivisections and hybrids in *The Island of Doctor Moreau* (1896)—and is more a straightforward allegory for the new Soviet regime than an exploration of the limits of human subjectivity. The same can be said for Eugène Ionesco's animal transformations in *Rhinoceros* (1959), a political allegory of resistance to a massive brutalization of social life. In both cases the animal is equated with the darkest, most vilified aspects of humanity.

WORKS CITED

Apollinaire, Guillaume. *Le bestiaire, ou, Cortège d'Orphée*. Paris: Deplanche, 1911.

Bataille, Georges. *Theory of Religion*. Trans. Robert Hurley. New York: Zone, 1989.

Borges, Jorge Luis. "La biblioteca de Babel." In *El jardín de senderos que se bifurcan*. Buenos Aires: Sur, 1941.

———. *The Book of Imaginary Beings*. Trans. Norman Thomas di Giovanni. New York: Penguin, 1980.

———. "El idioma analítico de John Wilkins." *La Nación* 8 (February 1942): 1.

Bulgakov, Mikhail. *The Heart of a Dog*. Trans. Michael V. Glenny. London: Collins and Harvill Press, 1968.

Cendrars, Blaise. *Moravagine: Roman*. Paris: Grasset, 1926.

Coetzee, J. M. *Elizabeth Costello*. London: Secker & Warburg, 2003.

Darwin, Charles. *The Descent of Man, and Selection in Relation to Sex*. London: John Murray, 1871.

———. *The Expression of the Emotions in Man and Animals*. London: John Murray, 1872.

———. *On the Origin of Species by Means of Natural selection; or, The Preservation of Favoured Races in the Struggle for Life*. London: John Murray, 1859.

de Andrade, Oswald. "Cannibalist Manifesto." Trans. Leslie Bary. *Latin American Literary Review* 19, no. 38 (July–December 1991): 38–47.

Deleuze, Gilles, and Félix Guattari. *Kafka: Toward a Minor Literature*. Trans. Dana Polan. Minneapolis: University of Minnesota Press, 1986.

Éluard, Paul. *Les animaux et leurs hommes, les hommes et leurs animaux*. Paris: Au Sans Pareil, 1920.

Ionesco, Eugène. *Le rhinocéros; pièce en trois actes et quatre tableaux*. Paris: Gallimard, 1959.

Kafka, Franz. *The Metamorphosis: Translation, Backgrounds and Contexts, Criticism*. Trans. Stanley Corngold. New York: W. W. Norton, 1996.

———. "A Report to an Academy." In *The Complete Short Stories of Franz Kafka*, trans. Willa Muir and Edwin Muir. London: Vintage, 1983.

Norris, Margot. *Beasts of the Modern Imagination: Darwin, Nietzsche, Kafka, Ernst, and Lawrence*. Baltimore, Md.: Johns Hopkins University Press, 1985.

Moore, Marianne. *Collected Poems*. New York: Macmillan, 1951.

Minotaure. Ed. Albert Skira and Tériade. New York: Rizzoli International Publications, 1981.

Rilke, Rainer Maria. "Black Cat." In *The Selected Poetry of Rainer Maria Rilke*, trans. Stephen Mitchell. New York: Random House, 1982.

———. "The Eighth Elegy." In *Duino Elegies; The Sonnets to Orpheus*, trans. Stephen Mitchell. New York: Vintage International, 2009.

———. "The Panther." In *The Selected Poetry of Rainer Maria Rilke*, trans. Stephen Mitchell. New York: Random House, 1982.

Skarimbas, Yannis. *To Θείο Τραγί*. Athens: Nefeli, 1993.

Wells, H. G. *The Island of Doctor Moreau*. London: William Heinemann, 1896.

Woolf, Virginia. *Flush: A Biography*. New York: Oxford University Press, 1998.

4. ANTIQUITY

DAVID DAMROSCH

Analyzing modernism should not lead us to fall into a presentism that limits our ability even to understand the recent modernisms themselves. In the absence of a deeper temporal context, historically local choices may be mistaken for inherent or inevitable features of modernity and then of modernism; twentieth-century British or Bengali writers may come to represent modernism tout court.

No one ever lived in antiquity. People live only in the present, and in that sense every culture has always been modern at any given time. Yet an awareness of modernity is far from universal, and it can take many different forms. Every landscape bears the traces, and the scars, of earlier eras, but these traces may be prominent or obscure, and they may or may not loom large in people's consciousness. For some cultures, the distant past is no real issue: its echoes are faint, or they are rarely listened to. Conversely, the monuments and memories of the past can be pervasive, and people may feel closely connected to their ancestors, still fundamentally part of their spiritual and material world. To have a sense of oneself as a modern, however, depends on an active awareness of a premodern era that is understood to have been significantly different from one's own time. In such circumstances, particular weight is often given to the foundational era of antiquity as a prime point of reference, whether for emulation or opposition or both, and so modernity can be said to emerge in dialectical relation to antiquity as its buried twin.

As a literary movement arising both within and against modernity, modernism involves a sense of "an acceleration, a rupture, a revolution in time" (Latour, *We Have Never Been Modern*, 20). Yet for many writers this rupture is a qualified one shadowed by the presence of a distant past to which they remain inextricably tied. Born amid political upheaval and social stress, modernism precipitates out as a crisis of language and of representation, bound up with a fraught but often highly productive relation to the past. These well-known characteristics are prominent in the following fairly little-known passage, probably written around 1900, which can help us think freshly about the more canonical "high" modernists and their struggle for self-definition over against their contemporaries and the distant past alike:

> If only I had unknown phrases, sayings that are strange, novel, untried words, free of repetition; not transmitted sayings, spoken by our ancestors! I will wring out my body of what it holds, to release all my words; for what was said is repetition, when what has been said has already been said! There should be no pride about the literature of the men of former times, or what their descendants discovered! What I say has never been said. . . . I speak these things just as I have seen them.

Our author seeks out strange, unknown phrases, in terms comparable to Baudelaire and Mallarmé's gesturing toward medieval *grimoires* or the retro-mysticism of Huysmans's Des Esseintes, while at the same time seeking to "make it new" in a Poundian sense. Like a good imagist, our author will speak the truth of his own observations, avoiding the clichés of the ancestors whom he repeatedly evokes even while claiming to have left them far behind. His new language will be given psychic and even somatic force by a quasi-expressionist wringing out of language from his body; we may think here of Joyce's Shem the Penman, mixing ink out of his urine and excrement in order to scribble his "nameless shamlessness" on "the only foolscap available, his own body" (Joyce, *Finnegans Wake*, 182, 185). Our author writes in opposition to those he sees around him—let us say, his self-satisfied contemporaries, comfortable in their graffiti-free skins, who fail to experience the pleasurable anguish of the modernist's divided self: "If only I knew what others ignore," he declares, "to say it and have my heart answer me, so I might explain to it my grief, shift to my heart the load on my back . . . and sigh 'Ah' with relief!"

This passage encapsulates a range of themes typically associated with Anglo-American and continental modernism, but its actual provenance is very different. It was written not in London or Paris but in Egypt, and the date I've cited wasn't the more recent 1900 but the earlier one: 1900 BCE. This is the prologue to "The Lamentations of Khakheperre-sonbe," preserved in a collection made in the Eighteenth Dynasty but written earlier. W. K. Simpson and others (*The Literature of Ancient Egypt*, 212) believe that it was likely composed in the late nineteenth century BCE, toward the end of the Twelfth Dynasty or in the chaotic period following the dynasty's collapse, resonantly known today as the "Second Intermediate Period." This was a time of civil strife and economic decline (vividly described in the body of the lamentation), a period in which the nostrums of the older wisdom tradition were wearing thin. An alternative possibility is that Khakheperre-sonbe was actually writing much later, not detailing his own observations at all but merely plundering older texts in order to display his rhetorical skill (Lichtheim, *Ancient Egyptian Literature*, 146), in which event this would be a pseudomodernist text or, we might even say, a protopostmodernist pastiche.

By invoking Khakheperre-sonbe, I don't mean to collapse four millennia of cultural history into a single timeless schema or to deny the exceptional density of modernist production by the Anglo-American and continental writers who continue to serve as prime reference points for field-expanding discussions such as those in Mao and Walkowitz's *Bad Modernisms* (2006) and Wollaeger and Eatough's *Oxford Handbook of Global Modernisms* (2013). Ancient modernisms are often more tentative and ephemeral than the broad movement that gained momentum around our modern 1900, but they are all the more interesting for their challenges to the dominant attitudes toward language and history that reigned around them. The ancient modernisms, whether briefly glimpsed in Khakheperre-sonbe's prologue or fully elaborated in Ovid and Apuleius, can help us resist the common identification of modernism as only a period concept, constructed by a select group of fin-de-siècle writers and their immediate heirs, against whose values all other modernisms are to be assessed.

This tendency persists even in a good deal of work that seeks to globalize modern studies. Thus in his introduction to the *Oxford Handbook*, Mark Wollaeger stresses the importance of "decentering modernism" by developing a global view that doesn't simply map European modernism onto the world at large. The volume includes essays on all sorts of writers, from the Balkans to Vietnam, who have been left out of discussions of modernism. Yet Wollaeger notes only in passing that most of his contributors presuppose that modernism centers on a "core period of about 1890 to 1945" although "they are willing to identify other instances of modernism coming either earlier or (more often) later" (14). This generous "willingness" to find other instances of modernism mostly extends back only as far as Baudelaire in the 1850s or forward to later non-European modernisms. Though the contributors emphasize postcolonial modernists' transformative creativity, across the volume the modernist movement takes on overtones of a *mission civilisatrice* spreading enlightened disillusionment around the globe.

I would like to propose that if we are ever to break from this kind of neoimperial modernism, we should attend to the variety of global modernities that can be explored across time as well as space, a perspective adumbrated over the past decade by Susan Stanford Friedman. Though her own work centers on Western and postcolonial modernisms of the past century, she understands herself as focusing on just some among the many modernisms that have emerged at different times as well as places. As she says in her article "Periodizing Modernism,"

> rethinking the periodization of modernism requires abandoning what I have called the "nominal" definition of modernity, a noun-based designation that names modernity as a specific moment in history with a particular societal configuration that just happens to be the conditions that characterize Europe from about 1500 to the early twentieth century. The "relational" mode of definition, an adjectivally-based approach that regards modernity as a major rupture from what came before, opens up the possibility for polycentric modernities and modernisms at different points of time and in different locations.
>
> (426)

She argues that modernity often arises in the context of empires and conquest, in times and places as disparate as the Roman Empire, Tang Dynasty China, and the Abbasid Caliphate (433). Modernism of one kind or another typically accompanies a given modernity's emergence: as Friedman elsewhere puts it, "Every modernity has its distinctive modernism" ("Planetarity," 475).

Even a "nominal" definition of modernity need not confine itself to just the last few centuries. In his classic study *Five Faces of Modernity*, Matei Calinescu traces the roots of the term "modernity" back to the fifth century CE, when the Latin *modernus* began to displace the older νεώτερος/*neotericus*, in a heightened contrast to *classicus* or *antiquus* (14). Though Calinescu concentrates on later texts that use or imply the term "modern," he adds an important qualification: "Of course, I am fully aware that such a limitation is artificial and that the 'consciousness of modernity' is not tied down to the use of a specific word or of a set of phrases, similes, or metaphors that obviously derive from it" (10). For literary studies of modernism and modernity, anywhere we find written texts we have a key precondition for the development of a self-consciously modern perspective, a factor clearly evident in Khakheperre-sonbe's highly intertextual lament. As the Egyptologist Jan Assmann has remarked, "Historically, the invention of written language marks the turning point in which 'modernity,' as we know it today, began: 'Writing creates history where myth was'" (cited in Richter, review of *Dynamics and Change*, par. 2).

Analyzing modernism should not lead us to fall into a *presentism* that limits our ability even to understand the recent modernisms themselves. In the absence of a deeper temporal context, historically local choices may be mistaken for inherent or inevitable features of modernity and then of modernism; twentieth-century British or Bengali writers may come to represent modernism tout court. In the following pages, I will look at some of the ways in which antiquity was construed in the ancient Near East and the classical Mediterranean world and then conclude by suggesting how an attention to ancient modernities can aid us in comparative study of global modernisms in our own era as well.

Ancient writers knew that they were heirs to centuries or even millennia of previous artistic endeavor. The Assyrians of the seventh century BCE thought of themselves as modern by comparison to the Babylonians, who had dominated Mesopotamia before them. They were immensely proud of the novel strategies and innovations in weaponry that had enabled them to bring Babylon under their rule and to build the greatest empire ever known in the region. Ashurbanipal boasted of receiving tribute from King Gyges of Lydia, "a distant country," he declared, "whose name the kings, my fathers, had never heard" (Luckenbill, *Ancient Records of Assyria and Babylonia*, 2:297). The Babylonians in turn saw themselves as modern by comparison to the Sumerians, whom they had supplanted in the early second millennium BCE, but even the Sumerians hardly thought of themselves as ancients. Four thousand years ago, the world's first known patron of literature, the Sumerian king Shulgi of Ur (r. 2094–2047 BCE), already proclaimed himself to be the preserver and restorer of an ancient literary heritage. "I am no fool," he says in one of his ebullient self-portraits, "as regards the knowledge acquired since the time that mankind was, from heaven above, set on its path: when I have discovered . . . hymns from past days, old ones from ancient times. . . . I have conserved these antiquities, never abandoning them to oblivion." He ordered the old poems to be added to his singers' repertoire, "and thereby I have set the heart of the Land on fire and aflame" ("Šulgi B," lines 270–280).

Most significant among these antiquities was a group of poems about his ancient predecessor Gilgamesh, who had reigned in Uruk, thirty miles from Ur, six centuries before him. Shulgi's scribes' versions of these archaic Sumerian poems became the basis for the *Epic of Gilgamesh*, first in its Old Babylonian version of c. 1600 BCE and then in the "Standard Version" attributed to Sin-leqe-unnini (c. 1200 BCE). In this self-consciously modern rewriting of the older epic, Sin-leqe-unnini presents Gilgamesh himself as the recoverer of ancient stories:

> He saw what was secret, discovered what was hidden,
> he brought back a tale of before the Deluge.
> He came a far road, was weary, found peace,
> and set all his labors on a tablet of stone.
>
> (George, The Epic of Gilgamesh, 1)

Here, Gilgamesh's literary achievements get as much attention as his actual adventures.

A full consideration of ancient writers' relations to their own antiquity could encompass a wide variety of issues. For the writers of a particular time and place, were their ancient predecessors primitive or sophisticated? If primitive, were they innocent and authentic, or had their lives been nasty, brutish, and short? Was antiquity preliterate or already the site of enduring writings? Was it a world of tribes and clans, or of independent city-states, or of a great early empire? What mixture did it involve of what we would now think of as myths versus legends or verifiable history? Just as we are increasingly inclined to speak of modernisms in the plural, we need to be attentive to the wide variety of prior antiquities that existed already within antiquity itself. In the following pages, I will focus on three antinomies that seem particularly suggestive for later modernisms too: for a given culture or group of writers trying to define themselves as modern, was antiquity *their own* or *someone else's*? Was it *single* or *multiple*? And was it *shallow* or *deep*? These antinomies can give us a basis for comparative study of the varieties of modernism that can be traced within early periods as well as over time.

To return to my opening example, for Khakheperre-sonbe antiquity was his own country's foundational history, not the past of some privileged "reference culture" (Denecke, *Classical World Literatures*, 4) such as Greece was for Rome or China was for Japanese writers. Egypt's antiquity was a chthonic past, and it was singular in nature, at least in theory. In actual fact, Egypt had a multiethnic population, and the Nile Delta differed significantly from Upper Egypt to the south. Yet the legendary founder of the First Dynasty, Menes, had united Upper and Lower Egypt into a single oxymoronic entity, "The Two Lands" (*Tawy*), embodied by the kings' dual crown, and the kingdom was taken to have had a singular history ever since. By Khakheperresonbe's time this was a history of great depth. Scribes in the nineteenth century BCE were already heirs to a thousand years of textual tradition, and they loved to study the works of their famous predecessors, whose images adorned the walls of temples and tombs. So strong was the ideology of continuity that few Egyptian writers would have thought of their era as clearly distinct from past times, but periods of social and political turmoil could yield a modern self-awareness, haunted by a lost—but still very audible—past:

> I have heard the words of Imhotep and Hardedef,
> Whose sayings are recited whole.
> What of their cult places?
> Their walls have crumbled,
> Their cult places are gone,
> As though they had never been.
> . . . .
> Make holiday; do not weary of it.
> Lo, none is allowed to take his goods with him,
> Lo, none who departs comes back again.
> (Simpson, *The Literature of Ancient Egypt*, 332–333)

Preserved on the wall of a thirteenth-century tomb, this "Song of the Harper" was composed as early as 2000 BCE; it is probably the oldest surviving example of a poem on the present-centered theme of "carpe diem." So strong is the poet's evocation of loss that it is easy to miss the fact that he does still possess his predecessors' works, which are "recited whole"—read aloud from papyrus scrolls—and so this poem takes shape within a sense of antiquity's simultaneous loss and preservation.

Then as now, the antiquity that mattered most for writers was the era of foundational literary productions that they knew and had to deal with. As Jan Assmann has said of Egyptian scribal culture:

> The emergence of the classics altered the tense of culture. . . . The past was the time of the "classics." It was not a primal age that always remained the

same distance away from the progressive present—a distance that was not temporal but ontic; this was an historical past, whose distance from the present was observable and measurable.

(Assmann, *Cultural Memory and Early Civilization*, 77)

Imhotep and Hardedef were not mythic culture founders like Prometheus in Greece or Quetzalcoatl in Mesoamerica. Imhotep served as vizier to the Third Dynasty king Djoser in the twenty-seventh century BCE; a century later, Hardedef was a son of the pyramid-builder Cheops. Imhotep's fame was sufficiently lasting for the Greeks to have known of him long afterward (as "Imuthes"), and while his sayings have since been lost, we still have portions of Hardedef's maxims today. The Harper's Song thus looks back to sages who had lived six and seven centuries before the poet's own time. If the proposed datings are correct, the poet would have been roughly contemporary with Khakheperre-sonbe, in which event we have evidence of a modernist sensibility extending beyond a single writer during a time of upheaval.

By contrast with the Egyptian scribes, the biblical writers of the exilic and postexilic periods were located very differently in relation to the past. Antiquity for them was only partly their own, extending from the patriarchal age through the time of Moses and the entry into the Promised Land. Equally, they knew how closely their own culture was connected to the histories, and the literatures, of the empires that so often controlled their destinies. From Genesis to Proverbs, Job, and the Song of Songs, the more literary books of the Bible owed much to Egyptian and Babylonian models, and those cultures' foundational eras had an effective history for the Israelites themselves. So in contrast to the Egyptian scribes' singular antiquity, the biblical writers were heirs to three major bodies of ancient traditions, which differed considerably in their historical depth. Their direct Abrahamic and Mosaic heritage was revered but also relatively shallow, unlike the far deeper Egyptian and Babylonian traditions to which they were also reacting. Culturally indebted to the imperial societies that were often oppressing them, the Hebrew writers didn't have the luxury, or the limitations, of an assumption of continuity with Egyptian or Mesopotamian history, and they adopted foreign models with a mix of admiration and distance, transforming and even parodying them in the process.

The Mesopotamian and Egyptian cultures had great historical depth, and they exaggerated it still further; the Sumerian King List stretches back tens of thousands of years. Yet rather than regretting their youth in a world of gerontocratic prestige, the Hebrew writers sometimes chose to present their antiquity as even shallower than it was, as a mark of their continuing closeness to God and his covenant. Thus the modernizing, revisionist book of Deuteronomy (26:5) describes Abraham as the direct father of the contemporary community: "A wandering Aramaean was my father, he went down to Egypt and sojourned there, he and just a handful of his brothers at first, but soon they became a great nation, mighty and many." Reciting this history, the community enters directly into it: "The Egyptians abused and battered us, in a cruel and savage slavery. Then we cried out to the Lord, the God of our ancestors. . . . So the Lord brought us out of Egypt with a mighty hand and an outstretched arm, with great terror, and with signs and wonders" (Deut. 26:6–8). These signs and wonders included drowning Pharaoh's army and slaying the Egyptians' firstborn sons: this was making it new with a vengeance.

By the Hellenistic age, antiquities were multiplying all around the Mediterranean. Whereas the only antiquity that really mattered for Virgil and Ovid was Greek, by the time of Apuleius in the second century CE the floodgates of history had opened up. Born in Madauros in North Africa of mixed Numidian and Berber parentage, Apuleius was sent as an adolescent to study philosophy in Athens and then to Rome to study law. In the prologue to his *Metamorphosis* (or *Golden Ass*), his narrator describes himself as a linguistic acrobat, performing "much as a circus-rider leaps from one horse to another" (1). He comically excuses his provincial Latin by asserting that his style is distorted by his bilingual fluency—not in North African Punic but in the culturally prestigious language of Greek.

Like Virgil and Ovid before him, Apuleius revered Homer, "that godlike creator of ancient poetry among the Greeks," who sang "of him who had attained the highest virtues by visiting many cities and gaining acquaintance with various peoples" (169). His asinine hero's wanderings become a parodic odyssey, and Lucius claims that even though he lacks Odysseus's powerful intellect, his metamorphosis into animal form has allowed him to overhear the fund of stories he now retells. In a striking moment in the middle of the book, he attempts to flee a band of robbers, carrying on his back the beautiful Charite, whom the bandits have been holding hostage, and she imagines that their tale will one day become an ancient classic in its own right:

I shall have a picture painted of this flight of mine, and consecrate it in the atrium of my house. This unprecedented theme, "A noble maiden escaping captivity on an ass's back," will be on view, will be heard in common gossip, and will be immortalized by the pens of learned men. You too will have your place among the wonder-tales of old, cited as an example from real life to inspire our belief that Phrixus swam across the sea on a ram, that Europa straddled a bull. If it is true that it was Jupiter who bellowed in the form of a bull, there may lurk within my donkey some human identity or divine personality.

(116–117)

Remarkably, Charite anticipates that once their tale acquires the authority of antiquity, it will inspire skeptical moderns to believe again in the truth of the ancient Greek myths themselves.

The ass's body does, of course, conceal a human, but freeing him will take the power of a much more ancient divinity than Odysseus's patron Athena: Lucius will need the aid of Isis, the Egyptian goddess of the moon and mistress of transformation. Already in his prologue, Apuleius invites his reader to enjoy his "Greekish tale" (*fabulam Graecanicam*), "as long as you don't disdain to run your eye over Egyptian papyrus inscribed with the sharpened point of a reed from the Nile" (1). In the climactic eleventh book, Isis appears to Lucius in a dream vision, granting his fervent wish to be restored to human form, on condition that he be initiated into her mysteries and become her servant. Her speech is filled with references to the antiquity of her cult, and she reveals that she has been worshipped in many forms around the world:

I am the mother of the world of nature, mistress of all the elements, first-born in this realm of time. . . . In one land the Phrygians, first-born of men, hail me as the Pessinuntian mother of the gods, elsewhere the native dwellers of Attica, Cecropian Minerva . . . the Eleusinians, the ancient goddess Ceres.

(220)

Yet amid all these linguistic metamorphoses, her Egyptian name is ultimately the real one: "the Egyptians who flourish with their time-honoured learning—worship me with the liturgy that is my own, and call me by my true name, which is queen Isis" (221).

Apuleius's Greco-Egyptian syncretism was not uncommon in the eastern Hellenistic world. Funerary portraits from Fayyum in Egypt depict the features of the deceased with Roman realism, even when (as in figure 4.1) a toga-clad youth is being guided into the underworld by Thoth and a mummified

FIGURE 4.1 Funerary portrait from Fayyum, Egypt, second century CE.

Osiris. In this painting, the deceased's head is framed in a hieroglyphic inscription offering him safe passage into the afterlife. Resting his weight on
his left foot, he bends his right knee, ready to step into the next world. His
passage will be assisted by the powerful spells contained in the sacred scroll
he holds, much as Lucius's initiation is performed by priests equipped with

hieroglyphic scrolls, "books headed with unfamiliar characters . . . in the shape of every kind of animal" (233).

The Fayyum image suggests a harmonious combination of traditions, but the world of Apuleius's *Metamorphosis* was violent, uncertain, and endangered on all sides. Apuleius satirizes many forms of human venality and corruption, but he also mobilizes Egyptian antiquity against two growing threats to morality: skepticism and monotheism, each rewriting history in alarming ways. Just as Calinescu would say of our more recent modernists (41), Apuleius's modernism is formed in opposition to the threatening modernity around him. Apuleius is quite serious about the divine power of the ancient religion that frees Lucius from his animalistic self. His *Metamorphosis* is aimed squarely at the cultivated secularism of Roman sophisticates like Ovid, whose *Metamorphoses* presents the ancient Greek gods as little more than literary conceits or tropes, colorful characters whose stories offer opportunities to probe purely human concerns and to display his poetic virtuosity. Nor does Apuleius favor the rationalism of his contemporary Marcus Aurelius, raised like him on Homer and on Neoplatonism, for whom it was an open question whether the gods did or didn't actually exist. It is surely no coincidence that the first character to fall victim to the power of witchcraft in Apuleius's tale is a hapless oldster named Socrates.

Yet also of concern to Apuleius is a very different kind of history: the monotheism that was starting to take hold in Rome and in his adoptive city of Carthage, where a group of Christians were martyred in the year of his death. Rejecting every religious tradition but their own and subjecting even Judaism to radical revision, the Christians were asserting a singular salvation history dating back to the creation of the world. During his wanderings, Lucius encounters a dissolute miller's wife, who "despised and ground beneath her heel the powers of heaven; instead of adhering to a sure faith, she sacrilegiously feigned bold awareness of a deity whom she proclaimed to be the only God. By devising empty ceremonies she misled the people at large, and deceived her hapless husband by devoting herself to early-morning drinking"—evidently communion wine—"and day-long debauchery" (170). Among the many peoples whom Isis lists as worshipping her under different names, Jews and Christians are not included.

Apuleius's modernism arises amid the tectonic shifting of competing antiquities just beneath the surface of the present. As the denouement of his story shows, this multiplicity can be liberating as well as troubling. Whether their antiquity was singular or multiple, homegrown or imported, shallow or deep, writers of earlier eras had almost always been playing the historical hand that had been dealt them. For Hellenistic writers, antiquity was becoming less a given, more a matter of choice. Punic culture was evidently still thriving in second-century Madauros (Bradley, *Apuleius and Augustine Rome*, 41–58), and Apuleius made a deliberate decision to leave that cultural world behind even after returning from his studies abroad; he made further choices when he sought initiation into the mystery cults of Isis and also of Dionysus. Very different from Apuleius in his particular choices but similar to him in having choices to make, Tertullian was born in Carthage during Apuleius's years there; raised as a pagan, he then opted for Christianity, as later did Augustine, also a Carthaginian of Punic heritage.

One of the most modern features of the Hellenistic age, then, is the unusual freedom that people had to choose between competing antiquities—a factor bound up with empire, as Friedman emphasizes. In this late imperial context, writers such as Apuleius clearly show one of Calinescu's prime indices of modernism: "the total freedom of individual artists to choose their ancestors at their own discretion" (8). This Hellenistic modernizing process would be reversed with the consolidation of Christian orthodoxy, which ratcheted antiquity back down to a nearly singular form, sidelining classical antiquity or harmonizing it as closely as possible to biblical history. But the modernizing multiplication of antiquities resumed in the Enlightenment and reached a new level of openness in the late nineteenth century, a development comically encapsulated in Gilbert and Sullivan's *Pirates of Penzance* (1879). There Major-General Stanley, having recently acquired a country estate, asserts his kinship with the ancestors buried in its chapel. Describing himself as "their descendant by purchase," he asserts that "with the estate, I bought the chapel and its contents. I don't know whose ancestors they *were*, but I know whose ancestors they *are*" (14).

I hope that the examples discussed in the preceding pages can suggest the interest for global modernist studies of ancient literatures, which already show an intense and varied engagement with antiquity as a prime ground of self-definition. Taken together, the earliest modernities open up a range of terms that can be useful in analyzing contemporary modernisms as well. Shoring up their ruins with fragments of the antiquities available to them, the Euro-American modernists similarly enlist their distant ancestors in the struggle with their contemporaries and their more recent predecessors. They find their way among antiquities that are variously local or imported, shallow or deep, though rarely if ever still singular or simply given a priori. Yeats, Joyce, Pound, and Eliot all have to reckon with a dual antiquity, both biblical and classical, but they diverge widely beyond that base, with Yeats but not Joyce turning to Irish antiquity, Pound to Confucius and the *Shi Jing*, Eliot to Sanskrit studies, and Joyce ransacking *The Book of the Dead* in order to mold the *Wake's* H. C. Earwicker into "the Bug of the Deaf" (134).

In China, the writers of the New Culture movement of the 1920s worked against the Confucian classics not only by turning to modern Europe but also by extensive programs of translation of classical Greek authors, including Homer, Plato, and Aeschylus. Lu Xun and his brother Zhou Zouren reworked Herodotus and Plato in their fiction, even as Lu Xun's madman fears the vengeance of an official whose ledgers he has trodden underfoot: Gu Jiu, "Mr. Ancient Old" (2). Their counterpointing of classical Chinese and Greek can be compared to Ezra Pound's converse blending of Greek and Chinese antiquities, as when in Canto LIII he describes the emperor Yu receiving tribute in the form of sycamores, river stones, " 'and grass that is called Tsing-mo' or μῶλυ"—the plant that Hermes gives to Odysseus to protect him from Circe's spells (Pound, *Selected Cantos*, 64). A page later, Pound records the ancient inscription *hsin jih jih hsin*, the basis for his famous slogan "Make it new." As we read next to the Chinese characters:

Tching prayed on the mountain and
wrote MAKE IT NEW
on his bathtub
Day by day make it new

(65)

Pound doesn't add any Greek gloss to this phrase, but if we are aware of the multiplicity of modernist antiquities, we may also hear an echo of the climactic statement in Revelation 21:5, proclaimed by God from his throne in the New Jerusalem at the very end of the New Testament: Ἰδοὺ καινὰ ποιῶ πάντα—"Behold, I make all things new."

A full exploration of global modernisms will need to bring together studies of early modernities and their different antiquities in many parts of the world, which to date have mostly been explored separately by scholars based in different regions, whether Matei Calinescu for Europe, Satya Mohanty for medieval India, or Jan Assmann on ancient Egyptian modes of preserving and transforming cultural memory. A whole new old world awaits modernist studies today.

WORKS CITED

Apuleius. *The Golden Ass*. Ed. and trans. P. G. Walsh. Oxford: Oxford University Press, 1994.

Assmann, Jan. *Cultural Memory and Early Civilization: Writing, Remembrance, and Political Imagination*. Trans. David Henry Wilson. Cambridge: Cambridge University Press, 2011.

Bradley, Keith. *Apuleius and Augustine Rome: Historical Essays*. Toronto: University of Toronto Press, 2012.

Calinescu, Matei. *Five Faces of Modernity: Modernism, Avant-Garde, Decadence, Kitsch, Postmodernism*. Durham, N.C.: Duke University Press, 1987.

Denecke, Wiebke. *Classical World Literatures: Sino-Japanese and Greco-Roman Comparisons*. Oxford: Oxford University Press, 2013.

Friedman, Susan Stanford. "Periodizing Modernism: Postcolonial Modernities and the Space/Time Borders of Modernist Studies." *Modernism/modernity* 13, no. 3 (2006): 425–443.

———. "Planetarity: Musing Modernist Studies." *Modernism/modernity* 17, no. 3 (2010): 471–499.

George, Andrew, ed. and trans. *The Epic of Gilgamesh: A New Version*. London: Penguin, 1999.

Gilbert, W. S., and Arthur Sullivan. *The Pirates of Penzance; Or, The Slave of Duty*. New York: Chappel, 1911.

The Holy Bible. New Revised Standard Version. New York: Meridian, 1994.

Joyce, James. *Finnegans Wake*. London: Penguin, 2012.

Latour, Bruno. *We Have Never Been Modern*. Trans. Catherine Porter. Cambridge, Mass: Harvard University Press, 1993.

Lichtheim, Miriam. *Ancient Egyptian Literature: A Book of Readings*. Vol. 1, *The Old and Middle Kingdoms*. Berkeley: University of California Press, 1975.

Luckenbill, D. D. *Ancient Records of Assyria and Babylonia*. 2 vols. 1926–1927; repr. Chicago: University of Chicago Press, 1989.

Lu Xun. "A Madman's Diary." In *The Complete Stories of Lu Xun*, trans. Yang Xianyi and Gladys Yang, 1–12. Bloomington: Indiana University Press, 1981.

Mao, Douglas, and Rebecca Walkowitz, eds. *Bad Modernisms*. Durham, N.C.: Duke University Press, 2006.

Mohanty, Satya P. "Alternative Modernities and Medieval Indian Literature: The Oriya *Lakshmi Purana* as Radical Pedagogy." *Diacritics* 38, no. 3 (2008): 3–21.

Pound, Ezra. *Selected Cantos of Ezra Pound*. New York: New Directions, 1970.

Richter, Hedwig. Review of *Dynamics and Change. 2nd Annual Seminar, Bielefeld Graduate School in History and Sociology*. H-Soz-u-Kult, H-Net Reviews. April, 2010. https://www.h-net.org/reviews/showrev.php?id=30045.

Simpson, W. K. *The Literature of Ancient Egypt*. 2nd ed. New Haven, Conn.: Yale University Press, 2004.

"Šulgi B." Electronic Text Corpus of Sumerian Literature (ETCSL), text 2.4.2.02. http://etcsl.orinst.ox.ac.uk.

Wollaeger, Mark, and Matt Eatough, eds. *The Oxford Handbook of Global Modernisms*. New York: Oxford University Press, 2013.

5. CLASSIC

TSITSI JAJI

When Plaatje discovered that many of the proverbs he had heard educated black South Africans quoting were not merely part of the English language but taken directly from Shakespeare, he formulated an interpretation of the bard as a source of "sayings" rather than as a man of the theater. This interpretation effectively recruits the function of Shakespeare into the cultural context of South Africa, where many indigenous languages were rich in proverbs and where quoting such sayings or their English counterparts was a mark of prestige.

The overwhelming consensus in the global North at the end of the nineteenth century held that Africa was fundamentally, even ontologically primitive. Its traditions might be celebrated as inspiration and instigation and its ancient civilizations prompt uneasy awe, but rare indeed was the notion that Africa might produce, or have produced, classic art.[1] Nor were African-descended peoples in the diaspora, whose gradual emancipations continued to drag against access to modernity (1791 in Haiti . . . 1834 in Britain . . . 1848 in France . . . 1865 in the United States . . . 1899 in Brazil . . .), any more likely to lay legitimate claim to the classic. Given their ex-centric position in relation to the hegemonies of taste and style dictated by a global minority of largely white European and North American men, black perspectives on the classic are necessarily novel. As W. E. B. Du Bois put it, invoking Pliny the Elder in his 1920 *Darkwater: Voices from Within the Veil*, "Semper novi quid ex Africa" (32).[2] While the classic might seem to be the opposite of the modern, I argue that for black artists it was a strategy of modernism, one that I call "classic black."

My grounding assumption is that "classic *black*" can and does teach us something new about the relation of the classic to modernism. Recalling the work of LeRoi Jones (later Amiri Baraka) and Nathaniel Mackey in worrying the line of distinction between jazz as noun or verb, I want to think about how the classic, as the seeming obverse of the popular, the vernacular, the "in," might also function as a sort of verb, a way of making meaning and value. Such a consideration should not imply a reactionary call to prioritize elite forms over those with mass appeal. Rather, I want to insist on the diversity of black subject positions, motivations, and artistic practices in order to enrich conversations about the role of black cultural production, particularly music, in modernism. Examples of popular black culture inspiring "high" modernism are well known, but at the same time that T. S. Eliot was quoting the Johnson brothers and Cole's "Under the Bamboo Tree," contemporaneous discourses on music, value, and the role of the past were unfolding among an array of artists of African heritage. Many of these black artists articulated tensions and countercultures of modernity from outside the popular. Attending to *global* black reinventions of the *classic* is a necessary supplement to rich scholarship on popular and vernacular black musics like the blues, ragtime, jazz, *son*, and beguine. As this essay shows, even in seemingly elite forms of black expression, "their special power derives from a doubleness, their unsteady location simultaneously inside and outside the conventions, assumptions, and aesthetic rules which distinguish and periodise modernity" (Gilroy, *The Black Atlantic*, 73).

I will not venture to arbitrate what is and is not a classic: this question has already been debated by such able critics as T. S. Eliot, Frank Kermode, John Maxwell Coetzee, and Ankhi Mukherjee. Instead, I am interested in the work that the notion of the "classic" accomplished for black artists deeply concerned with the sonorous worlds of music, oratory, and linguistics at the beginning of the twentieth century. What did these thinkers use the "classic" for? I approach this question through two case studies, a composition by Samuel Coleridge-Taylor (1875–1912), a musician of British and Sierra Leonean heritage, and an essay by Solomon Tshekisho Plaatje (1876–1932), a writer, activist, and linguist of Batswana South African heritage. While there is much excellent scholarship on African American modernism, I have chosen these two figures precisely because they are *not* African *American*, yet they demonstrate strategies that could be termed globally or transnationally black.

Race serves as a useful optic for these two figures separated by nationality and medium *only* because of the rise of an internationalist movement that linked organized protest against local forms of racial oppression to a global intentional phalanx of allied struggles. This movement crystallized in a modest yet signal gathering, the Pan African Conference of 1900. Fifty-three delegates of African heritage gathered in a diverse assembly that included two attendees from India and fifteen participants of European heritage (Sherwood, *Origins of Pan-Africanism*, 279–288). The conference evinced a new will to make common cause in protesting the most egregious forms of racial discrimination and colonial violence. This orientation stood in contrast to earlier back-to-Africa movements that had seen emigration as an alternative to reform and had in fact relied on colonial logics.[3] To identify as black in this global sense meant partaking in a shared political and ethical project. It was a significant act of self-making as fundamentally modern, an embrace of the call first articulated at the 1900 conference to address *the* "problem of the Twentieth Century . . . the colour-line." In other words, blackness was under renovation at the turn of the century, repurposing discourses rooted in black religious missions, African colonization schemes, and Ethiopianist romance for an emerging global consciousness. Print media ranging from newspapers to musical scores to anthologies were crucial modes of instantiating this consciousness. These print forms captured the simultaneity of contemporaneous expressive cultures and circulated key strategies and tropes. Identifying with a global black struggle, then, became an important way to signal that one was *A New Negro for a New Century*, as one editorial team put it.

What exactly the term "classic" designates is slippery to say the least, and the distinctions between classic, classical, and classicism bring to mind the same definitional debates as the modern/modernity/modernism quandary Susan Stanford Friedman has mined. The classic may be that which has been judged over time to hold merit, excellence, or importance. It implies enduring value or interest, rewarding repeated attention, yet often is distinguished because it is memorable. It may simply be an elegant style impervious to the vicissitudes of fashion, as in "classic black." Yet time is not the only distinguishing factor. As Frank Kermode notes, the term "classic," first coined by Aulus Gellius to refer to works deemed canonical, is defined by a power differential: "*Classicus . . . scriptor, non proletarius*: the classic writer is distinguished from the rabble" (15). We are reminded, then, that the classic assumes an act of sorting, classifying objects by rank, or into groups that share attributes, properties, affinities.[4] While the roots of the term in English can be traced back to Middle French, current usage in modern French emphasizes that classics are models of excellence suited for study (in class). They are works that conform to ancient or traditional approaches to form and style or, more broadly, are practices that follow an established convention.[5] Common to all of these usages is the occluded role of power: to make a classic, one must have the (cultural) capital to assign value. Analogously, the classic is that which is vested with such capital. Here we note that it is no accident that this essay focuses on male authors, as the critical power to assign value as a classic, even the insurgent power of black artists, was highly gendered. Contemporaries such as the Afro-British composer Amanda Aldridge (under the pseudonym Montague Ring), the South African activist Charlotte Maxeke, and the African American author Georgia Douglas Johnson could not claim access to the cultural platforms of their male counterparts. This essay investigates how early twentieth-century black artists who shared a project of vindicationist racial uplift countering centuries of expropriation and prejudice used the "classic" and what their work does to make the term available as a keyword for other instances of global modernism.

SAMUEL COLERIDGE-TAYLOR'S AFRICA: ROMANCE OR CLASSIC

Samuel Coleridge-Taylor's *Twenty-Four Negro Melodies* represents what I would call his most self-consciously and globally black modernist work. Here the "classic" functions not so much as a noun but as an operation, a curatorial procedure that preserves and heightens the appeal of the "simple" materials of folk music and adds a protective layer of cultural prestige to guard it against the looming erosion of value in the face of modern industrialization, urban migration, and racial terror. Coleridge-Taylor is perhaps as unlikely a representative modernist as Booker T. Washington was before Houston Baker's virtuosic reading in *Modernism and the Harlem Renaissance* (1987).[6] As the son of an absent Sierra Leonean doctor and a British mother who raised him, Coleridge-Taylor's musical education placed him in elite circles in a comparatively less racially charged environment than the colonies or the United States at the time. However, British audiences implicitly expected that "Coalie," as he was taunted when young, would offer music with an exotic tinge. His early works appear to have done so within the bounds of the conventional Victorian forms he mastered. However, his career tracks the development of a globally informed black identity over the decade between 1895 and 1905. Increasingly, he viewed African American and African folk music (especially the spirituals) as an urtext limited in its circulation only by its "extreme brevity and unsuitability for the ordinary amateur." The compositional techniques he had honed at the Royal Academy of Music would allow him to transform these folk melodies into works that would survive a rapidly changing present by entering a standard repertoire. In short, he would make them "classics."

Coleridge-Taylor was not only present but also prominently featured at the 1900 Pan African Conference. The conference was an important turning point in his consciousness, and thus he is an ideal figure for considering how transnational black consciousness inflected the uses and valences of "the classic" in the early twentieth century. Music was remarkably central to the gathering. The conference convener, Henry Sylvester Williams, had taught music before emigrating from Trinidad to England; the director of the Fisk Jubilee Singers, Frederick Loudin, was in attendance; and several of Coleridge-Taylor's vocal works were performed, including two from *African Romances*, an 1897 suite of settings of Paul Laurence Dunbar poems. The suite's title is Coleridge-Taylor's rather than Dunbar's. While he attaches "African" to both the suite and the first piece, "An African Love Song," none of the poems specifically refers to Africa. Race is only evoked through quaint descriptors like "dusky" and "swarthy"; nonetheless, the young composer sees in his collaboration with Dunbar an alluring and novel expression of ethnic identity. Just as his musical aesthetics are solidly late romanticist here, literary romance is the dominant mode of Coleridge-Taylor's other large work with Dunbar, the 1898 *Dream Lovers: An Operatic Romance*, for two male and two female characters, chorus, and orchestra. This operetta is actually set in Africa (Madagascar). Apart from tropes of ethnic sympathy it is the successful marriage plot and harmonic resolution that predominate. One is tempted to read the marriage plots joining the African and African American characters as presaging international black solidarity, but the conventional diatonic harmonic language, balanced musical forms, and lack of any non-European melodic material do not convincingly support such a reading. In these works, as in his wildly popular oratorio on Longfellow's *Song of Hiawatha*, his musical innovation (or light exoticism) does not override his mastery of form. Despite the hint at the spiritual "Nobody Knows the Trouble I've Seen" in its opening theme, *Song of Hiawatha* was embraced for its singability, familiar exoticism, and colorful orchestration. It was a staple (or temporary classic) of the British secular choral repertoire, with the score selling hundreds of thousands of copies, and the work was recorded and regularly performed until the Second World War.

It is not until Coleridge-Taylor's later works that a more substantive engagement with African American, Caribbean, and African material becomes apparent, and he joins in an established discourse that viewed the Negro spiritual as an urtext of black musical (and religious) creativity.[7] In 1904, Coleridge-Taylor presents a more decisive turn toward African and Afro-diasporic *musical* content in his *Twenty-Four Negro Melodies* op. 59, reworking melodic themes culled from ethnomusicological studies and collections of spirituals into a set of virtuosic pieces for piano. I would argue for our considering this an example of a modernist practice of global black expression. The fact that Booker T. Washington provided a three-page introduction for that collection indicates how Coleridge-Taylor's music not only reflects but also reinforces transnational black collaboration. Several years earlier the composer first heard spirituals when the Fisk Jubilee Singers toured England. His foreword to the opus 59 score acknowledges that it was "the world renowned and deeply lamented Frederick J. Loudin, manager of the famous Jubilee Singers, through whom I first learned to appreciate the beautiful folk music of my race." Coleridge-Taylor deftly articulates his theory of classic-ing through compositional craft, and it is worth quoting at length:

> The Negro Melodies in this volume are not merely *arranged*—on the contrary, they have been amplified, harmonized and altered in other respects to suit the purpose of the book. I do not think any apology for the system adopted is necessary . . . What Brahms has done for the Hungarian folk-music, Dvořák, for the Bohemian, and Grieg for the Norwegian, I have tried to do for these Negro Melodies. . . . The actual melody has in every case been inserted at the head of each piece as a motto.[8] The music which follows is nothing more nor less than a series of variations built on the said motto. Therefore my share in the matter can be clearly traced, and must not be confounded with any idea of "improving" the original material any more than Brahms' Variations on the Haydn Theme "improved" that.

Coleridge-Taylor stands at the intersection of nineteenth-century European theories of *Volksmusik* that reflected an inborn national spirit, American traditions of collecting and transcribing spirituals, and the rise of ethnomusicology as a discipline. Yet by traversing these distinctions, which had been variously used to hierarchize and sentimentalize race relations, he effectively upends these historical conventions. He thus introduces a modernism that is radical because it takes a global range of black vernacular creativity seriously enough to treat it as a "classic." Insisting that he is not "improving" these songs but doing what Brahms (who had died only a decade earlier) did with an already beautiful theme by a composer of what music historians call the classical era also made a claim for the status of the black musical sources as classics.[9]

An extended discussion of the compositions themselves is not feasible in an essay of this length. However, it is crucial to note that although Coleridge-Taylor's dissimulating preface suggests that he is making the melodies suitable for "the ordinary amateur," his pieces would be difficult for any but the most gifted of pianists. This is apparent in the nearly ubiquitous use of octaves for both the right-hand melodies and the left-hand accompaniments, sometimes at rapid tempi (as in "Going Up" and "My Lord Delivered Daniel"); the many arpeggiated and rolled chords that stretch a tenth or more (as in "They Will Not Lend Me a Child! or *A Ba Boleki Nwana!*"); and large leaps required in the left hand (bringing to mind the virtuosic stride pianists of the following generation). Like Washington, Coleridge-Taylor knew the art of talking out of both sides of his mouth: they displayed Baker's "mastery of form" in slyly putting one over racists too quick to dismiss black talent.

Coleridge-Taylor's cataloguing of differences between the "African Negro" and the "American Negro" and his proposal that both were more easily integrated into a "Caucasian" aesthetic than other "native" non-European musics may strike us as problematically conservative. Yet he carefully indexed sources for his melodies: Henri Junod's ethnomusicological collection *Les chants et les contes des Ba Ronga*, a West African song collected by Victoria Randall, and Loudin's performances, which introduced him to African American spirituals. These detailed citations reflect an impulse to classify and demonstrate scientific authority that was very much in step with contemporaneous African American assertions of the ability to "originate and scientifically arrange good music."[10] Coleridge-Taylor's use of African American, African, and Caribbean folk music anticipated the call that the New Negro movement would issue a generation later to embrace the spirituals but also, less often, African sources for their modernist aesthetics. Locke, writing in 1925, chided African Americans to take up African art, although he noted that their motivations would be different from those of European artists of a generation earlier. He wrote:

what the Negro artist of to-day has most to gain from the arts of the [African] forefathers is perhaps not cultural inspiration or technical innovations, but the lesson of *a classic background*, the lesson of discipline, of style, of technical control pushed to the limits of technical mastery.

A more highly stylized art does not exist than the African. . . . [If] the present vogue of African art should pass, and the bronzes of Benin and the fine sculptures of Gabon and Baoulé, and the superb designs of the Bushongo should again become mere items of exotic curiosity, *for the Negro artist they ought still to have the import and influence of classics* in whatever art expression is consciously and representatively racial.

(256, 267; my italics)

In other words, black artists who presented their work as "consciously and representatively racial" were necessarily motivated by different interests than modernist Europeans, for whom African art had been an epiphany, to use Simon Gikandi's term. Locke viewed the European modernist turn as emerging in a moment that was experiencing the "marked decadence and sterility in certain forms of European plastic art expression, due to generations of the inbreeding of style and idiom [plagued by] the exhaustion of imitating Greek classicism" (258–259).

Coleridge-Taylor's turn to African and African American folk music would seem to be just the sort of move Locke would later recommend. As a keyword for Coleridge-Taylor's transnational black modernism, "classic" remains rooted in its shared etymology with "classification" and with that "class" of works judged over time to merit being taught, emulated, and passed on to succeeding generations.

SOLOMON TSHEKISHO PLAATJE: STANDARDIZING THE CLASSIC

Sol T. Plaatje is best known for his diary documenting the Anglo-Boer War, his collagelike nonfiction work *Native Life in South Africa* (1916), and his novel *Mhudi: An Epic of South African Native Life* (completed in the early 1920s but only published in 1930). Born to Tswana parents and raised at the German mission where they worked, Plaatje had an unusual ear for language and music, and he mastered nine languages. Our interest lies in the intersection of his careers as a linguist and a writer. Plaatje was deeply concerned about the distortions introduced into indigenous South African languages like his mother tongue, Setswana, as they transformed from oral to written languages via the dual processes of colonization and evangelization. Three pressing concerns occupy his writings on linguistics in the modern era of colonial expropriation and racial segregation. First, the miscarriages of justice that indigenous South Africans faced when their encounters with the state were mistranslated by official interpreters. Second, the confusion created by multiple orthographies for indigenous languages that were the direct result of competing systems among various missions. And third, the dual problem of cultural amnesia whittling away at younger generations' knowledge of deep language structures like proverbs and idiomatic expressions and, simultaneously, the cultural isolation of those whose lack of command of English limited their access to reading material. I have discussed elsewhere Plaatje's essays on the need for competent court interpreters and his enthusiasm for the standardized notation of tonal languages enabled by a cutting-edge new system: the International Phonetic Alphabet.[11] Here, however, I propose a close reading of (an English translation of) the introduction to his translation of Shakespeare's *Comedy of Errors*, *Diphosho-phosho*, which was published in 1930 along with three other plays he translated. The introduction reflects Plaatje's belief that a "classic" was defined by its translatability across not only languages and historical periods but also across colonial power differentials.[12]

I want to argue for reading Plaatje's theory of translation as a *critical* discourse, one that locates his work within the hermeneutic and evaluative processes most fundamental to the "classic" as that which is *judged over time* to be "of *acknowledged* excellence or importance," to turn to the *OED*'s primary definition (my italics). For Plaatje, a translatable "classic" was a number of things: a finely wrought conduit through which one could pour "original" content, an echoing pipe down which to hiss biting satirical critique and indigenous parody on the Ellisonian "lower frequencies," and a two-way channel where "source" and "target" languages rewrote each other through exchanges of sociolinguistic value. What made the difference between a finely wrought translatable classic and a crude, quickly forgotten novelty was a careful and critical practice of translation as a multidirectional transaction, which is why Plaatje spends so much time on the broad questions of Setswana orthography.

The first indication that his approach to translation is as wily as those of his fellow modernists from Beckett to Pound lies at the top of the title page. The work is entitled "Mabolelo a ga Tsikinya-Chaka (The Sayings of William Shakespeare)." As David Schalkwyk and Lerato Lapula have noted, Plaatje's first encounter with Shakespeare was a live performance of *Hamlet*. When he discovered that many of the proverbs he had heard educated black South Africans quoting were not merely part of the English language but taken directly from Shakespeare, he formulated an interpretation of the bard as a source of "sayings" rather than as a man of the theater.[13] This interpretation effectively recruits the *function* of Shakespeare into the cultural context of South Africa, where many indigenous languages were rich in proverbs and where quoting such sayings or their English counterparts was a mark of prestige. Furthermore, the bard's name is phonetically transcribed as Shake-Spear and then translated literally into Setswana as Tsikinya-Chaka. Plaatje shakes the synecdoche of imperial prestige, England's most universally esteemed author, like a spear in the face of Dominion while simultaneously turning his back on the hegemony of the English language, taking Tsikinya-Chaka hostage for his project of vernacular modernism. The preface is itself a sly play on Shakespeare's title, for in cataloguing the various limitations, problems, and resulting misprisions occasioned by the legacy of an orthography invented for "religious literature," Plaatje depicts the missionary project as its own comedy of errors. Damning with faint praise, he notes that "Batswana authors find these orthographies useful in one way or another" but then raises one little frustration, a mere jot: the missing letter *j*. He goes on to explain its significance with an inside joke:

> In this book we have added the letter "j" to the missionary alphabet, so that we can distinguish words such as *nyalela* (marry my daughter) and *njalela* (give me some seed). Had we not done this, readers would misunderstand Antifoluse when he said to his younger brother, "*U njetse tinare*" ("You have partaken of my dinner"), and would think he was using vulgar language, when he was not. [*Nyetse*, a synonym of *nyalela*, would imply an inappropriate passion for dinner.]
>
> (383)

If missionaries are the originators of *written* Setswana, they are presumably among the readers who are likely to be duped by their own scriptive practices. Plaatje thus signifies on recurrent and inane Western stereotypes of Africans as sexually depraved, vulgar, and primitive. Such racism is already inscribed in the Western notations of Setswana, and it is the incestuous relation between colonial writing and colonial meaning making that would vandalize Shakespeare's text into a scandalous one were it not for the "minor" corrective Plaatje applies to the alphabet.

He continues by gnawing at the very root of British imperial pride, the purported lineage from Rome's hegemony to the Pax Britannia: "the 26 letters of the Roman alphabet used in all these books is insufficient for Setswana" (383).

The Setswana language, unlike antiquated English, for which an alphabet invented millennia ago suffices, demands the most modern of linguistic technologies. "That is why [he has] borrowed letters from the International Phonetic Alphabet, namely ŋ and ." Not finished, Plaatje's next paragraph adds another letter from the IPA, ɔ. Justifying this choice, he lists a number of examples, closing with the difference the new IPA character allows readers to recognize between the Setswana words for "steam" and "ignoramus." This is hardly an innocent choice: the first steam train in South Africa was introduced in 1860, and the development of railways rapidly gathered speed after the discovery of diamonds at Kimberley. Reminding his Tswana audience that there was only a slight (and hitherto ignored) difference between steam, a symbol of the industrial capitalism that had already cost South Africans so much, and the ignoramuses imposing it made for a piercing jibe.

The index of problems with existing mission-derived orthographies ended with a set of words Plaatje did not offer any remedy for, implying that even with the best tools of scientific linguistics, Setswana was too musical a language to be captured adequately by script: "in Setswana tone plays a very important role in that it conveys different meanings in words which look identical, such as *ditlhaka* (reeds) and *ditlhaka* (letters)" (383). Readers and killers were indistinguishable, pride and opening one's eyes might be mistaken for each other, and the difference between a hiding place and experience were only discernible by those who had a command of Setswana tones, largely native speakers. While outsiders proudly wielding the authority of their letters risked getting lost among the "native" reeds, the savvy reader could look forward to an entertaining treat: this trickster introduction was just the warm-up for an entire comedy of errors.

In the following section, Plaatje avows, "It has not been an easy task to write a book such as this, it has been both difficult and intricate" (383). Dwelling on the difficulty of his labor in translating Shakespeare, Plaatje calls to mind the ways that translation and difficulty were core values for "high" modernism. Similarly, Plaatje's choice to call his novel *Mhudi* an epic reminds us of the genre's significance for Joyce, Stein, Pound, and others. However, Plaatje's motivation for taking on this difficult task was the alarm shared by many of his compatriots. "Tau's Setswana"—the language of Tau, the last ruler of the Barolong nation that Plaatje immortalizes in his novel—was rapidly being displaced by "the missionary language." Given that "Tau" also means lion, Plaatje here stages, yet again, the struggle over dynastic power, pitching the Tswana lion against the British lion. These examples show Plaatje's skill as a master of double entendre. Similar rhetorical strategies were mobilized by blacks in other parts of the globe to destabilize colonial and race relations. Such parodic linguistic strategies appear in works such as Kobina Sekyi's *The Blinkards* (1916), Claude McKay's *Constab Ballads,* and the brilliant outmaneuvering of minstrelsy in the work of Bert Williams and George Walker.

Yet if it appears that Plaatje was aligned with a stable, monolithic ethnic identity, his next critique exposes the dangers of confusing linguistic pride with ethnic chauvinism. It is a truism that the most fundamental damage wrought by colonialism was the conscription into global capitalism. Plaatje had detailed in his *Native Life in South Africa* how economic exploitation from hut taxes to land expropriation to coerced labor in the mines were unraveling black life in the early twentieth century. On a more personal level, Plaatje the writer faced a lifelong struggle to raise the funds to publish his work. Many of his shorter writing projects (such as a 1921 pamphlet entitled "The Mote and the Beam," which Plaatje sold during his tour of North America at twenty-five cents a copy) were intended to underwrite longer works such as the Shakespeare translations, his novel, and what he considered his most important life's work: a collection of Setswana proverbs. Shifting the object of his critique from language to capital, Plaatje reports in the introduction on the difficulties of publishing. He notes how, when he found himself unable to meet the costs of printing the translation, he first appealed to a number of "well-to-do Batswana," supposing that "when they heard that this was for a book in their own language they would stop simply asking for a book in Setswana and instead make it possible for it to be printed" (384). However, they were not willing to infuse the capital needed to translate Shakespeare, rendering it a Setswana classic. Despite the self-interested miserliness of his compatriots, he found an Indian and four Europeans willing to fund the publication. Thus, Plaatje's translation became a multiracial, even global exercise in modernist translation.

A similar frustration with the lack of interest among the Batswana appears to frame his closing anecdote. He recounts the perplexity of a certain old man who, observing Plaatje and his fellow linguist D. M. Ramoshoana laboring late into the night, asks "What is it that you gain from your witchery . . . working tirelessly on your books, when the rest of the people are asleep?" (385). Ramoshoana replies: " 'There are presently about 300 African languages which have their own printed books. If I die having translated one of Shakespeare's plays into Setswana I shall rest in peace, because I will have done something *for you*' " (385; my italics).

In Ramoshoana's address to a man of an older generation who believes "witchery" and literacy are twin arts of the night, Plaatje seems to stage an encounter between the ancient and the modern. Yet there is little antagonism here. Rather, Ramoshoana proposes a bond, linking the old man's aging to his own eventual death and implying that just as the old man seeks a peaceful night's rest despite his anxiety over these mysterious scribblers, so too Ramoshoana hopes to "rest in peace" after his death. But he also suggests that the translation of Shakespeare's classic into Setswana does something for the old man, who by all appearances is illiterate. However, this certain old man was first recognized for his mastery of Setswana verbal art, for it is at a moment when Ramoshoana and Plaatje are "puzzled by a problem [in their translation work that they summon] a certain man who was going past" them and seek his assistance. Literacy is irrelevant to the ethical relation between the three. Ramoshoana and Plaatje consider their translation of "the sayings of Shake-Spear" an offering to the Setswana language and the Batswana people and a work that parallels earlier generations' bequest of a vast repertoire of Setswana proverbs. Transferring value and prestige across exponential differentials of power—between the world of letters and the world of primary orality, between the imperial literary canon and an indigenous emergent orthography—was a project of such anticolonial bravado that the resulting entanglement of *The Comedy of Errors/Diphosho-phosho* can be considered a modernist classic in the tradition of classic black.

NOTES

1. See Gikandi, "Africa and the Epiphany of Modernism"; and Archer-Straw, *Negrophilia.*

2. Du Bois, perhaps quoting from memory, reformulates the original, "Ex Africa semper aliquid novi," which is used in a notably different context, Pliny's zoological discussion.

3. On predecessors of pan-Africanism as a formal movement, see Appiah, *In My Father's House*; Gilroy, *The Black Atlantic*; and Hamilton, "Introduction."

4. The *OED*'s entries for "classic," (noun) "class" (noun and verb), and "classify."

5. *Tresor de la langue francaise*, entries for "classique."

6. Baker shows how the Wizard of Tuskegee achieved a "mastery of form," bending the taste for racial caricature and minstrelsy among white Southerners (and Northerners) resistant to real advancement for blacks to hold their attention to his proposals for education while at the same time signifying or, as Zora

Neale Hurston might have called it, "lying" to assure black audiences of his good faith.

7. See Richards, "A Pan-African Composer?"

8. *The Souls of Black Folk*, published the previous year by Du Bois, includes incipits from spirituals at the head of each chapter, a practice also adopted by other black modernists including Alain Locke, James Weldon Johnson, and Langston Hughes.

9. Later music historians identified "Haydn's" theme as the "Chorale St. Antoni," of debated authorship, but it is still regularly referred to by the name Brahms gave it.

10. See Ramsey's discussion of James Trotter in "Cosmopolitan or Provincial?"

11. See Jaji, *Africa in Stereo*.

12. Isabel Hofmeyer's *The Portable Bunyan* is an important precedent for my reading.

13. See Schalkwyk and Lapula, "Solomon Plaatje, William Shakespeare, and the Translation of Culture."

WORKS CITED

Archer Straw, Petrine. *Negrophilia: Avant-Garde Paris and Black Culture in the 1920s*. London: Thames & Hudson, 2000.

Appiah, Kwame Anthony. *In My Father's House*. New York: Oxford University Press, 1992.

Baker, Houston. *Modernism and the Harlem Renaissance*. Chicago: University of Chicago Press, 1987.

Coetzee, J. M. "What Is a Classic? A Lecture." In *Stranger Shores: Literary Essays*. New York: Penguin, 2001.

Coleridge-Taylor, Samuel. *Twenty-Four Negro Melodies Transcribed by the Piano by S. Coleridge-Taylor*. Opus 59. Boston: Ditson, 1905.

Coleridge-Taylor, Samuel, and Paul L. Dunbar. *African Romances*. Opus 17. London: Augener, 1897.

———. *Dream Lovers: An Operatic Romance*. Opus 25. London: Boosey, 1898.

Du Bois, W. E. B. *Darkwater: Voices from Within the Veil*. 1920; repr. Mineola, N.Y.: Dover, 1999.

———. *The Souls of Black Folk*. New York: A. C. McClurg, 1903.

Eliot, T. S. *What Is a Classic?* London: Faber and Faber, 1945.

Friedman, Susan Stanford. "Definitional Excursions: The Meanings of Modern/Modernity/Modernism." *Modernism/modernity* 8, no. 3 (2001): 493–513.

Gikandi, Simon. "Africa and the Epiphany of Modernism." In *Geomodernisms: Race, Modernism, Modernity*, ed. Laura Doyle and Laura Winkiel, 31–50. Bloomington: Indiana University Press, 2005.

Gilroy, Paul. *The Black Atlantic: Modernity and Double Consciousness*. Cambridge, Mass.: Harvard University Press, 1993.

Hamilton, Ruth Simms. Introduction to *Routes of Passage: Rethinking the African Diaspora*, vol. 1, part 1, ed. R. Simms Hamilton. Lansing: Michigan State University Press, 2006.

Hofmeyr, Isabel. *The Portable Bunyan: A Transnational History of* The Pilgrim's Progress. Princeton, N.J.: Princeton University Press, 2004.

Jaji, Tsitsi. *Africa in Stereo: Modernism, Music, and Pan-African Solidarity*. New York: Oxford University Press, 2014.

Jones, LeRoi. "Swing—from Verb to Noun." In *Blues People: Negro Music in White America*. New York: Morrow, 1967.

Kermode, Frank. *The Classic: Literary Images of Permanence and Change*. Cambridge, Mass.: Harvard University Press, 1983.

Locke, Alain. "The Legacy of the Ancestral Arts." In *The New Negro: Voices of the Harlem Renaissance*, ed. Alain Locke, 254–268. New York: Simon and Schuster, 1992.

Mackey, Nathaniel. "Other: From Noun to Verb." In *Jazz Among the Discourses*, ed. Krin Gabbard, 76–99. Durham, N.C.: Duke University Press, 1995.

McKay, Claude. *Constab Ballads*. London: Watts, 1912.

Mukherjee, Ankhi. "'What Is a Classic?': International Literary Criticism and the Classic Question." *PMLA* 125, no. 4 (2010): 1026–1042.

Plaatje, Solomon Tshekisho. "Introduction to *Diphosho-phosho* (translation of *The Comedy of* Errors." In *Sol Plaatje: Selected Writings*, ed. Brian Willan, 381–385. Athens: Ohio University Press, 1998.

——. *Mafeking Diary: A Black Man's View of a White Man's War*. Ed. John Comaroff. London: James Currey; Athens: Ohio University Press, 1973.

——. *Mhudi: An Epic of Native South African Life*. Marianhill: Marianhill Press, 1930.

——. *Native Life in South Africa*. 1916; repr. Essex: Longmann, 1987.

——. *Sechuana Reader in International Orthography (with English Translations)*. London: University of London Press, 1916.

Ramsey, Guthrie. "Cosmopolitan or Provincial? Ideology in Early Black Music Historiography, 1867–1940." In *Black Music Research Journal* 16, no. 1 (Spring 1996): 11–42.

Richards, Paul. "A Pan-African Composer? Coleridge-Taylor and Africa." *Black Music Research Journal* 21, no. 2 (Autumn 2001): 235–260.

Schalkwyk, David, and Lerato Lapula. "Solomon Plaatje, William Shakespeare, and the Translation of Culture." *Pretexts: Literary Cultural Studies* 9, no. 1 (2001): 9–26.

Sekyi, Kobina. *The Blinkards*. London: Heinemann, 1974. (First performance, 1915)

Sherwood, Marika. *Origins of Pan-Africanism: Henry Sylvester Williams, Africa, and the African Diaspora.* London: Routledge, 2011.

Washington, Booker T., Fannie Barrier Williams, and Norman Barton, eds. *A New Negro for a New Century: An Accurate and Up-to-Date Record of the Upward Struggles of the Negro Race.* Chicago: American Publishing House, 1900.

6. CONTEXT

CHRISTOPHER BUSH

The global turn puts conflicting methodological pressures on modernist studies' desire for context. On the one hand, it reinforces (albeit with an extra political charge) the field's dominant tendency to valorize histori- cal context against that aesthetic autonomy said to have been valued in the bad old days. On the other hand, the very idea of the global implies new conceptions of history so unimaginably vast and complex that we can hardly rely on them to perform their traditional function of explanatory, clarifying, context.

One of the most memorable passages in Benedict Anderson's classic ac- count of nationalism, *Imagined Communities*, is his reading of the scene in José Rizal's *Noli me tangere* (1887) in which our protagonist, Juan Crisóstomo Ibarra y Magsalin, having returned from a seven-year stay in Europe, expe- riences an uncanny disidentification with the gardens of his native Manila. Anderson returns to this scene fifteen years later in a collection of essays whose title, *The Spectre of Comparisons*, is taken from the very same passage in Rizal's novel, in which the gardens are, for Juan Crisóstomo, "shadowed automatically . . . inescapably by images of their sister gardens in Europe. He can no longer matter-of-factly experience them, but sees them simultane- ously close up and from afar. The novelist arrestingly names the agent of this incurable vision *el demonio de la comparaciones*" (Anderson, *The Spectre of Comparisons*, 2).[1]

Texts such as Rizal's make explicit the extent to which the spectral dis- location of the local has been a constitutive experience of modern life. It is telling that the most influential theorist of nationalism of the last thirty years should repeatedly return to a scene in which the experience of national be- longing is defined not by the centripetal imagining of community but by the spectral presence of other, distant nations—or, rather, other nations at once near and far.

How does one read such a text in *its historical context*? In so many ways, any credible reading of a loosely autobiographical novel about life under colonialism, a novel that has since come to be treated as the defining literary work of the world's twelfth most populous nation, knowledge of which in the West is generally thin, demands such contextualization. Yet the novel's power as a literary work, even its status as a *national* classic, derives from the fact that its "own" historical context was not entirely its own. Is it, then, right or even desirable to render close, only close, what had seemed at once near and far, to cure, with our hindsight and in the name of historical fidelity, the text's "incurable vision" and thus reanimate, with wounds healed, a work that had, after all, greeted us "noli me tangere"?[2]

The global turn puts conflicting methodological pressures on modernist studies' desire for context. On the one hand, it reinforces (albeit with an extra political charge) the field's dominant tendency to valorize historical context against that aesthetic autonomy said to have been valued in the bad old days. On the other hand, the very idea of the global implies new conceptions of history so unimaginably vast and complex that we can hardly rely on them to perform their traditional function of explanatory, clarifying, *context*. Thinking about modernism more globally should require not simply multiplying the number of contexts (Spain for the Spanish, Korea for the Koreans) but also considering the dynamic interactions between these various contexts and, ultimately, confronting "the world" as the context of interpretation. This can be discouraging because whatever else it has been or may become, "the world" will always remain something you can be accused of not having fully taken into account. "Context" thus comes to function less as the recovered slipper for Cinderella's foot and more as the inadequately singular name of an ever-receding horizon, a problem rather than a solution.

If thinking globally required first knowing the whole of the world and then reading any given text in relation to that knowledge, we would indeed be in trouble. But the global need not be understood as the sum total of all that is knowable about the world. The challenge of reading modernism more globally is often more a question of how we know than of how much. That is, we might frame the global not as a problem of inclusivity or scale but rather as a perpetual challenge to the comforting connotations of con-text, of what we put with what, and why. The world is not a pregiven unity waiting to become an object of more or less accurate knowledge, not a completed *fact* that lifts the scales of the national from our eyes, but an interpretive attitude that initiates new dialectics of insight and blindness.[3] For better and worse, this means anyone studying "the world" participates in (or, if you prefer, is complicit in) its realization.

Such an interpretive attitude is historically justified if we believe that the impossible horizon of the global already haunted modernism. Indeed, I began with Rizal to suggest how the global might be understood in this way, as a *qualitative* problem at the heart of (for example) everyday, ostensibly national, modernity. It is perhaps unsurprising that an anticolonial text would be self-reflexive about its "peripheral" location in the world.[4] But what happens at the "center," where one might assume the specter of comparisons is more easily kept out of the magic circle of the here and now? Consider, for example, as a kind of asymmetrical pendant to Rizal, the near-contemporaneous but differently doubled public garden in an oft-quoted passage in Oscar Wilde's "The Decay of Lying" (1889), in which the character Vivian explains that the Japanese aesthetic sensibility so prized by his *japoniste* contemporaries is not local to Japan at all. "In fact," he explains,

> if you desire to see a Japanese effect, you will not behave like a tourist and go to Tokio [*sic*]. On the contrary, you will stay at home and steep yourself in the work of certain Japanese artists, and then, when you have absorbed the spirit of their style, and caught their imaginative manner of vision, you will go some afternoon and sit in the Park or stroll down Piccadilly, and if you cannot see an absolutely Japanese effect there, you will not see it anywhere.
>
> (82)

The unlikeliness of this juxtaposition of Rizal and Wilde—the *engagé* and the aesthete—says a lot about what we talk about when we talk about context. Rizal's novel was published just two years before Wilde's essay. During the intervening year Rizal spent several months in Japan, whose modernization he imagined as a possible alternative to Euro-American hegemony.[5] Rizal then traveled throughout the United States and on to Europe, where he would spend ten months at the British Museum reading room working on his second novel, *El filibusterismo* (1891), precisely when Wilde was writing his essay.[6]

Now, I do not wish to suggest any *direct* connection between Rizal and Wilde (although, who knows?)[7] but simply to point out how selective conventional notions of historical context are and that this selectivity has conceptual consequences. Vivian's remark is of course meant to debunk naive notions about the truth-value of the "imitative arts," but in doing so it acknowledges the role Japanese art was playing in the aesthetic education of modern Europe. Wilde no doubt had seen Japanese effects in Piccadilly, and this was the work of (an admittedly rather benign) specter of comparison as surely as that moment in the garden in Manila was a European effect.

Fredric Jameson's "Modernism and Imperialism" famously links modernist formal innovation to the increasing importance of imperial networks: "daily life and existential experience in the metropolis—which is necessarily the very content of national literature itself, can now no longer be grasped immanently; it no longer has its meaning, its deeper reason for being, within itself" (51). In the age of high imperialism (whose consolidation Jameson links to the 1884–1885 Berlin Conference), the real economic and political foundations of social life become something modern metropolitan experience itself "constitutively lacks": no matter how much one learns, travels, or empathizes, these foundations remain "an outside like the other face of a mirror." This constitutive absence is, according to Jameson, "the dilemma, the formal contradiction, that modernism seeks to solve." Or, "better still," he quickly specifies, "it is only that new kind of art which reflexively perceives this problem and lives this formal dilemma that can be called modernism in the first place" (51). Although predating "modernism" in the narrow sense, the juxtaposition of Rizal and Wilde (with the mediator Japan) restages the formal dilemma Jameson describes as central to thinking about literary modernism in more global terms: should metropolitan and colonial experience be understood as completely unrelated, as two sides of the same mirror, or in yet some other way? Figuring their relationship as two faces of the same mirror has the advantage of suggesting their simultaneity and interdependence but has the clear disadvantage of reifying their separation, suggesting two things that cannot know each other and cannot be known at the same time.

The similar and related figures of dislocation in Rizal and Wilde show not a clear opposition between representations of the naked truth of exploitation in the colonies and the always unconscious, essentially unknowable effect of the colonial in the metropolis but rather different configurations of the immanence and absence of "the world" in any given place. Rizal's and Wilde's perhaps parallel-seeming universes were, I have suggested, empirically more proximate, even interconnected, than might first appear. Such a claim does not, however, exclude the formal dimensions of modernism as defined by Jameson but rather transforms a large opposition (metropolis/colony) into a series of graduated, local oppositions. Modifying Jameson's argument in this way allows us to take more seriously the rich empirical knowledge of, and complex aesthetic engagement with, the colonial that is often *explicitly* present in the corpus of metropolitan modernisms and, at the same time, to allow for the possibility of "modernism" (even on Jameson's terms) on the periphery. Rather than thinking of colony and metropolis as the *other* of each other, they might more productively be thought of as each other's *context*. Or, more carefully, as both *other* and *context*. What does it mean, then, to study a modernist work in *its historical context*?

ITS?

Eric Hayot's claim that "no one is really a New Historicist any more" ("Against Periodization," 742) because everyone is de facto a New Historicist seems especially apt with respect to modernist studies, a field that defined itself as a break from a broadly New Critical consensus toward a New Historicist consensus, bridging the Great Divide of low and high cultures and sending scholars to the archives of the BBC, the FBI, and 1920s *Vogue*.[8] There is a particularly strong temptation, then, for modernist studies to approach the problem of context in rather binary terms: one either *reduces* or *restores* a text to its historical context. In many respects the study of literary modernism went straight from New Criticism to a kind of thinned-out New Historicism that often bypasses the cultural-anthropological density and the debates about the nature of historical evidence that had characterized New Historicist studies of early modern literature (see Gallagher and Greenblatt, *Practicing New Historicism*).[9]

Any claim to read a text in terms of *its* context is a claim to reveal or restore a preexisting propriety, in opposition to the inaccuracy, even violent dispossession, of *not* reading in this way. Yet the effects of this seemingly descriptive possessive pronoun can be no less violent, as when someone is told to sit down in "his" seat or a woman is told that she should know "her" place. The very fact that propriety needs to be asserted is often an indicator that things might be, perhaps already are, not so. Assertions of contextual priority are at least as performative as constative and should, accordingly, be understood not just in terms of how well they (re)align text and context but also in terms of what allows them to be efficacious in the first place: who speaks, to whom, how, and (ahem!) in what context. There are therefore legitimate concerns about the potential for "context" to be wielded as a blunt instrument that effaces the specificity of any given text, especially when context is assumed to be something already known and easily looked up in a history book, as when literature is used to *illustrate, represent,* or *reflect* a context but, by contrast, the context *explains* the literature.

Jameson's essay suggests an alternative sense of context at once sophisticated and dissatisfying in ways that will be familiar to most literary scholars. The essay's claim that modernism emerged most forcefully in areas defined by uneven development is undeniably insightful: Joyce's Dublin, Musil's Vienna, and Faulkner's Yoknapatawpha County come immediately to mind. It is not too difficult to extend this model beyond the modernist canon when considering works whose geopolitically "peripheral" status compels them to describe their "own" context extensively and whose very emphasis on the local reveals an other-directedness: even in a straightforwardly sociological sense, such works are in part intended for cosmopolitan audiences that are and are not "theirs."[10] (Moretti's concluding *Modern Epic* with a reading of Gabriel Garcia Marquez's *One Hundred Years of Solitude* is a paradigmatic example of such an extension of Jameson's method.)

Yet to the extent that one accepts the argument that peripherality is constitutive of modernism in general, the lessons of uneven, peripheral, and colonial/postcolonial literatures should redound upon the modernism of the metropolis, recalling the specters of comparison that haunts, for example, the London not only of *Heart of Darkness* but also of *Mrs. Dalloway.* The crucial point is that thinking globally about the "context" of a work in terms of any geopolitical plotting requires abandoning the prioritization of the local and the simultaneous. This is not to abandon the solid ground of history for speculative freefall but to acknowledge that the ground of history itself is ever shifting and still remains largely unmapped.

HISTORICAL?

Invocations of the priority of context are almost always implicitly about *historical* context, and historical context is almost always by default national-historical (if not more spatially localized): things that happened at the same time and close by are treated as mattering more than those that happened at another time or at a distance. The reductio ad absurdum of this tendency is to imagine as the ideal interpretive model a Google Glass mounted on the author's face.[11] Correspondingly, critiques of contextualization often question the value of the national as a spatial limit and of simultaneity as the ideal historical horizon.[12] Yet even if one wants to prioritize national context, any serious consideration of the nation reveals it to be more than a geographically bounded space (even in those rare instances where a nation-state has a relatively longstanding spatial continuity). Not only did the valorization of the national emerge in an international context,[13] but even the internal logic of the national is not governed by simultaneity, instead invoking pasts and futures with which it can claim some identity. Anderson famously discusses the importance of imagined simultaneities for a sense of national belonging, but he also emphasizes the pull of other times: that "reverse teleology" (*The Spectre of Comparisons*, 257) that, as in Michelet, "claim[s] to speak *for* generation after generation of dead 'French' men and women who did not know themselves to be such" as well as that drive to become "the forefathers of the race of the future," a future of which we like to imagine, as Max Weber wrote in 1895, that, if "we could *rise from the grave* thousands of years from now," we would find that "the future recognizes in our nature the nature of its own ancestors" (in *The Spectre of Comparisons*, 361; emphases added). An essential feature of national identity is that it does not happen all at once: it claims to speak to and for the unborn and the dead. This is something other than historical context in the conventional sense, then, in that it takes seriously the often very real effects of how things really were *not*.

The national subject must project not only simultaneity and a common future but should also, like the ideal poet in T. S. Eliot's "Tradition and the Individual Talent" (1919), live "in what is not merely the present, but the present moment of the past" (*Selected Essays*, 11). While this most canonical formulation of the canonical would seem quite remote from the concerns of a globalizing modernist studies, especially one informed by colonial literatures and postcolonial theory, the homology of Eliot's essay with the structure of national time merits closer scrutiny. Eliot asserts that "the historical sense involves a perception, not only of the pastness of the past, but of its presence" (4). To be truly modern, poets should write not only with a distinct sense of the present but also "with a feeling that the whole of the literature *of Europe* from Homer and *within it* the whole of the literature of *his own country*" are essential contexts of the present, contexts whose "simultaneous existence . . . composes a simultaneous order" (4; emphases added). Poets should, therefore, be "set . . . for contrast and comparison, among the dead" (4), but it should be emphasized that these (European, national) dead populate the "simultaneous" past of the poet's present as surely as do the crowds flowing over London Bridge. Eliot famously ends with the assertion that the poet must live "in what is not merely the present, but the present moment of the past," must be "conscious, not of what is dead, but of what is already living" (11).[14]

This would seem a profoundly conservative position, and in many respects it is. Any fair reading of Eliot should, of course, acknowledge the extent to which for him the past is something that can, indeed must, change if it is to endure: "the past . . . [is] altered by the present as much as the present is directed by the past" (5). But however strong an emphasis we might choose to put on the dynamic elements of Eliot's sense of tradition, the present remains, for him, defined by its relationship to the past. What weighs on a poet with a sense of tradition (that is, any poet who is truly a poet) are the "great difficulties and responsibilities" of the past, even if that past is unusually present, even changeable. The essay has little to say about the future, which might also fairly be said to present "great difficulties and responsibilities" and indeed might more obviously be altered by the present.[15] Indeed, it is tempting to read Eliot's essay as a calculated inversion of the logic of the avant-garde: a call to usher new pasts into the world through aesthetic innovations guided by a strong ethical commitment to those possible pasts.

My point, then, is not to contrast a present defined by what actually was with a present defined by what is actually going to happen but to note two differently dynamic senses of the present as haunted by the "already living" of some other age. What, then, is the historical context of Eliot's essay? Is Eliot an American contemporary of *Winesburg, Ohio* or a European contemporary of *La symphonie pastorale*? Is it mere provocation to note the essay was published the same year as *Les champs magnétiques* (think of the importance of the chemical metaphor in Eliot's account of impersonality) and "In the Penal Colony" (think of the importance of impersonality and tradition)? In what sense is Eliot's essay contemporaneous with *Broken Blossoms*, Felix the Cat, or the founding of Bauhaus? If we value *the work's* historical context (rather than our contemporary tastes), then shouldn't we view Eliot as belonging to the age of Carl Spitteler (the Swiss winner of the Nobel Prize for Literature that year)? These are all interesting and I think legitimate questions, but none expands the map of modernism very far. And most of them, correspondingly, consider "Eliot's" context to be defined by what we today most often remember about the period.

What was happening in world history in 1919? What futures animated the present of that year? Hitler's first speech to the Deutsche Arbeiterpartei and the founding of the Italian fascist movement loom large in retrospect, but at the time few could have known they would have a greater impact on the future than the Sparticist uprising in Berlin, the founding of the Hungarian Soviet Republic, or Tragic Week in Argentina. What of the enormous futures suggested by the outbreak of the Turkish war of independence, the Egyptian revolution, the March First independence movement in Korea, and the May Fourth movement in China? Are we certain that none of this is relevant to the thoughts of a well-read man sitting down to reflect on tradition in 1919?[16]

This list of events might do more than simply add new information to the histories we already tell. For example, 1919 might be understood not as a date primarily "between the wars" but as a watershed year in the history of nationalist revolutions and anticolonial wars (the British alone saw the start of the Anglo-Irish War and the third Anglo-Afghan War), conflicts fueled, precisely, by the failures of the most obvious world-historical events of 1919: the signing of the Treaty of Versailles and the formation of the League of Nations. The Second World War then becomes less the parenthesis that closes the "interwar" period and more the immediate precursor of the Chinese Revolution of 1949 and the wave of anticolonial wars of the 1950s.

In this context, we might think of Eliot's essay neither as a singular instance of modernist innovation nor as particularly reactionary but rather as an example of global debates about tradition during that period. Within a European context, Valéry and Benjamin come to mind, but we might also think of Eliot as a contemporary of Hu Shi or Mohammed Iqbal. Indeed, viewed in relation to this period's anti-Western questioning of the universality of "modernity," Eliot's Eurocentrism might be understood not as an *affirmation of* but precisely a regionalist *resistance to* universalist modernity. This allies Eliot with right-wing cultural pessimism, of course, but also with many anticolonial thinkers.[17] Even this hasty sketch suggests how geographical and historical horizons are interwoven, how different pasts and futures within the present of 1919 recede and jut forth as we expand and contract the map on which we locate it.

Confirmation of such an idea can be found on the other side of the mirror, as it were, in a major work of postcolonial theory that links the critique of historicism to futurity in ways that have implications for modernist historiography, Dipesh Chakrabarty's *Provincializing Europe*. Chakrabarty offers a complex and nuanced critique of historicism of which I will here foreground one specific aspect, namely his Heidegger-derived claim that "All our pasts . . . are futural in orientation" (250).[18]

While the (new) historicist critique of New Criticism (so indebted to Eliot) presented itself as undoing *the violence of decontextualization* by restoring lost and silenced worlds, the work of Chakrabarty (and many other postcolonial critics) foregrounds *the violence of historicization*, which tells non-Westerners that "contrary to whatever they themselves may have thought and however they may have organized their memories, *the historian has the capacity to put them into a time we are all supposed to have shared, consciously or not*" (74; emphases added). The language here closely parallels Anderson's account of Michelet, quoted above, but Chakrabarty's work affirms the extent to which historicization can be not a *restitution* of context (or even a *reduction* to context, as some antihistoricist critics would have it) but the imposition of previously alien interpretive values (not least among which is the value of "historical context" itself).

For Chakrabarty, "historical" evidence is "produced by our capacity to see something that is contemporaneous with us . . . as a relic of another time or place. The person gifted with historical consciousness sees these objects as things that once belonged to their historical context and now exist in the observer's time as a 'bit' of that past" (238). In colonial contexts, then, historicism can entail not so much respect for historical difference as an often violent means of asserting the distance between, and the interpretive irrelevance of, for example, things that are historically simultaneous and even spatially proximate. History puts the "peoples without history" in their place.

That place is most often the nation, but such nations are themselves often uncertain, haunted places. As already suggested above, despite the fact that the classic Andersonian account of nationalism emphasizes the ways in which nations create relative unity out of diversity, his work also emphasizes the extent to which producing this unity requires exclusions and even *internal* divisions, separating off what truly is or is not of the present. While all nations are torn between these centripetal and centrifugal pulls, for those understood to be "belated" or "peripheral" there are additional challenges. The imagining of these communities requires not only unifying their local space and time into a national history but also negotiating their uncanny sameness and irksome difference compared to the unmarked (not peripheral, not belated, that is, European/North American) nations. If the belated nation differs too much, then it is not yet modern, perhaps not even yet a nation; if it is too similar, then it has merely succeeded in becoming a copy, unreal, doomed to be haunted by the specter of comparisons.

That is, not only does historicism *impose* contexts unknown to those on "the periphery" to whom those contexts supposedly belong, but it also helps block from view, for those in "the center," the ways in which their "own" time and place is connected to others, "stop[ping] the subject from seeing his or her own present as discontinuous with itself" (Chakrabarty, *Provincializing Europe*, 239). Historicism sorts the elements of any period according to what truly belongs to it and what merely happened to exist or occur at the same time. This distribution of contemporaneity is in many ways what Jameson's essay seeks to account for, portraying geopolitically peripheral literatures as defined by the violence of uneven development and metropolitan modernism (precisely to the extent it is "modernism") as defined by an experiential fragmentation whose geopolitical causes must remain unknowable as such.

I have already argued that Jameson's essay reifies the distinction between the colonial and the metropolitan, rendering the former essential to the latter but also banishing it offstage. Overstating the unknowability of the periphery predetermines history beyond the national and the metropolitan as detectable only in the mode of form-structuring absence. However insightful it is in other respects, this model obscures the "actually existing cosmopolitanisms of the past" (in the metropolis and elsewhere) while at the same time barring the colonial or even peripheral from full participation in modernity: if modernism is defined by the impossibility of any direct experience or knowledge of the colonial, then the colonial can never be modernist.[19] "Modernism" is thus defined by the repression or ignorance of its full historical context, and any literature that recognizes, much less thematizes, that context is by definition not modernism.

Such an account is clearly troublesome for the agenda of "global modernism." Rather than opposing the directness of colonial geopolitical experience to the (aesthetically rich) alienation of the modernist metropolitan, we should respect the dialectical tensions structuring both. Just as the metropolis did not have an entirely unconscious relationship to the periphery, so too peripheral experience was itself defined by elsewheres at once unknowable and inescapable. It is useful to recognize the referential geopolitical consciousness of "modernism" and right to recognize the geopolitical unconscious of the colonial.

For Jameson, all literature under capitalism is necessarily formally constituted by what it cannot represent, its "political unconscious."[20] What is specific to modernism, in his account, is that what is there unrepresentable is the tendentially global basis of social life. This is "unrepresentable" in at least two distinct senses: it is subject to a system of ideological prohibitions and distortions, to be sure, but it is also unrepresentable because of its sheer scale and complexity. That is, confronting the global character of modernism requires a recognition of facts but also a coming to terms with a perhaps genuinely irresolvable problem of representation. While in many respects the globalization of modernist studies represents an affirmation and extension of the field's overwhelmingly (new) historicist values, it should then also be understood as a challenge to those values. The global turn should encourage reflection on context as such.

CONTEXT?

"Restoring" some putatively original context can be an effective means of shaming alternative readings; however, claiming that a text is a perfect expression of "its context" is but another way of saying one is incapable of learning anything from it. Ironically, such restorations regularly contradict what we can know about authorial intent. To the extent we understand "modernism" as precisely a form of literature that does not seek to reflect its "context" in any immediate way, we are often going against authorial intent when we prioritize the local and immediate whereas, strangely enough, the very refusal of proximate context determinacy can be understood as a kind of fidelity, even a kind of historicism. "Historical context" need not valorize the alignment of a text to what was contiguous or synchronous.

Conversely, critiques of contextualism, whatever they might explicitly claim, involve less a denial of the value of context as such than the proposal, more or less explicit, of alternative contexts. Most such critiques are simply opposed to granting primacy to contemporaneous historical factors, preferring instead a history of genre, the psychological profile of an author, or affinities with a philosophical text, for example. These too reduce. Not all reductions are equal, of course, but an abstract charge of "reduction" in some absolute sense is meaningless because interpretation is never a question of reducing or restoring as such but of what is brought to bear and what is not: a composite of inclusions and exclusions, so no hermeneutic or ethical preference can be given a priori to either.

In Jonathan Culler's quotable formulation, "Meaning is context-bound, but context is boundless."[21] Despite the fact that so much of the pushback against "theory" in general and deconstruction in particular claims to be about a *return* to context, deconstruction was and remains deeply engaged with the problem of context, challenging readers to take responsibility for deciding which contexts they prioritize in any given . . . context? This responsibility is shirked when the value of reading a text in "its historical context" is claimed to be the nonpartisan restitution of something pregiven. Which history? Whose history? What bounds do we impose on boundlessness when we claim to put a text in "its" context?[22]

Moreover, one of the fundamental insights of deconstruction is that the impossibility of fully accounting for context is a necessary precondition of language. That is, it is not the case that context should, ideally, be fully de-terminable because in fact words can only function if they are *not* bound to and fully definable by any single context.[23] Any signifying element must be repeatable, indeed in almost every instance must be a repetition: any text fully determined by "its" context would be incomprehensible. In ways specific to their identification as "literature" (however defined), literary texts too are always destined to be reinscribed in "an infinity of new contexts" (Derrida, *Limited Inc.*, 12)—at least with a little luck, since the alternative is oblivion. In this way, the deconstructive problems of iterability and grafting are at the heart of historicism: potentially infinite reinscription is both the precondi-tion of historicism (meaning is context bound) and a challenge to any of its specific claims (context, it turns out, is boundless).

Different fields of literary study have, at different periods in their history, manifested greater or lesser anxiety about the unresolvable problems that structure their methods. At times, these "theoretical" issues are relatively easy to ignore; at other times they become "practical," even urgent. Although the global turn in modernist studies has largely been driven by historicist values, I would argue that it begs theoretical questions with which the field has never really fully engaged. For despite the literary corpus of modernism being well represented in most forms of literary theory, the field of modernist literary studies itself has never really been defined by a theory moment. "Theory" in general and deconstruction in particular get lumped in with New Criticism for the common sin of insufficiently valuing and understanding context. The effect of this dismissal has been impoverishing not only for "theory" but also, I want to suggest, for the contextualizing, historicizing impulses of modernist studies as it is generally practiced.

I am suggesting not a "return" to theory but a recognition of the profound methodological challenges posed by taking "the global" as a "context," specifically for the study of the period we call modernism, much of whose literary production was generated by and was about, precisely, an inability to grasp the local and immediate. Recall, for example, Bertolt Brecht's famous remark (cited several times by Walter Benjamin) that "less than ever does a simple reproduction of reality say anything about that reality. A photograph of the Krupp factory or the AEG reveals next to nothing about these institutions ... The reification of human relations—the factory, for example—means that they are no longer given. So in fact something must be 'constructed,' something 'artificial,' 'posited' " (Brecht, "Der Dreigroschenprozeß," 161–162). Today, when two-thirds of Krupp's sales are outside of Germany and the corporation has offices on every continent (including in almost every nation in Africa), the difficulty of representing such an institution might be more quantitatively spectacular or more acutely felt, but it is hardly new.[24] The globalization of modernist studies does not represent the imposition of contemporary concerns on an earlier period, but neither is it simply the restitution of how things really were. Hence the unsatisfying because ultimately disingenuous quality of the opposition of "reduction to" and "restoration of" context. The former decries abuse, the latter asserts justice, but both appeal to a knowable original, naturalized textual condition when in fact such a condition is not the real concern of either.

Reading literature globally can involve reading more (it almost certainly does) or bigger (it often does), but accepting these as the only possibilities pushes us to accept the pseudo-opposition of distant and close reading, superficial and deep reading. To read *Mrs. Dalloway* in the context of twenty modernist city novels from around the world circa 1910–1930 will no doubt produce a different sense of the novel than reading it in the context of twenty contemporaneous novels written in and about England—or reading it in the context of Woolf's diaries and letters—and there might be good reasons to value the latter approaches over the former. But it is not the case that the former has no sense of historical context while the latter does, that the former is superficial and the latter deep. "Context" has always been ruthlessly selective, a fact to which our familiarity with, even affection for, particular Procrustean beds should not blind us.[25] Reading modernism globally need not mean *less* context any more than it must mean *more*; it is simply different, and the truth and value of that difference depend entirely on the specifics of any given "global" reading.

CONCLUSION

As modernist studies attempts to globalize it can embrace the apparent contradictions of a twofold approach. On the one hand, we can respect conventionally formulated claims about historical context and engage in empirical research about what modernism was. Modernism *was* global in ways that can be known through relatively straightforward historicization, and we should not underestimate the extent to which a less myopic sense of historical context can transform the ways we read even the most familiar texts. On the other hand, modernism's global context was and remains something that cannot be fully grasped through knowledge saturation. We need theoretical, even speculative models of what modernism was, is, or might still become, even when the facts have not yet caught up.[26] The very impossibility of the global as context can encourage a vigorous reconsideration of the more positivistic ways in which "context" has been deployed as a hermeneutic tool and as value. After all, grasping the importance of race in Stein or empire in Joyce surely required *both* an assertion of verifiable historical facts *and* some theoretical imagination. The former was not a *reduction* to context but an end to the refusal to consider clearly relevant facts; the latter was not mere cleverness but the development of the critical tools necessary to disclose a modernism that is historically grounded even if it might have been quite unrecognizable to Stein or Joyce themselves. It is not inconsistent to think we might both need to know more and to have better ideas.

"We can't do everything," they sigh. Certainly not, but must we therefore keep doing the same things? A truly global study of modernism is no doubt impossible, but shouldn't the degree to which modernist studies has been so utterly *possible* be a source not of pride but embarrassment? Much of the world has been living this impossibility for some time, forced to experience and to understand itself as part of "the world."[27] If today the gardens of Europe themselves can no longer be experienced matter-of-factly, are at once near and far, is it because the specter of comparisons has just escaped the tomb of context—or was it empty all along?

NOTES

1. In Harold Augenbraum's recent translation, the passage reads: "The botanical garden drove away these delightful memories [of childhood] and the devilry of comparison placed him back in front of the botanical gardens of Europe, in those

countries in which one needs a great deal of will and even more gold to bring forth a leaf and make a flower open its calyx . . . Ibarra looked away, to the right, and there saw Old Manila, surrounded still by its walls and moats, like an anemic young girl wrapped in a dress left over from the grandmother's salad days" (Rizal, *Noli me tangere*, 54). The edited volume *Grounds of Comparison* (2003) includes several discussions of how *demonio* ought to be translated, including a concession from Anderson himself that the choice of "specter" was "a real mistake." Noting that the Spanish word has crossed over into Tagalog, he writes that the correct connotation is rather "pest": "Comparisons are like that, they buzz, and buzz, and refuse to go away or to be quiet. Irritating and distracting, but not spectral" (Anderson, *Grounds of Comparison*, 245n1).

2. In addition to being the statement from the resurrected Jesus to Mary Magdalene (John 20:17) that became a common subject of European painting, *noli me tangere* is also a medical term for cancer of the eyelid, an otherwise obscure term that, as numerous critics point out, was known to Rizal, an ophthalmologist. One of the English translations of the novel renders the title as *The Social Cancer*.

3. As Sanjay Krishnan writes, "a central task for literary or cultural analysis that seeks to understand globalization as a historical process is exploration of the formal struggles and textual strategies through which the global is instituted as a perspective" (*Reading the Global*, 2). For an important recent study of literary world making, see Hayot, *On Literary Worlds*.

4. On literary historiography in relation to the problem of "the periphery," see especially Schwarz, *Misplaced Ideas*.

5. On Japan as a model for late nineteenth-century alternative modernities, see Bush, *The Floating World*.

6. Researched in London and written in Spanish, this second novel of "the first Filipino" would be published in Belgium (the first had been published in Berlin). On his ship to the United States, Rizal met the Japanese activist and novelist Shigeyasu 'Tetcho' Suehiro (1849–1896), an important figure in Japan's Freedom and People's Rights Movement and a major writer in the genre of the political novel. The two traveled together on and off throughout the United States and on to Europe. When Suehiro returned to Japan he would publish two political novels set in the Philippines, *Nankai no daiharan* (South Sea typhoon, 1891) and *O-Unabara* (The great ocean, 1894), both modeled on (some say almost plagiarizing) Rizal's novels. See Hayase, "Japan and the Philippines"; and Saniel, "José Rizal and Suehiro Tetcho."

7. See, for example, Hill, "Crossed Geographies: Endo and Fanon in Lyon": "Figures of international repute pass each other unnoticed if the conventions under which we labor don't allow a meeting" (93).

8. I here use "modernist studies" to refer broadly to the interdisciplinary ways of studying literary modernism identified with the Modernist Studies Association and the journal *Modernism/modernity* over the past fifteen to twenty years. For brief overviews of changes in the field over this time, see Mao and Walkowitz, "The New Modernist Studies"; and, more recently, James and Seshagiri, "Metamodernism."

9. Consider, for example, the relative absence of such major New Historicist touchstones as Claude Levi-Strauss, Clifford Geertz, and Michel Foucault in modernist studies. Who are the major *theorists* of modernist New Historicism?

10. Often further confirmed by, for example, the text's very genre or language. With Rizal: a *novel* written in *Spanish*.

11. Almost no contextualist would endorse this, of course, any more than those advocating a more global approach to literary studies would consider total knowledge of all things on the planet a prerequisite to reading. But the former has been naturalized to such an extent that its limitations and occasional absurdities are accepted as inevitabilities, even virtues.

12. For a range of critical treatments of "context," see the articles in the 2011 *New Literary History* special issue on the topic, edited by Felski.

13. See especially Appadurai, *Modernity at Large*; Chatterjee, *The Nation in Fragments*; and Hill, *National History and the World of Nations*.

14. The "already" of the "already living" is here not anticipatory (as in: "tickets go on sale tomorrow and people are *already* lining up") but rather asserts the persistence of what might be mistaken for dead and gone (as in: "all of philosophy is *already* contained in Plato").

15. A few words substituted, and the poet must live "in what is not merely the present, but the present moment of the future." Such a poet must be "conscious, not of what has not yet been born, but of what is already living"—but here "already" in the anticipatory sense.

16. It was precisely in 1919 that John Dewey traveled to Japan and then China, where he witnessed the emergence of the May Fourth movement and worked with his local advocate Hu Shih, whose name perhaps would remain unknown to Eliot but who, as a matter of principle, would be the object of the attacks in Eliot's *After Strange Gods* (40) as one of those in China who had "blazed a path for John Dewey" and thereby undermined the Anglo-Saxon-like continuity of what had previously been "a country of tradition."

17. On continuities between the European right and anticolonialism, see Bush, *The Floating World*; Jones, "The End of Europe"; and Moretti, *Signs Taken for Wonders*. For an overview of the May Fourth movement, see Schwarcz, *The Chinese Enlightenment*.

18. Few of the critics who make passing reference to Chakrabarty's title as a catch-phrase acknowledge his extensive and explicit debt to Heidegger's critique of historicism.

19. The phrase "actually existing cosmopolitanisms" is from Goodlad, "Cosmopolitanism's Actually Existing Beyond," 430. Goodlad has written about how Jameson's geopolitical models, otherwise so valuable to efforts to rethink her field of Victorian studies more globally, cannot be much interested in realism. Again, a model that in certain obvious ways limits our understanding of literature beyond the metropolis also limits in debatable ways how scholars categorize literature even within the metropolis: what "can be called modernism in the first place."

20. For a more detailed account of how this is and is not equivalent to an Althusserian "representation of the imaginary relationship of individuals to their real conditions of existence," see Jameson, *The Political Unconscious*.

21. Originally in *On Deconstruction* (1982), the formulation reappears in Culler's more recent *Literary Theory: A Very Short Introduction* (2011).

22. Far from asserting the autonomy of the text, Derrida's infamous claim "il n'y a pas de hors-texte" (regularly cited in its mistranslation as "there is nothing outside the text") is precisely what I would describe as a critique of *the autonomy of the context*: how texts mean is so profoundly determined by context that none of these "contexts" can be treated as if it were not itself also a text, that is: its meaning determined by context. This is the sense is which "there is no *hors-texte*": there are no out-texts, no pre-texts, but with-texts, the nature of that "with" always needing to be accounted for since nothing is a priori contextual rather than textual. The line in question is in *Of Grammatology* (158), but see also especially "Signature Event Context," in *Limited Inc*. Similarly, in what is perhaps Paul de Man's most well-known formulation of "undecidability," it is precisely a question of context: we justify reading a passage in one rhetorical mode rather than another based on our understanding of its context, but our understanding of the context is determined by how we read specific passages. See his "Semiology and Rhetoric," in *Allegories of Reading*.

23. Language—in the broad sense of any form of signification—requires what Derrida calls a "structural non-saturation" because "communication must be repeatable—iterable—in the absence of the receiver or of any empirically determinable collectivity of receivers" (*Signature Event Context*, 3, 7). "A written sign," he continues, "carries with it a force that breaks with its context, that is, with the collectivity of presences organizing the moment of its inscription" (9)—but not only *written* signs (cf. *Of Grammatology*).

24. See here Jameson's reflections on the modernist city novel in *The Geopolitical Aesthetic*, a work explicitly about the postmodern period.

25. See Moretti, "The Slaughterhouse of Literature"; and Levine, "For World Literature."

26. "History" is constantly changing, being reinvented or rediscovered, not just for theorists or literary critics but for professional historians. Nowhere is this more apparent than in the emergence of "world history" as an increasingly important field of historical study, one of whose most important consequences has been to provide an enormous amount of empirical evidence to support the idea that "modernity" might be reconceived in less Eurocentric ways. For a recent literature review, see Doyle, "Notes Toward a Dialectical Method."

27. Hence the relevance to modernist studies of so much postcolonial criticism, a field that has always struggled with the Eurocentric biases of the pseudouniversal categories of modernity. To globalize modernist studies is at the same time to provincialize it. And to provincialize, following Chakrabarty, means not simply to denigrate or to ignore but to recognize the particularity of "universals," the potential marginality of centers, and the potential reversibility of the near and far.

WORKS CITED

Anderson, Benedict. *The Spectre of Comparisons: Nationalism, Southeast Asia, and the World*. London: Verso, 1998.

———. *Imagined Communities*. London: Verso, 1991.

Appadurai, Arjun. *Modernity at Large: Cultural Dimensions of Globalization*. Minneapolis: University of Minnesota Press, 1996.

Brecht, Bertolt. "Der Dreigroschenprozeß." In *Gesammelte Werke in acht Bänden*, vol. 8. Frankfurt am Main: Suhrkamp, 1967.

Bush, Christopher. *The Floating World: Japoniste Aesthetics and Global Modernity*. New York: Columbia University Press, forthcoming.

Chakrabarty, Dipesh. *Provincializing Europe*. Princeton, N.J.: Princeton University Press, 2007.

Chatterjee, Partha. *The Nation in Fragments: Colonial and Postcolonial Histories*. Princeton, N.J.: Princeton University Press, 1993.

Cheah, Peng, and Jonathan Culler, eds. *Grounds of Comparison: Around the Work of Benedict Anderson*. New York: Routledge, 2003.

Culler, Jonathan. *Literary Theory: A Very Short Introduction*. Oxford: Oxford University Press, 2011.

———. *On Deconstruction*. Ithaca, N.Y.: Cornell University Press, 1982.

De Man, Paul. *Allegories of Reading*. New Haven, Conn.: Yale University Press, 1979.

Derrida, Jacques. *Limited Inc*. Evanston, Ill.: Northwestern University Press, 1988.

——. *Of Grammatology*. Trans. Gayatri Chakravorty Spivak. Baltimore, Md.: Johns Hopkins University Press, 1977.

Doyle, Laura. "Notes Toward a Dialectical Method: Modernities, Modernism, and the Crossings of Empire." *Literature Compass* 7, no. 3 (2010): 195–213.

Eliot, T. S. *Selected Essays*. 1932; repr. New York: Harcourt, Brace and Company, 1950.

——. *After Strange Gods: A Primer of Modern Heresy*. London: Faber and Faber, 1934.

Felski, Rita, ed. *New Literary History* 42, no. 4 (Autumn 2011).

Gallagher, Catherine, and Stephen Greenblatt. *Practicing New Historicism*. Chicago: University of Chicago Press, 2001.

Goodlad, Lauren. "Cosmopolitanism's Actually Existing Beyond: Toward a Victorian Geopolitical Aesthetic." *Victorian Literature and Culture* 38 (2010): 399–411.

Hayase Shinzo. "Japan and the Philippines." *Philippine Studies* 47, no. 1 (1999): 30–47.

Hayot, Eric. "Against Periodization; or, On Institutional Time." *New Literary History* 42, no. 4 (Autumn 2011).

——. *On Literary Worlds*. New York: Oxford University Press, 2013.

Hill, Christopher. *National History and the World of Nations: Capital, State, and the Rhetoric of History in Japan, France, and the United States*. Durham, N.C.: Duke University Press, 2009.

——. "Crossed Geographies: Endo and Fanon in Lyon." Forthcoming in *Representations*.

James, David, and Urmila Seshagiri. "Metamodernism: Narratives of Continuity and Revolution." *PMLA* 129, no. 1 (January 2014): 87–100.

Jameson, Fredric. *The Geopolitical Aesthetic*. Bloomington: Indiana University Press, 1995.

——. "Modernism and Imperialism." In *Nationalism, Colonialism, and Literature*. Minneapolis: University of Minnesota Press, 1990.

——. *The Political Unconscious*. Ithaca, N.Y.: Cornell University Press, 1982.

Jones, Donna. "The End of Europe: Pessimistic Historiography in the Interwar Years and the Paradox of Universalism." *Clio* 39, no. 2 (2010): 187–212.

Krishnan, Sanjay. *Reading the Global: Troubling Perspectives on Britain's Empire in Asia*. New York: Columbia University Press, 2007.

Levine, Caroline. "For World Literature." *Public Books*. http://publicbooks.org/for-world-literature.

Mao, Douglas, and Rebecca Walkowitz. "The New Modernist Studies." *PMLA* 123, no. 3 (May 2008): 737–748.

Moretti, Franco. *Signs Taken for Wonders*. London: Verso, 1988.

———. "The Slaughterhouse of Literature." *Modern Language Quarterly* 61, no. 1 (2000): 207–228.

Rizal, José. *Noli me tangere*. Trans. Harold Augenbraum. New York: Penguin, 2006.

Saniel, Josefa M. "José Rizal and Suehiro Tetcho: Filipino and Japanese Political Novelists." *Asian Studies* 2, no. 3 (1964): 353–371.

Schwarcz, Vera. *The Chinese Enlightenment: Intellectuals and the Legacy of the May Fourth Movement of 1919*. Berkeley: University of California Press, 1990.

Schwarz, Roberto. *Misplaced Ideas: Essays on Brazilian Culture*. London: Verso, 1992.

Wilde, Oscar. "The Decay of Lying." In *De Profundis and Other Writings*. New York: Penguin, 1973.

7. COPY

JACOB EDMOND

By attending to modernist works that radically foreground copying and by recognizing similarly repetitive structures even in works that seek to resist sameness through strangeness, we can complicate the opposition between mass reproduction, consumer capitalism, and globalization, on the one hand, and modernist aestheticism, on the other.

"Make it new." The original, the foreign, the idiolectic—modernism has been told as a story of novelty, strangeness, and singular genius. And this story has been given new inflection as scholars have sought to emphasize the variety and global reach of modernisms in the plural. Yet "make it the same" might equally serve as the catchphrase of modernism. Modernism emerged out of a vast increase in copying, to which it responded through repetition, appropriation, and remixing, from Eisenstein's montage, Duchamp's ready-mades, Stein's repetitions as insistences, Picasso's and Braque's collage, Joyce's pastiche, Melville's Bartleby, Borges's Menard, and Burroughs's and Gysin's cut-ups to Xu Zhimo's translations and versioning, Gandhi's printing press, Sergei Tretyakov's newspaper as twentieth-century epic, and Kamau Brathwaite's audio and computer-graphic remediation and self-rewriting.[1] Even the slogan status of Pound's phrase "make it new" is the product of later critical appropriations, and the phrase itself is a translation, a copy of a centuries-old text that was probably mistranscribed from a far more ancient source (North, *Novelty*, 162–171; Shaughnessy, *Sources of Western Zhou History*, 7). The copy's centrality to modernism is increasingly legible in the early twenty-first century, when reproduction triumphs over production in the billions of everyday acts through which we produce and consume links and likes on Facebook, Twitter, Weibo, and other social media.

But the copy is hardly new. Oral poetry was and is built on repetitions of plots, rhymes, and stock phrases. Manuscript culture produced individualistic acts of repetition, variation, and remixing. Copying and annotation are central to many traditions, from Chinese literature and philosophy to biblical hermeneutics. Medieval poetry in Europe and East Asia depended on repeated forms and conventions, and early modern theater in England developed through competitive copying and versioning of plays, plots, and characters. At a more basic level, copying is fundamental to the acquisition and use of language.

Despite copying's ubiquity, what counts as a copy and the pace and intensity of copying have changed in response to technologies, from writing, print, and audio recording to digital computing, and as a result of new transportation and communication linkages and the institutions of trade and empire that have increased the adoption and adaptation of cultural material from afar. The copy, as I will refer to it here, is both a literary device and a conceptual framework through which to rethink global modernism: an artistic strategy encompassing such techniques as pastiche, stylization, cut-and-paste, collage, montage, remediation, performance, translation, and the appropriation of form, plot, theme, titles, and the like; and a technological, economic, and geopolitical context in which copying becomes a cultural dominant.

Modernism has often been seen as a site of resistance to the emergence of the copy as a cultural dominant. The emphasis in Anglo-American modernism on making it new has been influentially read as deriving from the need "to produce something which resists and breaks through the force of gravity of repetition as a universal feature of commodity equivalence" (Jameson, "Reification and Utopia in Mass Culture," 136). Yet by attending to modernist works that radically foreground copying and by recognizing similarly repetitive structures even in works that seek to resist sameness through strangeness, we can complicate the opposition between mass reproduction, consumer capitalism, and globalization, on the one hand, and modernist aestheticism, on the other. The copy thereby provides a way to negotiate the ongoing rift between readings of modernism—and between parts of modernist practice—that emphasize sociological, technological, political, and economic context and those that stress the particularity and singular genius of modernist works.

The copy—more than its apparent cousins, influence, imitation, mimesis, adaptation, and translation—also offers a means to question global modernism's temporal and spatial hierarchies. These hierarchies emerge from what Rey Chow has termed a "mimetic desire, responsive and oriented toward the West's imposition of itself on the Rest" (*The Age of the World Target*, 83). Understood in these terms, to write of non-Western, peripheral, or global modernism is to articulate this mimetic desire "to speak in the other's language in order to be recognized by the other" that is the West. Within the "make it new" rhetoric of modernism, mimetic desire "imposes a historical lag between the other's behavior and one's own. To be caught up in mimetic desire requires one invariably to be 'behind the times'" (Hayot, "Chinese Modernism," 157). The copy, by contrast, does not "privilege being temporally 'first'" (162). Hence the "strategy of re-writing" not only attempts, as in some avant-garde practice, "to short-circuit or interrupt the text's own representational construction" (Murphy, *Theorizing the Avant-Garde*, 263, 293); it also undoes the structure of mimetic desire that shapes the way we think modernism transnationally. Just as the "anti-theatrical" theater of Brecht and other modernists was a means of "keeping under control and mediating the theatrical mimesis" (Puchner, *Stage Fright*, 25), so copy works to denaturalize the framework of originality, innovation, and mimetic desire in approaches to global modernism.

THE SAME NEWS THROUGHOUT THE WORLD

To think global modernism through the copy is to highlight the various technological, geopolitical, and historical materialisms that have reinvigorated modernist studies and especially to draw together two still arguably "separate and non-communicative" approaches: on the one hand, a focus on new technologies of reproduction and communication; on the other, transnationalism (Collier, "Imperial/Modernist Forms," 487).[2] Read in this vein, for example, Joyce's *Ulysses* adopts the newspaper's collage effect and global reach not just in the "Aeolus" episode but also, for instance, where an advertisement in a newspaper used for butcher wrapping shifts Bloom's thoughts suddenly to Zionist settlements in Palestine. Read similarly, the conclusion to the "Oxen of the Sun" episode responds to the rise of global English by developing a dialect of modernism founded on racial mimicry while also asserting the public domain of speech in response to the expansion of international copyright (North, *The Dialect of Modernism*, 32; Saint-Amour, *The Copywrights*, 184–185).

But to focus on the copy is equally to recognize the problem with such global perspectives, which reduce individual texts to examples of larger phenomena through "the magic of mimesis wherein the replication, the copy, acquires the power of the represented" (Taussig, *Mimesis and Alterity*, 16). Charles Altieri criticizes the new modernist studies for seeing copies everywhere, for adopting an "analogical model" that "stresses only similarities." Altieri invites us to consider "the difference between showing how Henry James's work shares some characteristics with the telegraph, and showing how James thought about working out ways to have his style take on telegraphic properties," as the difference between analogy and "a dialectical account of how those purposive actions worked through specific and general problems" ("Afterword," 778). In seeking to emphasize larger historical, technological, and geopolitical forces and contexts such as those I have invoked here, scholars of global modernism risk underplaying the poetics and materiality of modernist texts and modernists' active engagements with and responses to new technologies, media, and globalization. Yet analogical thinking—what Walter Benjamin called the "historical hallucination of sameness" (*Selected Writings*, 208)—is also a central theme of modernism, fed by the rise of the commodity economy and new technologies, such as telegraphy, that enabled copies to be propagated rapidly around the world. Addressing the poetics of the copy provides a way to bridge the divide between modernist text and context by calling attention to the iterative devices through which modernists respond to and reconfigure the larger rise of copying culture in modernity, including the intertwining of the copy with imaginings of the global.

Paul-Louis Couchoud exemplifies such intertwined imaginings of new media, cross-cultural appropriation, and globalization in his conflation of modern media's capacity to copy, the Western tradition of imagining East Asian cultures as inherently imitative, and Euro-American modernism's tendency to find in East Asia a distorted copy of the West and hence a "privileged site for witnessing the increasingly global character of a modernity" (Bush, *Ideographic Modernism*, 114; Bush, "Modernism, Orientalism, and East Asia," 196). Couchoud was instrumental in introducing the haiku to Europe, and he explained his promotion of the Japanese form by citing new global convergences wrought by technologies of reproduction and communication, "the telegraph, the daily paper and the cinematograph," through which the "same news is known . . . throughout the world" (*Japanese Impressions*, 9–10). For Couchoud, this "same news"—combined with the West's shock at Japan's defeat of Russia in 1904–1905, broadcast around the world by telegraph—also resulted in a new recognition of cultural iteration. Any "problem . . . on one side of the planet" could now be seen to have "repeated itself, in essence, on the other side" (11). The haiku form not only spread worldwide thanks to the copying potential of new technologies and media but also embodied the increased speed of global communication through a "rapid impression" that "instantly strikes us" (38). Couchoud's haiku is, then, the perfect form for the world of global linkup that Lamartine had anticipated as early as 1831 when he wrote that through the newspaper, "Thought will spread abroad in the world with the rapidity of light: instantly conceived, instantly written, instantly understood, at the extremities of the earth" ("The Polity of Reason," 68–69). And indeed Couchoud reports that it is "the journalists who write the haikai. The war with Russia brought forth hundreds of them" (*Japanese Impressions*, 38).

Couchoud's imagining of global repetition through new media, the rise of a non-Western great power, and a traditional Japanese poetic form is repeated, through the intermediary of F. S. Flint, in Ezra Pound's better-known mimicry of haiku poetry (Carr, "Imagism and Empire," 70–72, 80). Pound inaugurated imagism as a poetry of the "instant," which "instantaneously" conveys a "sense of freedom from time limits and space limits," precisely the qualities of rapidity and spatial transcendence through which Couchoud linked the haiku form to the telegraph and the newspaper (Pound, "A Few Don'ts," 200). Like Couchoud, Pound also implicitly connected the minimalism of the haiku to the minimalism required for the telegraphic journalism of war reporting, criticizing in his imagist manifesto a "Turkish war correspondent" for using "ornament" (202). The haiku as both a non-Western traditional form and the form of modern media and globalization matched Pound's own oxymoronic desire to make "news that STAYS news," to make copy that would be perpetually copied (Pound, *ABC of Reading*, 29).

As it was first published, Pound's most famous haiku-like poem, "In a Station of the Metro," typographically isolates the colon and period:

The apparition   of these faces   in the crowd   :
Petals   on a wet, black   bough   .

Here, the punctuation marks appear almost as separate words and so invite the reader to sound them out as in a telegraph: "The apparition of these faces in the crowd colon / Petals on a wet, black bough stop." In support of this unorthodox reading, one might note Pound's interest in rhythmic signaling systems, as evidenced by his later writing on the Balunda "drum telegraph" (Golston, *Rhythm and Race*, 85) and by the way Pound's "METRO Hokku" employs a form of juxtaposition similar to what Marinetti had a year earlier named "wireless imagination" (*l'immaginazione senza fili*), alluding to the recently invented "wireless telegraph" (*telegrafo senza fili*). Pound's poem also suggests the short dots and long dashes of Morse code through the single and double dots of the isolated period and colon and through the rhythmic repetitions and variations of the text, in which the prosodic echo between the title and first line runs in counterpoint to the equation, signaled by the colon, between the two lines of the poem proper, which are rhythmically contrasted.

To claim that Pound's poem resembles a telegram might seem to actualize Altieri's hypothetical example of how "the 'New Modernist Studies' fails the old modernism" and to ignore willfully Pound's own railing against "similarity or analogy . . . likeness or mimicry," especially "the copying or imitating" that he associates with new technologies such as the cinematograph (Pound, "Vortex," 154; Pound, "Vorticism"). Yet attention to the intertwined levels of copy poetics at work in Pound's poem tells a different story, allowing one to see how the poem is "at once photographic and antiphotographic," how it both mimics and responds to the pressures of new technologies and globalization in its imaginary traversal of spatial and cultural divides (Bush, *Ideographic Modernism*, 65). The global vision is reinforced in the poem's original publication context by Harriet Monroe's editorial on Tagore, which calls for a break with Anglo-American provinciality in the face of the "bigness of the world" ("Editorial Comment," 25), and by the final line of the immediately preceding poem, "Let there be commerce between us" (Pound, "A Pact," 12). Although referring to Pound and Whitman, the line in this context underscores the dependence of Pound's haiku-imagist poem on East/West commerce and on the parallel between a Western modernist's appropriation of a Japanese form and the poem's two juxtaposed lines. The poem conveys a sense of encoding, equation, and translation—as in the process of telegraphy—through the colon, through the teleportation of a form from Japanese to English, through the juxtaposition of urban modernity and rural image, Paris and East Asia, and through its aural and syntactic repetitions.

But Pound also puts pressure on such assertions of sameness and instant connectivity, undoing their certainties through further acts of repetition. Pound signals his refusal of exact equivalence, encoding, and copying by replacing the colon with a semicolon and regularizing the layout in later printings of the poem, so eliminating the explicit equation between the poem's two lines and the telegraphic voicing of the punctuation.[3] Recognizing this change, of course, requires attention to the poem's multiple material embodiments, its many copies—the contrast, in particular, between the poem's initial publication in *Poetry* and later versions. Pound himself famously stressed the process of versioning, rewriting, and telegraphic condensation, describing how the poem emerged out of two much longer poems of "second intensity," thereby claiming "In a Station of the Metro" as both an essence and a copy (Pound, "Vorticism"). Pound's poem works dialectically between a global vision of the copy and an enfolding of the copy, photography, telegraphy, and the adopted set form of the Japanese haiku into an assertion of singularity. Reading Pound's poem through the copy illustrates how globalization and new technologies of reproduction and communication shape the dialectic between originality and mere repetition in modernism. Engendered by the rise of the copy as a cultural dominant, this dialectic also helps explain modernist historiography's ongoing division between, at its crudest, sui generis singularity and technological or economic determinism.

Taking the copy as a central device and problematic of modernism also extends modernism's historical range by deprivileging being temporally first and so revaluing later copy works that respond to a new wave of globalization and copy-enabling technologies. For example, in 1997, the Chinese poet Yang Lian remediated the layered repetitions of his poem *Dahai tingzhi zhi chu* 大海停止之处 (Where the sea stands still) into a HyperCard and HTML collaboration with the Anglo-Canadian poet-programmer John Cayley. Using Cayley's theory of digital poetics—itself developed in dialogue with classical Chinese poetry and Poundian poetics—Yang later cited their collaboration in arguing that Chinese writing was particularly suited to computer-based poetry, thereby appropriating Western modernism's approach to new media through the so-called Chinese ideograph. Many other late twentieth- and early twenty-first-century poetic works foreground copying and repetition, as in Yi Sha's idiosyncratic and irreverent translations of poems from world literature and the Chinese tradition, which are rapidly disseminated online, provoking the ire of traditionalists (Inwood, "Yi Sha," 9); Kenneth Goldsmith's transcriptions of traffic and weather reports and an entire issue of the *New York Times*; and Hsia Yü's newspaper page cross-outs (Hsia Yü et al., "Cross It Out").

Perhaps the most prolific of all recent exponents of copy works, the Russian poet and artist Dmitri Prigov produced a series, entitled *Telegrammy* (Telegrams), that reiterates the telegraphic imagination of the early twentieth century while comically taking Pound's vision of imagist condensation to absurdist extremes, as in the telegram in his series attributed to Dostoevsky: "STUDENT COMMA KILLED OLD WOMAN COMMA WITH AXE COMMA ANGUISHES TERRIBLY STOP" (СТУДЕНТ ЗПТ УБИЛ СТАРУХУ ЗПТ ТОПОРОМ ЗПТ МУЧИТСЯ УЖАСНО ТЧК; Prigov, untitled artist's book, n.p.). Prigov's condensation of the essence of *Crime and Punishment* is just one in a series that includes pieces attributed to Tchaikovsky ("EMOTIONAL DEVELOPMENT COMMA CRISIS COMMA . . . STOP TRAGIC FINALE STOP"), Pushkin ("UNCLE COMMA SICK STOP"), Stalin, and the Voice of America (untitled artist's book, n.p.; *Grazhdane!*, 230–233). In his *Telegrams*, Prigov satirizes modernism's overturning of the nineteenth-century classics through an insistence on telegraphic compression while also connecting these Russian classics to the ideology of the Soviet state (and its Cold War enemy) as represented by the officially regulated medium of the telegram. Yet by uniting an official medium and officially sanctioned great artists with the samizdat medium of typescript pasted onto art-quality paper, Prigov also targets the cultural mythologies of the samizdat text, according to which each scrap of semilegible, laboriously copied typescript on poor-quality paper contained treasured words of repressed expression.

Prigov produced his *Telegrams* in the late 1970s and early 1980s, around the time that he began using the term "conceptual" to refer to his work. The Russian theorist Boris Groys had first brought the term to prominence in the samizdat literary community in a 1977 essay in which he introduced British and American conceptual art via Borges's fictional copyist hero Pierre Menard, who reproduces *Don Quixote* "word for word" but whose copying of Cervantes produces a text "almost infinitely richer" than the original (*Ficciones*, 49, 52). Borges's story highlights how even an exact copy differs over time and between contexts and media: the narrator perceives the "traces" of the "handwriting of our friend," Menard, within the "final," printed *Don Quixote* (54). Just a few years before Borges wrote his story, Mikhail Bakhtin had named this process of continuous change "re-accentuation" and made it central to his account of discourse in the novel (*The Dialogic Imagination*, 421–422). Groys's act of copying and recombination—remixing Borges and conceptual art—continues this process of reaccentuation and in turn inspired further acts of copying, versioning, and remediation, such as Prigov's *Telegrams* and his many repetitions and versionings of Pushkin's *Eugene Onegin*. Such acts of explicit copying reflect on the processes of repetition that characterize canonization and cross-cultural appropriation, as in Prigov's reframing of Menard's strategy as a way to comment on Russian nationalism, romanticism, and samizdat culture and as part of his presentation of Russian conceptualism as more conceptual than Western conceptualism (Prigov, "Conceptualism and the West").

Menard returns as the prototype for the rise of conceptual writing in the English-speaking world (especially in Canada and the United States) in the 2000s (Dworkin, "Fate of Echo," xlv). These conceptualists make Menard's poetics of echo central to a retrospectively generated canon of modernist conceptual writing that includes such works as Yeats's "Mona Lisa," a transcription of a passage from Walter H. Pater's *Studies in the History of the Renaissance* lineated into free verse by Yeats and used to open the *Oxford Book of Modern Verse: 1892–1935* (Dworkin and Goldsmith, *Against Expression*, 576–577). Such uses of Menard affirm how Borges's "text already inscribes within itself, intimately and unavoidably, the analytic and epistemic protocols for its discursive and narrative permutation into the theoretical complexity of the critical field called world literature" (Kadir, "World Literature," 300–301). Where Djelal Kadir here offers Borges's story as an antidote to fungible world literature, however, Menard and his travels indicate a more complex playing with fungibility and the uniqueness of each instantiation of even the same text.

The dialectic between the generalizing claims of the copy—finding the same everywhere—and the unique materiality of each instantiation inheres in modernism's use of the copy to respond to media and globalization and in attempts to read modernism as a response to these forces while recognizing the particularity of each iteration. Even the most exact repetition contains differences. These differences undo the artificial separation of a repeated text or object from its context or medium of iteration, highlighting the contingent nature of language and culture, text and media, which are not clearly defined objects but intertwined "social experiences of meaning," "nodes of articulation along a signifying chain" (Gitelman, *Always Already New*, 148; Dworkin, *No Medium*, 32). To address modernism through the copy means confronting the relation of the global conceived as a generalizable series of copies to the "ideology of disembodiment," "transcendental data," and translatability that dominates today's digital imaginary but which is already recognizable in Couchoud's vision of the "same news . . . throughout the world" (Hayles, *How We Became Posthuman*, 192; Liu, *Local Transcendence*, 211–236; Pressman, "Reading the Code").

VARIETIES OF SAMENESS

"In today's divided world, to discover varieties of sameness is to give in too easily to the false promises of a level playing field," writes Gayatri Spivak ("Rethinking Comparativism," 611). Yet to discover only differences is to give up the possibility of thinking relations between things. The dialectic of the copy not only illuminates this problem but also offers a possible methodological solution. If, as Spivak suggests, "we start from an assumption of linguistic equivalence, which rests on language's capacity to inscribe," then we should recognize that to inscribe is also to copy, to iterate (614–615).

Language's iterability offers grounds for comparison and a way to find commonality between the two major competing models for thinking modernism on a global scale. The copy is at the heart of the influential account of global modernism associated with Fredric Jameson, Franco Moretti, and Pascale Casanova, who draw on Immanuel Wallerstein's world-systems theory in order to explain modern literary history as the product of a world that is "*one, and unequal*" (Moretti, "Conjectures on World Literature," 56). As Moretti emphasizes, this model is explicitly focused on accounting for the production of "*sameness*" through the "*diffusion*" of cultural forms from the global economic and geopolitical "core" to the "periphery" (Moretti, "Evolution, World-Systems, *Weltliteratur*," 114–115). Moretti's prescription for "distant reading" is the tracking of copies (through the wavelike propagation of the novel form, for example) across space and time (Moretti, "Conjectures on World Literature," 56–58). Such accounts emphasize the sameness of the copy as the formal representation of cultural hegemony.[4] But even more influential have been studies that stress the changes texts undergo as they move—through copies, translations, and versioning—beyond "their culture of origin" (Damrosch, *What Is World Literature?*, 4) and related counterhegemonic accounts that highlight diasporic circulation in "transnational contexts marked by difference" and the proliferation of "hybrid" and "translocal poetics" as copies are produced, circulated, and reframed in new contexts (Edwards, *The Practice of Diaspora*, 7; Ramazani, *A Transnational Poetics*, xii–xiii). Despite stressing difference rather than sameness, this alternative model of cultural "circulations" shares with world-systems theory an attempt to account for and address forms of iteration.[5] The contrasting readings of iteration as either a source of creative adaptation or slavish imitation reflect the tension between making it new and mimetic desire in global modernism.

Modernist copy works suggest an alternative to both paradigms for thinking global modernism. They treat dissemination and circulation neither as merely a system of domination imposed on the periphery by the center nor through a generalized counterhegemonic account of hybridity or translocalism. Instead, copy works suggest a fundamental upheaval in the value system of originality and mimetic desire upon which both accounts of global modernism are built.

Take, for example, Lu Xun's foundational work of Chinese modernism and modern vernacular Chinese literature "Kuangren riji" 狂人日记 (Diary of a madman). Lu Xun's short story echoes and reframes Gogol's "Zapiski sumasshedshego" (Diary of a madman), which is in turn indebted to Cervantes (Tambling, *Madmen and Other Survivors*, 29–30). One might treat these instances of appropriation as examples of how writers on the peripheries or semiperipheries of China and Russia responded to Western Europe's hegemonic status in nineteenth- and twentieth-century modernity. Or one could take the example to be a case of global circulation that undermines such center-periphery accounts by illustrating the networks of linkage and affiliation whereby so-called peripheral literatures communicate with one another rather than only with the center. In doing so, one would undoubtedly also stress the transformative ways in which Cervantes's talking dogs become Gogol's and then Lu Xun's literary pets. In one reading, we emphasize the mimetic desire for recognition on the center's terms. In the other, we acknowledge the creative adaptations through which globalization undermines the center-periphery binary.

Read through the poetics of the copy, however, these texts, like Menard's fictional copying of Cervantes, challenge the assumptions of originality and genius upon which both accounts are built. Although it could be read as an example of foreign imitation or creative adaptation, Lu Xun's story is also specifically about copying and exact repetition. Attending to Lu Xun's emphasis on repetition and reinscription clarifies what we might gain from rereading modernism through the copy.

Lu Xun's and Gogol's stories both describe the delirium of sameness, of finding exact copies everywhere, as in the discovery that "four thousand years" of Chinese history can be paraphrased in two words—"eat people"—

or that "Spain and China are one and the same country" since if one writes "Spain on a piece of paper, it comes out as China" (Lu Xun, *Lu Xun quan ji*, 454; Gogol', *Polnoe sobranie sochinenii*, 211–212). The importance of the copy is itself suggested in the device of a story written from the perspective of a madman, a perspective that, as in Cervantes's *Don Quixote*, interrogates the notion of mimesis by undermining the reader's confidence in the text's description of the world. Through the madman's revelation that the practice of "eating people" has been repeated over thousands of years, Lu Xun connects uncertainty about mimesis to the act of copying. This endless copying is also performed through the related iterative device of repetition. The phrase "chi ren" 吃人 (eat people) is repeated no less than twenty-eight times in a story of fewer than five thousand characters (that is, over one percent of the text is made up of the words "eat people"). The iterated phrase enacts the madman's discovery of a "whole book filled with two words—'Eat people'!" (满本都写着两个字是 "吃人" !; 447). Lu Xun further emphasizes copying and repetition by presenting the story as a partial copy made from a diary and, implicitly, as a remediation from manuscript to print. The editor-narrator claims to have "copied out a part to serve as a subject for medical research" (撮录一篇，以供医家研究; 444). The story is not only about an imagined unveiling of a vast history of cannibalism—and, allegorically, an attack on repressive and inhumane aspects of Chinese society—but itself suggests a modernist project that consumes foreign examples and turns them to new uses. Lu Xun consumes the body of Gogol's text "Diary of a Madman" while also taking a bite out of *Dead Souls*'s focus on the inhuman institution of serfdom, which extends macabrely and absurdly in Gogol's story to the ownership of the dead. Lu Xun's story identifies such parasitism not just as the problem of China and Chinese history but also as a digestive model for Chinese modernism.

Lu Xun's emphasis on copying through both the narrative frame and phrasal repetition gives a different inflection to readings of his appropriative practice. Whether we treat Lu Xun's appropriation as an act of imitation or creative genius, we remain committed to originality and innovation as the terms of recognition within global modernism's framework of mimetic desire. Yet Lu Xun's stress on exact reproduction suggests another perspective. Just as Lu Xun's madman undoes any sense of historical development or progress by maintaining that the same two characters are repeated unaltered across four thousand years, so attending to repetition, reproduction, and copying as modernist practices undoes the privileging of originality, origins, temporal priority, and progress in commonplace accounts of modernism. Lu

Xun's allegorical presentation of Chinese culture as entrapped and unchanging in contrast with the progress of Western modernity is turned on its head: Chinese repetition becomes the condition of modernity at large.

Contemporary scholarship on global modernism has attacked the tendency to approach Euro-American modernist appropriations by the likes of Pound as works of original genius while at the same time treating non-European or so-called peripheral modernisms as derivative or belated. Rather than simply reversing the direction of influence, however, copy works interrogate the underlying framework of mimetic desire. The question ceases to be, as Friedman wryly asks of Picasso's and Van Gogh's copies of African and Japanese art, "who . . . is derivative of whom?" ("Planetarity," 484; similarly, Bush, "Modernism," 201) and instead becomes: is derivativeness or originality the sole basis for thinking global modernism?

The anxiety central to East Asian modernism about copying Western models and about copying, rather than escaping, tradition can be considered not just as a response to Western hegemony but as part of a general anxiety about the copy, new media, and globalization, an anxiety equally present in the appropriative poetics of Pound or Joyce. One can thus address the worry that reading a work such as Lu Xun's "Diary of a Madman" as "modernist" reduces twentieth-century Chinese literature to "a diluted story about repetition" not by insisting on its innovations but by recognizing the centrality of the copy to modernism *in toto* (Tang, "Lu Xun's 'Diary of a Madman,'" 1,222–1,223).

The copy not only highlights overtly iterative practices but also offers a way to rethink a much broader range of modernist work. I have tried to suggest these broader implications by singling out, in Pound's poem and Lu Xun's short story, modernist texts that are not obviously copies of anything but which are more commonly thought of as acts of artistic adaptation. Copy works are in one sense a specific subset of modernist practices that foreground the technologies of reproduction and the forces of globalism and commodity capitalism that shape modernity. But copy works also open our eyes to copies everywhere. The copy allows us to recognize the delirium of sameness in modernism, as much as the obsession with innovation, and so to write and think global modernism differently.

NOTES

1. The latter few examples may require some glossing. For Xu Zhimo's use of translation and commentary as part of his modernist poetics, see Saussy, "Death and Translation." On the collage poetics of Gandhi's printing press in South Africa, see

Hofmeyr, *Gandhi's Printing Press*, esp. 69–88. Tretyakov described the newspaper as the "epic and bible of our days" (Tret'iakov, "Novyi Lev Tolstoi," 33). On Brathwaite's poetics of versioning, see Josephs, "Versions of *X/Self*."

2. On these two tendencies in recent modernist studies, see also Mao and Walkowitz, "The New Modernist Studies"; Ardis, "Editor's Introduction," vi–vii.

3. On the history of the poem's publication and the changes in its punctuation and layout, see Ellis, "The Punctuation of 'In a Station of the Metro,'" 204–206; Chilton and Gilbertson, "Pound's 'Metro Hokku,'" 225–231; Brinkman, "Making Modern *Poetry*," 34–36.

4. E.g., Moretti, "Evolution, World-Systems, *Weltliteratur*," 120; Owen, "What Is World Poetry?"; Owen, "Stepping Forward and Back."

5. "Circulations" is Friedman's term. See Friedman, "Planetarity," 482–483; Friedman, "World Modernisms," 503. Other related terms include "webs" (Ballantyne, "Race and the Webs of Empire") and "relation" (Glissant, *Poetics of Relation*; Shih, "Comparison as Relation"). World-systems and circulation models of global modernism are contrasted in, inter alia, Hayot, "On Literary Worlds," 131; Friedman, "World Modernisms," 501; Boehmer, "How to Feel Global," 601.

WORKS CITED

Altieri, Charles. "Afterword: How the 'New Modernist Studies' Fails the Old Modernism." *Textual Practice* 26, no. 4 (2012): 763–782.

Ardis, Ann. "Editor's Introduction: Mediamorphosis: Print Culture and Transatlantic/Transnational Public Sphere(s)." *Modernism/modernity* 19, no. 3 (2012): v–vii.

Bakhtin, Mikhail. *The Dialogic Imagination: Four Essays*. Ed. Michael Holquist. Trans. Caryl Emerson and Michael Holquist. Austin: University of Texas Press, 1981.

Ballantyne, Tony. "Race and the Webs of Empire: Aryanism from India to the Pacific." *Journal of Colonialism and Colonial History* 2, no. 3 (2001). http://www.muse.jhu .edu/journals/journal_of_colonialism_and_colonial_history/v002/2.3ballantyne .html.

Benjamin, Walter. *Selected Writings*. Vol. 4, *1938–1940*. Trans. Edmund Jephcott et al. Ed. Howard Eiland and Michael W. Jennings. Cambridge, Mass.: Belknap, 2003.

Boehmer, Elleke. "How to Feel Global: The Modern, the Global and the World." *Literature Compass* 9 (2012): 599–606.

Borges, Jorge. *Ficciones*. New York: Grove, 1962.

Brinkman, Bartholomew. "Making Modern *Poetry*: Format, Genre, and the Invention of Imagism(e)." *Journal of Modern Literature* 32, no. 2 (2009): 20–40.

Bush, Christopher. *Ideographic Modernism: China, Writing, Media*. New York: Oxford University Press, 2010.

————. "Modernism, Orientalism, and East Asia." In *A Handbook of Modernism Studies*, ed. Jean-Michel Rabaté, 193–208. Chichester: Wiley-Blackwell, 2013.

Carr, Helen. "Imagism and Empire." In *Modernism and Empire*, ed. Howard J. Booth and Nigel Rigby, 64–92. Manchester: Manchester University Press, 2000.

Casanova, Pascale. *The World Republic of Letters*. Trans. M. B. DeBevoise. Cambridge, Mass.: Harvard University Press, 2004.

Chilton, Randolph, and Carol Gilbertson. "Pound's 'Metro Hokku': The Evolution of an Image." *Twentieth-Century Literature* 36, no. 2 (1990): 225–236.

Chow, Rey. *The Age of the World Target: Self-Referentiality in War, Theory, and Comparative Work*. Durham, N.C.: Duke University Press, 2006.

Collier, Patrick. "Imperial/Modernist Forms in the *Illustrated London News*." *Modernism/modernity* 19, no. 3 (2012): 487–514.

Couchoud, Paul-Louis. *Japanese Impressions*. Trans. Frances Rumsey. London: John Lane, 1921.

Damrosch, David. *What Is World Literature?* Princeton, N.J.: Princeton University Press, 2003.

Dworkin, Craig. "The Fate of Echo." In *Against Expression: An Anthology of Conceptual Writing*, ed. Craig Dworkin and Kenneth Goldsmith, xxiii–liv. Evanston, Ill.: Northwestern University Press, 2011.

————. *No Medium*. Cambridge, Mass.: MIT Press, 2013.

Dworkin, Craig, and Kenneth Goldsmith. *Against Expression: An Anthology of Conceptual Writing*. Evanston, Ill.: Northwestern University Press, 2011.

Edwards, Brent Hayes. *The Practice of Diaspora: Literature, Translation, and the Rise of Black Internationalism*. Cambridge, Mass.: Harvard University Press, 2003.

Ellis, Steve. "The Punctuation of 'In a Station of the Metro.'" *Paideuma* 17, no. 2–3 (1988): 201–207.

Friedman, Susan Stanford. "Planetarity: Musing Modernist Studies." *Modernism/modernity* 17, no. 3 (2010): 471–499.

————. "World Modernisms, World Literature, and Comparativity." In *The Oxford Handbook of Global Modernisms*, ed. Mark Wollaeger and Matt Eatough, 499–525. New York: Oxford University Press, 2012.

Gitelman, Lisa. *Always Already New: Media, History, and the Data of Culture*. Cambridge, Mass.: MIT Press, 2006.

Glissant, Édouard. *Poetics of Relation*. Trans. Betsy Wing. Ann Arbor: University of Michigan Press, 1997.

Gogol', N. V. *Polnoe sobranie sochinenii*. Vol. 3. Moscow: Akademii nauk SSSR, 1938.

Goldsmith, Kenneth. *Day*. Great Barrington, Mass.: Figures, 2003.

Golston, Michael. *Rhythm and Race in Modernist Poetry and Science*. New York: Columbia University Press, 2007.

Groys, Boris. "Ekzistentsial'nye predposylki kontseptual'nogo iskusstva." *37* 12 (1977). Reprinted in *Moskovskii kontseptualizm*, ed. Ekaterina Degot' and Vadim Zakharov, 332–342. Moscow: World Art Muzei, 2005.

Hayles, N. Katherine. *How We Became Posthuman: Virtual Bodies in Cybernetics, Literature, and Informatics*. Chicago: University of Chicago Press, 1999.

Hayot, Eric. "Chinese Modernism, Mimetic Desire, and European Time." In *The Oxford Handbook of Global Modernisms*, ed. Mark Wollaeger and Matt Eatough, 149–170. New York: Oxford University Press, 2012.

——. "On Literary Worlds." *Modern Language Quarterly* 72, no. 2 (2011): 129–161.

Hofmeyr, Isabel. *Gandhi's Printing Press: Experiments in Slow Reading*. Cambridge, Mass.: Harvard University Press, 2013.

Hsia Yü 夏宇, Hung Hung 鴻鴻, Ling Yü 零雨, Yung Man-Han 阿翁, and Tseng Shumei 曾淑美. "Cross It Out, Cross It Out, Cross It Out: Erasurist Poetry from Taiwan's *Poetry Now* (Issue #9, Feb. 2012)." Trans. Dylan Suher and Rachel Hui-Yu Tang. *Asymptote* (April 2012). http://www.asymptotejournal.com/visual/hsia-yu-et-al-cross-it-out-cross-it-out-cross-it-outerasurist-poetry-from-taiwans-poetry-now.

Inwood, Heather. "Yi Sha: Running His Race in the 'Ninth Lane.'" *Chinese Literature Today* 2, no. 2 (2012): 6–10.

Jameson, Fredric. "Reification and Utopia in Mass Culture." *Social Text* 1 (1979): 130–148.

Josephs, Kelly Baker. "Versions of *X/Self*: Kamau Brathwaite's Caribbean Discourse." *Anthurium: A Caribbean Studies Journal* 1, no. 1 (2003). http://scholarlyrepository.miami.edu/anthurium/vol1/iss1/4.

Joyce, James. *Ulysses: The Corrected Text*. Ed. Hans Walter Gabler, Wolfhard Steppe, and Claus Melchior. London: Bodley Head, 1986.

Kadir, Djelal. "World Literature: The Allophone, the Differential, and the Common." *Modern Language Quarterly* 74, no. 2 (2013): 293–306.

Lamartine, Alphonse de. "The Polity of Reason." In *The Polity of Reason; or, The Rationale of Government*, 65–136. London: H. G. Clarke, 1848. Translation of "Sur la politique rationnelle" (1831). In *Mémoires politiques 1*, 355–390. Vol. 37 of *Oeuvres complètes de Lamartine*. Paris: chez l'auteur, 1863.

Liu, Alan. *Local Transcendence: Essays on Postmodern Historicism and the Database*. Chicago: University of Chicago Press, 2008.

Lu Xun 鲁迅. *Lu Xun quan ji* 鲁迅全集. Vol. 1. Beijing: Renmin wenxue, 2005.

Mao, Douglas, and Rebecca L. Walkowitz. "The New Modernist Studies." *PMLA* 123, no. 3 (2008): 737–748.

Marinetti, F. T. *Manifesto tecnico della letteratura futurista*. Milan: Direzione del movimento futurista, 1912.

Monroe, Harriet. "Editorial Comment: The New Beauty." *Poetry* 2, no. 1 (April 1913): 22–25.

Moretti, Franco. "Conjectures on World Literature." *New Left Review* 1 (2000): 54–68.

———. "Evolution, World-Systems, *Weltliteratur*." In *Studying Transcultural Literary History*, ed. Gunilla Lindberg-Wada, 113–121. Berlin: Walter de Gruyter, 2006.

Murphy, Richard John. *Theorizing the Avant-Garde: Modernism, Expressionism, and the Problem of Postmodernity*. Cambridge: Cambridge University Press, 1999.

North, Michael. *The Dialect of Modernism: Race, Language, and Twentieth-Century Literature*. New York: Oxford University Press, 1994.

———. *Novelty: A History of the New*. Chicago: University of Chicago Press, 2013.

Owen, Stephen. "Stepping Forward and Back: Issues and Possibilities for 'World' Poetry." *Modern Philology* 100, no. 4 (2003): 532–548.

———. "What Is World Poetry? The Anxiety of Global Influence." *New Republic* (November 19, 1990): 28–32.

Pound, Ezra. *ABC of Reading*. London: Faber, 1951.

———. "A Few Don'ts by an Imagiste." *Poetry* 1, no. 6 (March 1913): 200–206.

———. "In a Station of the Metro." *Poetry* 2, no. 1 (April 1913): 12.

———. "A Pact." *Poetry* 2, no. 1 (April 1913): 11–12.

———. "Vortex." *Blast* 1 (1914): 153–154.

———. "Vorticism." *Fortnightly Review* (September 1, 1914): 461–471.

Pressman, Jessica. "Reading the Code Between the Words: The Role of Translation in Young-Hae Chang Heavy Industries's *Nippon*." *Dichtung-digital* 37 (2007). http://dichtung-digital.de/2007/Pressman/Pressman.htm.

Prigov, Dmitrii. "Conceptualism and the West." Interview by Alexei Alexeyev [Aleksandr Sidorov]. Trans. Michael Molnar. *Poetics Journal* 8 (June 1989): 12–16.

———. *Grazhdane! Ne zabyvaites', pozhaluista! Raboty na bumage, installiatsiia, kniga, performans, opera i deklamatsiia / Citizens! Please mind yourselves! Works on Paper, Installations, Books, Readings, Performance, and Opera*. Ed. Ekaterina Degot'. Moscow: Moscow Museum of Modern Art, 2008.

———. Untitled artist's book comprising three folded leaves from the series *Telegrammy* (*Telegrams*). Moscow, 1981. Held in the British Library, London.

Puchner, Martin. *Stage Fright: Modernism, Anti-Theatricality, and Drama*. Baltimore, Md.: Johns Hopkins University Press, 2002.

Ramazani, Jahan. *A Transnational Poetics*. Chicago: University of Chicago Press, 2009.

Saint-Amour, Paul K. *The Copywrights: Intellectual Property and the Literary Imagination*. Ithaca, N.Y.: Cornell University Press, 2003.

Saussy, Haun. "Death and Translation." *Representations* 94 (2006): 112–130.

Shaughnessy, Edward L. *Sources of Western Zhou History: Inscribed Bronze Vessels.* Berkeley: University of California Press, 1991.

Shih, Shu-mei. "Comparison as Relation." In *Comparison: Theories, Approaches, Uses,* ed. Rita Felski and Susan Stanford Friedman, 79–98. Baltimore, Md.: Johns Hopkins University Press, 2013.

Spivak, Gayatri Chakravorty. "Rethinking Comparativism." *New Literary History* 40, no. 3 (2009): 609–626.

Tambling, Jeremy. *Madmen and Other Survivors: Reading Lu Xun's Fiction.* Hong Kong: Hong Kong University Press, 2007.

Tang, Xiaobing. "Lu Xun's 'Diary of a Madman' and a Chinese Modernism." *PMLA* 107, no. 5 (1992): 1222–1234.

Taussig, Michael T. *Mimesis and Alterity: A Particular History of the Senses.* London: Routledge, 1993.

Tret'iakov, Sergei. "Novyi Lev Tolstoi." In *Literatura fakta: Pervyi sbornik materialov rabotnikov LEFa,* ed. N. F. Chuzhak, 29–33. Moscow: Federatsiia, 1929.

Yang Lian 杨炼. "Dahai tingzhi zhi shiShi yu diannao: Changkai zhongwen de neizai shijian" 大海停止之时———诗与电脑：敞开中文的内在时间. *Ershiyi shiji* 二十一世纪 56 (1999): 90–92.

Yang Lian, and John Cayley. *Where the Sea Stands Still.* A bilingual performance reading with Hypercard projections based on *Dahai tingzhi zhi chu* 大海停止之处, by Yang Lian, trans. Brian Holton (London: Wellsweep, 1995). Institute of Contemporary Arts, London, May 27, 1997. A subsequently published HTML version of the work is available online: http://programmatology.shadoof.net/works/wsss /index.html.

8. FORM

JAHAN RAMAZANI

Although the foreign form–local content model may seem to have taken "dominion everywhere" in studies of literary globalization, it looks, like Stevens's jar, "gray and bare" when held up against the richly chromatic prism of individual poems.

Imagine, if you will, rewritings of Wallace Stevens's first line of "Anecdote of the Jar," recasting it in a global register as an allegory of the migration of form: not "I placed a jar in Tennessee" but "I placed a sonnet in India," or "I placed a film in Iran," or "I placed MTV in China," or "I placed a novel in Africa."[1] Or perhaps "I placed haiku in America," or "I placed Safavid architecture in India," or "I placed African masks in Paris." Forms—shaping aesthetic patterns, structures, configurations—travel from one part of the world to another. "Precisely because they are abstract organizing principles," observes Caroline Levine, "shapes and patterns are iterable—portable. They can be picked up and moved to new contexts."[2] As modernity has sped up and intensified such movement, an insistent question for globalist cultural scholarship is how to understand this movement and its effects. Stevens's amusing allegory may help conceptualize the encounter between foreign form and local environment. In the case of the jar, the introduction of an alien form is transformative:

The wilderness rose up to it,
And sprawled around, no longer wild.

The jar was round upon the ground
And tall and of a port in air.

The internal rhyme of "Surround" with "around," "round," and "ground" son-
ically dramatizes the jar's in-forming mastery of the once wild native environment. It's almost as if native peoples were worshipping a newly arrived
god ("rose up to it"). In a largely unrhymed poem, the final stanza's triple
end rhyme with "air" emphasizes and mocks the new form's assumption of
"dominion everywhere. / The jar was gray and bare." In keeping with longstanding representations of the American South as exotic, its lushness and
wildness continuous with the global South's (Greeson, *Our South*), this environment is untamed and unruly (a "slovenly wilderness") until the ordering
principle of the jar arrives and takes control. The intruder's unnaturalness
("gray and bare") may result in sterility ("did not give of bird or bush") but
is also the source of its power over the local environment. In a poem that
represents an alien form's imperial takeover of a wilderness, the poem's own
form—quatrains in tetrameter, comically simple diction, encircling phonemes—bears some resemblance to the jar's. But the poem also marks its
difference in the sonic and imagistic ironies it directs at the jar's inflated sense
of its significance.

One of the most pervasive models for "world" and "global" literature has
been the formula *foreign form and local content*. New literature issues, we are
told, from the introduction of a jarlike foreign form into a local environment.
Franco Moretti, who frequently makes use of this paradigm in his studies of
the novel, cogently distills it in "Conjectures on World Literature" and other
essays collected in *Distant Reading* (2013). Building on Fredric Jameson's
reading of the Japanese novel and on Immanuel Wallerstein's world-systems
theory, Moretti proposes what he calls "a *law of literary evolution*: in cultures
that belong to the periphery of the literary system (which means: almost all
cultures, inside and outside Europe), the modern novel first arises not as an
autonomous development but as a compromise between a western formal influence (usually French or English) and local materials" (50). Borrowing from
various critical studies to track "the wave of diffusion of the modern novel"
on four continents over two hundred years, Moretti asserts that "when a culture starts moving towards the modern novel, it's *always* as a compromise
between foreign form and local materials," "west European patterns and local
reality" (52, 57). He modulates Jameson's binary law as "more of a triangle:

foreign form, local material—*and local form*. Simplifying somewhat: foreign *plot*; local *characters*; and then, local *narrative voice*" (57). Even so, as he discusses further examples, the abstractive formal dimensions of a text are almost entirely associated with the Western metropole and raw materials with the peripheries. If you are interested in the history of world, not national, literature, you are going to see Western waves, their "uniformity engulfing an initial diversity: Hollywood films conquering one market after another (or English swallowing language after language)" (60). *Engulfing, conquering, swallowing*—like Stevens's jar, the foreign form takes dominion over the local wilderness.

Moretti is preoccupied with the novel, but what happens to the foreign form–local content paradigm when put to the test with other genres, such as poetry? In response to previous critics who have raised this question, Moretti cites the spread of Petrarchanism (110), and in my view, modern and contemporary poetry offers some further confirmation.[3] As the model would predict, poetic forms sometimes travel one way to new environments and are loaded with local materials, if "local" is used in Jameson and Moretti's elastic sense, which includes the subnational, national, and regional as opposed to the "foreign" or "global." A number of anglophone poets from around the world could be ventriloquized thus: "I placed the sonnet in Jamaica" (Claude McKay), "I placed epic in Barbados" (Kamau Brathwaite), "I placed terza rima in Saint Lucia" (Derek Walcott), "I placed dramatic monologue in Uganda" (Okot p'Bitek), "I placed projectivism in Oceania" (Craig Santos Perez), and so forth. Caribbean, African, and Indian poets, I've argued elsewhere, adapted modernist syncretism, fragmentation, heteroglossia, and other formal principles to their local environments: witness the diverse Caribbean and Kashmiri uses that Kamau Brathwaite and Agha Shahid Ali make of T. S. Eliot's modernist strategies.[4] Nor is this pattern exclusive to anglophone works. To cite examples culled from *The Oxford Handbook of Global Modernisms* (2012), three critics show that Algerian, Palestinian, and Turkish poets access the oral, older modern, and Islamic aesthetics of their own traditions through the symbolist poetics of Baudelaire, Rimbaud, and Mallarmé (Talbayev, "Berber Poetry," 82; Lazarus, "Modernism and African Literature," 240–241; Ertürk, "Modernism Disfigured," 531). Following colonial patterns of cultural influence, francophone and anglophone modernist poetic forms were exported from the West to the so-called peripheries. Although Pascale Casanova, criticizing Moretti, proposes the terms "dominant and dominated" instead of center and periphery and "structure" instead of system, she, too, advances diffusionism ("Literature as a World," 80n14, 80). In her account of the Nicaraguan poet Rubén Darío's *modernismo* as a variant of symbolism, for example, she sees him as having performed "the deliberate Frenchification of Spanish poetry, down to the phonemes and syntactic forms" (88). Wielding symbolic power entails the transfer of literary forms from the site of greatest cultural capital to disempowered "local" sites, such as Latin America. Thus far, it would seem the foreign form–local content model has much to show for itself in theorizing world, planetary, or global literature.

But poetry also reveals the paradigm's one-sidedness and other inadequacies. First, the jar's "dominion" over the slovenly local wilderness is in part a methodologically produced illusion. The model of the Eurocentric wave doesn't merely reveal monolithic diffusion from the West; it occludes countercurrents. Consider Moretti's view that "after 1750 the novel arises just about everywhere as a compromise between west European patterns and local reality" (*Distant Reading*, 57). Doesn't the rest of the world have any "patterns" of its own? Moretti quotes Jameson as discussing the fit between "the raw material of Japanese social experience and the abstract formal patterns of Western novel construction" (49). But this literary-critical paradigm is in danger of "re-inscribing a hegemonic cultural centre" despite the aspiration to globalize literary studies (Beecroft, "World Literature Without a Hyphen," 88); that is, it risks reinforcing an imperial episteme in which the West is associated with control and conceptual order and the east with "raw material," as if local content resembled the land, sugar, labor, and spices expropriated under colonialism. Even Moretti's more nuanced triangle assigns technique to the West and consigns the rest to voice. Whether the novel, which writers such as Chinua Achebe, Salman Rushdie, and Marjane Satrapi meld with long-lived local narrative and pictorial traditions, or poetry, which has local and often ancient forms in many different parts of the world, the "peripheral" culture brings more to the table than local content and voice. In the creation of cubism, African and Oceanic art contributed not just raw materials but abstractive forms that were generative for modernist pictorial and sculptural styles. At the same moment, Kandinsky's study of Muslim Arab art, ornament, and calligraphy in Tunisia helped propel his turn to abstraction. Through imagism and subsequent literary movements, Chinese and Japanese formal principles became integral to the juxtapositional and compressed structure of modernist poetry. South Asian culture plays a crucial role in modernist perspectivism, as in works such as E. M. Forster's *A Passage to India* and Eliot's *Waste Land*. "Forms are the abstract of social relationships," Moretti claims, "so, formal analysis is in its own modest way an analysis of power" (59). If so, then to represent Western forms as "engulfing" and "swallowing" local sites and agents is to grant those "peripheries" little power, either symbolic or conceptual. "The West, for Moretti," as Susan Stanford Friedman writes, "is the site of discursive creation, while the non-West is 'local materials,' a center/periphery binary that ignores the often long histories of aesthetic production among the colonized" ("World Modernisms," 502). Casanova grants more agency to writers from "dominated" cultures in seizing cultural capital, but she, too, assumes that form typically travels from the European center outward.

Perhaps more surprisingly, the foreign form–local content paradigm plays a major role in loco-centric statements that may seem to contradict it. The so-called *bolekaja* critics ("Come down let's fight!" in Yoruba), for example, argued that some African poets, in anticipation of Moretti's wave metaphor, "trim their sails to the modernist squalls from the West" (Chinweizu et al., "Towards the Decolonization of African Literature," 37). Unduly influenced by the "wild and purposeless experimentation of some decadent Western poets," these African poets such as Christopher Okigbo and Wole Soyinka are said to import an "obscurantist cesspool" of difficult forms—arcane diction, contorted syntax, writerly instead of oral structures, privatist instead of communal language—into an environment where they did not belong (Chinweizu et al., 30). Even as the *bolekaja* critics argue African poetry should be based in indigenous oral traditions, thus recognizing the prior existence of forms outside the West, they dichotomize foreign form and local content, seeing them as incompatible.

Similarly, Brathwaite argues in *History of the Voice* that Western forms such as the sonnet and iambic pentameter, having traveled to the Caribbean and other parts of the former British Empire, are ill suited to non-European environments and experience. The Jamaican Claude McKay "allowed himself to be imprisoned in the pentameter" (275n17), Brathwaite claims; in keeping with Moretti's triangle of foreign form with local content and local voice, "the only thing that retains its uniqueness"—that is, the only locus of Caribbeanness in such poems—"is the tone of the poet's voice," as heard in sound recordings (275). But even as Brathwaite contends that poets should look not to the sonnet but to calypso and other local folk forms for inspiration, and even as he concedes the crucial role that Eliot's speech rhythms played in helping him and other poets creolize their poetry, he relies on and reinforces the binary of foreign form and local content. The pentameter, in his view, "carries with it a certain kind of experience, which is not the experience of a hurricane. The hurricane does not roar in pentameter" (265).

But such dichotomizing of foreign form and local content oversimplifies. As if in retort to Brathwaite's lecture, Walcott's frightening and tumultuous "Hurucan," a poem that uses the local Taino (Arawak) root of the English word, begins:

> Once branching light startles the hair of the coconuts,
> and on the villas' asphalt roofs, rain
> resonates like pebbles in a pan.
>
> (423)

If it does not roar, this hurricane at the very least rumbles in the pentametric variations of these lines. And elsewhere, in Walcott's *Omeros*, the hurricane roars in terza rima, a form forged in Dante's fourteenth-century Tuscany. Or rather the hurricane sighs, zithers, rattles, winds, thuds, and lurches:

> all the village could do was listen to the gods in session,
> playing any instruments that came into their craniums,
> the harp-sighing ripple of a hither-and-zithering sea,
> the knucklebone pebbles, the abrupt Shango drums
> made Neptune rock in the caves. Fête start! Erzulie
> rattling her ra-ra; Ogun, the blacksmith, feeling
> No Pain; Damballa winding like a zandoli
> lizard, as their huge feet thudded on the ceiling,
> as the sea-god, drunk, lurched from wall to wall, saying:
> "Mama, this music so loud, I going in seine,"
> then throwing up at his pun. People were praying.
>
> (52)

This hurricane, propulsively riding the momentum of Dante's interlinked rhyme, also rages in the outrageousness of Walcott's puns ("hither-and-zithering" as well as "in seine"), the onomatopoeic effects of alliteration ("rattling her ra-ra"), strong rhythms ("made Neptune rock in the caves"), hard enjambments ("zandoli // lizard"), abrupt shifts in syntax, and rolling hexameters. With other postcolonial poets, Walcott has adapted, remade, and refreshed terza rima, pentameter, hexameter, and other such "alien" forms.

After all, if the hurricane could not roar in pentameter, then presumably neither could Western poets bespeak their experience in haiku, tanka, ghazal, pantoum, and other such imported forms. Tell that to Ezra Pound, Amy Lowell, Adrienne Rich, John Ashbery, and Paul Muldoon. Despite the diffusionist wave, formal currents cross.

When Moretti and other theorists argue for the one-way global spread of the Western novel, their distantly read examples don't always support the terms of their argument. In one footnote, Moretti quotes the critic Ken Frieden as saying that "Yiddish writers parodied—appropriated, incorporated, and modified—diverse elements from European novels and stories" (51n13). If so, then far from being engulfed by the European novel, Yiddish writers actively remade it in accordance with their own narrative traditions and techniques. In another footnote, he quotes Jale Parla as saying that "the early Turkish novelists combined the traditional narrative forms with the examples of the western novel," so Turkish writers, it turns out, themselves have form, not only local content or voice, and their inherited narrative forms transform the European novel (52n15). Yet another quotation embedded in a footnote raises questions about the model it ostensibly validates: the first Dahomean novel, according to Abiola Irele, "is interesting as an experiment in recasting the oral literature of Africa within the form of a French novel," but here again, two discrepant forms are being fused, not a form and a content, and the result is a change in both (52n17). Moretti makes some allowance for "diversification," but he sees "convergence" and "diffusion" as paramount from the eighteenth century onward (129–131). Although postcolonial "hybridity" is often criticized, it and related ideas of creolization, vernacularization, indigenization, and interculturation are more capable of registering the intricate meldings of transnational forms than is the foreign form–local content model of diffusion.

"Distant reading" has the advantage that it can survey developments across not just a handful of canonical novels but an enormous corpus, "the other 99.5 per cent" (66). Moretti is right that literary scholars base their claims about a genre's evolution on a small number of examples. But consider what made this small subset of canonical works distinctive in the first place. When largely forgotten works are compared with critically favored examples in the same genre, in many cases the less-well-known works more passively replicate the formal codes and conventions than their better-known counterparts. More aggressively remaking genres, poems by Stevens, Moore, Yeats, and Eliot stand out against the bulk of poetry published in early twentieth-century literary journals. Little wonder that foreign-form diffusionism finds itself confirmed in panoramic surveys. The governing tropes of Moretti's scientific model aren't neutral but skewed toward normativity and therefore are ill suited to close contact with works that actively trouble and twist inherited forms.

What further limitations does the particularly form-intensive genre of poetry reveal, and what alternatives might it suggest? For one thing, the principle of "distant reading" is especially incongruous with the study of poetry: if you're reading poetry at a distance, you're not reading it as poetry. Poetry has been associated more than any other genre with close reading partly because of the small-scale intricacies and textures that help constitute poems and that disappear when works are viewed at a remove. Besides, the assumption that form can be extracted from content is anathema to poetry, in which form and content are more thoroughly melded than in perhaps any other genre. For many poets, as Robert Creeley declared, "Form is never more than an extension of content" (in Olson, "Projective Verse," 240). *How* a poem says what it says is no less essential to its identity as a poem than *what* it says. Indeed, in many a poem the main idea—I love you, I mourn my loss, I am in awe of nature—isn't especially original: it's the linguistic, formal, and imaginative freshness and vividness that make many a poem.

Further, the multifacetedness of form in poetry calls for nuanced analysis. As we've seen, Jameson refers to the novel's "abstract formal patterns," and Moretti substitutes "foreign *plot*" for "foreign form," but if the equation of "form" with "plot" simplifies the novel—which has other vital elements down to the level of syntax and sentence—it tells us even less about poetry.[5] A survey of the plot or argument of thousands of poems says little about them as poems. One way of salvaging distant reading for poetry is to consider poetic genre the macro-level equivalent to novelistic plot. Mapping the global migration of the sonnet, ballad, haiku, sestina, ghazal, and other such forms has long been an aspect of literary history ("form is precisely *the repeatable element of literature*," Moretti states [86]), and much more such mapping remains to be done. But as we track these migrations at the macro level, we need to keep in mind that a poem's fixed form is often only a part—not necessarily determinative—of what is going on in the work's multiple layers. "Epic in adapted terza rima" could be said to be the "form" of Walcott's *Omeros*, but as we've seen, this scarcely begins to suggest the array of formal elements mobilized in the poem, from the mixing of discursive registers between creolized English, French-based patois, and Standard English to paronomasia, chiasmus, and personification of a hurricane in the guise of Afro-Caribbean and classical gods. The same goes for works in "open forms." The "form" of Allen Ginsberg's "Howl" is to be found not only in its macro-level open structure but also in its insistent use of anaphora ("who . . ."), ellipsis ("Zen New Jersey"), mixed registers of diction ("who studied Plotinus Poe St. John of the Cross" and "Let themselves be fucked in the ass"), asyndeton ("yack-etayakking screaming vomiting whispering facts") and polysyndeton ("facts and memories and anecdotes and eyeball kicks and shocks of hospitals and jails and wars"), oxymoron ("hydrogen jukebox"), zeugma ("waving genitals and manuscripts"), allegory ("Moloch!"), metonymy ("unshaven rooms"), personification ("negro streets"), long, cascading, rhythmically loaded lines (indebted to Whitman and the Bible), syntactic parallelism and compression, and a whole array of sonic devices such as alliteration and assonance (49–51, 54). The form of a poem is no less its figurative language, rhythm, tone, syntax, registers of diction, and so forth than it is its overall structure. The evolutionary tracking of a single "device" such as the detective clue, albeit a smaller-scale unit than genre, hardly seems adequate to this multitudinous formal array (Moretti, *Distant Reading*, 77). Form needs to be pluralized and disaggregated in the analysis of its migratory patterns.

Another way of breaking up the monolithic foreign form–local content paradigm, or FFLC, would be to consider alternative configurations. There may also be works of foreign form and foreign content, or FFFC, such as Eliot's *Waste Land*, Yeats's "Lapis Lazuli," Pound's *Cantos*, Olson's *Maximus Poems*, and Walcott's *Omeros*—poems that draw on formal resources from various parts of the world and that reach for a planetary scope. In addition, there may be local form and foreign content, or LFFC, as exemplified by Louise Bennett's poems in orally performative Jamaican Creole but addressing midcentury news of the Nazi invasion of Europe. Perhaps Agha Shahid Ali's ghazals are also "local" in form, insofar as they are written in a monorhymed structure widespread in the Muslim Indian subcontinent in which he was born, and "foreign" in content, insofar as they take in war, imperialism, and so forth on a worldwide scale. There may even be local form and local content, or LFLC, as in Bennett's patois poems about local emigration, poverty, politicians, race relations, and so forth, or in Brathwaite's "Rites," a tour de force in West Indian Creole about a 1948 cricket match at Kensington Oval in Bridgetown, Barbados.

But as we trace such local-foreign configurations, we must acknowledge that poetry's complex tessellation often makes it difficult to distinguish FFLC from

FFFC in any hard and fast way, and each from LFFC or LFLC. Let's not forget that all FFFC poems have "local" bearings, such as the Whitmanian models behind Pound and Olson or the Saint Lucian code switching in Walcott; that Bennett's poems, if seemingly LFLC and LFFC because strongly Jamaican in orality and language, are still organized by British ballad stanzas while their foreign news is always screened through local preoccupations and their local experience impinged on by distant pressures; that the local form in Ali's LFFC ghazals looks back not only to Urdu but to Persian and Arabic sources, welded to Eliotic modernist disjunctiveness and syncretism, and their foreign content bears traces of a localizable Kashmiri Shia background; and that the use of Caribbean vernacular in Brathwaite's LFLC "Rites" and other poems is indebted to Anglo-modernism and their local content transatlantically striated by the Middle Passage. If Brathwaite's LFLC can be flipped around into FFLC or LFFC, Ali's LFFC to FFLC, Bennett's LFFC and LFLC into their mirror opposites, and if even Walcott's FFFC can be seen as its chiastic obverse, then these mirror-image initialisms point up the slipperiness of "foreign form and local content" and its variants. A pluralized, four-part tracking structure is surely more promising than the monolithic FFLC schema, representing a first step toward a more flexible and multidimensional model for charting global aesthetic flows. But even as we deploy it, we must bear in mind that, given the complexities of poetic form and of local-global enmeshments, most poems will fit into several of these slots at once, and no amount of long-distance squinting can accurately reduce them to one or the other.

I've mentioned many poems in passing, but now let's look closely at two works, one modernist, the other contemporary, one American, the other postcolonial British, to see how these questions of local and foreign, form and content, play out in specific examples. As suggested by its title, Marianne Moore's "England" (1920) is a poem that slyly poses as monolocational in subject but quickly turns out otherwise. After two and a half lines about England, a coordinating conjunction abruptly swivels elsewhere:

> and Italy with its equal
> shores—contriving an epicureanism from which the
> grossness has been
>
> extracted: and Greece with its goats and its gourds, the nest of
> modified illusions:
> and France. . . .

Of this poem that deploys and subverts cultural stereotypes, we might say its syntactic form is American—paratactic, even egalitarian in straddling one culture and another—that its metrical structure (unrhymed quatrains of twenty, fifteen, twenty-two, and eighteen syllables) Americanizes classical syllabics, that its occasional use of a colloquial register "in plain American which cats and dogs can read" is American, albeit mixed with words and phrases like "epicureanism," "continents of misapprehension," and "cataclysmic torrent," all spilling forward in the headlong rush of heavily enjambed lines. So what at first seemed to be "local content" may instead look "foreign" on further reading, in a poem of localized form, or LFFC. But the jump from the national to the regional or hemispheric calls into question the kinds of cultural groupings that the poem, like taxonomic criticism, makes use of:

> and the East with its snails, its emotional
>
> shorthand and jade cockroaches, its rock crystal and its
>   imperturbability,
>   all of museum quality. . . .

We are asked to recognize the familiar East Asian animals and objects that might be housed in a museum, but as for the putative psychological characteristics of "the East"—"emotional // shorthand" and "imperturbability"— how are these "of museum quality"? Clearly something has gone awry in the poem's syntactic straddling of discrepant cultures and locations. America is affectionately yet wryly described in skewed stereotypes: supposedly "there are no proof readers" and "no digressions," and no language even (a "language-less country"), but this presumably "American" poem, which we thought was going to be about "England" but turns out to be globally comparative and closes with a meditation on America in its global relationality, vigorously demonstrates both digression and precision in language. If responding defensively to views of America as culturally deficient, Moore bespeaks a nationalism that shades into transnationalism. By poem's end, she may have convinced some readers that she is making a case for American exceptionalism—America as the only place where the best qualities of China, Egypt, Palestine, and elsewhere are to be found. But she pulls the rug out when she says of such "superi- / ority," not accidentally one of only two words split violently in the poem by an enjambment (the other, no less wittily, "con- // clusions"): "It has never been confined to one locality." Although Moore speaks from America (local content), she reveals that her national culture can only be conceptualized comparatively (foreign content). Indeed, given that enjambment, syllabics, and zeugma go back to the ancients, we could also see the form as having global bearings. Like many a modernist poem, Moore's can be seen as FFLC, LFFC, LFLC, or FFFC but is more accurately understood as a complex amalgam of all at once.

What if we looked at a poem that represents itself as steadfastly joined to one specific locale instead of peregrinating across the world like Moore's trickily named "England"? "The Punjab" (2011), a poem by the Indian British poet Daljit Nagra, concerns the poet's familial homeland:

> Not 'The'—just 'Púnjab'!
> Was there once upon before partition a Púnjab
> whole? A Pan-jab of Hindu, Sikh, Muslim, anything?

In the assertive first line, the speaker-as-native-informant demands omission of the British definite article. But his Indian British pronunciation places him at a diasporic remove from the homeland he claims: the Punjabi stress, as the poem later emphasizes, is on the second syllable ("Punjaaab"). Further eroding the appearance of locally anchored authority, the assured tone dissolves in questions and uncertainties about Punjabi history and identity. An integral facet of its form, the quick tonal modulations position the poem's voice both within (the) Punjab and outside it, both locally and extrinsically. As in Eliot's relation to Prufrock, Nagra's to his speaker is one of both proximity and ironic distance. Although the talismanic place-name Punjab seems to confer local authenticity, it spirals beyond the local in interlingual wordplay, extravagant punning (and jabbing)—"Pan-jab," "Punjamentalist," "Punjaaab," "Punglanders"—that recalls Joyce's *Finnegans Wake*. The poem is built around the pun on "pun" and "Punjab," as if the very place-name invited such verbal acrobatics. When the speaker's questions about Punjabi identity twist into a Peter Piper–like alliterative tongue-twister, the poem ridicules claims to authentic representativeness and at the same time stereotypes of Punjabis as lascivious and fanatical:

> To play the pipes of a Punjamentalist—
> must I pin a badge, must I drop my pants—
> must I join a junta and jab-jab-jab for my Púnjab!?

Where is the poem's form-content amalgam now? It's in (the) Punjab, in an Asian British account of it, and in a field of translingual puns and sonic play that includes Spanish. The poem is both locally fixed on (the) Punjab and self-mockingly hyperbolic and extrinsic in its performance of that locality.

The toponym fastens the poem to a specific location with five rivers ("If it's five for the 'punj' and it's 'jaaab' for a river," in a cross-cultural riff on Elvis's "Blue Suede Shoes"), but a language of homage to rivers is hardly exclusive to this site, as emphasized by the refrain:

That old man river calls you loud and long
from a land that you loved in a lullaby

The refrain both bespeaks nativist longing and mocks it in a pseudo–negro spiritual. The love of the land is displaced into a song that, echoing an African American source, shows that nostalgia to be stranded in foreign forms that mediate the speaker's relation to his homeland (so too the references to the English nursery rhyme "Row, Row, Row Your Boat" and the American minstrel song "Swannee River"). In subsequent iterations of the refrain, the land is rosily idealized ("*the rainbow glows*") yet sternly withheld ("*but you'll never know the land or the song*"). Through its insider knowledge, place-names, Punjabi words, and comic persona, which implicitly voices South Asian robustness over against English restraint (even while sending up such stereotypes), the poem lays claim to Punjabi rootedness in form, tone, language, and content. At the same time, its interlingual punning, its alliteration and internal rhyme, its code switching among Standard English and Punglish and Punjabi, its intergeneric melding of African American spiritual with literary poem, and its riotous allusions to Western literary texts ("jump aboard / for your unplucked jut-land, your bee-glade Indusfree!") situate even this regionally focused poem within a global matrix of forms, words, sounds, and places. To say that its humor is "Punjabi" or "Anglo-Punjabi," that its hetero- and polyglot mixing of discourses or its ironized speaker is "modernist," either to localize or to globalize it exclusively, would be to oversimplify the complexly translocal intermixing of language, place, and identity that drives the poem. Poems such as Nagra's and Moore's, outstripping "foreign form and local content," demand a more supple and nuanced critical vocabulary for the relations of foreign to local and form to content.

We may well be unable to forsake entirely the foreign form–local content paradigm in mapping the transnational migrations of literary techniques and strategies amid the intensified globalization of the twentieth and twenty-first centuries. But in tracing literary flows, we should at least decenter it by multiplying the configurations of local and foreign, form and content. To reduce world literary transmission to this single structure is to occlude the mutually transformative nature of intercultural literary dialogue. It is also to limit "form" to one scale, when it ranges from the minute adjustments of enjambment and tone to the larger patterns of genre and argument. Although the foreign form–local content model may seem to have taken "dominion everywhere" in studies of literary globalization, it looks, like Stevens's jar, "gray and bare" when held up against the richly chromatic prism of individual poems. As we turn a poem over and over, it is likely to reveal a kaleidoscopic range of local-foreign configurations no matter how firmly situated within the local or how foreign its form or content may at first appear. In their intricacy and complexity, poems vividly illustrate the inextricability of form from content and of local from foreign. Instead of abstracting world literary evolution as a one-dimensional and one-directional model or scientific law, our form-content analysis should—taking its cues from poems—aspire to be polyphonic and multilayered, moving nimbly back and forth between micro and macro, local and global. Another way to enrich our vocabulary for exploring global literary migration is to reenergize the formal discourse of poetics: it can help make visible the many-sidedness of imaginative works—a multiplicity that may disappear if viewed from too great a distance yet that helps poems live in and beyond their moment and their places of origin. As Pound showed in adapting an ancient Chinese inscription for the modernist imperative, sometimes an especially old vocabulary serves to "make it new."

NOTES

1. See Kenneth Koch's famous poem "Variations on a Theme by William Carlos Williams."

2. According to Levine, all historical uses of the term "share a common definition: 'form' always indicates *an arrangement of elements—an ordering, patterning, or shaping*" (*Forms*, 3). My use of the term is largely consonant with Levine's, though I see "form" and "genre" as intertwined rather than sharply distinct in their portability (13). Form is the subject of much new scholarship; in addition to Levine, recent overviews and discussions include Wolfson, "Form"; Attridge, *Moving Words*; Theile, "New Formalism(s)"; and Bogel, *New Formalist Criticism*.

3. Moretti cites and responds to previous critics in "More Conjectures," in *Distant Reading* (107–119).

4. Ramazani, *A Transnational Poetics*, chap. 5. "Traveling poetry" is the subject of chap. 3.

5. Recent work by Moretti's Stanford Literary Lab has been applying computational methods to the smaller-scale aspects of novels, such as the syntax and verbs of sentences, insofar as they can be correlated with an overarching genre or style; see, e.g., Sarah Allison et al., *Style at the Scale of the Sentence*.

WORKS CITED

Allison, Sarah, et al. *Style at the Scale of the Sentence*. Pamphlets of the Stanford Literary Lab. June 2013. http://litlab.stanford.edu/LiteraryLabPamphlet5.pdf.

Attridge, Derek. *Moving Words: Forms of English Poetry*. Oxford: Oxford University Press, 2013.

Beecroft, Alexander. "World Literature Without a Hyphen: Towards a Typology of Literary Systems." *New Left Review* 54 (2008): 87–100.

Bogel, Fredric V. *New Formalist Criticism: Theory and Practice*. New York: Palgrave Macmillan, 2013.

Brathwaite, Kamau. *History of the Voice*. Revised and reprinted in *Roots*, by Kamau Brathwaite, 190–304. Ann Arbor: University of Michigan Press, 1993.

Casanova, Pascale. "Literature as a World." *New Left Review* 31 (2005): 71–90.

Chinweizu, Onwuchekwa Jemie, and Ihechukwu Madubuike. "Towards the Decolonization of African Literature." *Transition* 48 (1975): 29–37, 54, 56–57.

Ertürk, Nergis. "Modernism Disfigured: Turkish Literature and the 'Other West.'" In *The Oxford Handbook of Global Modernisms*, ed. Wollaeger, 529–550.

Friedman, Susan Stanford. "World Modernisms, World Literature, and Comparativity." In *The Oxford Handbook of Global Modernisms*, ed. Wollaeger, 599–525.

Ginsberg, Allen. "Howl." In *Selected Poems, 1947–1995*, 49–56. New York: Harper-Collins, 1996.

Greeson, Jennifer Rae. *Our South: Geographic Fantasy and the Rise of National Literature*. Cambridge, MA: Harvard University Press, 2010.

Lazarus, Neil. "Modernism and African Literature." In *The Oxford Handbook of Global Modernisms*, ed. Wollaeger, 228–245.

Levine, Caroline. *Forms: Whole, Rhythm, Hierarchy, Network*. Princeton, N.J.: Princeton University Press, 2015.

Moore, Marianne. "England." In *The Poems of Marianne Moore*, ed. Grace Schulman, 141–142. New York: Viking-Penguin, 2003.

Moretti, Franco. *Distant Reading*. London: Verso, 2013.

Nagra, Daljit. "The Punjab." In *Tippoo Sultan's Incredible White-Man-Eating Tiger Toy Machine!!!*, 34–35. London: Faber, 2011.

Olson, Charles. "Projective Verse." In *Collected Prose*, ed. Donald Allen and Benjamin Friedlander, 239–249. Berkeley: University of California Press, 1997.

Ramazani, Jahan. *A Transnational Poetics*. Chicago: University of Chicago Press, 2009.

Stevens, Wallace. "Anecdote of the Jar." In *The Collected Poems of Wallace Stevens*, 76. New York: Random House, 1954.

Talbayev, Edige Tamalet. "Berber Poetry and the Issue of Derivation: Alternate Symbolist Trajectories." In *The Oxford Handbook of Global Modernisms*, ed. Wollaeger, 81–108.

Theile, Verena. "New Formalism(s): A Prologue." In *New Formalisms and Literary Theory*, ed. Theile and Linda Tredennick, 3–28. New York: Palgrave Macmillan, 2013.

Walcott, Derek. "Hurucan." In *Collected Poems, 1948–1984*, 423. New York: Farrar, Straus, and Giroux, 1986.

——. *Omeros*. New York: Farrar, Straus, and Giroux, 1990.

Wolfson, Susan. "Form." In *The Princeton Encyclopedia of Poetry and Poetics*, 4th ed., ed. Roland Greene, Stephen Cushman, et al., 497–499. Princeton, N.J.: Princeton University Press, 2012.

Wollaeger, Mark, ed. *The Oxford Handbook of Global Modernisms*. With Matt Eatoughs. New York: Oxford University Press, 2012.

9. LIBRARIES

B. VENKAT MANI

Modernist registers of innovation, transformation, and dissociation from the ancient and the classical are particularly suited to augment the role of libraries as sociopolitical texts; the collector and the collected, the consumer and the consumed, the object and the subject undergo various transformations.

W. G. Sebald's *Austerlitz*, published in 2001, recounts the story of Jacques Austerlitz, who arrived in England in 1939 as part of the Kindertransport from the former Czechoslovakia. Speaking to the narrator, Austerlitz proclaims his interest in the "tendency towards monumentalism evident in law courts, penal institutions, railway stations, and stock exchanges" (30). In the novel, Austerlitz's search for monumentalism culminates in detailed descriptions of a library: the Bibliothèque Nationale de France. *Austerlitz* weaves fact and fiction, personal memory and history, and verbal and visual representation to create a narrative about the recuperation of the past. It is simultaneously a fascinating account of public spaces, extending the historical phenomena of the nineteenth century—colonialism, imperialism, and the establishment of a world market—into the twentieth century's two world wars and the Holocaust. The novel begins in the transitory space of a railway station, but it ends in the classificatory space of the library, where historical and contemporary knowledge is collated, preserved, and disseminated. Bookended by the Antwerp Centraal Station and the Bibliothèque Nationale, *Austerlitz* suggests that the time of modernism is a time of transition and transformation, order and chaos, knowledge and ignorance. The novel asks readers to consider the relationship between national histories and the national collecting of books.

Modernism had a special relationship with libraries, as Sebald's novel suggests and as many other works can show us.[1] Libraries, I argue in this essay,
are historically conditioned, culturally fashioned, and politically charged institutions. Modernists' engagement with libraries in their works unfolds these
multiple facets. We normally distinguish between books and institutions, but
many modernist works show us that aesthetic representations of libraries
have in fact augmented their position as sociopolitical agents. Institutions
may create the occasion for books, but books have also helped generate the
meaning and power of institutions.

As a programmatic dissociation with the ancient and the classical and a renewed engagement with the present, modernism's pluralistic manifestations
in art, architecture, cinema, and literature are associated with many features.
Modernism provides new ways of expressing the autonomy of the self; it also
registers systematic renegotiation of the self within the collective. Modernism resists realist representation to promote imaginations of futurity through
originality, innovation, avant-gardism, experimentation, and subjectivity. In
Literary Worlds, Eric Hayot suggests that a modernist work "would have to assert a total ontological rejection of the normative world-view of its era" (132).
Hayot's comment captures the shift of focus in recent scholarship, especially
in the first decade of the twenty-first century: instead of presenting modernism as a phenomenon exclusive to metropolitan centers of Western Europe or
the United States, there is an attempt to understand not merely its reception
but also its appropriation and renegotiation in multiple literary and cultural
traditions around the world. Recent scholarship draws attention to the lin-
guistically and geographically diverse genealogy of modernism. By examining European modernism in tandem with developments in Asia, Africa, and
Latin America, scholars have begun to position modernism vis-à-vis nations
connected to Europe through the history of colonialism and empire building and have shed new light on the transnational dimensions of modernism
(Kapur, *When Was Modernism?*; Bharucha, *Another Asia*). Simon Gikandi locates the literary form of the postcolonial experience "solely—in the language
and structure of modernism" ("Modernism in the World," 420). Susan Stanford Friedman asks for a rethinking of the periodization of modernism to
avoid the exclusion of "the agencies of writers, artists, philosophers, and other
cultural producers in the emergent postcolonial world" ("Periodizing Modernism," 427). The translocalization of modernism is also evident in studies of
literature marked by large-scale migration—willful and forced—into Europe

after the Second World War. In *Cosmopolitan Style*, Rebecca Walkowitz sutures the discussion of modernist aesthetics and style in contemporary literature with political features of home, belonging, and cultural citizenship through cosmopolitan interventions in the so-called national styles of modernism. These examples are by no means exhaustive, yet they serve to illustrate transformations in the conceptual and spatial expansion of knowledge about modernism. The fixation on English, American, and European writers is now giving way to multicentered, multidimensional, multidirectional, and multilingual understandings of modernism.

This new conceptual, spatial, and temporal awareness in current scholarship is beneficial for making a case for libraries in studies of modernism. To be sure, libraries are also multiply signified. As I have discussed elsewhere,[2] the term "library" has multiple meanings: a house of books, a catalog of titles, a publication series, and, more recently, a virtual space, a digital collection. The definition of the book as "codex"—a technological device with hand-copied or printed pages that can be turned—has now given way to the digital or e-book with a virtual, rather than a physical, identity. Like readers, libraries do not stand outside of the sociopolitical fabric of society. The house of books, the Bibliothek—especially public, but also private—is far from a neutral space. Libraries are sites rife with the politics of literacy and sanctioned illiteracy, historical contingencies that condition accumulation and classification, circulation and distribution, patronage and accession, orderly organization and disorderly contention. If public libraries, sometimes along with museums, serve as major institutions of various forms of local, national, regional, or transnational representations, private libraries come to represent the individual features and idiosyncrasies of their collectors.

Given the diversity of modernist innovations and interventions, it would be difficult to claim that there is a categorically "modernist" approach to libraries. It will, however, be productive to identify instances where modernist thinkers and authors draw attention to libraries as "medial" institutions—as institutions that collect and circulate books and other media of knowledge dissemination—which acquire a far greater intellectual and cultural iconicity than the physical space that they occupy. An attention to the "medial" nature of libraries can serve three purposes: first, it can augment our understanding of "books" as a medium and institution of knowledge and entertainment and assist in asking if there was, in an age of technological innovations such as the telegraph, telephone, radio, and cinema, a shift of sensibility for older media and sources of knowledge and information such as books and libraries. Second, print-cultural explorations of modernism can amplify the "public-

ity" of the modernist movement by drawing our attention to the transformation of social spaces. While extant scholarship has generated interest in
the institutionalization of modernism through the city,[3] the factory (Wirth
and Ciesielski, *Die moderne Fabrik*), the train station (Presner, *Mobile Modernity*), and the film theater (Feiereiss, *Die Wiener Trilogie und ein Kino*), to
name just a few, the library somehow has remained outside the scope of the
critical spectrum. Were modernist texts able to articulate—as Sebald puts it—
the "chronic dysfunction and constitutional instability" (279) that coincides
with the otherwise seemingly absolute and perfect concept of a library? Were
modernist authors able to use libraries to express, paraphrasing Hayot, a refusal and rejection of a normative worldview? And finally, a curiosity about
depictions of books and libraries in modernist texts can assist in expanding
the "inventory"—borrowing from Chartier's politicization of the term in *The
Order of Books*—of modernist interventions and innovations in postcolonial
literatures. To what extent did modernist works mobilize libraries to give
expression to the unevenness of literary circulation? How did modernism
and its postcolonial literary interpretations reflect on the linguistic, aesthetic,
and epistemic violence caused by dominant nationalist paradigms? How did
modernism set the tone for the creation of a transnational expansion of ideas
through books and libraries?

To approach these questions, let us briefly turn to Walter Benjamin: jour-
nalist, essayist, chronologist, and above all, book collector.

Walter Benjamin's media-theoretical writings reflected on the many new media of the twentieth century: film, advertisement, radio plays, newspapers,
magazines, and even the telephone. But it is in his writings on books that
his understanding of the medium appears with quintessential wit and play-
fulness. From commentaries on bestsellers and masterpieces, to modernist
French authors such as Charles Baudelaire and André Gide, and to classical
European authors from Cervantes to Goethe, Benjamin was very aware of the
media through which literature is accessed. Especially in the last years of the
Weimar Republic (1928–1932), he published several essays on books. Apart
from his essay on dime novels of the nineteenth century, children's books,
and reading trends among Germans during the time of the writing of German classics (*Medienästhetische Schriften*), Benjamin wrote his most famous
essay on "Unpacking my Library" ("Ich packe meine Bibliothek aus").

Written on the occasion of moving into a new, partially furnished apartment after his divorce with his wife Dora (Lewandowski), Benjamin's essay
"Unpacking my Library" focuses on the ways in which a personal library

becomes the site of transformation of the collector and the collected, the consumer and the consumed, the subject and the object. Benjamin locates such transformative forces between the tedious agony of organization and collation and the euphoric ecstasy of the acquisition of books. Benjamin begins his essay with a declaration of an act: the act of unpacking his books, before they find their places on bookshelves. He invites his readers to join the chaos of a library that is dispersed in crates and on the floor, a library that has not taken the form of what is associated with the word: an orderly arrangement of books on display. Benjamin associates this dispersed, strewn-about disorderliness with the chaotic energy of the passion for book collecting. Benjamin's essay is thus not about the collection itself: "what I am really concerned with is giving you some insight into the relationship of a book collector to his possessions, to collecting, rather than the collection" ("Unpacking My Library," 59–60).

Arbitrary modes rather than exact knowledge, randomness of passion rather than the programmatic energy of rationalism, thus set the tone for Benjamin's reflections. He calls attention to the "dialectical tension between the poles of order and disorder" in the life of a collector (60). What informs his own text, his own recounting of the act of collecting books, as they lie strewn around in his apartment, is a distinct dialectical tension between "fate" and "freedom." Counterbalancing this tension, as Benjamin further proposes, is the torque of "memory" that resounds in the very act of collecting. Benjamin draws a direct connection between remembering and book collecting: "Every passion borders on the chaotic, but the collector's passion borders on the chaos of memories" (60). To collect is to reconstruct the past, "to renew the old age," but that renewal is dependent on the fate of an object: it is taken from one's collection and becomes part of someone else's, and the person who acquires it accumulates a sense of "freedom" in receiving, borrowing, or even purloining a work from someone else's collection, in order to give a new meaning to the object in the new collection. This is where the art of collecting books becomes a question of accessibility to them, which Benjamin further connects with the act of writing. Having declared earlier that "Collectors are physiognomists of objects" (60), Benjamin states—referencing the protagonist of Jean Paul's novella *Schulmeisterlein Wutz* (1790)—"Writers are really people who write books not because they are poor, but because they are dissatisfied with books they could buy but do not like" (61). This is a remarkable moment of shift in Benjamin's essay. His recollection of cities where he acquired specific books, catalogs that informed him of particular books, and memories of coming across those catalogs all become part of the action of collection. In the specific kind of physiognomic exercise carried out by collectors, many moments of chance are involved: the chance of coming across a particularly treasured object, the chance of having that object available for purchase, and the chance that the object will actually be acquired by the collector. Benjamin's reflections on fate and memory culminate in a sense of a peculiar kind of "freedom" that for him is associated with the act of collecting:

> One of the finest memories of a collector is the moment when he rescued a book to which he might never have given a thought, much less a wishful look, because he found it lonely and abandoned on the market place and bought it and gave it its freedom—the way the prince bought a beautiful slave-girl in the Arabian Nights. To a book collector, you see, the true freedom of all books is somewhere on his shelf.
>
> (64)

It is hard to miss the gendered political tension that is part of Benjamin's imagination of the freedom that involves the particular "rescuing" of books. The personal library—a confined space—can hardly be seen as a site of freedom from the openness of a market; the condescension invoked by the emancipation of a beautiful slave girl by a prince similarly implies a further exploitation of sexualized labor. Acknowledging these tensions actually helps in identifying the ineluctable power dynamic that is an essential part of any library, private or public. Libraries are founded upon the collector's sense of an epistemic privilege, a desire to grant an object a new meaning, function, and ambition. It is hardly a surprise that in Benjamin's essay the thrill of collection, the excitement of acquiring a new and less-circulated item, the heroic sense of purchasing "freedom" for an "enslaved" book and granting it emancipation on one's own shelf, toward the end is also accompanied by the sense that a collector's work might never really be recognized during his lifetime "but, as Hegel put it, only when it is dark does the owl of Minerva begin its flight, only in extinction is the collector comprehended" (67).

Benjamin's essay calls upon its readers to focus on many issues, especially on the dialectical relationship between order and chaos. But what the reader cannot miss is the dialectical tension between dissemination (*Zerstreuung*) and accumulation (*Sammlung*). The entire act of collection simultaneously becomes an act of de-collection, of anticipating a collection. At the center of Benjamin's essay is a personal library, which becomes a reflection of the collector's inclinations, proclivities, and even idiosyncrasies. And the freedom of books, as well as the freedom of the collector, stays embedded in equations of asymmetrical power.

Benjamin's reflections are one instance of a quintessentially twentieth-century relationship with books and libraries. The benefits of the proliferation of the publishing industry in the nineteenth century, in tandem with widespread literacy, the rise of the book market, the expansion of public libraries, and the availability of cheap editions, all augmented public access to books and libraries by the early twentieth century. The classical iconicity of books and libraries—exemplified for example in the opening scene of Goethe's *Faust*, part 1, where books are the sole property of the intellectual and are at once portrayed as great sources of knowledge but also as dreary and morose with obscure wisdom—undergoes a gradual displacement. Private libraries come to represent the new *Bildungsbourgeoisie*; they become spaces that reflect personal passions and idiosyncrasies, which in turn are historically conditioned. Public libraries transform as well. The political purchase of royal libraries of the nineteenth century is recast in the public, democratic currencies of the twentieth century through libraries real and imagined, where multiple social actors claim their stakes, and not entirely in harmonious ways. Modernists have not remained oblivious to these transformations. The multiple significations of "the library"—as an idea, an institution, as well as a material/physical space—have found expression in modernist literature from around the world. Modernist registers of innovation, transformation, and dissociation from the ancient and the classical are particularly suited to augment the role of libraries as sociopolitical texts; the collector and the collected, the consumer and the consumed, the object and the subject undergo various transformations. Paying attention to aesthetic representations of libraries can assist in deepening our understanding of libraries as well as of modernism.

In the next section, let us turn to a few examples from literary texts—some canonized as classics of European modernism, others that condition and redefine modernism in specific historical, linguistic, and cultural contexts—to see how understanding global modernism through libraries can be productive. Instead of arranging the authors chronologically, to follow rules of literary history, or alphabetically, as would be expected from an essay on a library, it might be better to follow a Benjaminian chaos, which would hopefully help reveal the role of a library as an agent of the multidirectional, multicentered, and multilinguistic facets of modernism.

In the "Telemachus" chapter of James Joyce's *Ulysses*, the tension between Buck Mulligan and Haines is palpable, among others, through Haines's in-

ability to comprehend much of what Mulligan conceives as important under-
takings for the day. Mulligan's suggestion to Stephen, "Today the bards must
drink and junket. Ireland expects that everyman this day will do his duty"
(18), reminds Haines of his own duty, that he has to visit the National Library
of Ireland (18). Haines, who "intends to make a collection of [the Irish] sayings if you will let me," creates an anthropological subject of investigation and
study. The National Library invites the reader to examine the fractured sensibilities of national subjugation and cultural pride; the multiple references to
many libraries all over Dublin in the novel reiterate these sensibilities.

If Haines's access to the National Library of Ireland facilitates his epistemic
privilege over Buck Mulligan—of collating and classifying everyday speech
to produce folkloric knowledge—Virginia Woolf's lack of access to a university library would reveal asymmetrical power over its gendered subject. In *A
Room of One's Own*, Woolf describes standing at the entrance of the Trinity
College Library at Cambridge, hoping to read essays by Charles Lamb or perhaps even to take a look at the manuscript of Thackeray's *Esmond*, when she
is informed that "ladies are only admitted to the library if accompanied by a
Fellow of the College or furnished with a letter of Introduction" (8). There is
no room for a woman author in the library unless legitimized by male com-
panionship, leading her to curse the library, with full awareness of the apathy
of the institution of learning: "That a famous library has been cursed by a
woman is a matter of complete indifference to a famous library" (8).

The expression of such hierarchies of access, indeed the politics of accessibility and inaccessibility, can be followed in the postcolonial context in two
novels, one originally composed in Hindi, the other in Arabic. The Hindi novelist Amritlal Nagar's historical novel *Karavata* starts in 1854, when the protagonist Bansidhar makes three life-altering decisions at the age of nineteen:
to renounce his early achievements in Farsi, Arabic, and Sanskrit; to learn English; and to move out of the northern Indian city of Lucknow to Calcutta, the
new center of political and economic power in India. Lady Nancy Malcolm—
Bansidhar's father's acquaintance—promises to write a letter of introduction
addressed to Mr. Pincot, an East India Company official in Calcutta, albeit
not without stipulating a condition. Bansidhar must acquire for her and for
Mr. Pincot "rare Sanskrit manuscripts." An acquaintance directs Bansidhar
to Raina Pandit, a Kashmiri migrant in Lucknow, who reportedly owns the
best collection of books in northern India but since the arrival of the British
in the city has stopped caring about them. When Bansidhar enters Pandit's
library, he finds himself surrounded by books stacked from floor to ceiling—

in Arabic, Farsi, Sanskrit, Kashmiri, and Bangla. Bansidhar tricks Pandit into selling him a few illustrated copies of the *Kamasutra, Bhagavad-Gita,* and *Mahabharata* at a bargain price. Books from Pandit's library soon find themselves on the shelves of Lady Malcolm in Lucknow and of Mr. Pincot in Calcutta. Bansidhar is all set to embark upon his colonial *Bildung* (Nagar, *Karavata,* 36–38).

In Nagar's novel, the library of a British East India Company official, through its acquisition of native (ancient Indian) texts, assures the entry of a colonial subject in the social text of modernity. By contrast, the Sudanese writer Salih al-Tayyib instantiates how the library of a colonial subject is formed through the suppression and rejection of local knowledge. Tayyib's novel *Season of Migration to the North* (*Mawsim al-Hijrah ilā al-Shamāl,* 1962) starts with the narrator's return to his home in a village in Sudan after he has spent seven years in England. The narrator's interaction with the civic life of the village is filtered through his recent memories of England and his curiosity about the life of Mustafa Sa'eed, his doppelganger. At the end of the novel, the narrator gains access to the secret of all secrets when he opens the iron door of Mustafa Sa'eed's rectangular room. He finds "shelf upon shelf, with books, and more books and yet more books" (Tayyib, *Season of Migration,* 135). Sa'eed's library includes an eclectic collection of works by Thomas Mann, Thomas Carlyle, Rudyard Kipling, G. W. F. Hegel, and Harold Joseph Laski, among many others. In addition, the library holds copies of the Bible and the Koran in English and other books, all in English, authored by Mustafa Sa'eed, with titles ranging from *The Cross and Gunpowder,* to *Rape of Africa,* to *Colonialism and Monopoly.* "Not a single Arabic book. A graveyard. A mausoleum. An insane idea," the narrator utters in fury and embarrassment (137).

The private library as a site of contestation of Eastern and Western knowledge systems is at the heart of *The New Life* (1998), a novel by the Turkish Nobel laureate Orhan Pamuk. Set in Turkey in the mid-to-late 1980s, Pamuk's novel centers on a fictitious book, also called *The New Life.* At the beginning of the novel, as the young protagonist Osman first discovers "the book," the effect is visceral, mesmerizing, radically transformative. Osman's search for the author of "the book" and the sources of its creation leads him to the private library of Uncle Rıfkı, a railroad engineer who in fact turns out to be the author. Rıfkı's library contains books as diverse as Ib'n Arabi's *Seals of Wisdom,* Dante's *La vita nuova,* and Rainer Maria Rilke's *Duino Elegies,* among many others (Pamuk, *The New Life,* 257–258). Both Osman and Rıfkı transform in Pamuk's novel into Borgesian "men of the Library." The readers (admirers) of the book authored by Rıfkı recognize its multiple social lives, and for them, "Life," "book," and "world" become inseparable. The book's detractors fear its social impact. Their self-proclaimed leader, Dr. Fine, is in an "all-out battle against printed matter" (83) and thinks of Gutenberg as "one of the pawns of the Great Conspirator" (107).

These examples of literary engagements with libraries, readers, and books unfold the aesthetic affinities and liaisons between geoculturally diverse interpretations of modernism while simultaneously highlighting the mutually enriching synergy between the terms "library" and "modernism."

I started this essay with a brief reading of a novel by a German British author. Let me end with a discussion of another novel, *Ja, sagt Molly* (Yes, says Molly), by the Turkish-German author Kemal Kurt. Born in 1947 in Çorlu, Turkey, Kurt moved to Germany in 1972 and worked as an essayist, photographer, author of children's books, translator, and television writer. Kurt's novel bears distinct marks of large-scale human migration in the late twentieth century; it simultaneously creates an archive of a multidirectional and multilingual modernism through a literary inventory. If the title is a direct citation of the last lines of Joyce's *Ulysses*, the frame story refers to another classic modernist text, "The Library of Babel," by the Argentine modernist Jorge Luis Borges. As is well known, Borges's narrator organizes the library in indefinite, infinite, hexagonal units. Noticeably, the Library *follows* the Universe: it appears in parentheses, contained in punctuation marks as the other signifier of the universe, as the universe's alias, a nomenclature used by undefined "others." Borges splits the perceivers of the universe and the library, yet, by approving that the universe can indeed be called a library, he blurs the distinction between the two, presents them as interchangeable. It is at this point that the narrator confesses his belonging to a community of "men of the Library" who went looking for "a book"—a single book nonetheless—a "catalog of catalogs" (Borges, "The Library of Babel," 112).

In Kurt's novel, characters from literary texts around the world turn into the Borgesian "men of the Library" who go out looking for a book of all books—"das totale Buch" (*Ja, sagt Molly*, 11)—which would simultaneously serve as an epitome and extract of all other books. The novel begins on a rainy evening in a city with many names: "Eine Stadt mit vielen Namen: London vielleicht, Paris oder Berlin. Oder auch New York, Tokio, Dublin, Istanbul, Toronto, Kalkutta, Kinshasa, Ulan Bator, Samarkand, Astrachan" ("London, maybe, Paris or Berlin. Or also New York, Tokyo, Dublin, Istanbul, Toronto,

Calcutta, Kinshasa, Ulan Bator, Samarkand, Astrakhan"; 10). Having established its global locations, the narrator, referring to Borges's "The Library of Babel," declares that the "regressive method" suggested by the "blind librarian" where, in order to locate book A, one has to look for book B, will not suffice. And so he begins the writing of that all-encompassing book, which tells the story of the twentieth century through conversations among characters from over 150 literary works written in about twenty-five languages. The opening scene brings the reader to the apartment of Leopold and Molly Bloom (Joyce, *Ulysses*). Molly, who is about to go to bed, finds Gregor Samsa (Kafka, *The Metamorphosis*) on the foot of her bed. At first astonished by Gregor's presence in her bedroom, Molly ends up inviting him to bed, and as she lies down, Gregor starts his erotic foreplay, slowly discovering her body as he discovers his own sexuality, which was symbolically denied to him in scene 2 of *The Metamorphosis*, when his mother and sister remove the framed picture of the lady in a fur boa (a reference to Leopold von Sacher-Masoch's *Venus in Furs*) from his room. Molly relents to his sexual advances with "*Ja, ich will Ja*" (10), and thus the last sentence of Joyce's classic, "yes I said yes I will Yes" (Joyce, *Ulysses*, 933), becomes the opening line of the story of the twentieth century.

As the reader tries to fathom whether the sexual intimacy between the human Molly and the vermin Gregor is the start of the process of Gregor's rehumanization or a magical-realist intercourse between species, the novel turns to Jimmy Herf and Congo Jake (Dos Passos, *Manhattan Transfer*). This transfer from Dublin to New York is punctuated in Kurt's novel by italicized insertions of important global events, telegraphically communicated as headlines of newspapers: the Boxer Uprising is crushed by interventionist forces (*Ja, sagt Molly*, 18), Guglielmo Marconi succeeds in transatlantic wireless transmission of radio waves (20), the financial crisis of 1929 hits the United States (21), Einstein introduces the theory of relativity (22), the plague spreads in India (23), and San Francisco experiences devastation through the earthquake and fire (23). In the midst of these moments of scientific discoveries and financial and natural disasters, Congo reads in the *New York Times* that the "Library of Babel" is full, that there is no more room for any more books, and under the directorship of a blind librarian a commission of select librarians is making a decision about selecting that one book that will represent all forms of modernism (24).

From this point on, Kurt's novel recreates the twentieth century through an engagement with its literary history. Disparate and unexpected conversations inhabit the novel: Hans Castorp (Thomas Mann, *The Magic Mountain*) experiences the violence of the First World War with O-Lan (Pearl S. Buck, *The House of Earth*), who finds a copy of Flaubert's *Madame Bovary* in his pocket (39); Clelia Oitana (Cesare Pavese, *The Beach*) tells Meuersault (Albert Camus, *The Stranger*) that as a woman she finds herself alone in a library (44); Zneno Cosini (Italo Svevo, *Zneno Cosini*) criticizes the Nobel Prize as "one named after the founder of the first weapon of mass destruction in the world" to Harry Haller (Hermann Hesse, *Steppenwolf*) as Hitler comes to power (51); Martin Marco (Camilo Jose Céla, *The Hive*) discusses the expansion of libraries and the significance of books with William of Baskerville (Umberto Eco, *The Name of the Rose*) (57) during the aftermath of the Second World War; and between the Arab-Israeli Six-Day War and the assassination of Ché Guevara, Saleem Sinai (Salman Rushdie, *Midnight's Children*), David Caravaggio (Michael Ondaatje, *The English Patient*), and Lord Jim (Joseph Conrad, *Lord Jim*) meet—where else?—in the house of Mr. Biswas (V. S. Naipaul, *A House for Mr. Biswas*), as Stevens (Kazuo Ishiguro, *Remains of the Day*), immaculately dressed, serves them tea (70–71).

This is by no means an exhaustive reading of this complex and fascinating novel. Suffice it to say that throughout the rest of the narrative, a variety of actors converge and diverge to reflect on the state of literature and literary criticism as they present books and libraries as historically conditioned and politically charged. Punctuating these conversations is the slow foreplay between Molly and Gregor, which becomes more intense as the twentieth century ends. Toward the end of the novel, after the fall of the Berlin Wall and as violence against foreigners rises in Germany, Gregor fantasizes yet another transformation. He wants to be an oil beetle so he can turn Molly crazy (*verrückt*) by releasing cantharidin (127). Meanwhile a host of intoxicated characters—Rosario (Alejandro Carpentier, *The Kingdom of this World*), Lambert Strether (Henry James, *The Ambassadors*), Gora (Rabindranath Tagore, *Gora*), Babbitt (Sinclair Lewis, *Babbit*), Sagoe (Wole Soyinka, *The Interpreters*), Piggy (William Golding, *Lord of the Flies*), Malte Laurids Brigge (Rainer Maria Rilke, *Malte Laurids Brigge*), Querelle (Jean Genet, *Querelle*), and others—join a procession (125), shouting the slogan, "To the Library! To the Library!" ("Zur Bibliothek! Zur Bibliothek!", 129). As Czechoslovakia splits into the Czech and Slovak republics and the World Trade Center bombing takes place in New York City, Gregor thinks of ancient Indian erotic texts, *Ananga Ranga* and *Kamasutra*, and discovers Molly's "Yoni" (132–133). The entire history of the twentieth century and the sexual foreplay between Molly and Gregor reach their climax as the crowd of characters reaches Taksim Square, Istanbul, where the library burns in flames.

The libraries depicted in these novels transform modernism—formally and substantially—presenting it at times as a system of exchange and at other times as a difficult conversation about the historical burden of socioeconomic and political domination between Western centers and non-Western peripheries. On the one hand, these examples of engagements with libraries reveal modalities of asymmetrical power and epistemic violence; on the other hand, they point at the diverse temporalities of modernism whereby formal appropriations of modernism are localized to challenge and unravel the permanence of domination and subjugation. Paying attention to the various forms in which libraries emerge in modernist texts, as "myth, order, space, power, imagination, home, to borrow a few keywords from Alberto Manguel's wonderful characterization in *The Library at Night*, assists in identifying questions of propriety and patronage within the libraries while revealing at the same time modes of affiliation to and appropriation of modernism in various contexts.

To sum up, engaging with the modernist imagination of libraries as part of a larger print-cultural approach to global modernism serves many purposes. First, it underlines the process, material, and subject, along with the space of reading. Second, the "medial" nature of the library, when subject to scrutiny, reveals the constantly moving boundaries between fact and fiction, history and memory, collection and dispersion, order and chaos. Third, the silent order of the libraries is quickly unraveled to reveal the "constitutional instability," which becomes a driving force of modernist texts. Fourth, such an approach assists in challenging normative periodization that turns non-Western modernism into a derivative discourse, into a unidirectional flow from Western centers to non-Western peripheries. Finally, a print-cultural approach to modernist texts does not merely decenter Europe; it deepens the understanding of the imbricated relationship between modernist aesthetic approaches and texts while simultaneously making us aware of the multicentric, multidimensional, and multilingual nature of modernism. Shaping this decentered approach is a specific form of "bibliomigrancy," the physical and virtual migration of books from one geocultural space to another (Mani, "Bibliomigrancy").

The story of modernism is not a single story. It consists of multiple stories of creation and innovation, interrogation through reformulation, local disposition and worldly orientation. Much like libraries—and it does not have to be the perfect library of all libraries as in Borges—the order and system is coincidently interrupted with contesting narratives of disorder and purposeful disarrangement. As Sebald reminds us, every moment of monumentalism comes with its own set of absurdities. As Benjamin makes us realize, dissemination becomes part of dispersion, and as Kurt reveals through his differential calculus of global modernism, historical chronology is productively interrupted by a renewed circulation of literary works.

NOTES

1. See also Cowan, "W. G. Sebald's *Austerlitz* and the Great Library." Cowan's essay provides an excellent commentary on the fictionalized interpretation of history that is central to Sebald's work.
2. For a longer discussion of libraries and books and in conjunction with world literature, see Mani, "Bibliomigrancy" and "Borrowing Privileges."
3. There are many studies of modernism and the city, starting with Georg Simmel's seminal essay "Die Grosstädte und das Gesistesleben." See also Gold, *The Experience of Modernism*; Holston, *On Modernism and Modernization*; Hyde, *Constitutional Modernism*; and Umbach and Hüppauf, *Vernacular Modernism*.

WORKS CITED

Benjamin, Walter. "Ich packe meine Bibliothek aus." 1931. In *Medienästhetische Schriften*, ed. Detlev Schöttker, 175–182. Frankfurt am Main: Suhrkamp, 2002.

———. *Medienästhetische Schriften*. Ed. Detlev Schöttker. Frankfurt am Main: Suhrkamp, 2002.

———. "Unpacking My Library: A Talk About Book Collecting." Trans. Harry Zohn. In *Illuminations*, ed. Hannah Arendt, 59–67. New York: Schocken, 2007.

Bharucha, Rustom. *Another Asia: Rabindranath Tagore and Okakura Tenshin*. New Delhi: Oxford University Press, 2006.

Borges, Jorge Luis. "The Library of Babel." Trans. Andrew Hurley. In *Collected Fictions*, 112–118. New York: Penguin, 1998.

Chartier, Roger. *The Order of Books: Readers, Authors, and Libraries in Europe Between the Fourteenth and Eighteenth Centuries*. Stanford, Calif.: Stanford University Press, 1994.

Cowan, James L. "W. G. Sebald's *Austerlitz* and the Great Library: History, Fiction, Memory." *Monatshefte* 102, no. 1 (2001): 51–81.

Feiereiss, Kristin, ed. *Die Wiener Trilogie und ein Kino: Drei Wohnbauten in Wien und ein Kino in Dresden*. Berlin: Aedes, 1998.

Friedman, Susan Stanford. "Periodizing Modernism: Postcolonial Modernities and the Space/Time Borders of Modernist Studies." *Modernism/modernity* 13, no. 3 (2006): 425–443.

Gikandi, Simon. "Modernism in the World." *Modernism/modernity* 13, no. 3 (2006): 419–424.

Gold, John Robert. *The Experience of Modernism: Modern Architects and the Future City, 1928–53*. London: E & FN, 1997.

Hayot, Eric. *On Literary Worlds*. Oxford: Oxford University Press, 2013.

Holston, James. *On Modernism and Modernization: The Modernist City in Development, the Case of Brasilia*. Notre Dame: Helen Kellogg Institute for International Studies, University of Notre Dame, 1984.

Hyde, Timothy. *Constitutional Modernism: Architecture and Civil Society in Cuba, 1933–1959*. Minneapolis: University of Minnesota Press, 2013.

Joyce, James. *Ulysses*. 1922. London: Penguin, 2000.

Kapur, Geeta. *When Was Modernism? Essays on Contemporary Cultural Practices in India*. New Delhi: Tulika, 2000.

Kurt, Kemal. *Ja, sagt Molly*. Berlin: Hittite Verlag, 1998.

Lewandowski, Joseph E. "Unpacking: Walter Benjamin and his Library." *Libraries and Culture* 34, no. 2 (1999): 151–157.

Manguel, Alberto. *The Library at Night*. New Haven, Conn.: Yale University Press, 2008.

Mani, B. Venkat. "Borrowing Privileges: Libraries and the Institutionalization of World Literature." *Modern Language Quarterly* 74, no. 2 (2013): 239–260.

———. "Bibliomigrancy: Book-Series and the Making of World Literature." In *The Routledge Companion to World Literature*, ed. Theo D'haen David Damrosch, and Djelal Kadir, 283–296. New York: Routledge, 2011.

Nagar, Amritlal. *Karavata* [The turn]. Delhi: Rajapala, 1985.

Pamuk, Orhan. *The New Life*. Trans. Güneli Gün. New York: Vintage International, 1998.

———. *Yeni Hayat*. Istanbul: Illeştim Yayınları, 1994.

Presner, Todd. *Mobile Modernity: Germans, Jews, Trains*. New York: Columbia University Press, 2007.

Sebald, W. G. *Austerlitz*. Trans. Anthea Bell. New York: Modern Library, 2011.

Simmel, Georg. "Die Grosstädte und das Gesistesleben." In *Die Grosstadt. Vorträge und Aufsätze zur Städteausstellung*, Jahrbuch der Gehe-Stiftung Dresden, Band 9, ed. Theodor Petermann, 185–206. Dresden: v. Zahn & Jaensch, 1903.

Tayyib, Salih al-. *Season of Migration to the North*. Trans. Denys Johnson-Davis. Portsmouth, N.H.: Heinemann, 1976. Translation of *Mawsim al-Hijrah ilā al-Shamāl*. Beirut: Dar al-Awdah, 1969.

Umbach, Maiken, and Bernd Hüppauf, eds. *Vernacular Modernism: Heimat, Globalization, and the Built Environment.* Stanford, Calif.: Stanford University Press, 2005.

Walkowitz, Rebecca. "Sebald's Vertigo." In *Cosmopolitan Style: Modernism Beyond the Nation*, 153–170. New York: Columbia University Press, 2006.

Wirth, Siegfried, and Günter Ciesielski, eds. *Die moderne Fabrik in Vergangenheit, Gegenwart und Zukunft.* Karl-Marx-Stadt: Rektor der technischen Hochschule, 1986.

Woolf, Virginia. *A Room of One's Own.* San Diego, Calif.: Harcourt, 1981.

10. OBSOLESCENCE

MARK GOBLE

Modernism persists for us today largely as an aesthetic of obsolescence, which is not just a sign of its advancing age but a crucial and originary aspect of its character that we now understand with greater clarity precisely because we no longer feel required to insist on modernism's novelty as the most important measure of its value.

Imagine what modernism will look like in another hundred years, well into the century after the one in which it flourished in so many literary and artistic genres, across so many media, and from all corners of the increasingly global culture that modernism's early masterpieces simultaneously anticipated and, at times, decried. Maybe nothing much is left to change: with the emergence of "the new modernist studies" powerfully mapped by Douglas Mao and Rebecca Walkowitz, critics now have access to a far more historically responsive and conceptually flexible set of terms and genealogies for talking about modernism in contemporary ways.[1] The "new" modernism extends beyond the decades of the early twentieth century and reflects the work of countless figures once abandoned or never even known by another generation and the canon it produced. Where earlier critics of modernism such as Clement Greenberg or Hugh Kenner seemingly had endless energy for delimiting what kinds of art could really count as modernist or for debating whether the era belonged to Ezra Pound or someone else, few recent figures working in the field would champion or even countenance a return to the midcentury preoccupations that almost made modernism into a relic—isolated and anachronistic, redolent of a vanished, lifeless epoch cut off from a changing world—as artists, theorists, and academics of the 1960s, 1970s, and 1980s increasingly conceptualized *their* time as "postmodernity." The book that you are reading, on the other hand, is evidence that modernism is alive and well, or at least not dead. By turning its attention to a broader range of authors, movements, periods, and continents, modernist studies has aggressively pursued what Mao and Walkowitz characterize as "temporal and spatial expansions" that have inspired compelling projects too numerous to list. Modernist studies, put another way, seems to have faced the prospect of its obsolescence and realized the promise of one of modernism's own most contentious bits of propaganda: "Make It New." Which is only possible, as Pound would certainly admit, if you have something old already at your disposal.

I am not concerned here with the possibility that modernism may someday finally be obsolete nor with the perhaps inevitable future when its survival, like that of other, earlier aesthetic modes such as neoclassicism and romanticism, is, well, academic—as a feature of syllabi and survey courses that figures in the deeper logic of the contemporary moment but nowhere near the surface of its artistic practices and cultural affairs. I am interested instead in all the ways that forms of obsolescence—both anxious and aspirational— are part of modernism's project from the beginning and speak to many of the conditions that helped bring it into prominence in the first decades of the twentieth century and beyond. It might even be the case that modernism persists for us today largely as an aesthetic of obsolescence, which I would like to argue is not just a sign of its advancing age but a crucial and originary aspect of its character that we now understand with greater clarity precisely because we no longer feel required to insist on modernism's novelty as the most important measure of its value. As Michael North has recently reminded us, "the pretense to independence that is that basis of modernism clashes everywhere with the fact of dependence on the past," and "though modern art is supposed to be absolutely new and different without compromise, its advent is often announced as if it were the return of something long exiled."[2] Modernism, especially in its most ambitious literary forms, has regularly functioned as an archaeology of mythic correspondences and reanimations of dead pasts that point to futures that look a lot like the ruins of a present we are trying to escape. We need only think of all the cultural material that Eliot recycles in *The Waste Land* or all the histories that Pound wants to revitalize in *The Cantos*. A certain style of "high" modernism is largely predicated on skillful and arcane invocations of obsolete traditions, mobilized at least in part to compensate for the unrelenting emptiness of time itself. "Quick now, here, now, always—" writes Eliot in "Burnt Norton," "Ridiculous the waste sad time /

Stretching before and after."[3] For many Anglo-American writers after World War I, thinking about obsolescent forms of art and culture—Homeric epics, Provençal lyrics, Jacobean dramas—provided an alternative language of expression at a moment when the future loomed as a perpetual and enduring crisis, "catastrophic or intolerable," as T. J. Clark puts it, "an epoch formed from an unstoppable, unmappable collision of different forces" and the wars, technologies, ideologies, and genocides they made.[4] If this is the history that comes with modernism, then maybe we should be glad its time has passed.

The modernist period's fascination with obsolescence should be distinguished from its related interests in various models of antiquity and other iconographies of cultural tradition. I would like to focus instead on obsolescence as a more specialized phenomenon of technology and the accelerated temporalities of modern life it comes to register. Obsolescence is an invention of industrial modernity. While words and things had been described as obsolete in English since the Renaissance, it is not until the nineteenth century that "obsolescence" is used to characterize a quality of objects and the processes that render them outmoded as a result of technological development. The nominalization that makes for "obsolescence"—apart from any instance of the obsolete—suggests a more pervasive sense of being somehow too soon outside of or behind the times, abandoned by the sheer scale and speed of the productive forces put in motion across England, Europe, and, later, the United States in the late eighteenth and early nineteenth centuries. It is no accident, in other words, that a more conceptually abstract and portable idea of obsolescence emerges with the rise of an economy based increasingly on what Marx, writing in *The Grundrisse* (1857), termed "productive consumption."[5] Thus the perception of a commodity's obsolescence, notwithstanding its actual durability or usefulness, provides one of modern capitalism's central drives and, as Jennifer Gabrys argues, "creates a loop between production and consumption . . . where consumption provides the necessary dissolution of products in order to spur new production."[6] Or as Marx observes: "Consumption accomplishes the act of production only in completing the product as product by dissolving it."[7] The industrial technologies and economies of scale that make it possible to manufacture goods in unimaginable abundance by the middle of the nineteenth century—the Victorian excess that many modernists condemn with flair and passion—just as certainly demand that these same goods must be abandoned before their time, which, from the perspective of capital, has been too long already.

"The rose is obsolete," writes William Carlos Williams in the seventh poem of *Spring and All* (1923), where he labors to bring an exceedingly dead metaphor back to life as an artifact of modernist depiction. He then goes on to talk of roses anyway:

> but each petal ends in
> an edge, the double facet
> cementing the grooved
> columns of air—The edge
> cuts without cutting
> meets—nothing—renews
> itself in metal or porcelain—

The lines break radically and unnaturally across the grammar of the sentences and the hackneyed symbolism they invoke by way of absolute denial. Rendered in a hard material—this rose, of course, is "cutting" edge—Williams's rose feels like a manufactured object, mass produced for simple decoration but rewarding, in its formal structuring and crystalline complexity, the more sustained attention we would give a work of art. Summing up the literary tradition that the poem is salvaging from obsolescence, the speaker later says that "love is at an end—of roses," a circular construction that conflates austere perception and sappy projection in a kind of productive consumption, borrowing from Marx, that at last inspires a positively cosmic vision of poetic fancy. "From the petal's edge a line starts / that being of steel / infinitely fine, / infinitely / rigid penetrates the Milky Way." This rose is obsolete, but it finally takes dominion beyond the earth from which its raw materials are taken and out of which its natural referent grows.

We could find analogs to Williams in a range of modernist expression from the early twentieth century and see variations on the ways in which the materiality of technology was embraced as an alternative to aesthetic obsolescence. Still, Fredric Jameson would insist that underneath it all remains "this transfer of the temporality of capitalism" and "its ever-more-rapid style and fashion changes" to the "dynamics of artistic modernism," which is why, for Jameson at least, modernism itself is "an immense negative process" that can only promise newness in bad faith since it is beholden to the "same boom-and-bust cycle of some desperate movement from markets saturated with commodities to new markets and new commodities alike."[8] His disdain for modernism is considerable and significant, particularly in that he seems scandalized that modernism has managed to survive the postmodernity that should have made it obsolete. Modernism in the present is not a canny or potentially disruptive version of what Raymond Williams, in a different idiom of Marxist criticism, would have characterized as "residual" for its implicit challenge to the "dominant" forms of a contemporary moment.[9] The surprising durability of modernism as a category of both aesthetic judgment and cultural critique instead seems to Jameson positively retentive, a weird regression in the present to an even starker, more complete surrender to the rhythms and imperatives of the market. Postmodernism now looks in retrospect like a righteous but unfinished purge: Jameson writes, "in the midst of all the healthy movements of disgust and revulsion, indeed, to the very sound of windows breaking and old furniture being thrown out, we have begun in the last few years to witness phenomena . . . that suggest a return to and the reestablishment of all kinds of old things, rather than their wholesale liquidation" (1). It is not just that modernism is obsolete but that we have become obsessive hoarders of its objects and imperatives, unable to move beyond the spurious "value of the New that seems to preside over any specific or local modernism worth its salt" (121).

Jameson will be decidedly unhappy, then, if the future turns out like William Gibson pictures it in *Count Zero* (1986), the second novel in the "Sprawl" trilogy that began with *Neuromancer* (1984), where Gibson helped contribute to the mythology of postmodernism by coining the term "cyberspace." *Count Zero* is set in a decade near the end of the twenty-first century and features all the variety of details that encode its genre as science fiction: artificial intelligences are real and sentient beings, human users can connect their neural pathways directly to the web, and most of the world's nation-statues have faded as sovereign entities, replaced by ambitious corporate entities that simultaneously pursue bleeding-edge strategies for market dominance alongside feudal designs on status, grandeur, and virtual immortality. And modernism is in vogue, at least for Herr Josef Virek, a capitalist and collector, possessing "wealth on another scale of magnitude," who approaches a disgraced art curator with a offer she cannot refuse.[10] Virek hopes to upload his consciousness to a computer network large and complex enough to sustain his being forever, and he suspects that the hardware he needs in fact exists because he has discovered that somewhere on Earth, or in the space stations orbiting it, an "AI" has been producing some curious artifacts that not only suggest a version of a mind at work but one with a sense of history and taste that is plainly obsolete:

> Marly [the curator] stared. Box of plain wood, glass-fronted. Objects . . .
> "Cornell," she said . . . "Cornell?"
> "Of course not. The object set into that length of bone is a Braun biomonitor. . . ."
> But Marly was lost in the box, in its evocation of impossible distances, of loss and yearning. It was somber, gentle, and somehow childlike. It contained seven objects.
> The slender fluted bone, surely formed for flight. . . . Three archaic circuit boards, faced with mazes of gold. A smooth white sphere of baked clay. An age-blackened fragment of lace. A finger-length segment of what she assumed was bone from a human wrist, grayish white, inset smoothly with the silicon shaft of a small instrument that must once of ridden flush with the surface of the skin—but the thing's face was seared and blackened.
> The box was a universe, a poem, frozen on the boundaries of human experience.
>
> (14–15)

Like an actual Joseph Cornell box, such as 1945's *Hotel Eden* (figure 10.1), the AI in *Count Zero* has made a work of art invoking several of modernism's most familiar strategies and principles. Gibson imagines a work of late twenty-first-century *bricolage* that seamlessly inserts the detritus of an age we cannot yet quite imagine—what exactly does a "Braun biomonitor" do? how impossibly advanced are these "archaic circuit boards," having had another century or so of Moore's law to condition their increasing speed and power?—into an aesthetic program whose every subroutine we know by heart. There are still, it seems, "no ideas but in things," just as Williams once insisted, and the allure of materiality remains provocatively affecting long into a high-tech future where a bit of "small instrument" once wired into a body can seem as worn and homespun as a cardboard parakeet or uncoiled spring. Gibson's appreciation may be overwrought ("the box was a universe"), but the idea that we perceive an aura of timelessness and presence in an artwork's formal structure is something we know as dogma according to Greenberg, Michael Fried, or Stanley Cavell.[11] Or borrowing from another idiom of modernism,

FIGURE 10.1 Joseph Cornell, *Hotel Eden*.
Source: © The Joseph and Robert Cornell Memorial Foundation / Licensed by VAGA, New York, NY.

we might note that when Eliot argues that the artists should be "perfected me-diums" reflecting "a continual extinction of personality," he certainly did not have an AI out of cyberpunk in mind. But Gibson's anachronistic, simulated modernism suggests an aesthetic of technology that answers Eliot precisely, if only we can wait another couple hundred years for it to emerge out of the past. Jameson himself contrasts Gibson's writing "to an exhausted modern-ism" and argues that "cyberpunk constitutes a kind of laboratory experiment in which the geographic-culture light spectrum and bandwidths of the new system are registered." In the case of *Count Zero*, however, the only "new" seems like another form of obsolescence that has not been modernized, that has been retrofitted for another time.

Or put another way, Gibson conceives an AI that didn't just manage to become sentient but to become Walter Benjamin. Like the figures about whom Benjamin writes in his essay on "Surrealism"—and, it bears mention, influences on Cornell—we see an artist who "can boast an extraordinary discovery" insofar as they "perceive the revolutionary energies that appear in the 'outmoded.'"[12] Benjamin's writings represent modernism's most intensive and exhaustive encounter with obsolescence, which informs not only his elaborate archaeologies of nineteenth-century modernity in *The Arcades Project* but also his essays on storytelling, mimesis, and "The Work of Art in the Age of Its Technological Reproducibility," as well as the project that became *The Origin of German Tragic Drama*, where he is everywhere concerned with the "antique qualities of the baroque" that make it so uncannily contemporary.[13] Gibson even echoes Benjamin on aura—"the unique phenomenon of distance"—in the way that these belated Cornell boxes provide for an "evocation of impossible distances" that has little to do with the hundreds of miles they may have already traveled down from orbit over Earth. In her wonderful account of "digital rubbish," Gabrys borrows from Benjamin a methodology she links to his singular practice of "natural history" to reflect on "the fossilized commodities in the obsolete arcades of [Paris]"; here he found in objects variously "decaying" or "outmoded" what she terms "concrete facts about past cultural imaginings."[14] Gabrys herself is interested in the sorts of technological commodities that Gibson and other cyberpunk writers have long traded on, and by seeing the way that their future obsolescence gets projected onto even the latest gadgets, she helps us track the legacy of the modernist aesthetic I have been exploring here. "Obsolete objects," Gabrys notes, evoked for Benjamin "a kind of prehistory when they fell out of circulation, at which time they could be examined as resonant material residues . . . of economic practices." More importantly, Benjamin's attention to obsolescence, in all its many modern forms, tried to slow down or perhaps more radically disrupt the very notion of what "progress" under capitalism really looks like in order "to demonstrate the contingency and transience of commodity worlds." Or as Joel Burgess puts it, the modernist fetish for obsolescence, despite the ahistorical nostalgia it may risk, can generate "a series of relations between past and present as a function of the aura of datedness that its objects produce."[15] Obsolescence seems to work for modernism even when the point is that it doesn't.

We can see this in a contemporary project that very much has modernism in its retrospective view. Produced in 2011 by Jung von Matt, a Hamburg-based

FIGURE 10.2 Jung von Matt, "The Museum of Obsolete Objects."
Source: Jung von Matt / next, Hamburg.

digital ad agency, "The Museum of Obsolete Objects" (figure 10.2) was part
of YouTube's "Brand Channel" initiative, which allowed "marketers to create
a bespoke interface, customizing the look and feel of their presence on the
site" in order to "provide the opportunity to create truly persistent relationships" with customers online.[16] The ephemerality of so much digital culture is
an abiding preoccupation of Jung von Matt's project, which commemorates
a series of older technologies—such as the abacus, electronic calculator, telephone, fountain pen, telegraph, phonograph, and typewriter—that speak to
the contemporary world of media in which they have *all* been replaced by the
computer, just as some of them once replaced their predecessors (calculator
for abacus, telephone for telegraph). In other words, a specter is haunting
"The Museum of Obsolete Objects": the specter of new media obsolescence,
which corporations such as YouTube must find a way to overcome in order
to make possible both "truly persistent relationships" and the profits that
come with brand loyalty. What are the chances that any "marketers'" online
presence—no matter how bespoke—will endure for as long as even the most
short-lived obsolete technology that Jung von Matt identifies? The floppy
disc, according to the "Museum," survived for thirty-five years, from 1960 to
1995. Will YouTube, founded in 2005, last till 2040?

I am finally less interested in this popular culture of obsolescence than in
the more rarefied ways that a project like "The Museum of Obsolete Objects"
invokes a patently modernist iconography. Given the tropism toward dead

media objects in Jung von Mott's "museum," the inclusion of an eggbeater seems at first an odd choice—of all the implements and gadgets in the world, why this particular object? Though I cannot be sure, I would venture that one of Jung von Mott's designers is showing off a bit of training in art history and quoting one of Man Ray's more iconic photographs of his early, Dada phase, specifically, the 1918 image entitled *L'homme* (though he titles a later print of the same photograph *Femme*, and the two names are used somewhat interchangeably in discussions of Man Ray, which is of course the point) (figure 10.3). This Man Ray photograph is one of many artworks from this period that helped fashion an early modernist idiom of technofetishism, a deliberate play with the hybrid mechanics of quasi–human sexuality put to work amid the turning gears and pistons of such works as Francis Picabia's *Machine Turn Quickly* (*Machine Tournez Vite*) from 1916 or, more famously still, Duchamp's *Large Glass*, which incorporates his *Chocolate Grinder* painting from 1914 in its lower panel.

Jung von Mott's especially pristine eggbeater is also curious because it obviously and demonstrably still works. We can click to see a Flash video that shows it beating eggs, its functionality unimpeded by the countless electric mixers that have come after it. Its obsolescence, then, is a matter of our no longer *wanting* to use it, which is different than saying it is no longer useful. Obsolescence does not inhere in objects as a property of their being in the world but rather is a quality that we project upon them, an aura of uselessness and inefficiency that we could dispel or disbelieve if we insisted. It seems right, in fact, to think that most obsolete things *must* still work, just not for us—this, after all, is the scandal of "planned obsolescence," where commodities are designed to fail, aesthetically if not functionally, before their time is really up.

We might say that "The Museum of Obsolete Objects" gives us a collection of what Heidegger would call "broken tools," which are ultimately the *only* tools we ever come to feel and know. As Graham Harman writes in his exploration of this concept, first laid out by Heidegger in *Being and Time*, "equipment in action operates in an inconspicuous usefulness, doing its work without our noticing it. When the tool fails, its unobtrusive quality is ruined. There occurs a jarring of reference, so that the tool becomes visible *as* what it is . . . emerging into the sun only in the moment of their breakdown."[17] For Harman and other "speculative realists" such as Quentin Meillassoux and Ray Brassier, this Heideggerian drama of perception marks only the first step toward getting past the privileging of human beings—over the "substance"

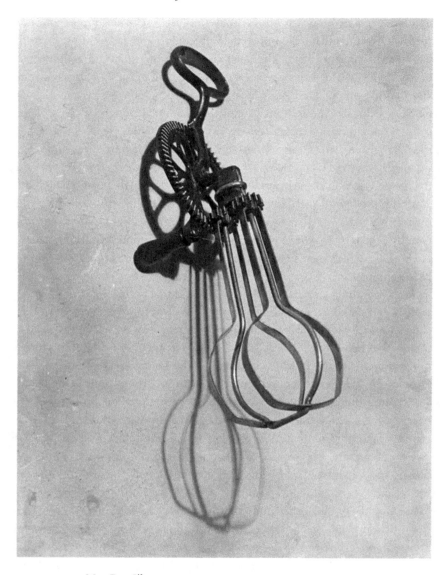

FIGURE 10.3 Man Ray, *L'homme.*
Source: © Man Ray Trust / Artists Rights Society (ARS), NY ADAGP, Paris 2015.

of objects for Harman, over the mathematics and scale of time and space for Meillassoux—that has shaped the whole history of philosophy and theory as they critique it. At the very least, Harman's reading of Heidegger's famous account in chapter 16 of *Being and Time* of how "entities within-the-world" announce themselves can provide a way of understanding modernism's fascination with technological innovation as more than just a reflection—a kind of mimetic investment after all—of its twentieth-century context.

Heidegger argues that a tool can be what he terms "un-ready-to-hand"— which is to say, broken and thus actively perceived—for many different reasons, but what we term obsolescence corresponds best to Heidegger's "obstinacy." As he writes in *Being and Time*:

> In our dealing with the world of our concern, the un-ready-to-hand can be encountered not only in the sense of that which is unusable or simply missing, but as something un-ready-to-hand which is *not* missing at all and *not* unusable, but which "stands in the way" of our concern. That to which our concern refuses to turn, that for which it has "no time," is something *un*-ready-to-hand in the manner of what does not belong here, of what has not yet been attended to. Anything which is un-ready-to-hand in this way is disturbing to us, and enables us to see the *obstinacy* of that with which we must concerns ourselves in the first instance before we do anything else.[18]

Let me point to a single turn in this passage that registers the complex temporality of the tool or object whose obsolescence, as a kind of "obstinacy," we find ourselves facing. At first, we have "no time" for it, and while it's always risky to assume that Heidegger uses common phrases with their common meanings in mind, here, at least, it seems plausible to suggest that having "no time" for, say, a manual eggbeater *does* mean that we're frustrated by the prospect of its slowness and inefficiency. From this, we project onto the object a more pervasive aura of anachronism, "in the manner of what does not belong here." But this anachronism is perversely forward looking, as if pulling us not *back* in time to when all eggbeaters were mechanical but pushing us toward a *future* moment when we *will* attend to "what has not yet been attended to." The apprehension of an object's obsolescence, in this story, seems finally to reveal that we are constantly failing to pay attention to the things we use until the moment when their brokenness throws us into an existential awareness of them, an awareness that we know, at some level, we should have had already in the past.

This is a logic far trickier than the one we might fashion from Williams's dialectic of the emergent and the residual, but it nonetheless helps clarify how modernism can treat obsolescence as both a failure of a technology to stay current and as an apotheosis of technology that makes art possible. Consider, in this respect, a series of photographs that Walker Evans made just

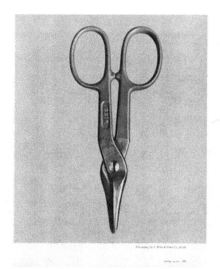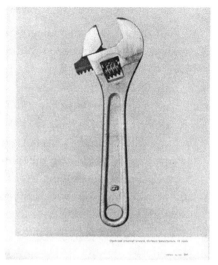

FIGURE 10.4 James Agee, *Beauties of the Common Tool.*
Source: The Metropolitan Museum of Art, Walker Evans Archive, 1994 (1994.258.223; 1994.258.228)
© Walker Evans Archive, The Metropolitan Museum of Art.

after World War II, when he would have had ample reason to reflect on how modernism and its technologies were aging with the century they helped fashion. Published in July 1955, "Beauties of the Common Tool" (figure 10.4) appeared in *Fortune,* where Evans had previously placed images throughout the 1930s, including some that eventually made their way into James Agee's *Let Us Now Praise Famous Men.* His introduction to the photo-essay assigns a catalogue of Machine Age virtues to the objects in the succeeding pictures: these common tools provide "a kind of offbeat museum show for the man who responds to good, clear, 'undesigned,' forms"; "aside from their functions—though they are exclusively wedded to their function—each of these tools lures the eye to follow its curves and angles, and invites the hand to test its balance"; "all the basic small tools stand, aesthetically speaking, for elegance, candor, and purity."[19] It is likely that Evans is also here remembering another "offbeat museum show" that appeared at the Museum of Modern Art a few years before Evans's own American Photographs at MOMA solidified his standing as one of America's preeminent modernists: in 1934, Philip Johnson's Machine Art became the first major art exhibition devoted entirely to works of contemporary design, from industrial components and tools to scientific instruments and even human appliances. Indeed, the family resem-

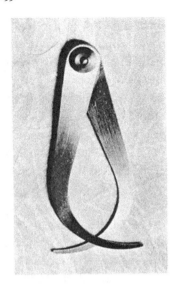

FIGURE 10.5 Philip Johnson, "Machine Art."
Source: © The Museum of Modern Art / Licensed by SCALA / Art Resources, NY.

blance between Evans's photographs from "Beauties of the Common Tool"
and some from Johnson's *Machine Art* (figure 10.5) catalog are telling. But
if Evans's photographs of 1955 are gesturing back to a "machine art" of 1934,
they do so obliquely and ironically; there is a feeling of premature "postmodernism" in way these photographs of tools also allude to some of his own
from the 1930s, such as the closely cropped portraits from *Let Us Now Praise
Famous Men*. I am especially tempted to anthropomorphize and project a
human visage onto the tin snips, placing eyes in the handles and tracing the
bridge of a nose down the blades. Whether we see these pictures as portraits,
it remains the case that for all the functionalism he ascribes to their aesthetic
character—as "undesigned" forms "wedded to their function"—he addresses
them, in prose at least, as oddly feeling and virtually alive, which only underscores the pathos of their tangible outmodedness as "common tools" in
a world of high technologies that are aggressively designed commodities.
"Who would sully the lines of the tin cutting shears . . . with a single added
bend or whorl? Or clothe in any way the fine naked impression of heft and
bite in the crescent wrench . . . ?" These tools may be almost indestructible as
material artifacts, but Evans makes them sound sensitive and easily offended.
Like heroines in a Victorian melodrama, their moral and aesthetic "purity"

is endangered by what Evans calls "design-happy manufacturers" who would have them tarted up with corrupting decorations or "tampered with" so brazenly that a "beautiful plumb bob" is made to look "suspiciously like a top space ship." To borrow again from Williams, spaceships represent some of the most spectacularly "emergent" forms of new technology in these first decades of the Cold War. Evans is writing in the year that inaugurates the Space Race between the United States and the Soviet Union, with both nations announcing their intentions to build ballistic missiles capable of putting satellites into orbit. There is nothing necessarily obsolete about a crescent wrench in 1955, but it perhaps is no longer a useful tool for fighting global communism.

The same nostalgic tone pervades much of Evans's work at *Fortune* after World War II and helps us track how modernism as such comes to deal with the specter of its potential obsolescence in the period. A photo-essay on "These Dark Satanic Mills" of the industrial Northeast—"factories and shops of America's industrial age of innocence"—can look past an often violent history of labor politics and economic exploitation and instead describes abandoned cotton mills as good places "to find some mellow Americana." "The Auto Junkyard" Evans explores in another essay is "rich in tragicomic suggestions of the fall of man from his high ride." Here are other titles Evans uses to organize his increasingly melancholic imagery of American modernity growing old: "A Beautiful Factory Vanishes," "Vintage Office Furniture," "The Last of Railroad Steam," The Twilight of American Woolen," "Before They Disappear." The signs of a more modern modernity are abundant, and nowhere are the consequences of progress more visible than in the ruination, as Evans sees it anyway, of a prior epoch of modernity that now appears antique.

This phase in Evans's long career might readily be taken to mark the earliest moments of the contemporary genre of "ruin porn," which has become one of the most prominent aesthetics for depicting the obsolescent landscapes of industrial modernity in the West. And like Evans's own sad nostalgia for an "age of innocence" that somehow manages to survive the politics behind a manufacturing economy of "Satanic Mills," the aestheticizing regard for what capitalism has left behind can all too easily structure a blindness toward the full complexity of the present—a variation on the anthropological primitivism that Johannes Fabian argues is invariably employed "for the purpose of distancing those who are observed from the Time of the observer."[20] That said, we can gain a more critical perspective on Evans's turn toward obsolescence by noting that it coincides, in both chronology and subject matter, with the work of Bern and Hilla Becher, who begin their photographic project of documenting the "typologies" of industrial buildings in Europe and the United States shortly after marrying in 1957. What salvages the Bechers' work from any intimations of the nostalgia that colors Evans's postindustrial photography is both its excessive rigor and sheer excess: hundreds and thousands of programmatically composed black-and-white photographs made over several decades, with little stylistic development or alteration. The Bechers' many books and exhibitions have accumulated an archive of minutely observed details about the anonymous architecture of heavy industry, which they understand as an increasingly obsolete sector of the global economy in much of the West. As Bern Becher recalled before his death, they were interested in "a kind of nomadic architecture" that "had a comparatively short life—maybe 100 years, often less, then disappears."[21] Becher here does not overtly link this epoch to that of modernism, but it remains implicit in the way their imagery recalls the "New Objectivity" of German photographers in the 1930s; it also plays more slyly with the documentary aesthetics of August Sander and his portrait series on "People of the Twentieth Century."

The Bechers themselves regularly downplay the documentary nature of their agenda and see their work in far more abstract terms. Or still more pointedly, they insist in high modernist fashion that the most important content of the images are their own protocols and formal operations for making pictures. For Michael Fried, this makes for a remarkably absorptive mode of photography that depends on "the isolation and 'silhouetting' of the individual objects, the consistency of lighting, the duration of the exposure of the black-and-white film, [and] the choice of an elevated view-point that enables the object to be photographed head-on."[22] These are features of Evans's photographs in "Beauties of the Common Tool" as well, where any sense of a world in which these tools could still be used has been obscured, if not obliterated. Such decontextualization might be just what it takes, or so these pictures argue, to render these obsolete technologies into works of art, but this is the same logic that makes it hard to grasp the Bechers' buildings or Evans's tools as parts not just of a world but of an industrial economy able to provide the West with an iconography of the bleeding-edge modernity it once pretended to monopolize.

In this respect, an aesthetics of obsolescence continues to pattern a way of looking at the presence and persistence of technology as a shared phenomenon of global modernity in the twenty-first century. Indeed, the spectacle of obsolete technologies—in all their decaying bulk and toxic materiality—has come to provide contemporary artists with compelling imagery to reflect upon the legacies of modernism not just as a surprisingly durable network of cultural practices but also as a set of ideologies that have reified the idea of technical and scientific innovation as a Western project against which the timelessness or slower temporalities of other peoples, places, and nations are reckoned. This is not to say that older forms of primitivism do not remain a part of modernism today nor that a decidedly postmodern set of anxieties about the hypermodernization of various Asian cultures in particular have gone away—as first Japan in the 1980s and now China, South Korea, and Singapore are feared and fetishized for leaving "us" behind. The bleeding edge in obsolescence, by contrast, appears in works that increasingly imagine how both technologies and the histories of consumption and production they make real are connected within a global ecology where the extreme disposability of the recently outmoded gives modernism a new afterlife as something retrograde and uncanny.

Consider this ancient iPhone (figure 10.6), meticulously aged and rendered as a relic by the Japanese artist Maico Akiba, one of many technological artifacts in her 2013 series *One Hundred Years After*, in which she paints items to look like salvage from a landfill from an imagined future where archaeologists are assembling a picture of our present from its ruins. Such a project resonates with any number of postapocalyptic visions of the contemporary— think of the talking children's doll that Charlton Heston's astronaut finds at the end of *Planet of the Apes*—but Akiba's iPhone is particularly powerful because it reflects so sharply on the speed with which the consumer-electronics industry pursues a form of "accelerationism" as a marketing device.[23] As we can see from its rounded back and edges, this is an iPhone 3G and so already "ancient" for its makers at Apple, which discontinued making them in 2010. Another century or so of projected wear and material decay gives form and texture to the obsolescence that Apple no doubt hopes that we perceive already in last year's model. The fact that Akiba shows an iPhone that is fully charged and ready to make calls is thus part of the joke. Its "obstinacy," to return to Heidegger, might even let us appreciate the old-fashioned modernism of Apple's commodity aesthetic, which derives almost entirely from Bauhaus principles and the minimalism that Dieter Rams made his signature as an industrial designer at Braun starting in the 1960s.

We see another version of what a global modernism can make of obsolescence in Gibson's most recent novels, which have been set squarely in the present and where his twentieth-century tastes have become pronounced and more austere. The protagonist of 2003's *Pattern Recognition* wears a "fanatical

FIGURE 10.6 Maico Akiba, from One Hundred Years After.

museum-grade replica of a U.S. MA-1 flying jacket, as purely and iconic a garment as the previous century produced."[24] Except it didn't: though fanatically accurate in the smallest details of design, the jacket Gibson describes was only ever made in green, not black, as worn in *Pattern Recognition*—a mere technicality that was corrected by the actual Japanese clothing company mentioned in the novel, which put a version of the jacket into almost immediate production and now sells a whole line of "William Gibson" coats and accessories based on classic twentieth-century work wear.[25] His latest novel, *Zero History* (2010), features a "secret brand" of jeans and work wear as one of its several "MacGuffins," as Hitchcock called his finally useless predicates for narrative action. The clothes are styled to embody an absurd excess of functionality and, though made from heavy fabrics "loomed in Japan" on antiquated machines, their maker is finally discovered in Chicago, where she labors among "the ruins of American manufacturing" as if better to impart the aura of an epoch that no longer requires workers, across much of Europe and the West at least, to dress in denim built to last for decades. "I saw that an American cotton shirt that had cost twenty cents in 1935," Gibson's designer says near the end of the novel, "will be better than almost anything you can buy today. But if you re-create that shirt, and you might have to go to Japan to do that, you wind up with something that needs to retail for around three hundred dollars." The novel has a longing for "people who remembered how to make things," and this adds a note of Rust Belt melancholy to what has always been a familiar theme in Gibson's writing: the power and appeal of a residual materiality in digital culture that may not promise "disembodied consciousness" with quite the same abandon that it did in the 1990s but that remains beholden to the fantasies of an information economy that still has a great deal of trouble processing what might be somewhat euphemistically called its externalities. Thus the hyperbolic and expensive obsolescence of the commodities worn by Gibson's technological elite find their dialectical reflection in the "e-waste" that Edward Burtynsky and others have made into a familiar trope in contemporary documentary photography. Burtynsky is only one of many photographers working in a super-large-format style of realism—which is aided by the seamless integration of analog and digital imagery—that operates at a scale of immersive detail and allover attention to the picture plane informed by abstract expressionism and postwar minimalist painting.

In an image from his photo book *China* (2005), Burtynsky wants to confront his viewers with the consequences of the computer industry's relentless

FIGURE 10.7 Edward Burtynsky, from *China*.
Source: © Edward Burtynsky, courtesy Nicholas Metivier Gallery, Toronto / Von Lintel Gallery, Los Angeles.

pursuit of perpetual and continuous obsolescence, which has accelerated in the iPhone era to reduce a technological "generation" to merely eighteen months (figure 10.7). And while the idea of such harrowingly productive consumption goes back at least to Marx and the *Grundrisse*, the term "planned obsolescence" does not enter the language of design and marketing until 1954, when it was coined by the industrial engineer Brookes Stevens at the very moment when modernism itself was becoming widely codified and taught by figures such as Clement Greenberg, who tracked each season's trends with a ferocious dedication to whatever seemed most pure in its commitment to innovation. Just as Vance Packard's *The Waste Makers* (1960) was lamenting an economy of "progress through planned obsolescence" as an increasingly dangerous "manipulation" of American consumers, Greenberg was offering one of his most doctrinaire articulations, in his essay "Modernist Painting," of the need for artists to "make it new." However suggestive this historical proximity may be, it mistakes the attitude toward "old" and obsolescent art that Greenberg saw as absolutely critical for modernism's project. Thus the point of "Modernist Painting" is to dismiss as merely shoddy "journalism" the notion that "each new phase of Modernist art should be hailed as the start of a whole new epoch . . . marking a decisive break with all the customs and conventions of the past."[26] Instead, what Greenberg celebrated as truly "Modernist"—here, for the first time, he capitalized the term—was the much less newsworthy proposition that "Art is . . . continuity, and unthinkable without it" (93). Far from rendering outmoded figures and traditions obsolete, Greenberg's modernism, in an argument analogous to Eliot's in "Tradition and the Individual Talent," was positively obsessed with aesthetic forms and systems of meaning that cultures left behind, and that "lacking the past of art, and the need and compulsion to maintain its standards of excellence, Modernist art would lack both substance and justification" (93).

Modernist studies has largely abandoned both Greenberg's restrictive terminology and the narrow prejudices and historical narratives that, as he might say, it justified. At the same time, I would not be so quick to abandon his sense that modernism's value is just as much a product of the past that it recycles as the new ground that it discovers. Though it comes to us as something of a relic already worse for wear, modernism might be even more important to us now if it can help us come to terms with all the ways that its technologies—and the cultures that they have shaped—will persist for decades, even centuries, after most people have forgotten their emergence. Modernism began with obsolescence, which is one reason why, perversely enough, it was built to last for the duration.

NOTES

1. Douglas Mao and Rebecca L. Walkowitz, "The New Modernist Studies," *PMLA* 123, no. 3 (May 2008): 737–748.

2. Michael North, *Novelty: A History of the New* (Chicago: University of Chicago Press, 2013), 149–151.

3. T. S. Eliot, "Burnt Norton," in *The Complete Poems and Plays, 1890–1950* (New York: Harcourt, Brace & World, 1971), 122.

4. T. J. Clark, *Picasso and Truth* (Princeton, N.J.: Princeton University Press, 2013), 14–16.

5. Karl Marx, *Grundrisse: Foundations of the Critique of Political Economy*, trans. Martin Nicolaus (New York: Penguin, 1973), 90.

6. Jennifer Gabrys, *Digital Rubbish: A Natural History of Electronics* (Ann Arbor: University of Michigan Press, 2013), 96.

7. Marx, *Grundrisse*, 93. I am indebted to Gabrys's *Digital Rubbish* for calling this passage to my attention.

8. Fredric Jameson, *A Singular Modernity: Essay on the Ontology of the Present* (London: Verso, 2002), 129.

9. Raymond Williams, *Marxism and Literature* (Oxford: Oxford University Press, 1977).

10. William Gibson, *Count Zero* (New York: Ace, 1986), 11–12.

11. See especially Michael Fried, "Art and Objecthood" (1967), in *Art and Objecthood* (Chicago: University of Chicago Press, 1998), 148–172.

12. Walter Benjamin, "Surrealism: The Last Snapshot of the European Intelligentsia," in *Reflections: Essays, Aphorisms, Autobiographical Writings*, trans. Edmund Jephcott (New York: Schocken, 1978), 181.

13. Walter Benjamin, *The Origin of German Tragic Drama*, trans. John Osborne (London: Verso, 2009), 134.

14. Gabrys, *Digital Rubbish*, 5.

15. Joel Burges, "Adorno's Mimeograph: The Uses of Obsolescence in *Minima Moralia*," *New German Critique* 40, no. 1 (Winter 2013): 91.

16. "The Museum of Obsolete Objects," Jung von Matt, http://www.youtube.com/ser /MoooJvM. YouTube has since discontinued its "Brand Channels" initiative.

17. Graham Harman, *Tool-Being: Heidegger and the Metaphysics of Objects* (Chicago: Open Court, 2002), 45.

18. Martin Heidegger, *Being and Time*, trans. John Macquarrie and Edward Robinson (New York: HarperPerennial, 1962), 103.

19. Walker Evans, "Beauties of the Common Tool," *Fortune* (July 1955); also reproduced in *Unclassified: A Walker Evans Anthology* (New York: Metropolitan Museum of Art, 2000).

20. Johannes Fabian, *Time and the Other: How Anthropology Makes Its Object* (New York: Columbia University Press, 1983), 25.

21. See Michael Fried, *Why Photography Matters as Art as Never Before* (New Haven, Conn.: Yale University Press, 2008), 305.

22. Ibid., 306.

23. For more on "accelerationism," see Matteo Pasquinelli, "The Labour of Abstraction: Seven Transitional Theses on Marxism and Accelerationism," http://matteo pasquinelli.com/labour-of-abstraction-theses/Accelerationism.

24. William Gibson, *Pattern Recognition* (New York: Berkeley, 2003), 10–11.

25. More on William Gibson's collection with the Japanese clothing company Buzz Rickson's is available at http://bookshelf.wisebook3.jp/bookstore/h5/toyo enterprise/2500/#57.

26. Clement Greenberg, "Modernist Painting," in *The Collected Essays and Criticism*, vol. 4: *Modernism with a Vengeance* (Chicago: University of Chicago Press, 1993), 93. See also Rosalind Krauss, *The Originality of the Avant-Garde and Other Myths* (Cambridge, Mass.: MIT Press, 1986); and Michael North, *Novelty*, 144–171.

11. PANTOMIME

MONICA L. MILLER

*Contemporary artists of African descent use pantomimic gestures of perfor-
mance and racial play to send us backward and forward in time. They force
us to range across the globe, to travel between "Africa" as an idea and an
actual place, to reimagine modernist Paris through, for example, Harlem
Renaissance New York, to consider Toyko's transformation from Edo (its
name in the Tokugawa period) to "modernity" via modernist Paris (again)
and the Bronx in the 1980s.*

(META-)MODERNIST HARLEQUINS

Consisting of gesture, music, and costume, a pantomime can mean in and on
multiple registers, manifest differently across time and space. Because pantomime—the actor, the form—can be a metaphor for performativity and the
contingency of performance itself, it is impossible to conceive of it as truly
conventional or even temporally and spatially bound. The stage that I would
like to construct here is a place in which pantomime is noun, verb, or adjective and, as such, an act of translation, a part of the grammar of modernism
that in particular relates black and white, "Africa" and the "West," the visual
and the oral/aural, time and geography. Because pantomime is a phenomenon that employs masks and forms of minstrelsy, it functions as a particularly apt aesthetic within which to explore the politics of racial performance
and play that forms a signature and constitutive part of the modernist era.
The "actors" on this pantomimic stage will be contemporary images of the
black body that enact and then move beyond earlier key modernist moments,
changing the time, place, and space of modernism. As they convey blackness
in/for the modernist world and assert the central importance of blackness
to a sense of being and feeling modern, these images encourage us to think
critically about the global dimensions of twentieth- *and* twenty-first-century
art and aesthetics.

A short history of pantomime demonstrates that it has been, over time, a form of spectacular performance productive of a myriad of cultural and political effects and critiques. As the form evolved from Roman times to the late nineteenth century, pantomime included, according to the theater historian John O'Brien, "acrobatics, spectacle, song, dance, travelogue, slapstick comedy and special effects"; indeed, the pantomime in its heyday "exploited all the material resources that play houses had to offer in order to create a kind of fantastic world where spectacular transformations happened as a matter of course."[1] In ancient Rome, the *pantomimi*, elaborately masked professional actors and dancers, were almost as popular as the gladiators and charioteers of the imperial theater; as a theatrical form, pantomime was a multimedia experience that was designed to engage the ear and the eyes, to appeal musically and in terms of movement and scenic design.[2] These *pantomimi* coexisted with Roman mimes, who, often donning a patchwork tunic and a square-hooded cloak, were part of an improvised theater of social critique with sometimes violent political effects.[3] Pantomime outlasted the Roman Empire as a theatrical form and also as a vehicle of politics; up until the medieval period, it was occasionally banned because its theatricality often included political critique.[4]

Fully emerging in the Renaissance as popular comic theater that nevertheless preserved a societal analysis, commedia dell'arte was a form that pantomime took—its lead "clown" Harlequin became an heir to the *pantomimi's* antics.[5] An original character from the commedia dell'arte and star of the comic extravaganza in the eighteenth- and nineteenth-century pantomime named for him, the harlequinade, Harlequin encapsulates and performs a kind of self-interested, anarchic play. The masks (and costumes) that accompanied the commedia's characters—Harlequin, Pantaloon, Columbine—allowed them a freedom to transgress, mock, provoke, and entertain. Harlequin, the preeminent trickster, reflected and transcended the cultural and social milieu in which he was born. His mask, originally of white leather but later more frequently a black half-mask, with a "pimple on the forehead, a wrinkled brow, and arched eyebrows," often had, according to the commedia dell'arte historian Lynn Lawner, "features that may be read as Oriental and Negroid." Lawner further argues that Harlequin's physical presentation and disposition "seems to have incorporated European society's fear of, and fascination with, the 'other,' the foreign, the marginal, the different, and in the idiom of the time, the diabolic."[6] A figure of anarchy who in trickster tradition always wins out, Harlequin ushers us into a comic yet altogether serious world full of carnivalesque effects, reversals of status, power, and fortune.[7]

Perhaps the most recognizable, "conventionally" pantomimic character in the modernist era can be seen on the canvases of one of modernism's greatest artists, Pablo Picasso. As an alter ego in some of his best-known work from his rose period (1904–1906), the harlequin, along with the saltimbanque and clown (he used these three figures interchangeably), was, for Picasso, a figure of contrasts, a self-Other that he mused over immediately before finding his (and modernism's) most influential Other, Africa and African art. Picasso's multiple and highly varied renditions of harlequin figures manifest, on the one hand, his lifelong interest in the energy, anarchy, and passion of the circus, theater, music hall, and other forms of performance and spectacle; on the other hand, his depictions of these theatrical figures often render them in repose, solitude, or melancholy. The harlequin figures in *Au Lapin Agile* (1905) or *Famille de Saltimbanques* (1905) (both of which bear Picasso's own likeness) are thus complex symbols of a modern artist's alienation, folly, *and* explosive creative potential, figures of impressive technical skill and extreme agility who nevertheless can be despondent and morose. Judged by the art historian Theodore Reff to be "intimately related to Picasso's most important formal invention, Cubism," his harlequins are linked to cubist form partially via the symbolic of their costume, "bright colors and strongly marked patterns both fragment and conceal the underlying forms, assimilating them to a surface design of great decorative brilliance."[8] Additionally, I would argue, they also presage cubism in their complex affect, "a form of concealment that is also a form of revelation."[9] In none of his harlequin images does Picasso preserve the figure's traditional black mask—one could say that it emerges in a different form in modernism's masterwork, Picasso's most famous appropriation of Africa and its art(s), *Les Demoiselles d'Avignon* (1907) (more on these African masks later).

The first aesthetic movement born out of a "need to merge with the other,"[10] modernism has at its core a duality and ambivalence surrounding Africa and African-descended people and culture. Simon Gikandi explains this dynamic as both Freudian and Lacanian, if not as constitutive of our "modern" consciousness:

For modernism needed Africa as both a site of experimentation and projection, not as a cultural force. If Africa did not exist as a site in which the fears and energies of modernism could be projected, it would have to be invented; by the same token, modernism emerged as an important cultural movement because while it could not do without Africa, it did not know what to do with the blackness it saw in the mirror that was supposed to reflect its repressed side. Africa is the unconscious of modernism—its "absent cause"—a force whose presence can neither be negated nor endorsed and must hence be repressed.[11]

While modern "writers and artists were themselves aware of the duality of their desire for the other and its elusiveness," what they did not understand or take into account was that this ambivalence included a further, significant distinction between African people and culture. At the heart of a modernist approach to Africa and African art was the complication that the "modernists' desire for African art objects, even for an African, pre-modern mentality, was always blocked and often haunted by the apparitional and haunting presence of the African's body."[12] The African body, the way in which it is both desired and reviled, is the true issue at stake in rethinking modernist experimentation with blackness and black experiments in modernism. It is to this irreducible materiality and harlequinesque performativity of the African body and its masks that contemporary artists of African descent turn when re-dressing modernist appropriations of African and Afro-diasporic art and culture. In that this artwork explicitly takes up and works through some signature moments/instantiations of modernist visual culture, we might think of it as "metamodernist." A term recently coined by David James and Urmila Sheshagiri to describe contemporary writing that "incorporates and adapts, reactivates and complicates the prerogatives" of modernism (periodized as 1890–1940), "metamodernism" cheekily combines homage and critique as it works to create incisive, astute aesthetic statements about our current moment.[13] The artwork in the essay performs a similar gesture, enacting a kind of New World pantomime that comments on and resituates modernist space/time and the place of Africa within that calculation.

Pantomimic images abound in late twentieth- and twenty-first-century art from the African diaspora. Employing masking, mimicry, and minstrelsy, as well as ironic costuming, these images create a kind of stage for the examination, reassessment, and transcendence of modernism's aesthetic legacy in relation to African art and culture. For example, at first glance, Iké Udé's *Sartorial Anarchy #12* (2013; figure 11.1) could be the studio portrait of a harlequin character fresh from a performance in a contemporary commedia dell'arte. While this portrait names a sartorial anarchy as its subject, a closer examination of the image prompts us to see a series of extrasartorial modernist

FIGURE 11.1 Ike Ude, *Sartorial Anarchy #12*.
Source: Courtesy of the artist.

rebellions and disorders at work. Both the harlequin and stylist of this shoot, the Nigerian-born, New York–based artist Udé imports a number of distinctions into the image that matter for it as an assessment and performance of modernist black/white, Africa/the West relations, then and now—it is a metamodernist moment. As "sartorial" anarchy, Udé's portrait displays a riot of influences: he wears a replica of a nineteenth-century "traditional" harlequin suit, distinctive for its multicolored diamond pattern. He accessorizes this with a men's white cotton organdy jabot, from the eighteenth century, secured by a Victorian red stickpin cravat. A tuxedo jacket from the 1970s is on his shoulders, accented with flowered brooch from the 1960s; contemporary argyle socks and green leather loafers cover his feet. He stands on an antique Aubusson French rug from the late 1800s, perched between two antique armchairs whose provenance is unknown. On his face are "classic" glasses from the early twenty-first century, and his hair is styled in an extravagant "Ramhorn" style reminiscent of Harlequin's tri- or duo-corned "jester-type" hat. He looks into the distance, lips parted, contemplative, and maybe amused.

If "Africa is the unconscious of modernism" and if the "African's body" haunts the modernist aesthetic and engagement with the other, then Udé as Harlequin in this pantomimic *mise en scene* visualizes the modernist unsaid/unseen. One might say, if this portrait were a metamodernist conversation with Picasso, that Udé's harlequin portrait is, in fact, a manifestation of the missing or repressed black mask from the rose period's harlequin portraits, an instantiation of the "Africanness" of the cubist period that follows it, and much more. Taking it upon himself to "merge" African and other, doing so on and with his own performative body, Udé transforms the body from an appropriated symbol into a scene of pantomimic play. A riotous, colorful, critical vehicle, the African body here claims a past and a future that extends the "modern" both backward and forward, encompassing but not limited by the modernist Africa/West encounter. This harlequin, in contrast to those of Picasso, revels in his agentive creativity, appreciates the work that he has done—he smiles. As such, he both dons and disclaims a one-way cultural influence and progressive aesthetic teleology. This is not merely an image of a postcolonial and postmodern African writing back or "re-dressing" empire, nor is this simply a portrait of a modern, African artist reconsidering and appropriating Picasso's many harlequins or even his African masks. Instead this harlequin is involved in more of a remix than a rewriting, referencing the commedia dell'arte, histories of European and black dandyism, the modern artist and his multiple and many appropriative gestures, consumption/globalization, and a kind of postblack, Afro-futuristic "dream work" all in one go.[14] This Afro-cosmopolitan harlequin performs and is himself metamodernist.

A character in a W. E. B. Du Bois novel of 1928 described modern art/modernism as "the Congo flooding the Acropolis," a kind of deluge of difference, a world of otherness, sweeping over but not subsuming Europe's foundational history and aesthetic forms.[15] Udé as harlequin invites us to rethink the origin of "tradition" and to consider it, insistently, more from an African point of view—a flood out from Africa, so to speak. This "flood" has transtemporal consequences for assessing the place of blackness within modernism and in the contemporary period. When discussing his work and its postcolonial or racial possibilities, Udé always eschews talk about what kind of "blackness" he is promoting, saying:

> I'm happy not to do so-called "black/political art" that one is/was obliged to do, especially since the 1990s. I HATE the very idea; finding it insulting and particularly stunting to the poetic imagination. So there won't be any mention of the obvious—"black"/"Africa" . . . because *I am*. It is nothing short of totalitarianism of sorts that we are all expected to think and do art works invariably laced and based on a socio-political framework. This is obviously myopic for there ought to be as much room for artists such as myself who are primarily keen in doing poetically-inspired work that is individualistic, romantic, radically inventive, beautifully wrought, free of socio-political dogma, without boundaries of any kind.[16]

Tailoring the costume of a riotous Italian into a cosmopolitan suit, refusing to take on the label of difference ("black," "African"), Udé is here an unqualified aesthetic and cultural force. The composed anarchy of Udé's body and its *mise en scene* in his portrait functions as what Aldon Nielsen has called a kind of "double-fold"—a "postmodernity within modernity that is [the time and place of] diasporic blackness." Not merely a Du Boisian double consciousness centered on identity formation but a time-space phenomenon productive of aesthetic effects, the "double-fold" encourages us to think about the possibility of reorienting the origins and legacies of modernism in different moments and in other geographies.

MASKING AND MINSTRELS

As the real or symbolic transit to a black voice, the (black) mask holds a very special place in modernist art and aesthetics. Famously brought into the modernist milieu via the highbrow Musée d'Ethnographie at the Palais de Trocadero or the more lowbrow blackface minstrel theater, the black or African mask in wood or burnt cork transported white American and European artists and writers to Other worlds as far away as the African Gold Coast or as close as the "dark" interior of the modern mind. For artists like Picasso, Michael North avers, "the [African] mask is not really a cultural artifact, worn for the purposes of concealment or adornment, but a psychological revelation exposing what usually lies behind the face."[17] Described by its liminality, an African mask is capable of performing the modern condition, both revealing and concealing angst, cacophony, disillusion, and a fundamental disorder. As such, it put into relief a radical sense of difference in how the self, the Other, and the here and now looks and feels. When most famously imported into *Les Demoiselles d'Avignon*, the African mask dislocates (European) identity and in its blankness and inherent mystery unmoors the presumptive stability of conceptions of race, gender, sexuality, class, and geography. Asking a question soon to be current in other quarters, "What does Africa mean to me?", Picasso and friends answered: "Everything [symbolically, semiotically] . . . and nothing [in reality]."

The African mask exposed modern identity as performative and made manifest the fact that there was and would be a "dislocation between subjectivity and role" for both Europeans and Africans.[18] This ontological transformation manifested itself not only in the visual field but also in textual/oral/aural terms via another, previous instantiation of the black mask: blackface racial masquerade. Given blackface's pantomimic aspect—that it is a drama of costume, mask, song, and talk—the relation of the "mask" of blackness here to the performative body is one of perhaps even greater intimacy. Created by burnt cork and drawn on the face, blackface desires an intense closeness to the black body, so much so that it elicits a "black" voice from that body. Just as African masks were ubiquitous in modernist visual art, a multitude of black voices can also be heard emanating from burnt-cork countenances. The African mask in modernist art or as a modernist aesthetic obscures the material circumstances (the people and place) that created it; similarly, the blackface mask and voice fragments and disappears the supposedly "black" body behind it.

A key object and idea in one of European modernism's greatest works, the black mask and its volatility is also of enormous importance to one of American modernism's iconic "texts" or pantomimes, the 1927 film *The Jazz Singer*. By donning the black mask and singing in a black voice, Jack Robin or Jackie Rabinowitz, Al Jolson's blackface character in the film, makes a transaction: he exchanges the synagogue for the jazz club and uses his blackface mask, an approximation of blackness, to escape his Jewish immigrant background. His deployment of burnt cork and a stereotypical, (black) dialectical voice simultaneously allows him to communicate the emotional cost of this exchange by accessing the raw melancholy of the blues. Jack's habitation of a black body—his blackface and blackvoice—is here also catalytic, functioning as an intermediate between Jewishness and whiteness that is essential in the creation of his Americanness. By pretending to be black in an obviously false way, he obtains a whiteness and uncomplicated Americanness that is the opposite of (even a caricatured) blackness. As Michael Rogin insists, blackface performance renders black bodies as (black) holes, "silences their [black] voices and sings in their name."[19]

Jack's blackface masquerade, itself a kind of anachronism in the late 1920s, would like to ignore other masking "effects" that also took place during modernism, in particular the use of the black mask, both visually and orally/aurally, by artists and writers of African descent. Aware of the stakes of stepping into what the dialect poet Paul Laurence Dunbar called a "broken tongue," or of donning masks so useful in accessing the "exotic" other, black artists nevertheless claimed the mask and its voice as a selfsame mode of identity inquiry.[20] African American visual artists and writers such as Malvin Grey Johnson, Aaron Douglas, Langston Hughes, Nella Larsen, and Countee Cullen put on masks of blackness and in doing so also asked "What Does Africa Mean to Me?" For these artists, their African heritage and its distance from their reality yet its evidence in and on their bodies also rendered the black mask and black voice into a tool of performative identity, but one that enabled them to define "blackness" as *both* a construct and an experiential cultural, political, and social history. This duality turns on contradiction and creates pantomimic aesthetic effects that interrogate the status of the black mask and its voice as mere tools of concealment and ventriloquism.

Working through and beyond the modernist moment, Lyle Ashton Harris addresses questions of masking, voice, and mimicry in a series of related self-portraits, *Minstrel, 1987–88, Man and Woman #1, 1987–88*, and *Man and Woman #2, 1987–88*. Though appearing to be an uncomplicated reversal of the emblematic image of Al Jolson singing "Mammy" at the conclusion of *The Jazz Singer*, "Minstrel" looks beyond Jolson's melancholic angst. A boater hat perched on his head, in satirical whiteface, with lips closed instead of open in performance of a supplicating song, the minstrel in the photograph looks as much like a mime—silent and critiquing—as he does a minstrel. Simultaneously parodying Jolson yet at the same time indicating that this act exceeds its own Jolson reference, Harris here refuses a reading of Jolson's

FIGURE 11.2 Lyle Ashton Harris,
Minstrel, 1987–88.
Source: Courtesy of the artist.

FIGURE 11.3 Lyle Ashton Harris,
Man and Woman #2.
Source: Courtesy of the artist.

racial masquerade as an act of "pure longing."[21] Instead, with his pout and re-enactment of minstrel as mime, Harris describes Jolson as silly, even infantile.

Man and Woman #1 and #2, also in whiteface, expand this critique, trans-forming Harris's comment on blackface/whiteface from Jolson's appropria-tion to other crises of skin/mask famously analyzed by Frantz Fanon. Im-aging that "white masks fail to hide African skin . . . and turn African into European," these two portraits encourage us to focus on the black bodies as much as the "white masks" on display here. Giving the bodies the majority of the frame and presenting them unclothed, this black man and woman, though still, are hardly passive. They are not in a traditional pose of miming, and their bodies are muscular, taut, and full of potential. In Man and Woman #2, they become animated: the woman turns her head to face the camera with squinted eyes, and the man faces the camera and opens his mouth in a potent, performative, (silent) scream. Not a supplicating song, because it is so violently delivered, nor an "authentic" black voice, because it emanates from a powerful black body counterintuitively wearing a defiant white mask, this scream images the contradictions and consequences of playing in and with "African" masks and "black" voices. Productive of reversals and perhaps a cer-tain kind of freedom, this pantomime and its metamodern mimicry prepare us for something new—a differently raced, differently gendered, differently situated sounding of an anarchic blues.

THE WEST AND THE REST

A "mash-up" of late twentieth- and early twenty-first-century African Ameri-can hip-hop culture and the "floating world" of Tokugawa Japan during the seventeenth and eighteenth centuries, the paintings and performance art of the artist iona Rozeal brown (now known as iROZEALb) capture and extend the complex politics of the time and place(s) of the Euro-American modern-ist moment. When we look at Sin Titulo (2012–2014) we see not an anxiety of influence but rather an anarchy: an elaborately dressed, coiffed, and made-up geisha, she is not in "traditional" Japanese attire but in a combination of tat-tooed flesh and a white, fluffy fur coat.[22] Sporting two enormous Afro-puffs, gold chains, pearls, and iconic 1980s "door-knocker" earrings, her blackface "mask" is ever so carefully applied, the line between Asian and African Amer-ican simultaneously precise and besides the point. Framed like an original ukiyo-e woodblock print from the Tokugawa/Edo era, which depicted Japan's stylish "life deluxe"—geishas, courtesans, actors, and others involved in the performance of opulence—she performs as both the player and the instrument, in that her hair mimics bass speakers, her face a nut-brown violin. Without title (*sin titulo*) and perhaps actually impossible to define definitively, she practices an improvisational art of sound and style that confuses and complicates the time, place, and race of cultural influence. In this Afro-Asian pantomime, brown, like Udé and Harris, reanimates modernist Europe and America's appropriations of the Other, domesticating and transforming what was thought of as not-Europe, not-America.

Although the initial inspiration for this image was brown's discovery of the *ganguro*, a group of Japanese girls enamored of hip-hop who, in the late 1990s, adopted the clothing, hairstyles, swagger, and even the skin color of African American hip-hop artists and fans, her rendition of their masquerade goes well beyond portraiture and a critique of their cultural appropriation. Instead, brown's engagement with Japanese/African American culture transhistorically—the connection she makes between Edo-period Japan and late-capitalist America, the cultural and racial insularity of Japan and the globalization of hip-hop—forces us to look for connections and conjunctions between *both* cultures and places, across time and space. While brown seemingly specifically pivots between contemporary America and a premodern or modernizing Japanese past, her work also recalls an earlier fascination with Japan and the era of the "floating world" in late nineteenth- and early twentieth-century Euro-American modernist art and culture. "Japonisme" also captured the imagination of Walt Whitman, Alexander Dumas, and Oscar Wilde. In fact, Gertrude Stein famously (and cryptically) stated, while perhaps standing in front of the many African sculptures at her home, 27 Rue des Fleurus in Paris, "Culture is Japanese."[23]

Best known for her "afro-asiatic allegory," brown's paintings and performance pieces reference and mash up present and past moments of African American, Asian, and modernist cultural contact and exchange. As a child, brown was fascinated by very disparate forms of Japanese and Asian culture—she remembers her mother taking her to a formative performance of Kabuki theater, featuring Bandō Tamasaburō, a celebrated virtuoso performer of female roles (*onnagata*); brought up on *Sesame Street*, she also enjoyed Bunraku puppet theater. On weekends, she watched kung-fu films featuring Bruce Lee with her father; she loved Japanese animation too, including *Speed Racer* and *Kimba*.[24] Initially disturbed by the *ganguro*'s blackface when she encountered the phenomenon in graduate school, she took research trips to Japan and later Korea and China, where hip-hop has transformed from an exotic import to an increasingly popular form of indigenous popular culture. Her fieldwork in the Asian hip-hop scene and apprenticeship in traditional art techniques complicated brown's reception and depiction of blackface and "black" urban performance. Complaining at first that "they've [the *ganguro*] got white around their eyes and around their lips" and that they "immediately made me think of Al Jolson," brown decided not to parody or mock the *ganguro* but instead created an even deeper, pantomimic critique of appropriation, excess, and materialism, whether in contemporary, globalized hip-hop culture or Edo Japan (or somewhere in a Euro-American in-between).[25] Blacking up geishas and samurais and transforming them into MCs, brown's address of racial stereotyping is inseparable from her critique of both cultures' love of luxury and conflicted politics of gender and sexuality. Neither African American culture, Japanese culture, nor modernist culture, past and present, gets a pass here; instead brown's mash-up creates something new: a statement on and vision of modernity and its aesthetics or the difficulty, necessity, and complexity of cross-cultural engagement as a description of modernist art. These interconnected modernisms are sometimes depicted in metamodernist pantomime.

Not just an investigation of contemporary, globalized cultural flow and cross-cultural influence, brown's work is also an object lesson for the future of modernist literary and cultural inquiry. As Doyle and Winkiel insist in *Geomodernisms*, a fuller investigation of modernity and modernism will require discovering and recovering connections between the West and the rest or even two "minor" modernist spaces and places.[26] Though centered on Tokugawa Japan and contemporary African America, brown's "afro-asian allegory" also reminds us that Commodore Perry celebrated the "opening" of Japan in 1854 by putting on a minstrel show; at the same time we must consider that three of African America's preeminent "race men," James Weldon Johnson, Langston Hughes, and W. E. B. Du Bois, all traveled to Japan as part of their antiracist, people-of-color solidarity work.[27] When we think of these connections, not to mention Richard Wright's attendance at the 1955 Bandung Conference and his authorship of over four thousand haikus near the end of his life, we are encouraged to think, along with Doyle and Winkiel, of "interconnected modernisms—[which will necessitate] a rethinking of periodization, genealogies, affiliations, and forms."[28]

All of the artwork considered in this essay functions as provocation for this project as they use pantomimic gestures of performance and racial play to send us backward and forward in time. Simultaneously, they force us to range across the globe, to travel between "Africa" as an idea and an actual place, to reimagine modernist Paris through, for example, Harlem Renaissance New York, to consider Toyko's transformation from Edo (its name in the Tokugawa period) to "modernity" via modernist Paris (again) and the Bronx in the 1980s. Additionally, they ask us literally and figuratively to listen to a multitude of voices, to heed and discern harmony and dissonance. Such reconsiderations allow for the possibility of multiple modernisms as well as metamodernisms. In an article in the *New York Times* recently, the art critic Holland Carter writes, "Modernism was, and is, an international phenomenon, happening in different ways, on different timetables, for different reasons in Africa, Asia, Australia and South America."[29] To see, hear, and locate modernism and its constituents more clearly, to see the complexity of the work of modern artists and their contemporary heirs, we are going to have to enter into and live within a new metamodern, multiply modern pantomime.

NOTES

1. John O'Brien, "Pantomime," in *The Cambridge Companion to British Theatre, 1730–1830*, ed. Jane Moody and Daniel O'Quinn (Cambridge: Cambridge University Press, 2007), 103.

2. Mark Griffith, "Telling the Tale: A Performing Tradition from Homer to Pantomime," in *The Cambridge Companion to Greek and Roman Theatre* (Cambridge: Cambridge University Press, 2007), 32.

3. Hugh Denard, "Lost Theatre and Performance Traditions in Greece and Italy," in *The Cambridge Companion to Greek and Roman Theatre* (Cambridge: Cambridge University Press, 2007), 156, 158. See also Lynne Lawner, *Harlequin on the Moon: Commedia dell'Arte and the Visual Arts* (New York: Abrams, 1998), 16.

4. Lawner, *Harlequin on the Moon*, 16.

5. Maurice Sand, *History of the Harlequinade* (London: Martin Secker, 1915), 1:13. Cyril Beaumont, *History of Harlequin* (London: C. W. Beaumont, 1926), is suspicious of a *direct* connection between the Roman *pantomimi*, mimes, and the commedia dell'arte but nevertheless admits that comedy shares features across the ages.

6. Lawner, *Harlequin on the Moon*, 18.

7. Ibid., 23.

8. Theodore Reff, "Harlequins, Satimbanques, Clowns, and Fools," *Artforum* 10, no. 1 (1970): 30.

9. Ibid., 30. For more on Picasso's harlequins, see also Yves-Alain Bois, ed., *Picasso Harlequin, 1917–1937* (New York: Skira, 2009).

10. Simon Gikandi, "Africa and the Epiphany of Modernism," in *Geomodernisms: Race, Modernism, Modernity*, ed. Laura Doyle and Laura Winkiel (Bloomington: Indiana University Press, 2005), 32.

11. Ibid., 49.

12. Ibid., 40.

13. David James and Urmila Sheshagiri, "Metamodernism: Narratives of Continuity and Revolution," *PMLA* 129, no. 1 (January 2014): 93.

14. Monica L. Miller, "An Interview with Iké Udé: Mining the Opposition . . . Is My Great Refusal," in *Iké Udé: Style and Sympathies: New Photographic Works* (New York: Leila Heller Gallery, 2013), n.p.

15. W. E. B. Du Bois, *Dark Princess: A Romance* (Jackson: University Press of Mississippi, 1995), 20.

16. Iké Udé, personal communication, August 2013, italics added.

17. Michael North, *The Dialect of Modernism: Race, Language, and Twentieth-Century Literature* (New York: Oxford University Press, 1994), 63.

18. Kaja Silverman, qtd. in ibid., 70.

19. Michael Rogin, "Blackface, White Noise: The Jewish Jazz Singer Finds His Voice," *Critical Inquiry* 18, no. 3 (Spring 1992): 442.

20. Paul Laurence Dunbar, "The Poet," second stanza: "He sang of love when earth was young, / And Love, itself, was in his lays. / But, ah, the world, it turned to praise / A jingle in a broken tongue." See *The Complete Poems of Paul Laurence Dunbar* (1913).

21. Rogin, "Blackface, White Noise," 442.

22. http://www.edwardtylernahemfineart.com/artists/irozealb-iona-rozeal-brown/#/images/1/. Accessed November 5, 2015. Image is no longer available at this web address.

23. Christopher Bush, "The Ethnicity of Things in America's Lacquered Age," *Representations* 99 (Summer 2007): 74; Christopher Bush, "The Other of the Other?: Cultural Studies, Theory, and the Location of the Modernist Signifier," *Comparative Literature Studies* 42, no. 2 (2005): 164.

24. Lyneise E. Williams, "Black on Both Sides: A Conversation with iona rozeal brown," *Callaloo* 29, no. 3 (Summer 2006): 829.

25. "Iona Rozeal Brown's Afro-Japanese Mash-Up," Interview on NPR's Studio 360 (June 7, 2013), http://www.studio360.org/story/296845-iona-rozeal-browns_afro_japanese_mashup/.

26. Laura Doyle and Laura Winkiel, introduction to *Geomodernisms: Race, Modernism, Modernity*, ed. Laura Doyle and Laura Winkiel (Bloomington: Indiana University Press, 2005).

27. Crystal S. Anderson, "The Afro-Asiatic Floating World: Post-Soul Implications of the Art of iona rozeal brown," *African American Review* 41, no. 4 (Winter 2007): 662, 657.

28. Ibid., 66; Doyle and Winkiel, introduction, 3.

29. Holland Carter, "Lost in the Gallery Industrial Complex," *New York Times* (January 17, 2014), http://www.nytimes.com/2014/01/19/arts/design/holland-cotter-looks-at -money-in-art.html?ref=hollandcotter. Thanks to Iké Udé for this reference.

12. PUPPETS

MARTIN PUCHNER

Puppets require not only that we return to our earliest childhood experiences; they also demand a more global approach to modernism since many modernists were particularly intrigued by non-European puppets. But puppets are a particularly strange form of exoticism because puppet makers and users knew that puppets, dolls, and marionettes were not simply an import from the East. What was so thrilling about them, in the minds of many of their most loyal adherents, was that they were at home in Europe as well, although relegated to nurseries and folklore.

Why should we bother with puppets when it comes to modernism? As everyone knows, puppets are for children; they belong to the elaborate toy theaters favored by the Victorian bourgeoisie rather than to the provocative arts of the avant-gardes. Or they derive from the rude folklore of Punch and Judy shows, at home at fairs and roadside spectacles, rather than from the recherché performances in the coterie theaters of Europe's capitals. Finally, puppets and their relatives such as idols evoke faraway cults and cultures rather than the high arts favored by connoisseurs within advanced capitalist societies. But these three origins—children's games, street theater, and cult—are also the very reasons why puppets can point us to a crucial undercurrent within modernism.

Looking at modernism through the eyes of puppets also requires that we expand our notion of modernism both geographically and temporally. Puppets require not only that we return to our earliest childhood experiences; they also demand a more global approach to modernism since many modernists were particularly intrigued by non-European puppets. But puppets are a particularly strange form of exoticism because puppet makers and users knew that puppets, dolls, and marionettes were not simply an import from the East. What was so thrilling about them, in the minds of many of their most loyal adherents, was that they were at home in Europe as well, although relegated to nurseries and folklore. Inspired by global puppets, European modernists went to work excavating these nonhuman residues at the heart of Europe, finding there another version of the East. Even as puppets work as reminders of forgotten pasts, they were also integrated into the most futuristic scenarios in the form of robots and mechanized actors, adapting to the art of the first machine age. Identifying these various strands will require a reflection on children's puppets, modernist puppets in the theater, mechanized puppets, and global puppets. Puppets, it turns out, not only capture several crucial strands within modernism. They still exert a considerable influence on art, especially the theatrical arts, and thus have managed to extend modernist estrangement into the present.

CHILD'S PLAY

One could do worse than to start with Charles Baudelaire, whose eyes tended to catch phenomena outside the main currents of culture. In a short piece of prose, the narrator describes an encounter with a poverty-stricken child, whose only doll is a live rat: "In order to save money, the parents had torn the puppet directly from life [tiré le joujou de la vie elle-même]" ("Morale du Joujou," 585). The living rat is a perversion of the traditional puppet, which is only supposed to simulate a living person without itself being alive.

A similar short-circuit, Baudelaire continues, is at play in the well-known desire of children to tear open puppets. This desire is not simply one of destruction but also a form of curiosity, a metaphysical drive to peek inside the puppet and search for its animating force. This curiosity leads to an explosion of violence. Baudelaire writes:

> The child twists the limbs of the puppet, scratches and shakes it, smashes it against the wall, throws it on the ground. . . . Its wondrous life comes to an end. Like the troupes assaulting the Tuileries, the child undertakes one more effort: it breaks open the puppet, since it is the stronger of the two. But where is its soul? This is the beginning of melancholia and depression.
>
> (587; translation is mine)

The comparison with the revolutionary masses is perhaps somewhat melodramatic, but it speaks to the force behind this destructive drive. A quasi-revolutionary orgy of violence aims at the seat of the puppet's "wondrous life," its soul.

Baudelaire's story, culminating as it does in "melancholia" and "depression," points us not so much to modernist art as to modernist theory, that is, to psychoanalysis and in particular to Freud's essay on the uncanny (1919). This essay begins with the traditional definition of that term, namely that the uncanny points to the zone between living organism and lifeless object. Even though Freud goes on to reject that definition, replacing it with his own Oedipal theory, other theorists have taken it up, including Donald Woods Winnicott, with his notion of the "transitional object." Among the typical transitional objects he names are security blankets, teddy bears, dolls, and puppets, those early objects through which the infant learns to establish a proper subject-object relation. Winnicott found that the process through which such a relation is established invariably includes the destruction of the transitional object. Ultimately, transitional objects are themselves substitutes for the breast and can be seen as a link between the breast and proper objects. When seen from this perspective, dismembered puppets and dolls resonate with the violent process through which a subject-object relation had been established in early childhood. Like Freud, Winnicott takes us back into an early and rarely remembered childhood, but instead of an Oedipal drama, Winnicott presents us with a drama of objects, of the gradual constitution of objects and, by extension, of subjects.

It is perhaps not surprising that this use—or abuse—of puppets turned out to be crucial for a number of modernist artists, for whom the work of Hans Bellmer can serve as a convenient stand-in. Bellmer's wooden puppets, presented for the most part in photographs, originate in bourgeois nurseries, but they have developed a twisted sexuality. Mature sexual organs are shamelessly exposed through ruffled lingerie; torsos sprout too many legs, often partially amputated but nevertheless arranged in inviting poses; series of breasts and folds are presented for inspection and use. Puppets are treated at once as objects of perverse desire and as wooden mechanisms that can be rearranged, making every joint an invitation for creative twists and turns, an opportunity to exchange a bone for a piece of wood or to add this or that prosthetic limb to a distorted torso.

Do these puppets and, for that matter, all puppets seek to imitate humans? This question of mimesis turned out to be crucial for modernists intrigued by these silent creatures. It is true that puppets usually take their cues from the human physiognomy: head, complete with eyes, nose, and hair; a torso and two arms adorned with some sort of garment. Hesitantly, puppets bow and greet and go through other forms of human interaction; marionettes are even more agile, with their limbs slowly, if never surely, setting one foot before the next. Even dolls, though less mobile, can be enticed to move. There is no doubt that there exists some sort of family resemblance between puppets and humans.

But is this resemblance really captured by the doctrine of mimesis? When seen through that lens, puppets and marionettes are at best awkward creatures. In truth, they have their own distinct ways of moving, of behaving, their own distinct ways of being. They point as much away from the human as toward it. Hence the recurrent effect of the uncanny they evoke.

PUPPETS AND ACTORS

The modernist art for which puppets turned out to be crucial was not photography but theater. To the extent that modernism can be understood as an attack on mimesis it was particularly difficult to implement in the theater, an art form at whose center stands the live human actor seeking to imitate another human. In the widely quoted opening sentences from *The Empty Space*, Peter Brook writes: "I can take any empty space and call it a bare stage. A man walks across this empty space whilst someone else is watching him, and this is all I need for an act of theatre to be engaged" (9). If theater wanted to become truly modernist, it needed to do away with the human actor. The actor posed a number of problems for which the puppet offered itself as a solution.

One way this solution was articulated was in the language of control. The fact that theater is a collaborative art had long been a thorn in the side of those hoping to turn it into a high art form. The resurgence of puppet theater was therefore closely related to the control over the actor, and thus to the violence against the actor, especially since the emergence of the director's theater in the second half of the nineteenth century. This new type of director saw the actor as mere material from which the theatrical work of art had to be forged. The human actor has been dying a slow death ever since. Edward Gordon Craig compared the director explicitly with the puppeteer. In his manifesto "The Actor and the Über-Marionette" (1908), he critiques all collaborative theater and advances the thesis that theater can become a true art form only if all artistic decisions are unified in the figure of the all-powerful director. Collaboration is associated with the inchoate collision of divergent wills that makes any formal order, on which Craig's notion of the artwork is premised, impossible. And the larger the number of meddling participants, the greater the danger that accidents enter the artwork, spelling the end of art. Hence Craig's sharp polemic against collaboration and his urgent call to consider the actor as a marionette that must execute everything according to the skillful commands of the puppeteer.

Such fantasies of total control via the figure of the puppet infiltrated actual theater practice. William Butler Yeats forced actors into barrels on castors, which he moved around on stage by means of a stick (*Explorations*, 86ff.). Samuel Beckett even considered this reduced presence of actors too much and immobilized his actors in barrels, ashbins, urns, and mounds. Or else he turned them into test creatures, as he did in "Act Without Words I," subjecting them to the most cruel experiments. By the same token, many of the leading dramatists of the turn of the century, including Maurice Maeterlinck, Alfred Jarry, and Garcia Lorca, wrote their most important plays explicitly for puppet or marionette theater, even if those pieces are now mostly performed with live, human actors (see also Segel, *Pinocchio's Progeny*).

Before the background of this puppet-inspired perspective on modernism, one might remember the most famous play to bear a synonym for that word in its title: Henrik Ibsen's *A Doll House*. Ibsen did not envision a Craig-like master director, nor did he wish to confine his actors to barrels. Yet it must be significant that his *succès de scandale* revolves around a puppet—or doll—metaphor, by which the infantilization of Nora Torvald is signified.

It took a postmodern theater company, the New York–based Mabou Mines, to tease out the puppet-modernism hinted at in this play. In this production, called *Mabou Mines DollHouse*, which premiered in 2003 at St. Ann's Warehouse in DUMBO, a neighborhood in Brooklyn, New York, the most important feature was size. Notoriously, all male characters in this production were played by actors approximately four feet tall. The casting in *DollHouse* was but one component of an elaborate scheme to get at Ibsen's obsession with size, with everyone becoming a doll to everyone else, across size boundaries. The small men were, of course, sometimes used as dolls. This happened for example when Torvald flew through the air, carried by a stagehand as if he were a puppet or doll. Since Nora could not handle Torvald despite his small size, she had to carry her own Nora doll. Early on in the first scene, Nora seized the blond hair of a doll, made up to look like herself, and ripped open its head. It was a sudden gesture that encapsulated the violence of which Freud, Winnicott, and Baudelaire speak with respect to the search for the puppet's soul. In this case, what Nora found inside the skull was a macaroon, which she kept hidden in willful defiance of her husband's prohibition. In a remarkable performance by Maud Mitchell, Nora also moved and spoke like a manic puppet, her fast-talking baby voice amplified by an extraordinary sound system and design. The entire production took place on a miniature set, with toy chairs, toy beds, toy doors, toy pianos, toy everything, forcing the life-sized actors into the world of dead and animated puppets.

Nora's two children were made up to resemble dolls and are treated like dolls as well. However, the child actors seemed out of place in this uncanny toy world not because they weren't good but because they belonged to the toy world in the first place. They were its natural inhabitants and therefore could not contribute to the terror that results when adults, no matter what size, start playing at dolls.

I have been speaking of puppets and marionettes indiscriminately, but it is important to distinguish between them. Marionettes barely keep their feet on the ground since they are forever pulled upward; despite their grace, they are bad at walking, a motion that is essentially a controlled form of falling and hence dependent on gravity. Puppets and dolls, by contrast, collapse onto themselves unless human hands prop them up. The most important theorist of this distinction was a premodernist, Heinrich von Kleist. In an essay that has become rightly famous, "On the Marionette Theatre," Kleist, or, rather, his narrator, develops a theory of marionettes being "antigravitational" and sets the stage for the modernist polemic against actors by preferring marionettes to human performers. Kleist was not alone. Giacomo Leopardi and E. T. A. Hofmann likewise construct uncanny fables of life and death revolving around the animating principle of puppets, ghosts, dolls, and other creatures.

While marionettes are thus elegant and light, puppets are heavy, bulky, and barely budge. Yet some of the same artists invested in marionettes were drawn to puppets as well, including Garcia Lorca, who liked their popular, folkloristic provenance, and Luigi Pirandello, whose native Sicily is famous for puppetry. Indeed, in addition to demanding that his plays be performed by marionettes, Lorca also wrote several puppet plays, some for children and some for adults, in the crude style of Punch and Judy. It is in this return to folklore that we can see modernists reaching back into the past, tracing forgotten or marginalized practices in their own cultures, drawing on puppets as a resource for estrangement from within. This folkloristic interest set the stage for another orientation, namely that toward the East.

First prize for the crudeness associated with Punch and Judy–style folk-lore, however, goes to Alfred Jarry, who turned the actor performing *Ubu Roi* into a kind of puppet by confining him in a full-body costume. The origin of this figure lies in schoolday pranks, and the aesthetics of the play draws on the kind of violence common in puppet theater, a trace, probably, of the kind of violence with respect to puppets noted by Freud, Winnicott, and others working in psychoanalysis and recorded in Bellmer's photographs.

MACHINE PUPPETS

In the twentieth century, the marionette also becomes a matter of technology. In some sense the theater has always been a machine for creating illusions. The crane through which a god was hoisted onto the scene in Greek theater is an early example of this technology-driven nature of theater. Trapdoors and all kinds of flying machines followed, and the revolving stage, developed in the middle of the nineteenth century, created even more possibilities for stage effects. In the early twentieth century, Walter Gropius's model for a total theater (*Totaltheater*) constituted a first culmination of this mechanization and technologization of the theater apparatus.

This mechanization of the theater had profound effects on the live actor. More and more, the actor's body was treated as a mere instrument, as a question of mechanics. A landmark text in this regard is Diderot's *Paradoxe sur le comédien* (1777), which understands successful acting to be a matter of cold calculation through which actors evoke passions by quasi-mechanical means. As Joseph Roach has shown in his study *The Player's Passion* (1993), the history of acting can be seen as a battle between mechanical and organic approaches, a battle in which the mechanical theory of acting usually wins.

The first machine age promised to deal with recalcitrant actors by turning them into machines. Mechanistic metaphors were turned into reality by industrialization and the mechanical revolution. One culmination of this development was without doubt Vsevolod Meyerhold's biomechanics, which was described in the early years of the Soviet Republic as a veritable "Taylorization of the theater" (Korenev, "Principles of Biomechanics," 138). In his landmark book *Principles of Scientific Management* (1911), F. W. Taylor had argued that the energy expenditure of workers could be minimized through a scientific analysis of their motions. More generally, the mechanization and economization of motion meant that workers were now assimilated to the rhythms of machines, a principle exemplified in the assembly-belt production system in-stituted by Henry Ford. It was this combination of slow-motion analysis and the mechanization of workers that Meyerhold turned into a model for the modern, working actor (see also Rabinbach, *The Human Motor*).

Contemporary theater practitioners considered the Taylorization of the theater with a combination of fascination and repulsion. German and Amer-ican expressionism invented veritable horror scenarios of the increasing mechanization of actors, including Eugene O'Neill's *The Hairy Ape*, Sophie Treadwell's *Machinal*, Elmer Rice's *The Adding Machine*, and Georg Kaiser's *Gas*. Many films also consider mechanization a threat, including Fritz Lang's *Metropolis* and Charlie Chaplin's *Modern Times*. But in the theater the fear of mechanization is particularly existential. Film, after all, knows that it is itself a mechanical medium and therefore not in a position to attack mechaniza-tion tout court. Karel Capek's play *R.U.R.* (1921), of course, invented the term robot, the puppet of the first machine age. In this play, an engineer creates a company, Rossum's Universal Robots, which supplies the world with mass-produced robots. In the end, the creatures, the so-called universal robots, rebel against their creator, conquer the world, and learn how to reproduce themselves. The most extreme vision of a mechanized theater came, not sur-prisingly, from Marinetti and the futurists, who created theaters consisting only of machines or machine puppets. At the same time, the Bauhaus mem-ber Heinz Loew constructed the so-called mechanical stage, in which living actors would become appendices to machines. The living actor was barely tolerated or even banished from the stage entirely. What was once called a "lively art" threatened to be deprived of life (also see Auslander, *Liveness*).

The most popular treatment of a director turning an actor into a mari-onette, as Craig had demanded, or even an appendix to machines, as envi-sioned by Loew, is George Bernard Shaw's *Pygmalion* (1914) and its musi-cal version *My Fair Lady*. The title refers to Ovid's *Metamorphoses* and the story of the statue Galatea, which is brought to life by the gods, who take pity on Pygmalion's hopeless love for his creation (also see Gross, *The Dream of the Moving Statue*). Shaw turns this story of animating an inanimate figure into one that revolves around the training and transformation of the flower girl Eliza Doolittle. The theatrical implications are quite clear. In the preface, he writes:

I may add that the change wrought by Professor Higgins in the flower-girl is neither impossible nor uncommon. The modern concierge's daughter who fulfils her ambition by playing the Queen of Spain in Ruy Blas at the Théâtre Français is only one of many thousands of men and women who have sloughed off their native dialects and acquired a new tongue. . . . But the thing has to be done scientifically.

(9)

Eliza Doolittle is the prototypical actor, and Henry Higgins, her acting coach and director.

Like a director of Craig's ilk, Higgins will use his creature as a mere marionette, as raw material that must be variously animated and built up from scratch. His rigorous training program goes from posture to pronunciation in order to create Doolittle anew. All too soon, the creature rebels: Eliza Doolittle no longer wants to be a mere marionette and threatens to leave. Shaw could never quite make up his mind about the ending of the play. In the play version, Eliza elopes with Freddy, a hapless but well-intentioned society boy who is head-over-heels in love with her. Not content with this ending, Shaw wrote a narrative postscript in which he summarizes the further doings of his characters. Eliza and Freddy open an elegant flower shop but secretly rely on Higgins's old friend Colonel Pickering for support. No matter which of these endings one considers, the relation between Eliza and her erstwhile creator remains difficult. Al Hirschfeld captured this relation between Higgins and Eliza in his sketch for the playbill of both the original play and its musical version and pushes it one step further: Shaw is up in the clouds and pulls the strings of his marionette Higgins, who in turn controls his marionette Eliza (see also Shershow, *Puppets and "Popular" Culture*).

Shaw's play is not only a good example of the convergence of directorial control and marionette theater; *Pygmalion* also testifies to the convergence of marionette theater and machine theater. Even though his Pygmalion story does not feature robots, the training of Eliza, and thus the creation of this modern-day Galatea, depends to a great extent on technology, taking place in a laboratory equipped with the latest machines and devices. Higgins is reminiscent of mad, romantic scientists such as Dr. Frankenstein, but it is also clear that we are dealing not with invented machines and fanciful science but with an actual laboratory and existing apparatuses:

In this corner stands a flat writing-table, on which are a phonograph, a laryngoscope, a row of tiny organ pipes with a bellows, a set of lamp chimneys for singing flames with burners attached to a gas plug in the wall by an indiarubber tube, several tuning-forks of different sizes, a life-size image of half a human head, shewing in section the vocal organs, and a box containing a supply of wax cylinders for the phonograph.

(33)

This laboratory includes an odd combination of devices, such as medical implements (laryngoscope, cross-section of a human head), chemical equipment (burners, tubes), musical instruments (tuning fork, organ pipes), and ordinary writing utensils. In addition, we find the latest invention: a phonograph with wax cylinders. The reason for this assembly of instruments is that Higgins wants to build his new Galatea by means of a new, interdisciplinary science called phonetics; the crucial element of the refurbishing of Eliza Doolittle, after all, is language. Even Colonel Pickering, himself a linguist and expert in South Asian dialects, is impressed by Higgins's laboratory. "Higgins: Well, I think thats the whole show. Pickering: It's really amazing. I havnt taken half of it in, you know. Higgins: Would you like to go over any of it again. Pickering: No, thank you, not now. I'm quite done up for this morning" (34). Pickering is simply overwhelmed by the technology assembled by this modern-day Pygmalion.

Eliza Doolittle has no choice but to give herself over to the laboratory where she is being refurbished, a marionette in the age of mechanical reproduction: "you can turn her on as often as you like," Higgins boasts about the phonograph. And this is precisely what happens at the end of the play. In the last confrontation between the two, Eliza answers Higgins's melancholic musings, "I shall miss you, Eliza. . . . And I have grown accustomed to your voice and appearance," by saying: "Well, you have both of them on your gramophone and in your book of photographs. When you feel lonely without me, you can turn the machine on" (127). Earlier, Higgins had bragged: "I can turn your soul on." But in the end, all that Higgins has left is the mechanically reproduced voice. The living creature has left him (and the theater). *Pygmalion* threatens to become something like Beckett's *Krapp's Last Tape*, a play in which the tape recorder takes center stage and the human actor becomes merely its operator, the one who pushes the buttons.

PUPPETS OF THE EAST

Puppets are a means of displacing the actor from the center of theater, ushering in an estranged or uncanny theater that is in accordance with the antimimetic instincts of modernism. At the same time, they represented a folkloristic residue in the eyes of modernists hoping to estrange their own culture from within. But puppets allow for estrangement in another sense as well: geography. The uncanniness of puppets has often led to their being associated with the religious origins of theater (also see Nelson, *The Secret Life of Puppets*; Bell, *American Puppet Modernism*). Indeed, many of the theater makers who turned to puppets for control were intrigued by their worldwide cousins. These include Craig and Yeats but also Artaud and Brecht, among others. For them, puppets were not just antimimetic devices; they also opened Western theater to the world.

There has been much debate about this episode of Western theater makers turning to Asian theater practices. Without doubt this is a variety of Orientalism to the extent that these dramatists and directors sought solutions to their own problems in the East and thus very much looked at the East through the lens of those problems (also see Hayot, *Chinese Dreams*). And the way in which Artaud encountered Balinese theater, namely at a colonial exhibition, and Ernest Fenollosa got his hands on No theater were bound up with early twentieth-century globalization, the vestiges of Western imperialism. At the same time, this form of Orientalism, if we want to hold on to this term, has also been crucial for the establishment of theater studies as a discipline in the first decade of the twentieth century. Both the Brander Matthews Theater Collection at Columbia University and the Harvard Theater Collection boast various forms of Asian puppets, forming the scholarly equivalent to modernist theater practice.

The theatrical Orientalism of the first half of the twentieth century was only the opening act. In the postwar period, it was followed by what is usually called "intercultural" theater, a period of the deliberate mingling of theatrical styles. Peter Brook is perhaps the obvious person to identify as a crucial figure in this respect, and his *Mahabharata*, begun in the mid-1970s and first performed in 1985, spans the high time of this era. Brook's signature technique was that of mixing theatrical styles—and not just styles but also performers trained in different theatrical traditions. Tadashi Suzuki might be seen as a somewhat later example of the phase of intercultural theater as well. Something similar happened in scholarship. The best example here is the cooperation between Richard Schechner and Victor Turner, which inaugurated a new phase in the relation between anthropology and theater studies. Indeed, the intercultural paradigm is premised on producing cultural amalgamation, the merry mixture of cultural hybridity, or of analyzing such phenomena, often by using an anthropological paradigm. For the perspective I am offering here, one might describe it as a scholarly mixture of cultures, with Richard

Schechner now incorporating all kinds of performance practices, again primarily from South Asia but also East Asia, into theater studies and performance studies. Puppets were part of these developments.

A new phase of world theater has emerged in the post-1989 or post-9/11 world of global capitalism. It raises a somewhat different set of questions, many economic: how has theater, including intercultural theater, become a commodity that circulates globally? The most paradigmatic troupe to capture our current moment is the South African Handspring Puppet Theater, which has been doing the international circuit for over a decade. Using a large repertoire of puppets from crude Punches and Judys to awe-inspiring oversized creatures, Handspring draws on the puppets of Western modernism but confronts them with their global cousins, often to stunning effect. It is perhaps not surprising that the breakthrough success of this troupe was none other than a puppet-theater version of Jarry's *Ubu Roi*, the central theatrical event of modernist theater.

More recently, however, Handspring has discovered Broadway, Hollywood, and the international theater circuit, using *War Horse* as its vehicle. A touching story of a horse and a boy during World War I, with a satisfying happy ending, *War Horse* couldn't be further from modernism and its puppets, yet even here, in a show that was always destined for Hollywood, the puppet horse moves so beautifully and strangely that it almost redeems the show's pat storyline. This, no doubt, testifies to the peculiar effect of puppets and their modernist legacy: even when they are apparently used to imitate our world, they introduce an element of estrangement.

In this manner puppets have managed to preserve a modernist estrangement effect and carry it into our own era. The source of this effect is derived from the exotic origins of puppets, whether they are located in our own childhood, in folkloristic practices, or in the East. But in the end, this exotic provenance is only a secondary feature, for what makes puppets so strange is the fact that they don't belong to the world of the living. As objects demanding to be animated, they keep popping up, bringing something into our midst that we can never fully assimilate.

WORKS CITED

Auslander, Philip. *Liveness: Performance in a Mediatized Culture.* London: Routledge, 1999.

Baudelaire, Charles. "Morale du Joujou." In *Oeuvres completes*, ed. Claude Pichois, 1:581–587. Paris: Pléjade, 1975.

Bell, John. *American Puppet Modernism: Essays on the Material World in Performance.* New York: Palgrave, 2008.

Brook, Peter. *The Empty Space.* New York: Touchstone, 1968.

Craig, Edward Gordon. "The Actor and the Über-Marionette." In *On the Art of the Theatre,* 54–94. London: Heinemann, 1956.

Freud, Sigmund. "Das Unheimliche." In *Gesammelte Werke. Chronologisch geordnet,* ed. Anna Freud et al., 12:229–268. Frankfurt: S. Fischer, 1947.

Gross, Kenneth. *The Dream of the Moving Statue.* Ithaca, N.Y.: Cornell University Press, 1992.

Hayot. Eric. *Chinese Dreams: Pound, Brecht, Tel Quel.* Ann Arbor: University of Michigan Press, 2011.

Kleist, Heinrich von. "Über das Marionettentheater." In *Sämtliche Werke und Briefe,* 9th ed., ed. Helmut Sembdner, 2:338–345. Munich: Carl Hanser, 1993.

Korenev, Mikhail. "Principles of Biomechanics." In Alma Law and Mel Gordon, *Meyerhold, Eisenstein, and Biomechanics. Actor Training in Revolutionary Russia,* 135–138. Jefferson, N.C.: McFarland, 1996.

Nelson, Victoria. *The Secret Life of Puppets.* Cambridge, Mass.: Harvard University Press, 2003.

Rabinbach, Anson. *The Human Motor: Energy, Fatigue, and the Origins of Modernity.* Berkeley: University of California Press, 1992.

Roach, Joseph. *The Player's Passion: Studies in the Science of Acting.* Ann Arbor: University of Michigan Press, 1993.

Segel, Harold B. *Pinocchio's Progeny. Puppets, Marionettes, Automatons, and Robots in Modernist and Avant-Garde Drama.* Baltimore, Md.: Johns Hopkins University Press, 1995.

Shaw, George Bernard. *Pygmalion.* London: Penguin, 2003.

Shershow, Scott Culter. *Puppets and "Popular" Culture.* Ithaca, N.Y.: Cornell University Press, 1995.

Taylor, Frederick Winslow. *Principles of Scientific Management.* New York: Harper and Brothers, 1911.

Winnicott, Donald W. *Playing and Reality.* London: Tavistock, 1971.

Yeats, William Butler. *Explorations.* New York: Macmillan, 1962.

13. SLUM

DAVID L. PIKE

The slum can remind us of the way periphery and center are mutually constituting forces, and its absence from modernism per se can remind us of the literal absence of that relationship from modernism. The further we move from the traditional centers of modernism, however, the more we find other ways of thinking about the slum.

The word *slum* entered the English language through London cant, or underworld jargon, in the early nineteenth century. We might imagine the subsequent vagaries of the term moving something along the lines of the Victorian life of the "Improbable Impostor" Tom Castro, as recounted by Jorge Luis Borges in his early book *A Universal History of Infamy* (1935). Born Arthur Orton to a Wapping butcher in the "the drabness and squalor of London slums [*barrios bajos*]" (31), Castro runs off to sea as a youth, jumps ship at Valparaiso, Chile, and knocks around South America before finding himself in Australia, where on a "run-down corner" in Sydney he makes the acquaintance of the "genius" Ebenezer Bogle, a black servant, by helping the latter overcome his fear of traffic and cross a busy city street. Bogle persuades his obese friend Castro to return to London to impersonate the fit and trim military officer Roger Charles Tichborne, believed lost at sea. Tichborne's grieving aristocratic mother is deceived by the improbable impostor, but after her death the heirs bring suit against him. Aided by Bogle's genius—he convinces the jury that "Tichborne" has been the victim of a Jesuit plot—Castro wins the case, only to lose the impetus for the deceit when Bogle is struck dead by a carriage in Primrose Hill. Borges resurrects not only the slums and pennydreadful tales of the previous century, but he intimates quite strongly that they continue to circulate the trade routes of the world no matter what the writers at the heart of the empire may have decided. What began on the mean streets of a Victorian slum, he suggests in the diction of the Buenos Aires underworld, returns to upscale Primrose Hill as a preposterous feat of imposture that is both historical and literary. Needless to say, this is a very different literary genealogy than we have been accustomed to expect from modernism, which tends to define itself as the negation of the slum and its associated meanings.

The nineteenth-century English industrial city had no exclusive rights to urban poverty, either spatially or temporally, but it is possible to see in it the beginnings of a new mode of describing that poverty and of a new need to fix its time and place, for which the term *slum* was eminently suited. Among the European languages, *slum* is a much newer coining than the French *taudis* or the Spanish and Italian *tugurio*, the English *shanty*, the Portuguese *cortiço*, or even the American *tenement*, but that's partly because this older set of words is primarily descriptive and limited in scope to a single dwelling—a shack or a hovel, but also a shelter—or to a single building.[1] The unknown derivation of *slum* helps account for a symbolic power quite different from the descriptive combinative forms that the French, Spanish, Italians, Portuguese, and Germans, among others, use to describe poor and informal urban settlements more broadly: *quartier pauvre* or *bas quartier*, *barrio bajo* or *barrio suburbi[a]*, *quartieri bassi*, *bairro da lata* [tin], *Elendsviertel* or *Elendsquartier* (*Elend* meaning misery or wretchedness). The lack of any iconic quality has made the word easily adapted to a variety of languages: *slum* is current usage in, among others, Finnish, German, Slovakian, Swedish, and Tagalog. Moreover, since the United Nations reintroduced in the 1990s a term that had been effectively banned from the social sciences and the "habitat vocabulary," the word *slum* has returned to prominence worldwide in academic and policy discussions of urban poverty over a variety of apparently more neutral terms.[2] So, while a myriad of local and indigenous terms and practices exist, the slum looms over representations of urban poverty just as modernity and European modernism loom over local, marginal, and less codified or differently developing forms of modernity and modernism.

MODERNIST SLUMS

The slum is a modernist invention in several ways. First of all, in the philological sense it is a new coining, for it has no known etymology (Dyos, "The

Slums of Victorian London") and is distinct in meaning from prior, related words such as *ghetto* (a bordered, and traditionally walled, urban enclave for an ostracized community) or *court of miracles, holy land, rookery*, and other terms for particular urban spaces appertaining to or sheltering criminal, divergent, or otherwise marginalized communities. It is also a spatial invention, a fundamentally new concept of modern urban planning that facilitates the division of once integrated cities into discrete zones either worthy or unworthy of preservation, secure or dangerous, licit or illicit, above- or underground. And it is a literary invention that appears as a topos, especially in the novel, from the early nineteenth century, becomes a dominant motif in realism and naturalism in the second half of the nineteenth century, and is repressed almost wholesale in modernist literature of the first half of the twentieth century, to say nothing of modernist art and architecture. Because of this vexed relationship, the modernist slum can help us grasp what it would mean to expand the scope of modernism temporally, spatially, and generically, just as it can also help clarify the tensions and contradictions involved in that same expansion.[3] For, strictly speaking, global modernism can have no slums in it, or it ceases to be modernism.

So, the slum is a slippery concept. While a vehicle and consequence of modernity, it is also a repudiation of it, a sign of its failure or of resistance to its ostensible progress. If modernity is about how "all that is solid melts into air" and modernism is about giving apt expression to that feeling and process, the new, nineteenth-century usage of the word "slum" is all about solidity, about something so unmelting in air that it defies description and requires the physical act of demolition in order not to represent it but to make it disappear. You cannot enjoy a slum; you can only look away from it in horror while calling for its demolition. To be sure, you can get a lot of play from the act of looking with your eyes shielded or from staring with them so wide open that they risk being blinded by what they see. The first type of looking is usually called realism; the second, naturalism. Established as literary genres in the nineteenth century, these representational strategies persisted throughout the twentieth century in what we might term nonliterary discourses such as popular journalism, the social sciences, urban planning, and politics, where the slum is consistently if not obsessively present as a sign of an obstruction to the process of modernization or as evidence of its dangerous state of incompletion. Whether the discourse of outrage is mobilized to justify social inequality, real-estate speculation, and political oppression or in order to claim basic human rights for the poor and the dispossessed, it deploys the full range of the slum's negative power as an image of disease, filth, suffering, and hopelessness.

Modernism, in its canonical formulation, repudiated both of these strategies as the province of a played-out and misguided Victorianism. As Virginia Woolf put it in her polemical dismissal of the novels of Arnold Bennett, H. G. Wells, and John Galsworthy as "unworthy" of the right to be called "books at all" (and by "books" I presume she means here something like what we have tended to call "modernist" books): "In order to complete them it seems necessary to do something—to join a society, or, more desperately, to write a cheque" (*Mr. Bennett and Mrs. Brown*, 12). Realism, which sought to integrate the slum into the greater fabric of the cityscape, enforced a Whig narrative of history and a moral calculus widely considered to have been bankrupted by the end of the First World War, if not before: those worthy of being saved would be saved, those proved unworthy would be damned, and the slum would be either cleared or left behind. Naturalism, which limited its purview of the urban to the slum at its most prurient and most extreme, was concerned either to expose its threat to the broader social fabric it impinged upon but was distinct from or to describe in the full horror of its details the plight of those trapped within. But in so doing, it eliminated any trace of human agency or autonomy. For a modernist, the slum posed two problems. First, it restricted the call for social change to the elimination of what was not modern, even as the definition of "modern" was seen as, at best, complacent and conformist or, at worst, oppressive and imperialist. Second, as the epitome of what was not modern, it eliminated any positive alternative to status-quo modernity through the prejudgment of its own overwhelmingly visceral negativity.

An inverse relationship between the kind of materiality embodied in the slum and the kind of reality sought by modernists militates against their easy coexistence. Reading against the grain can restore slum materiality to modernist texts, but I want to argue that a more productive project is to explore the relationship between the two. The question to ask is not so much *where* the slum is in modernism as what its absence means and how we can make that meaning critically productive. A trace of the slum *is* there, certainly, when Gregor Samsa dies an unwanted vermin in *The Metamorphosis* (1915), the shell-shocked Septimus Smith tosses himself on the spikes of the iron fence enclosing the entrance to his lower-middle-class building in *Mrs. Dalloway* (1925), or Matthew O'Connor trawls through a fever-dream Paris in *Nightwood* (1936). The slum becomes, in this sense, what modernism can never name or represent directly, the truths it must only gesture at, because to describe them directly has been rendered impossible by the phenomenon of modernity. Here, it is the source of modernism's *Sprachkrise*, and all of the complex stylistic gyrations are always only there to create a no-space from which that truth, "the horror," can emerge without being named directly because to name it would vitiate the power, the very identity of the truth.

Modernism, as Adorno eloquently established, was, quite simply, the end of the road. Perhaps we could take the garbage cans inhabited by Nagg and Nell in Beckett's *Endgame* (1957) as a final, vitiated trace of the slum in the abstract space of the negation of everything, the last vestige of the possibility of representation, signifying by its presence the impossibility of representing anything else, its banality and ugliness reminders that we couldn't possibly still want anything to do with it anyway. But then, why couldn't we? As in *Endgame*, the ultimate truth of the slum remains a phenomenal one: the fact that people do live in it, no matter how unspeakable and unrepresentable it may be as an abstract quantity or aesthetic quality, and the fact that people do prefer living in it to not living at all. And this truth is what makes the slum such a powerfully enduring topos for the modernist imagination. Can we thus see in the project of the new modernisms an endeavor to rediscover some concept of life, of pleasure or happiness or utopia, in the experience of modernity, a grudging concession that these qualities will have to be discovered in modernity since the illusion no longer remains that we have anywhere else outside of modernity to look for them? High modernism was nothing if not ascetic and forbidding, and even when it might proffer the faintest hint of enjoyment, that hint must be bracketed and quarantined as far as possible. And always in terms of the slum: modernist sex and violence are given to us as sordid and perverse, and the most urban of the modernist writers tend to be the most sordid and perverse, the most slumming and gritty of all—Céline and Döblin, Miller and Barnes. No wonder modernists tend to give Joyce a free pass here; however difficult *Ulysses* or *Finnegans Wake* may be to read as novels, they at least make no apologies for the relief of laughter and small pleasures. Whatever else they may be doing, they are not slumming. Like urban representations before the invention of the slum, Joyce's Dublin exudes identical qualities, if in different keys, no matter where in the city one may be. If the modernist style is an attempt to reintegrate the city (or the world) through linguistic invention, the slum is the inevitable trace of its failure to do so. As long, that is, as we continue to judge modernism according to its own all-or-nothing formulations.

SLUM, BEFORE AND AFTER MODERNISM

There is a complex temporality to the slum as urban space and as concept. Historically, slums are a product of the processes that create big cities and segregate and condense the populations within them; slums are a direct consequence of modernization and industrialization. But slums are also temporally unstable since a slum is not generally purpose-built but the result of the informal conversion of existing urban dwellings or the occupation of an empty or underutilized urban space. Most commonly, slums arise in previously middle-class areas that have descended more or less rapidly into poverty. Moreover, since a slum, once labeled as such, will eventually be razed, redeveloped, or (more recently) gentrified, the material spaces tend to be transitory, although their legends frequently outlive their materiality. Most big cities will always have something we can call slums, but those slums will not always be the same ones. And because *slum* is a symbolic and relational term rather than a legal or purely descriptive designation, whether a neighborhood becomes or ceases to be a slum over time and whether a city becomes or ceases to be identified more or less broadly with its slums may have little or nothing to do with the material circumstances of that neighborhood or city. Also, because the slum is by definition a reused or appropriated space rather than a newly created one, it accumulates multiple and often contradictory meanings rather than the unified or coherent one that, say, a purpose-built row of terraced houses, a new suburb, or a unified apartment block might have. The latter forms may, as they are lived in, acquire contingent meanings in conflict with or contradiction to their original conception. But the term *slum* is a designation we give to an urban space whose dominant conceptual meaning has wholly ceased to dominate. Finally, the experience, or the representation of the experience, of living in a slum or visiting a slum can change radically depending on who is having the experience or performing the representation. One of the effects of a global modernism and a global modernity was a growing consensus discourse about the slum; one mark of being modern was the ability to recognize and employ that discourse, just as one mark of a cosmopolitan author was the ability to recognize and employ the discourses of modernism. At the same time, because it was a global discourse, it could be mobilized for a number of different purposes besides simply echoing the categorical definition of "slum."

A typical strategy of the new modernist studies has been to extend the temporal boundaries of the movement's core decades both forward and backward. A related strategy would consider also the effect of historical distance on how we read modernism. For example, one may conjecture as to how strongly the postwar descent of the neighborhood of Harlem into both material and representational slumdom may have influenced the oft-noted exclusion of the Harlem Renaissance from the modernist canon during that same period. How could postwar critics reconcile the vibrant urban portraits and the freighted ambiguity of pleasure and oppression, high art and low jazz, uptown and downtown, with the brutally infernal visions of Upper Manhattan and the South Bronx that dominated the cultural register from the 1960s until quite recently (and as they dominated the annals of sociology and urban planning from even earlier on)? How could the mixed registers of the Harlem Renaissance make any critical sense in a postwar America where popular culture was freighted with the utopian pleasures of suburbia and the dark urban horrors of film noir and where urban studies was ruled by Lewis Mumford's repudiation of the hellish megalopolis and the Chicago School's structural model of neo-Victorian moralism? Similarly, how could anything resembling a working-class or slum modernism be countenanced in a postwar Britain whose urban centers of working-class sociality had been bombed into oblivion and whose newly built council housing projects appeared either life-sapping prisons or concrete jungles breeding criminal delinquency? How could any middle ground be possible in a Cold War climate in which the CIA funded modernist art criticism and worked to undercut the legitimacy of figurative art and where any trace of conventional mimesis risked the taint of socialist realism and communism? The slum was either a death trap for the poor, a breeding ground for crime and radicalism, or simply nonexistent. If modernism had successfully repudiated the slum as the emblem of the literature it wanted to replace, the postwar reception of that modernism successfully eliminated any trace of the slum that a different approach might actually have been able to find within the culture of the years from 1890 to 1945.

One of the fallacies of conventional accounts of modernism by Woolf and others is to establish a certain year—usually sometime in the second decade of the twentieth century—as the absolute line of demarcation between one generation of writers—the Edwardians, or nonmodernists—and another— the Georgians, or modernists. As if, in Woolf's case, Wells (d. 1946), Bennett (d. 1931), and Galsworthy (d. 1921) had all ceased producing in 1910, as if no "modernist" had done anything before that year, and as if no one else somehow might have had a different relationship to that chronology. Certainly, it remains a persuasive periodization, and it perfectly accounts for what Woolf wanted it to account for: the sort of literature she was writing and wanted to be written and the ways in which she wanted it to be read. There are no slums in it, and she discounts even the thought of slumming out of it (when young Elizabeth Dalloway escapes eastward on the #11 bus, she barely makes it as far as the western edge of the City, much less all the way to the East End). But what happens when we periodize differently? What would a Victorianist modernism look like, and what would modernism look like if the postwar reception of modernism hadn't happened to it? What does it mean in this context when the Victorianist historian Seth Koven blithely ignores conventional periodization and begins his recent study *Slumming* with the simple statement that "For the better part of the century preceding World War II, Britons went slumming to see for themselves how the poor lived" (1)? That different periodization suggests a Victorianist approach to thinking about the question of modernism, but it also raises fascinating questions about the explicit repudiation of the material detail Woolf objected to so much in Bennett, for Koven justifies his timespan according to a shift in methodology in which the slum is not ghettoized but integrated into a broader critical framework. "To understand how elite men and women thought about the poor," he argues, "required me to reckon with how they thought about sex, gender, and themselves" (4).

Nor did all experimental or innovative writers between the wars feel the need to define what they were doing according to a break with the past. Among the "exercises in narrative prose" (15) collected in Borges's *Universal History of Infamy* and recounted in what he calls the "entonación orillera" ("popular accent," literally "accent of the outskirts") of working-class Buenos Aires are half a dozen from the nineteenth century, ranging from London's Arthur Orton to the gangs of New York and from outlaws on the Mississippi to Billy the Kid in the American West to Ching Shih, the so-called Widow Pirate of the China Sea, and spanning five continents, the seven seas, and more than a millennium of history. Typically, Borges claims from the start to be merely the "translator and reader" of an eclectic collection of sources, of which he cites the Victorian Robert Louis Stevenson, the early twentieth-century (but not modernist) G. K. Chesterton, the expressionist director Josef von Sternberg's "early films" (presumably the atmospheric lower-depths dramas *Underworld* [1927] and *The Docks of New York* [1928]), and "a particular biography of the Argentine poet Evaristo Carriego [1883–1912]" (15). *A Universal History of Infamy* constitutes something like a slum tour of the modernizing world, but one that finds in those slums not the negation of modernity but an alternate, nonmaterial, history of it that recounts both its infamous treatment of those it consigns there and the unique qualities of "infamy" exhibited by its inhabitants and visible nowhere else.

Periodizing modernism within some strand of Victorianism provides one strategy for reading it differently; it's a strategy that has been deployed in a highly productive manner, for example, in the recent literary, visual, and cultural production of steampunk, which attempts to imagine the twentieth century as if modernism had not occurred or had occurred very differently. What happens to modernism when we imagine it from the point of view of the nineteenth century—not the straw man that sat back and was shocked by its provocations but the one dreamed of by writers around the globe for whom alternative nineteenth-century modernities might still have been taking shape around them long into the twentieth century? And, by the same token, what happens to modernism when we filter out the distortions of the 1950s and 1960s? In many ways, the new modernist studies can be characterized as an often tacit answer to both of these questions: a post–Cold War taking-stock and a pre-1910 recuperation. It is telling that a leading light in both of these new narratives is the slum. As the Scottish novelist Jane Findlater (1866–1946) wrote around the turn of the century of a "slum movement in fiction" that she considered finally to have reached as close to "truth in their picture of slum-life" as such an approach could do, "it may be seriously questioned whether all attempts in this sort are in vain" (*Stones from a Glass House*, 187). If the slum in fin-de-siècle fiction marked the apogee of a certain kind of realism and the slum in postwar fiction worked to impede the recognition of any social content in modernism or the recognition of literature with any social content *as* modernist, how can we use the slum topos as a tool for rethinking the temporalities of modernism?

SLUM, ABOVE AND BEYOND MODERNISM

Rethinking the temporalities of modernism does not eliminate the years 1890–1945 any more than rethinking its geography eliminates London and the other imperial capitals as its centers of gravity. Borges's "rereading" (*Universal History of Infamy*, 15) of the past ranges through world literature from a base in Stevenson and Chesterton, just as the trajectory of the infamous impostor Arthur Orton takes him from London around the world as Tom Castro and back again as a resurrected Roger Charles Tichborne. Among the key functions played by the slum in the economy of modernity is as a migratory hub, the teeming point of ingress and egress of a city that would prefer its identity fixed in space and looking resolutely forward. That the underworld cant from which the term *slum* emerged has been variously attributed to Irish, Roma, and unknown impostors can help remind us that slums appear in cities primarily as a consequence of migration, be it internal or external. They are the parts of the city where its past and its future intersect or, rather, where that intersection is conventionally located and understood to be occurring. Such a process could be more strictly defined in the medieval ghetto, for example, where clear rules determined movement and restricted the rights of the ghetto population, even though in the everyday life of the city movement between the ghetto population and the rest of the city was in many circumstances more fluid and less clearly defined than in theory. But ghettoes, like city walls, are created in order to endure; slums are created in order to be eliminated. What happens to the population of a slum when the slum is demolished? Symbolically, it is eliminated; practically, it simply sticks around, hovering nearby and making a new slum, or it travels the global network of slum spaces, each one, as Borges slyly suggests, both identical in its qualities to its fellows and unique. Ghettoes testify to ossified power relations (or at least to the desire to have those relations ossified); slums testify to the instability of those same relations. "Mobility, not fixity" is central to the definition of the slum, asserts Koven (*Slumming*, 9), even as, I would argue, the function of the designation is to attempt to fix a single identity onto an essentially mobile phenomenon.

The slum is a prime location for the colony in the heart of the empire or for those elements of the colony that are the hardest to fix or control (as opposed, for example, to its commodities in the shop windows). Not only were slum and colonial outposts "linked in the British imperial imagination as places of freedom and danger, missionary altruism and sexual opportunity" (Koven, *Slumming*, 21), but the global mobility instantiated by empire was a major factor in the creation of slums, just as imperial forces tended to create slums within colonial cities by surrounding, containing, and newly framing old parts of those cities by new neighborhoods designed on the modernist model. So, the slum can remind us of the way periphery and center are mutually constituting forces, and its absence from modernism per se can remind us of the literal absence of that relationship from modernism. The further we move from the traditional centers of modernism, however, the more we find other ways of thinking about the slum, of negotiating between the modern colonial city and the mixed slums, just as they negotiate between the discourses of modernism and the other mixed discourses also available. And the more we seek alternate geographies of the traditional centers of modernism, the more we also find other ways of thinking about the slum, as when Monica Ali reverses Elizabeth Dalloway's bus ride in *Brick Lane* (2003) to bring her Bangladeshi family from Whitechapel to St. James's Park, a sightseeing tour by a family in local residence for thirty years and a daughter who insists that London is "where she's from." Nothing about the bus has changed in the eighty years between novels: same route, same double-decker design, same conductor taking their tickets. And nothing about the parks and palaces of the West End London Nazneen and her family see has changed either. The geography and the social divisions are identical, just as, Ali implies, the descendants of the Dalloways are; what has changed are the slum dwellers. But how do you narrate that turning of the tables, and is turning them as simple a process as riding the bus in the opposite direction? Ali needs the slum to underpin the liberatory anger and oppressive violence of Nazneen's tale, but she also needs Woolf's modernism in order to narrate an outside to that slum and to grant subjectivity and agency to Nazneen, her daughters, and her friends.

The novel concludes with another bus ride, this one exclusively female and only for fun. Blindfolded, Nazneen knows the bus is taking her somewhere, but we are kept in suspense about where *there* is, except that it is somewhere on the route. It turns out to be an ice-skating rink, an artificial modern recreation of the frost fairs held on the frozen Thames at irregular intervals between the fourteenth and early nineteenth centuries. "But you can't skate in a sari," she protests. "This is England," her friend tells her. "You can do anything you like." Ali introduces the operative cliché of skating on thin ice in order to resist it, only to substitute the more recent cliché of multiculturalism. What could be more persuasive evidence of having left both modernity and modernism behind than this last blithe assertion, the words with which the novel concludes? It's not hard to see it as a capitulation by Ali to the easy solutions of realist fiction, the happy ending, the ground firmly beneath the heroine's feet, with her rented ice skates the grudging but gracefully finessed concession to the tenuousness of the twenty-first century. But that would concede that modernism somehow still holds the key to the representation of reality, and Ali has just spent an entire novel enumerating the limits of modernism. Like Borges back in the 1930s, the vernacular reminds us that the black hole of the modernist slum sucks into itself what is most seductive about the slum for those with a foot still outside modernity. For the threat of being melted away is equally the promise of remaking yourself anew, and endlessly. And that threat is also the promise of vernacular literature, the one that never ends.

SLUM—TO USE THE VERNACULAR

Rejecting the slum novel for making of the slum a strange sensation rather than seeking to grasp its essence, Chesterton argued that "the kind of man who could really express the pleasures of the poor would be also the kind of man who could share them" ("Slum Novelists and the Slums," 281). Writing in 1905, Chesterton took his examples from theatrical melodrama, but it was the cinema that was best equipped to capture "the pleasures of the poor" and suggest the positive potentialities of the slum. And it is the popular cinema and other examples of what Hansen has termed "vernacular modernism" that constitute the largest body of slum depictions within the conventional time-frame of modernism, that have dominated the representation of slums since the end of that timeframe, and that are the most popular, if not the only, slum representations actually consumed by slum dwellers. Hansen stresses "the new physicality . . . the material presence of the quotidian" and the "new sensorium" that Hollywood and other world cinemas "produced and global-ized" along with images and sounds. "Even the most ordinary commercial films," she argues, "were involved in producing a new sensory culture." The context of the slum, however, complicates the spatiotemporal coordinates of this argument, for what the cinematic slum offered was not so much a new sensory culture as an *old* sensory culture. Or, better, it offered a way of repre-senting neither the old sensorium of realism nor the new, anodyne sensorium of modernity but a novel combination of the two. Where modernism was able to represent this combination only in the contradictory negation of an absent presence—the unspoken slum that localized a vanished truth that could not otherwise be enunciated—the spectacular visuality of vernacular modernism conjured an unforeseen meeting of conventional narrative, a rapidly codify-ing visual grammar, and what Trotter calls "low mimetic detail," or "*existence as such*" (*The Uses of Phobia*, 133, 126). The cinema's ability to register visual detail in the margins of the frame permitted the slum to appear in its every-day qualities as well as in the mythic qualities of its narrative function.

Even more than in the experimental modernist cinema of surrealism, im-pressionism, or Soviet montage, mainstream narrative cinema could narrate the slum while also simply documenting it. This is not to argue that there is a documentary quality to the cinematic slum—whether constructed in the studio or filtered through a camera, the actual urban spaces never appear *as such*—but to suggest that the qualities of the slum otherwise unavailable to modernist representation—the actual experience of living in them and the potential for agency and subjectivity within their spaces—did find their way into narrative cinema of the period in ways they were not able to do in other forms.

There is no single cinematic slum, and they range in their depiction from the symbolic hells of German expressionist city cinema to the outlaw paradises of the Hollywood musical to a hard-hitting naturalism that makes the lower-depths novels of Zola and Gissing feel restrained. In all of them we find the familiar tropes of the slum from popular literature: the power of invention admired by Borges in his infamous impostors, the transgressive sexuality and disregard for convention of Louise Brooks's Lulu or Musidora's Irma Vep, the powerful criminality of Mack the Knife and myriad other underworld gangsters and criminal masterminds, and the working-class sociality and community almost wholly absent from modernist literature. Of course, we also find all of the clichés and framing devices that work to keep us from taking these tropes too seriously: the concluding punishment of Lulu at the hands of Jack the Ripper or the restoration of order following any threat by the slum to flow out of its boundaries. The spatial qualities associated with the slum are especially amenable to suspense and to comedy, as in Chaplin's *Easy Street* and *The Immigrant* (both 1917), for the lack of order, the protean character, and the unpredictability associated with them in the nineteenth century are precisely those ingredients that also contribute best to the thrills and spills of slapstick.

The slum musical would take these contradictory qualities to their extreme. The musical slum was sufficiently stylized to vitiate any real sense of suffering or menace in the setting. The sheer artificiality of the scene—the saturated colors or glossy black and white, the conventionality of the action and types, the simultaneous repression of sexuality and foregrounding of desire and emotion in song—stresses the performativity of slum roles. The "Limehouse Blues" number in the 1946 revue film *Ziegfeld Follies*, performed by Fred Astaire and Lucille Bremer as a down-and-out Chinaman and a kept Chinawoman in a gaslit and foggy Victorianist set derived primarily from the world of D. W. Griffith's silent melodrama *Broken Blossoms* (1919), well exemplifies the multiple layers of artifice and mediation involved in vernacular modernism's evocation of desire. First, the song itself is performed in a basement bar by jazz singer Harriet Lee, whom we glimpse from outside through ground-level windows as her voice plays over the soundtrack. Foregrounded is an entire melodrama in miniature, with Astaire smitten by Bremer's yellow-sheathed comfort girl. Caught in a shootout subsequent to a robbery, he dies holding an oriental fan he has snatched from the broken window for the girl. The dance sequence occurs within his dying imagination, a red-tinged fantasia of Chinoiserie. Returned to "reality," we find the fan broken as the girl brings her patron, modeled on Peter Lorre's Mr. Moto, into the shop to buy the fan. When she finds it, broken, in Astaire's hands, she drops it to the ground. It's a performance, in other words, of the already derivative melodrama of Griffith's film twenty-five years earlier, abstracting the Victorianist elements of slum Orientalism, female virtue and vice, and unrequited desire into the dance within the dream. But even within the most lurid tragedy, the sequence argues, inhere beauty and fulfilled desire. That it's also a preposterous fantasy is part of the point.

Musical performance in the slums, however outlandish in premise, always reminds us that creativity, hope, and pleasure exist in the slums along with poverty, suffering, crime, and degradation. Indeed, it argues that the latter are fundamentally productive of the former, however unlikely the connection might appear in "realist" terms. That's a dangerous argument, especially made in aesthetic isolation, and this is one reason the modernists repudiated it so virulently, especially during the 1950s. Yet it was an essential ingredient in the popular film genres of modernizing postwar nations such as Mexico, where the *cabaretera* genre found a way to permit women to sing in public, through the fallen-woman scenario that brought them to the slum as cabaret performers; Brazil, where the enduring *chanchada* genre set romance among comic antics and samba singing in the favela; and postindependence India, where the early peak of the Bollywood musical combined slum narratives with intricate and exuberant playback musical sequences, as in the blockbuster hits *Awaara* (1951) and *Pyaasa* (1957). Especially when approached as a global phenomenon, the slum musical offers a vernacular modernism—formally experimental, self-reflexive, allusive, and genre blending—that was also highly popular. Without question, these films are negotiating the tensions between modernization and tradition; the very technology of the cinema provided a vehicle of modernity able to stand in for so many others.

That cinema-going was one of the most pleasurable and popular forms of everyday modernity should not be underestimated. In their complex investment in and distance from the economic forces of the big city, and in their reliance on but distance from the popular quarters of those cities, the movies could express the gamut of experiences and emotions encompassed by the slum rather than solely their powers of negation and destruction. The tradeoff, certainly, was in the overtly fantastic quality with which those experiences and emotions were represented, the kind of vernacular improvisation we hear in the first recorded usage of the word in Pierce Egan's *Boxiana* (1812), "The flowing harangue of a dusty cove . . . lavish with his slum on the beauties possessed by some distinguished pugilist." These slum fantasies are a far cry from contemporary exposés such as Mike Davis's *Planet of Slums* (2007), for which the slum operates as the topos for the very different desire for basic human rights. Can we conceive of a slum capacious enough to contain the fanciful panegyric of a ramshackle sportsman, the justified outrage of the contemporary activist, and the indelible traces of "experience as such" while flexible enough to account for all of their contradictions? I suggest that we can find it, as the Victorians used to say, just around the corner from the bright city lights or, as Borges suggested from Buenos Aires, in that modernism where the mean streets of East London can be found nestled amid the fashionable West End homes of Primrose Hill.

NOTES

1. *Taudis* derives through medieval French from the old Scandinavian word for a tent and originally referred to the cover placed over a shored boat; *tugurio* derives from the Latin word for roof; *shanty* from the French *chantier* ("a place where one sleeps and stores one's work things"); *cortiço* from the word for beehive; *tenement* from the Latin for "freehold," its primary English meaning—the American usage to describe an overcrowded apartment building built for poor people dates from the second half of the nineteenth century (*OED*).

2. For a nuanced account of the UN revival of the word "slum," see Gilbert, "The Return of the Slum."

3. I am adapting these categories from Mao and Walkowitz's characterization of the "temporal, spatial, and vertical directions" in which the new modernist studies has expanded in recent years ("The New Modernist Studies").

WORKS CITED

Ali, Monica. *Brick Lane*. New York: Scribner's, 2003.

Borges, Jorge Luis. *Historia universal de la infamia*. 1935. New York: Vintage Español, 2012.

———. *A Universal History of Infamy*. 1935. Trans. Norman Thomas di Giovanni. New York: Penguin, 1975.

Chesterton, G. K. "Slum Novelists and the Slums." In *Heretics*, 267–284. London: Bodley Head, 1919.

Davis, Mike. *Planet of Slums*. London: Verso, 2007.

Dyos, H. J. "The Slums of Victorian London." *Victorian Studies* 11, no. 1 (1967): 5–40.

Findlater, Jane Helen. *Stones from a Glass House*. London: James Nisbet & Co., 1904.

Gilbert, Alan. "The Return of the Slum: Does Language Matter?" *International Journal of Urban and Regional Research* 31, no. 4 (2007): 697–713.

Hansen, Miriam. "The Mass Production of the Senses: Classical Cinema as Vernacular Modernism." *Modernism/modernity* 6, no. 2 (1999): 59–77.

Koven, Seth. *Slumming: Sexual and Social Politics in Victorian London*. Princeton, N.J.: Princeton University Press, 2004.

Mao, Douglas, and Rebecca Walkowitz. "The New Modernist Studies." *PMLA* 123, no. 3 (2008): 737–748.

Trotter, David. *The Uses of Phobia: Essays on Literature and Film*. Oxford: Wiley-Blackwell, 2010.

Woolf, Virginia. *Mr. Bennett and Mrs. Brown*. London: Hogarth, 1924.

14. STYLE

JUDITH BROWN

Yet, with the invocation of the foreign or of the desert as the true site of style, one has to wonder: can a discussion of style and modernism avoid the familiar tropes of Orientalism, with its distant lands, its mystery, its foreign tongues, its tantalizing darkness? Does a focus on the unknown and mysterious—those things we acknowledge as central to any account of style—depend upon the colonial imagination, relying on its habits of thought, using distant lands to stand in for that language we cannot know?

Style is, on its surface, self-evident yet difficult to define. It suggests temporal aptness: the right line at the right moment, whether in fashion or interior design (or in any number of other stylish things). But it also refers, of course, to modes or manners of writing. When we talk about style in writing, we approach an aesthetic category almost too familiar to contemplate yet at the same time strangely unfamiliar. It is the unfamiliar in style that I address in the following pages. The unfamiliar has been a hallmark in critical accounts of style, as when Gilles Deleuze calls it "the foreign language within language" ("He Stuttered," 113). Style brings out the most foreign element of language: the foreign in Deleuze's phrase is foreign to itself, pushing language to its utmost extreme and altering its rhythm. Style makes language strange; it defies the informational demands of language and speaks in another key altogether. If style is foreign to language, then the effects of style make the writer foreign to her own text. This is less the death of the author, one might say, than her emigration to new and unknown lands, at work in an unknown tongue.

That style is foreign may seem counterintuitive: isn't style instead what makes writing familiar or recognizable? Surely we recognize a sentence by Virginia Woolf—its particular cadence, its dashes and exclamations—even if the particular work is new and unknown to us? Is style what is most familiar about the work of art, or is it what we can never understand about it? It's a strange predicament, to find no stable ground on which to approach the knowability of style. Style itself thus makes strange our capacity to question, makes unfamiliar what we imagine the familiar to be. Perhaps this is why the idea of the foreign, the unknown, and the evasive clings to the concept.[1] Jacques Rancière uses a geographical metaphor to capture this sense of the foreign as an unknown or distant land when he (citing Flaubert) defines it as "a work without substance: no longer the work as cathedral, but the work as desert" (*Mute Speech*, 115). It's at first a perplexing metaphor, this turn to the desert—vast, figuratively (if not actually) empty, indifferent to human concern—in contrast to the cathedral, that monument to human ingenuity and culture. Why is the desert, without ornamentation or artifice, the appropriate figure for style, rather than the more obvious cathedral with its sublime heights, its carved stone, its stained glass? For Rancière and the French literary tradition he cites, style is empty and without boundary: it is the other language of language that turns away from content or substance ("style has no substance," goes the adage). In fact, style, in its privileging of the surface, turns away from meaning itself and thus from any representational obligation. The desert comes to stand for uninterrupted surface or for the blank and otherworldly spaces that free rather than crowd the imagination. Further, the desert in this metaphor is not a repository for meaning like the cathedral, heavy as the latter is with belief and human striving, with ideology and history: in this way Rancière distinguishes style from the substantive or meaningful. The desert of style has much greater affinity with an imagined emptiness that cannot, like the soaring arches of a cathedral, be bent to a singular purpose.

I offer these examples not as definitive but as representative of a critical history that thinks about style through tropes of the unfamiliar. Style, in these and other critical accounts, seems to lift itself away from representation, from the real, or from history itself. Yet, with the invocation of the foreign or of the desert as the true site of style, one has to wonder: can a discussion of style and modernism avoid the familiar tropes of Orientalism, with its distant lands, its mystery, its foreign tongues, its tantalizing darkness? Does a focus on the unknown and mysterious—those things we acknowledge as central to any account of style—depend upon the colonial imagination, relying on its habits of thought, using distant lands to stand in for that language we cannot know? We might trace a lineage of style, as Deleuze and Rancière do, from Flaubert through Proust, writers who idealize the capacities of style to transform life into art. In what might be called the beginnings of modernism in the mid–nineteenth century, then, there was an "unprecedented and strategic emphasis on style" (Schlossman, *The Orient of Style*, 1) that signaled the transformation to what would become modernist aesthetics. An intensified interest in style suggested a fascination with the nonrepresentational capacities of language, the as-yet-unknown, and style became understood as a figure for the other in language.

Flaubert, Baudelaire, and Proust all turned to the Orient to figure this otherness in phrases such as "the poetic dazzle of the Orient" or "the Orient of style."[2] Perhaps the Orientalism of style isn't surprising given the nineteenth-century European context of the discussion, yet this figure persists and offers a way to understand one of our basic (and thus most powerful) terms for talking about artistic expression. Critical history and colonial history intersect, and they form the network of relations through which we understand style today.

When we turn from Europe and consider works produced across the globe, does our critical understanding of style shift? Does style continue to invoke the foreign and unfamiliar? How does style speak in other contexts? I argue here that style's foreign tongue continues to make strange the work of art and indeed offers a particularly relevant way of thinking about modernism as a global, transnational, or planetary movement, one that paradoxically incorporates a colonial history at the same time as it empties that history of its privileged meaning. Thinking critically about style inexorably delivers us into the unseen and inescapable quicksands of an Orientalist desert, as Western paradigms and colonial histories exert their centrifugal force. We can never be free from the ideological conditions of our reading, yet style offers us, I want to suggest, the possibility of an unfamiliar language, one potentially foreign to those conditions that structure our lives or our readings. Attending to style offers one way to avoid reiterating Western narratives of modernism: style is, after all, a manner of expression rather than an authoritative message. Indeed, it speaks without authority, without substance, without interest. Style in my argument enables a forgetting of the world, which is an essential, if unexpected, way of thinking transnationally.

How can that be? Style has always been transnational, is indeed intrinsically transnational. Nation-states, identities, and regulatory institutions—those ordering structures that orient and determine our experience of the world—are irrelevant to this other language without limit or border or rule or law. Style speaks most compellingly when the necessary (legal, ethical, economic, political) order in which we live our lives moves off the page and allows for something other to speak, something unfamiliar and not grounded in the world as we necessarily know it. To demonstrate what I mean, I'll look at two exemplary figures as case studies of sorts—one a fiction writer, the other a painter—whose styles speak subtly and invoke something other, something that unsettles the familiar and demands a kind of forgetting. R. K. Narayan is known as a writer of the local and is often claimed to be the quintessential voice of India. Amrita Sher-Gil—flamboyant painter, cosmopolitan, polemicist—claims herself as India's first modern artist. Both began their careers in the volatile years of late colonial India yet developed styles that smooth over the era's political complexity. Their texts are marked by understatement and a general aesthetics of quiet, even passivity. Why are they exemplary? These figures make style their central concern, and they do so in order to find a language that has not been coopted by political discourse. That is, they seek an unimagined space without idealizing the work of art, as perhaps Flaubert or Proust did, but instead enabling the foreign or otherworldly to make itself known. Indeed, they thematize the larger operations of style itself: what I'll call its blank gaze, its emptying capacity, and even what has been argued is its "nothing to say" (Barthes, *Writing Degree Zero*; Miller, *Jane Austen*; Leighton, *On Form*).

How might these figures resituate style and its critical elaboration as a fantasy of the Orient? How might they turn critical attention away from an Orientalist fantasy empowered by imperial history? Both navigate and elaborate in their works the paradoxes of style itself and more importantly demonstrate a way of thinking about style without political imposition or invisible ordering structures. This is not necessarily unique to these two particular figures, but I choose them for the encounters they stage between the known and unknown, for their reputations as major figures of early twentieth-century Indian arts, and because their work turns away from overt political content (that is, from art with instrumental desires) in favor of something that appears to be more passive. Indeed passivity is a central feature of their styles and becomes the sign of style itself.

Narayan, if you aren't familiar with his name, was among the first generation of professional English-language writers in India. Over his long literary career (he died in 2001 in his mid-nineties) he published (among other things) fourteen novels and hundreds of short stories, nearly all of which take place in the fictional South Indian town of Malgudi (you might compare it to Faulkner's Yoknapatawpha or Hardy's Wessex). Aware of the absence of

Indian models of novel writing and equally aware of the colonial legacy that guided his tastes, Narayan set out to create a distinctly Indian landscape and cast of characters, and he would create his own uniquely ironic voice. Choosing to write in English, he called himself and those other writers of his generation "experimentalists" ("English in India," 22) for taking up the English novel form and, with it, the English language.

Narayan's novels—insistently gentle, almost uniformly quiet (one study is titled "R. K. Narayan, the Unobtrusive Novelist")—have been consistently characterized as limpid, calm, unaffected, flat, and neutral. Makarand Paranjape argues that this is the strategy of his style: Narayan "solves the problem of representing India in English by crafting a style of artful plainness . . . a kind of deculturation, so that 'Narayanese' becomes a 'basic' language which may stand for itself or any other (Indian) language" (*Another Canon*, 42). He thus overcomes, Paranjape goes on to say, "the difficulty of containing, confining or reducing the multiculturalism and multilingualism of India [via] the restricted, simplified and flattened monolingualism of English." It's a fascinating idea: that by flattening a language, simplifying and paring it back to its most basic components, it might be "decultured," made more universal. Narayan does ease the reader's entry into his writing with his directness of expression, the brevity of his sentences, and with an immersion into the rhythms and textures of Malgudi. The surprising result, however, given the bareness of expression, is one of dreaminess; the word "enchanted" is frequently used to describe the fictional landscape he creates. Perhaps Paranjape's theory can account for the broad ways that English comes to speak this landscape, yet it doesn't get at the elusive or indeterminate quality of Narayan's writing, the dreaminess that his style evokes.

Narayan's style is perpetually self-effacing and ironic: this is particularly visible and is especially interesting, I think, in his depiction of writers. Writers, in Narayan, don't really write. They dream big dreams but then produce hackneyed poetry, or don't finish their writing, or don't even write at all (even in his self-representations, Narayan seems to emphasize all the ways he avoids the labor of writing). Perhaps it's part self-effacement and part irony that lead Narayan repeatedly to depict the failed writer, or the foolish writer, or the wannabe writer who lacks talent or initiative or material. Self-effacement is understood by Narayan as central to the act of writing (and we might recognize this style as that of impersonality). He most explicitly stages the absence that style demands as a kind of event, even a traumatic one, in his autobiographical novel *The English Teacher*.

The novel's protagonist, Krishna, is an ironically rendered, half-hearted teacher with huge and unrealized poetic ambition. The first half of the novel recounts the pleasures of his domestic life with his wife and child, his ineffectual attempts at writing, and his growing alienation from the aesthetic education that has formed him and that he is paid to espouse at the Albert Mission College. When his wife, Susila, becomes sick and dies of typhoid at the midpoint of the novel, the novel itself experiences a kind of break (sometimes it's referred to as a broken-backed novel). Not only is Krishna engulfed in grief, but as he attempts to contact his wife in the spirit world, the novel's terms of engagement shift. Krishna's proud secular rationalism is tested, and the notion of writing is itself transfigured. Susila's death alters the fundamental terms of the novel in its self-conscious rationalism and introduces a story about writing that speaks in another key altogether.

The link between Susila, death, and writing is made early in the novel. In a comic scene, Krishna complains that he has nothing to write about, so his wife suggests he model a poem on her. He agrees but writes down Wordsworth's "She Was a Phantom of Delight" ("She was a Phantom of delight / When first she gleamed upon my sight; / A lovely Apparition, sent / To be a moment's ornament," etc.) and then chides her for her forgetfulness when she doesn't recognize it from her English literary anthology (she was very impressed, thinking he'd written it on the spot). "Aren't you ashamed to copy?" she asks. "No," he replies. "Mine is entirely different. He had written about someone entirely different from my subject" (47). It's a scene that raises questions about original and copy and situates those questions within the context of colonial India and its practice of aesthetic education. Krishna insists that his repetition of Wordsworth can never be Wordsworth; it introduces a new subject in a new context and thus absents or negates the poem's very center. Reciting Wordsworth's poem, Krishna transforms Susila, envisioning her as the phantom of writing. And this is what she'll become.

When Susila dies, Krishna's notion of writing too dies. The death occasions an epistemological break at the center of *The English Teacher* that radically destabilizes its grounds of knowing (something like Mrs. Ramsay's death in Woolf's *To the Lighthouse*). Krishna, overwhelmed with grief, meets a psychic who offers to put him in touch, through writing, with the spirit of his dead wife. You might imagine the scene: a psychic medium renders himself entirely passive, emptying his ego and removing himself from the exchange between grieving husband and dead wife as he scribbles out her messages in pencil. Note the absence of authorial agency here: "Letters appeared on the paper. The pencil quivered as if with life. It moved at a terrific speed across the paper; it looked as though my friend could not hold it in check. It scratched the paper and tore the lines up into shreds" (113). The pencil is the powerful agent (bringing to mind the Latin origin of the word "style," the *stylus* or *stilus*), and the message seems made of pure energy, delivered with a kind of volatile force. The two men and the spirit wife are made passive in relation to the writing. Krishna must struggle to give up his secular beliefs, and even as he draws some solace from the encounters with his dead wife, his trust will be continually tested: "After a few moments, I asked, 'Do you remember the name of our child?' The pencil wrote: 'Yes, Radha.' This was disappointing. My child was Leela" (115).

How can a ghost be so forgetful? Rather than the omniscience of the spirit world, we have partial knowledge, weakly remembered and inaccurately expressed. Susila gets most of the facts wrong, and we'll remember that Krishna had said to his wife earlier, "I should be ashamed to have your memory." What is the significance of Susila's forgetfulness? And what could it have to do with style? It certainly demands, as the pencil erratically scrawls its message, a kind of faith, a forgetting of reason, and a rejection of material fact. This might be likened to automatic writing (the kind we associate with early Gertrude Stein), except that the writing is working against the notion of the automatic, the learned message repeated from memory or drawn from an unconscious informed by repressed desires or former wounds. The forgetting of material facts, of historical evidence (such as the name of their daughter), is part of the process of writing in this scene. This forgetting is required if Krishna is to communicate with his wife. She is teaching Krishna to become the medium, to make himself passive, so as to find a direct mode of expression that is not simply a reproduction of something already learned.

Here, he learns to listen to something foreign (in the figure of his wife) and to reject the literalism that obscures his ability to communicate with her, as it has obscured his attempts at writing. In the brief sessions in which her voice is rendered in frantic pencil marks on the page, Susila is teaching Krishna how to write in a key tuned to pleasure, not to fact. Rather than standing in as the mere subject of the poem, she figures its very possibility. Krishna discovers a way to empty Wordsworth's poem and to find a new, as-yet-unwritten place from which to write India. He learns by absenting himself, by giving himself over to style, as it were, to the otherness in language. Krishna begins the novel as a model of the self-disciplining rational subject, loyal to the clock and to his anthology of English literature. As the novel closes, he is a subject without occupation (he quits his job at the Albert Mission College), without responsibility (he has sent his daughter to live with his parents), and without borders, having successfully merged with the enabling phantom of his wife. This lesson of style turns on a negative principle, one that enables forgetting, unmaking, and detachment. The central event, then, in Narayan's autobiographical novel is the turn away from realism, fact, or materiality and toward a phantom who offers us an unexpected way to theorize style as a passive encounter with the otherworldly or foreign.

The generally placid surface of Narayan's fiction, its reticence on questions of empire, and its universalizing impulse, even as Narayan is seen as the quintessence of India, has led to charges of excessive niceness and passivity. And we can see Narayan's passive impulse in *The English Teacher*. Surprisingly, given the pleasant tone and the quiet comedy of his work—more evident in his other novels—we also recognize the impulse toward negation, perhaps best exemplified in Narayan's pervasive irony. Paul de Man might helpfully remind us here that irony turns on negation, on undoing, and on the gesture of turning away from one thing in order to suggest the shadow of another. Critics of Narayan's bland likeability simply do not attend to these shadows that define his style. V. S. Naipaul, for instance, accuses Narayan of indifference when he hears the older writer say, "India will go on." Annoyed by the very inactivity of this phrase, India will go on, Naipaul builds his case against Narayan's writing: "Out of a superficial reading of the past, then, out of the sentimental conviction that India is eternal and forever revives, there comes not a fear of further defeat and destruction, but an indifference to it. India will somehow look after itself; the individual is freed of all responsibility" (*India*, 15). Narayan's art, in this view, fails to live up to an ethical standard, one that employs protest and political rhetoric. The indifference of Narayan's style, captured in the phrase "India will go on," speaks of an understanding that goes beyond the political structure. This is not Gandhi's passive resistance, then, but something other in its indifference.

What can we say about this charge of indifference or passivity? I've already noted the relative indifference of style to material reality, to substance, or to plot. Style in Narayan becomes a way of speaking in a new register and without the restrictions that might otherwise govern a life. Indifference contains no message, no preference. It refuses hierarchy. This is what frustrates Naipaul. The work that asks nothing, that makes no demands, is perhaps indifferent because it is not tied to political will. It does something different; it insists on a communication of the unfamiliar and the noninstrumental. And it communicates it best to the passive subject, as Susila will teach Krishna to be.

The principles of style as they emerge in Narayan's work, then, may be understood as operative in style more generally: first, the impersonality of style, estranged from its author yet providing the work with a personality; second, the indifference of style to the identities or experiences of its subjects, even as it records lives lived within the framework of history; third, the language of reverie spoken by style, rather than realism, even as the work obeys the laws of representation; and, fourth, the unfamiliar or foreign in style that makes visible or audible the particularity of a text not necessarily reducible to time or place or ideology. Each principle requires a kind of forgetting, a nonrootedness in bounded spaces or subjectivities, a lifting away from the already-known.

If Narayan thematizes the alternative languages that writing might speak and the complicated pleasures that attend an encounter with the foreign, Amrita Sher-Gil may be said to revel in the sensual power of the painted image that speaks across time, nation, and identity. As an iconoclastic painter and rebel, Sher-Gil envisioned a life and an art without restriction. "I think all art," she writes, "has come into being because of sensuality: a sensuality so great that it overflows the boundaries of the merely physical. How can one feel the beauty of a form, the intensity or the subtlety of a colour, the quality of a line, unless one is a sensualist of the eyes?" This hardly sounds indifferent. Sher-Gil defied all ruling conventionality and all restrictions that might impede her aesthetic vision, her sense of what exceeds the limits of the physical. Her writing is big, ambitious, sometimes bombastic, but in her paintings, her aesthetic is controlled and detached from emotion. Her portraits suggest the detachment of its subjects, a governing indifference. A note she wrote to Jawaharlal Nehru is telling (in many respects): "I like your face, it is sensitive, sensual and detached at the same time" (*Letters*, 421). She brings this quality of impassive detachment to her portraits and creates a kind of aesthetic of indifference: "I am always attracted to people . . . who don't trail viscous threads of regret behind them" (419).

Conceived, as her father would say, in Lahore and born in Budapest, Sher-Gil stands, as one critic puts it, "at the cosmopolitan helm of modern Indian art" (Mathur, "A Retake," 515). She was, another critic adds, "cosmopolitan by reflex, with the confidence that came from the aristocratic, artistic and intellectual milieu into which she was born" (Ananth, *Amrita Sher-Gil*, 13). She spent her childhood in Hungary, then India (her mother was Hungarian and her father Indian), and her artistic training would take her back to Europe, where she entered the École des Beaux Arts in Paris at the age of sixteen. In Paris she engaged the aesthetic movements of the day, developing a taste for painters like Gauguin and Van Gogh, and then at twenty-one she decided to move back to India, whose people she would paint, almost exclusively, for the rest of her short life (she died, apparently of peritonitis, in Lahore at the age of twenty-eight).

Sher-Gil, a far more polemical figure than Narayan, explicitly wanted to write India in new, modern form. "Europe belongs to Picasso, Matisse and Braque and many others," she asserted in 1938. "India belongs only to me" (*Letters*, 491). Yet style, she discovers, involves a letting go: "I know . . . how difficult it is to surmount the barrier of the style one has adopted. And to 'let oneself go' once one has acquired the habit of severe & strict discipline is perhaps more difficult than to subordinate an unruly spirit to discipline" (475).

Perhaps Sher-Gil contemplates such a "letting go" in her 1934 *Self-Portrait as Tahitian* (figure 14.1), where the artist stands in the place of Gauguin's models. Paul Gauguin is faintly viewed as a shadow, perhaps even as an effect of Sher-Gil. She incorporates her elder-sensualist, makes him an effect of her illumination: he blends into her body yet seems to shelter her, pagoda-like. One might read him as looming or as threatening to overpower, but his transparency, his sandwiching between the portrait of Japanese women and the artist herself as modern primitive shifts the French painter as towering authority. In fact, he's empty: he's a medium, a tonal ground, a transition, rather, connecting past and present, collapsing them into the promise of an artistic future. Sher-Gil layers aesthetic histories, from Japanese antiquity to contemporary Paris, yet centered on the colonial subject, the artist as Tahitian. The portrait thus hinges on a complex fantasy that involves forgetting as it empties its source texts and creates new power relations, by placing us within intimate proximity to the calm, voluptuous, and emphatically present model/artist who appears indifferent to our gaze. There's much more to say about this painting, from its engagement with Orientalist or primitivist discourses, to its commentary on the power of influence, to its recognition of the deep representational history of the female nude. There is political content to be gleaned, to be sure, if one takes these categories into account, but Sher-Gil's style self-consciously floats free of the past, a willed forgetting, then, as the artist envisions new languages of expression.

FIGURE 14.1 Amrita Sher-Gil, *Self-Portrait as Tahitian*.
Source: Images courtesy of Vivan Sundaram.

In India, Sher-Gil would find those new languages as she turned her attention to portraying the grey-blue melancholy of the nation, to reimagining her chosen home on large canvases where she pictured groups of ghostly people. What moved her, she wrote, "was the vision of winter in India—desolate, yet strangely beautiful—of endless tracks of luminous yellow-grey land of dark-bodied, sad-faced, incredibly thin men and women who move silently looking almost like silhouettes, and over which an indefinable melancholy reigns" (*Letters*, 249–251). In *Hill Women* (figure 14.2) she presents us with such a ghostly group, standing in physical proximity but each figure remaining isolated, almost in seclusion, despite the touch of a hand and the reality of their shared material conditions. Blank gazes look before them, unseeing perhaps, and without will. Yashodhara Dalmia describes the painting as a "silhouette of women standing in grave silence reminiscent of tombstones . . . in effect an elegy to the living" (*Amrita Sher-Gil*, 75). Death intrudes into life in this portrait of austerity. This is a portrait, too, of survival, perhaps, or of life and death as permeable or interpenetrating conditions. We witness this portrait of shared fate that doesn't reject representation as such but alters its terms, what Dipesh Chakrabarty has called "pierc[ing] the veil of the real" (*Provincializing Europe*, 150). Sher-Gil discovers in her intensified form, color, and line a formal alternative to the real, a way of seeing that isn't documentary. She had expressed frustration with the "futility" of many depictions of India that she claimed betrayed no "human understanding"; she opposes these renderings to her own, founded on a new style to express the desolate yet strangely beautiful.

The language Sher-Gil would work to develop in her paintings was one of possibility and paradox, the merging of incompatible truths. Structuring contradictions will be a hallmark of sorts of Sher-Gil's work. *Three Girls* (figure 14.3) is a portrait of isolation, three figures suspended in time, their shadows on a dingy wall, no aesthetic history visibly supporting them or buoying them into their futures, as in *Self-Portrait as Tahitian*. There is no abstraction here. This is a painting that presents to us three figures, but its realism is altered, muted, made to speak a language of reverie rather than realism. Sher-Gil offers us visual simplicity in this picture of biding time, again, this winter in India. The women appear bored, perhaps, indifferent, listless; the painting is rich in its palette, suffused with color, even as it portrays a kind of lack, best illustrated by that open and vulnerable hand, an emblem perhaps of want, or of grace in the form of a *mudra*, the gesture of the hand that signifies multiply. Here we witness detachment, indifference, and impersonality. No hierarchy

FIGURE 14.2 Amrita Sher-Gil, *Hill Women*.
Source: Images courtesy of Vivan Sundaram.

FIGURE 14.3 Amrita Sher-Gil, *Three Girls*.
Source: Images courtesy of Vivan Sundaram.

governs this group, and no narrative is easily imposed. Style speaks as absence, something Sher-Gil was thinking about as she read Proust's "amazing book": "One has to be in a certain state of mind to be capable of enjoying it, a state of absolute calm with no preoccupations of any sort, not even interests outside it, a complete though receptive void . . . to enjoy the fantastically subtle & slow rhythm of Proust's style" (*Letters*, 475).

Two Girls (1939, figure 14.4) will more completely evade narrative itself in its explicit turn toward the emptying language of style. Sher-Gil returns to the female nude form but removes the layers of irony that characterized her earlier *Self-Portrait as Tahitian*. The girls, one standing and one seated, are sculptural in their smooth planes and simplified lines. One is swathed in white sheets, her dark skin balanced by the fragment of an ancient sculpture we see at the left. The standing girl has empty blue space in place of her eyes— a vacant gaze, then, without focus or intent. The jeweled color often favored by Sher-Gil is drained from this canvas—what remains are the blended siennas and umbers of skin tone and earth. Is this the work as desert? Form and color are simplified, and there is a quality of detachment despite the girls' physical relationship (one hand resting on a shoulder, indeed blending into the shoulder, the hip leaning in). The simple planes and lines of the portrait raise many questions; indeed questions here, rather than answers, demand the viewer's imaginative attention. Despite the solid lines and smooth planes of this painting, certainty itself must be forgotten. Is this a portrait of indifference or desire? What is this relationship depicted? What do these girls share? What imaginary gratifications or symbolic desires frame their relationship in time or in space? Does the longing include that of racial equality? Sexual desire? Is this another kind of self-portrait? A picture of the divided self—Hungarian and Indian—posed with ancient tradition? Or a future, positioned next to a past? A refusal of temporality itself? This is, I would argue, a painting of possibility, of the very condition of possibility. The style of the painting—its blankness, its empty gaze, its quiet palette—indeed creates the grounds for questioning and resists any impulse to determine these girls.

So what can style do—or undo—for us or for the study of modernism conceived transnationally? For one, style as a methodological entry point offers an unlimited horizon not tied, at least in determining ways, to a historical moment, nation, or political framework. Freed from the important work of ideological critique, we can observe a text's other languages, other loves, and other means of expression. Style might also deliver the difference that the transnational makes: the working with, alongside, and against the canon; the

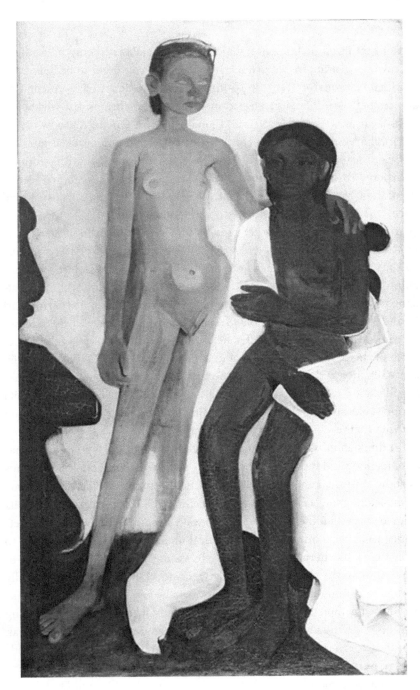

FIGURE 14.4 Amrita Sher-Gil, *Two Girls*.
Source: Images courtesy of Vivan Sundaram.

trace of tradition or influence; and the unpredictable alchemy of aesthetic borrowings drifting free of history. If modernism continues to be defined as a primarily formal movement pushing against the limits of representation and aesthetic tradition, its transnational reconception brings new vocabularies to bear, new particularities, and new demands. One of these would be a critical accounting of those concepts like style that quietly, even invisibly guide our reading. This is another way to reiterate Susan Stanford Friedman's assertion: "To simply read non-Western narratives is not enough; we need to think about their implications for narrative theory" ("Toward a Transnational Turn," 24) and, I would add, for aesthetics more broadly.

In Sher-Gil, we inevitably get a sense of impersonality or indifference: the models look away, their gaze often only legible in contradictory terms. Sher-Gil's art brings something new into the world that is neither mere representation nor revelation of the already there. Art thus alters the real by visualizing possibility through its other language of style. When the art critic Karl Khandalavala, Sher-Gil's friend and champion, compares her work to the serene image of the ancient Buddha, he captures something of this gaze, something of the productively empty, and something of Sher-Gil's legacy: "Miss Sher-Gil's men and women are not beautiful in a conventional sense but her simplification of form has much of that purity and balance which the Gupta period sculptors brought to their dreaming Buddhas. Her figures also dream but with their eyes wide open" ("Introduction," n.p.).

To think about style is necessarily to think beyond the boundaries of nation, identity, and history. To think about style in global modernism is thus to allow ahistorical musing, to confront the incomprehensible, to step away from meaning into a far more unstable realm. India will go on, these portraits seem to suggest indifferently. Style will always be embedded in discursive networks, will always be shaped by its critical moment, yet we should attend to its evasions, its alternative, even unlikely, visions. Let me return, by way of conclusion, to the closing lines of Narayan's novel. Krishna has successfully learned to communicate with the spirit world by emptying himself, by making himself completely passive. As the novel ends, he has a vision of standing with his wife: the now reunited couple are "gazing on a slender, red streak over the eastern rim of the earth. A cool breeze lapped our faces. The boundaries of our personalities suddenly dissolved. It was a moment of rare, immutable joy—a moment for which one feels grateful to Life and Death" (*The English Teacher*, 184). In these lines, I would venture, we discover ourselves at the ground of global modernism. Its ground is a ghost, a ghost who necessarily forgets and whose forgetfulness will seize and disturb the process of writing itself. With the view of a red streak over the eastern rim of earth, Narayan establishes a distant, even planetary understanding of the lesson learned by the English teacher. Sher-Gil's figures too dream, although their gazes give little away even as they open new and remarkable vistas of possibility. This, then, is the power of style, to take us to this window, to make us see and to make us hear—to make us sensible to—worlds not bound by our own.

NOTES

1. Critics including Walkowitz (*Cosmopolitan Style*), Ngai (*Our Aesthetic Categories*), Leighton (*On Form*), and Miller (*Jane Austen*) link style to the mobile, the evasive, and the evacuative.

2. Edward Said writes that in Nerval and Flaubert, the Orient "was not so much grasped, appropriated, reduced, or codified as lived in, exploited aesthetically and imaginatively as a roomy place full of possibility" (*Orientalism*, 181). Said, however, thinks about style as a mode of inhabiting authority, a "style of being": "style is not only the power to symbolize such enormous generalities as Asia, the Orient, or the Arabs; it is also a form of displacement and incorporation by which one voice becomes a whole history, and—for the white Westerner, as reader or writer—the only kind of Orient it is possible to know" (243).

WORKS CITED

Ananth, Deepak. *Amrita Sher-Gil: An Indian Artist Family of the Twentieth Century*. Munich: Schirmer/Mosel, 2007.

Barthes, Roland. *Writing Degree Zero*. Trans. Annette Lavers and Colin Smith. New York: Hill and Wang, 1967.

Chakrabarty, Dipesh. *Provincializing Europe: Postcolonial Thought and Historical Difference*. Princeton: Princeton University Press, 2000.

Dalmia, Yashodhara. *Amrita Sher-Gil: A Life*. New Delhi: Penguin, 2006.

Deleuze, Gilles. "He Stuttered." In *Essays Critical and Clinical*, trans. Daniel W. Smith and Michael A. Greco. Minneapolis: University of Minnesota Press, 1997.

de Man, Paul. "The Concept of Irony." In *Aesthetic Ideology*, ed. Andrzej Warminski, 163–184. Minneapolis: University of Minnesota Press, 1996.

Friedman, Susan Stanford. "Toward a Transnational Turn in Narrative Theory: Literary Narratives, Traveling Tropes, and the Case of Virginia Woolf and the Tagores." *Narrative* 19, no. 1 (2011): 1–32.

Khandalavala, Karl. Introduction. Quoted from *Shantaram's Bungalow*, http://www
.users.zetnet.co.uk/sparkes/edpics/amritashergil/amrita2.htm.

Leighton, Angela. *On Form: Poetry, Aestheticism, and the Legacy of a Word*. Oxford:
Oxford University Press, 2007.

Mathur, Saloni. "A Retake of Sher-Gil's *Self-Portrait as Tahitian*." *Critical Inquiry* 37
(2011): 515–544.

Miller, D. A. *Jane Austen, or The Secret of Style*. Princeton, N.J.: Princeton University
Press, 2003.

Naipaul, V. S. *India: A Wounded Civilization*. New York: Vintage, 2003.

Narayan, R. K. *The English Teacher*. Chicago: University of Chicago Press, 1945.

———. "English in India." In *A Story-Teller's World*. New Delhi: Penguin, 1989.

Ngai, Sianne. *Our Aesthetic Categories*. Cambridge, Mass.: Harvard University Press,
2012.

Paranjape, Makarand. *Another Canon: Indian Texts and Traditions in English*. New
Delhi: Anthem, 2009.

Rancière, Jacques. *Mute Speech: Literature, Critical Theory, and Politics*. New York:
Columbia University Press, 2011.

Said, Edward. *Orientalism*. New York: Vintage, 1978.

Schlossman, Beryl. *The Orient of Style: Modernist Allegories of Conversion*. Durham,
N.C.: Duke University Press, 1991.

Sher-Gil, Amrita. *Amrita Sher-Gil: A Self-Portrait in Letters and Writings*. 2 vols. Ed.
Vivan Sundaram. New Delhi: Tulika, 2010.

Spivak, Gayatri. *An Aesthetic Education in the Era of Globalization*. Cambridge, Mass.:
Harvard University Press, 2012.

Walkowitz, Rebecca L. *Cosmopolitan Style: Modernism Beyond the Nation*. New York:
Columbia University Press, 2006.

Walsh, William. "R. K. Narayan, the Unobtrusive Novelist." *Review of National Literature* 10 (1979): 59–69.

15. TRADITION

RACHEL ADAMS

The trans-American cohort that emerges out of Mexico City brings into view a different set of aesthetic and political commitments than those associated with the more familiar transatlantic modernist collectives. It prompts us to revise the more familiar story of modernism centered on Europe, in which "tradition" refers either to the cultures of outdated European ancestors or the aesthetics plundered from primitive regions of the world. Sharing an interest in formal innovation and the adoption of new or hybrid media, the Mexican modernists espoused a different relation to tradition as they aspired to produce an art that addressed the politics of revolution.

Modernism is often defined as the antithesis or repudiation of tradition. "No age can have been more rich than ours in writers determined to give expression to the differences which separate them from the past," wrote Virginia Woolf, "and not to the resemblances which connect them with it."[1] James Joyce's Stephen Dedalus remarked famously of his desire to escape from tradition, "history . . . is a nightmare from which I am trying to awake."[2] Situating the futurists "on the last promontory of the centuries!" F. T. Marinetti declared war on the institutionalized guardians of tradition: "we will destroy museums, libraries, academies of every kind." Theodor Adorno concurred when he remarked, "modernism negates tradition itself," and T. S. Eliot's influential "Tradition and the Individual Talent" sought to preserve the besieged concept via its dynamic engagement with history.[3] These views are reiterated by critics, for example, the retrospective survey of Astradur Eysteinsson, who writes decisively, " 'Modernism' signals a dialectical opposition to what is not functionally 'modern,' namely 'tradition,' " and "the self-conscious break with tradition must, I think, be seen as a hallmark of modernism."[4] Spanning more than half a century, writing from varied political and aesthetic investments, these diverse authors all conceive of modernism as a decisive break with tradition. But despite their differences, they share a vision of modernism that operates within a strikingly circumscribed geographical frame, one centered on major European cities such as London, Paris, and Berlin and radiating outward to the eastern United States.

In what follows, I will argue that the regionally specific nature of these authors' claims informs their account of modernism's relation to tradition in ways that have not yet been fully recognized. I ask what would happen to their understanding of tradition if we were to reorient familiar modernist geographies, centering them around different locales or tracing out more scattered and decentralized circuits of cultural exchange. I focus on the particular trans-American cohort that emerged out of Mexico City, where—for a brief period—authors, artists, critics, and policy makers sought to revitalize Mexico's ancient indigenous traditions in the service of a modern project of social, cultural, and political reform. Taking Mexico and the Mexicanist element in international modernism as an example, I hope that this essay can serve as a model that can be exported to the analysis of modernisms emerging from other understudied regions of the world. Doubtless each will have its own histories and agendas, but together these more geographically specific accounts will further destabilize the centrality of Europe within narratives of global modernism while providing alternative understandings of the meaning and function of tradition within modernism's aesthetic and political projects.

Like their better-known counterparts, Mexican modernists emerged from the devastating experience of war determined to repudiate European tradition. But where Europeans saw their traditions shattered and dispersed (Eliot's "fragments shored against our ruins"), Mexicans emerged from their ten-year civil war committed to reclaiming traditions that had been suppressed by a leadership in thrall to foreign influences. Postrevolutionary Mexicans rejected the Europhilia of the Porfirio Diaz regime, instead embracing their own history and culture with a nationalist fervor akin to that of the postcolonial societies of the later twentieth century. Where European modernists plundered the exotic cultures of Asia, Africa, and the Pacific Islands, Mexican modernists sought to recover indigenous traditions they saw as their own authentic heritage. Yet the strongly nationalist bent of the Mexican modernists did not make them provincial. Many of the artists and intellectuals involved with Mexican modernism were seasoned cosmopolitans who traveled abroad and engaged with cultural developments in other parts of the world. At the same time, Mexico was becoming a magnet for an international cohort of leftist scholars, authors, and artists attracted to the social and political projects of the postrevolutionary state, which saw culture as integral to social reform. These circuits of travel and exchange turned Mexico City into a trans-American bohemia that rivaled its counterparts in Greenwich Village, Paris, and London.

Despite the comparison to Europe and the United States, the Mexican bohemia was marked by significant disparities that shaped its participants' attitudes toward the traditions they incorporated into their creative expression. Although Mexico City was a cosmopolitan metropolis, much of the country remained untouched by industrialization and ravaged by the effects of civil war. If modernist expression arises in response to the conditions of modernity, these were different in Europe or the United States than they were in Mexico, which had only partially entered the industrial age. In the Mexican context, the distance between tradition and modernity, "primitive" and contemporary, felt greater but also more proximate. As Peter Wollen and Laura Mulvey argue, compared to European modernism, "'ancient' history was chronologically much closer and also in many ways culturally closer" in Mexico. Because "in the Mexican revolution, appeals to the pre-Conquest Indian past still had a political value . . . it was possible for political and artistic avant-gardes to overlap in Mexico in a way that they never could in Europe."[5] The view of tradition endorsed by this Mexican-inspired modernism was shaped by its emergence out of a largely agricultural national setting, one with a significant indigenous population that still spoke the languages and maintained the cultures of its ancient precursors. The revolution had mobilized these people with its promise of land redistribution, workers' rights, and vision of a more democratic Mexican state. Thus, while many Euro-American modernists embraced the dictum of an apolitical "art for art's sake," Mexicans saw art as closely tied to revolutionary goals for social and political reform.

When Mexico enters the conversation about international modernism, it is typically through the towering figures of the muralists José Clemente Orozco, David Alfaro Siquieros, and Diego Rivera, whose international training and reputations brought them into the circles of their Anglo-American and European counterparts. But the modernist community in Mexico was far broader and more heterogeneous, and the aesthetics of Mexican modernism more diverse, than is implied by this trinity. Women played an integral role in creating and sustaining the Mexican renaissance, a term coined by the Mexican anthropologist Anita Brenner. Many were important artists in their own right; others curated exhibits, arranged contacts, published articles, organized salons, and provided other occasions for informal gathering. Of these women, Katherine Anne Porter, Anita Brenner, and Tina Modotti are a particularly interesting trio. All three traveled to Mexico, where they found inspiration in the modernist embrace of Mexico's shifting social and political landscape. By charting their journeys to and from Mexico, we can track the spread of a Mexican element in international modernism. Their modernist work is both local, in that it could not have emerged anywhere but postrevolutionary Mexico, and global, in that it was attuned to events and cultural developments abroad.

THREE LIVES

Katherine Anne Porter

While most American participants in the high-modernist culture of the 1920s recognized travel to Europe as a crucial rite of passage, Katherine Anne Porter went to some lengths to distance herself from those circles. Although as a young woman she had wished to visit Europe, she did not make it there until 1931, when she sailed by an unconventional route that departed from the Mexican port of Veracruz. In Europe, she moved among the literary giants of her time and came away unimpressed, writing in her *Notebooks*:

> One evening a crowd gathered in Sylvia's bookshop to hear T. S. Eliot read some of his own poems. Joyce sat near Eliot, his eyes concealed under his dark glasses, silent, motionless, head bowed a little, eyes closed most of the time, as I could see plainly from my chair a few feet away in the same row, as far removed from human reach as if he were already dead. Eliot, in a dry but strong voice, read some of his early poems, turning the pages now and again with a look very near to distaste, as if he did not like the sound of what he was reading.[6]

Porter's tableau captures the end of an era. Decades later, she would express gratitude for having avoided the movement at its apogee. Her years in Mexico meant that she "missed more than half of the 'twenties in Greenwich Village; I missed the Hemingway epoch in Paris; and I think these are two of the luckiest misses I ever made."[7] Proudly asserting her artistic autonomy, Porter turns to Mexico as an alternative site of expatriate community.

While these memories are colored by the compensatory embellishments that often characterized Porter's self-representation, they nonetheless represent an effort to posit a different relationship to tradition than many members of her generation. Living in Mexico on and off between 1920 and 1931 left an indelible mark on her writing, her understandings of art and politics, and the subsequent course of her life. Porter's work as a reporter, reviewer, translator, and curator helped inform American and European audiences about the activities of the Mexican modernists. Her own writing was also deeply influenced by contact with Mexican indigenous traditions. Porter's indigenism landed her in a contradictory position. On the one hand, she recognized that the Mexican renaissance was responsible for introducing Mexico's traditions to the world; on the other, she believed that such attention exerted a corrosive effect on the pristine folk she so admired. She found the equanimity missing from her own life only in ancient precontact societies, and she came to believe that the revolution, which claimed to represent the Mexican people, had caused them more harm than good. She concluded that it endangered indigenous traditions and people by exposing them to the corrosive influence of modernity.

Porter's bleak and contradictory views are most apparent in her first short story set in Mexico. "María Concepción" (1922) illustrates the corrosive impact of the revolution and the impossibility of preserving native tradition from the encroachments of modernity. Porter begins by romanticizing her protagonist, María Concepción, whom she describes as "walk[ing] with the free, natural, guarded ease of the primitive woman carrying an unborn child."[8] But María's life is neither natural nor primitive. Her village is policed by local revolutionaries, and most of its population is employed by an American archeologist who promises "to uncover the lost city of their ancestors." Porter casts a skeptical eye on his project by adopting the perspective of the villagers, who see little value in the broken and dirty artifacts they are exhuming.

The story's political message rests on the contrast between the protagonist and her nemesis, María Rosa, who runs away with María Concepción's husband, Juan, and joins the revolutionary forces. María Rosa is brave and tenacious. She defies tradition by leaving home and bearing Juan's child out of wedlock. María Concepción is more closely tied to various forms of tradition. At a time when the church was associated with the antirevolutionary values of the Porfiriato, she is deeply religious and proud to have been married by a priest. The silent and long-suffering María Concepción remains rooted in place while Juan and María Rosa travel the countryside. When Juan deserts the army and returns home, he beats María Concepción and orders her to cook for him, which she does without complaining. As if to embody her own deadly stasis, María Concepción's child is stillborn.

Critics have tended to treat María Concepción's revenge as a feminist victory, if an ambivalent one. Ostracized from her community and enraged at Juan's betrayal, she brutally murders María Rosa. When the corrupt local police attempt to charge her with the murder, Juan and the other villagers come to her defense, justifying María Rosa's death as punishment for her immorality. The exonerated María Concepción assumes responsibility for María Rosa's newborn son and returns home with Juan. At the story's end, Juan contemplates his future with despair, knowing that with the death of María Rosa, his hope for change is extinguished. By contrast, María Concepción is satisfied by this return to the status quo, even though it means living with a faithless, abusive husband.

If there is a victory at the end of this story, it goes to the woman who embodies antirevolutionary values over the woman who fights for a different world. "María Concepción" thus condenses many of Porter's most pessimistic reactions to the revolution. Drawn to the promise that unionization and land redistribution were the first steps toward the creation of a more just society, she came to believe that the *campesinos* were incapable of fighting for their own rights. She idealized precontact rural folk and the traditions they embodied but wrote them into an impossible position whereby they were corrupted as soon as they encountered the forces of cultural or political modernization.

The combination of idealization and despair that characterized Porter's responses to indigenous tradition sounds much like modernist primitivism. To what extent, then, does it matter that her writing is set in Mexico? The difference is that Porter's primitivism grows directly from her exposure to the Mexican indigenists, who saw the turn to traditional folk aesthetics as a political gesture in keeping with the populist goals of the revolution. While she shares their blind spots, she also participates in a political project that involves not simply celebration of the primitive but a more general elevation of indigenous folkways, a project that was closely tied to Mexican agendas for social reform. Thus, via Porter's work we see how the recovery of tradition may be a political as well as an aesthetic project. "María Concepción" is about the ways the Mexican Revolution has failed the populations it claimed to represent, but it is also an instance of a modernism whose political and aesthetic project grew from an engagement with and a reworking of particular American traditions.

Anita Brenner

When Porter—the native Texan who went to Mexico—wrote an enthusiastic review of Anita Brenner's *Idols Behind Altars* (1929),[9] she created a concrete link to an author who—at age eleven—had completed a reverse migration when her family fled war-torn Mexico for Texas. Like Porter, the adult Brenner was drawn to the political and cultural promises of postrevolutionary Mexico, and she would eventually make it her permanent home. Through their work as writers, curators, and advocates, both women opened lines of contact between Mexico and the United States as well as between North America and more distant parts of the world. Brenner accepted this role more optimistically than Porter, fashioning herself as a cultural ambassador who championed Mexican artists and Mexican political causes abroad throughout her adult life. Whereas Porter sought purity in indigenous people and arts, Brenner affirmed *mestizaje* as Mexico's richest cultural tradition. Without denying the brutality of Spanish conquest, she found strength in the fusion of European and indigenous elements within the modern Mexican populace. And whereas Porter saw the corruption of the Mexican state as a reason to repudiate the revolution, Brenner sought to recuperate its legacy as a way of managing strained relations between the United States and Mexico.

Written for a foreign audience, *Idols Behind Altars* surveys Mexican art from precontact indigenous civilizations to the present. Its title, an allusion to the persistence of pantheistic beliefs despite the imposition of Christianity, is a metaphor for Brenner's understanding of the Mexican people, whose *mestizo* vitality comes from the mingled cultures of colonizer and colonized. *Idols Behind Altars* puts Mexico at the center of the history of American art. Brenner argued that, in contrast to a moribund Europe, Mexico was witnessing a creative resurgence akin to the artistic awakening that had taken place across the Atlantic five centuries earlier. As Mexican artists returned home from Europe to recover their native American traditions, they were shifting the history of art itself from established centers in Paris, Italy, and Spain to Mexico and the Americas.

Whereas Porter sought out the uncorrupted culture of the Mexican Indian, Brenner saw no possibility for such an escape from modernity. She recognized indigenism as a distinctively modern formation that entailed a recovery of "folk" traditions in response to contemporary aesthetic and political needs. Rather than fleeing from modernity, Mexican artists had been prompted by their encounters with modernism to reconsider the themes and traditions of their own American culture. As they translated modernism into a New World context, they envisioned their art working in the service of revolutionary politics. In Brenner's view, the Mexican artists were, at least in theory, at one with the people, rather than being elevated above them like their European counterparts. The Mexican renaissance thus introduced an alternative modernism, one that was politically engaged and attuned to the needs and values of a mass public. Its antecedents were to be found not only in ancient indigenous art but also in the traditional forms of the *corrido* and *pulqueria* murals, which had long been a means of self-expression for ordinary Mexicans. In the spirit of these popular forms, the new artists aspired to work collectively and anonymously and to use widely accessible visual media that did not require literacy for their meanings to be understood.

While the artist might express solidarity with the people, Brenner acknowledged that few Mexican artists could claim actual Indian ancestry. But where Porter saw this racial impurity as a sign of hypocrisy, Brenner believed biological kinship was less important than the fact that "nowhere as in Mexico has art so intimately been linked to the fate of its people."[10] Indeed, Brenner's position is consistent with Mexican understandings of race, which have more to do with class position than blood. Eschewing the European modernists' commitment to an autonomous and elevated art, the Mexican artists understood themselves as workers, and they aspired to represent the interests of working-class and rural audiences. Brenner took them at their word, emphasizing their dedication to indigenous traditions over their privileged backgrounds.

Idols ends somewhat surprisingly by turning from the attractions of Mexican art to Mexico's strategic position in the hemisphere. Throughout the book, Brenner describes the Mexican renaissance as not merely an explosion of artistic creativity but also the outgrowth of violent social and political upheaval that had enduring consequences for the entire region. Unlike Porter, who swung from extremes of enthusiasm to condemnation depending on her mood, Brenner consistently worked to strengthen cultural ties between Mexico and the United States in the hope that they would lead to improved political relations as well as a recognition of Mexico's centrality to the history of American art. Tradition was essential to her account of the Mexican renaissance. Its modernity constituted a break with a more recent past in which Mexican artists had been slavishly bound to their European counterparts. Rejecting those influences, the Mexican modernists were inventing new forms inspired by the recovery of native traditions that could become the source for an authentically American art.

Tina Modotti

Brenner and Porter both recognized the power of visual images to communicate the excitement of Mexico's cultural renaissance to foreign audiences. No matter how vivid their prose, these authors could not adequately describe the work of Mexican artists in words alone, and the murals, their most celebrated accomplishments, could not travel at all. It was through photography that the muralists' work became known in the United States, enabling them to receive lucrative commissions and international acclaim. Projects that incorporated written and photographic matter brought Brenner and Porter into contact with Tina Modotti, the Italian-born photographer whose artistic career was concentrated almost exclusively in Mexico. Modotti moved there in 1923 to establish a photographic studio with her lover, Edward Weston. Her beauty and vibrant personality made her the center of social gatherings and the inspiration for many in Mexico's artistic community. The increasing radicalism of Modotti's beliefs reverses the political journey of Porter and, to a lesser extent, Brenner. Whereas Porter's leftist commitments first drew her to Mexico, Modotti moved there because of her romantic and professional partnership with the apolitical Weston. Her growing politicization caused them to grow apart as she increasingly dedicated her art to politics, joining the Communist Party in 1927. In a letter to Brenner, she wrote that she aspired to photograph with "a class eye": "I look upon people now not in terms of race [or] types but in terms of *classes*."[11] Her subsequent photography fused the iconography of socialism and the formal concerns of Euro-American modernism, situating these international movements in a Mexican setting. Her career as a photographer ended in 1930 when she was accused of plotting the murder of President Ortiz Rubio and deported from Mexico.

Modotti can be identified as an American modernist because her formal experimentation and political commitments are grounded in New World settings. Her Americanist themes are evident even in still-life photographs that portray objects native to a New World landscape: the *flor de manita* reaching up like a gnarled, grasping hand; the asymmetrical, stunted geranium struggling to grow from a cracked pot; nopal cactus; stalks of sugar cane; corn; and the calla lily, which became a signature of Diego Rivera. The deepening of

Modotti's political commitments is evident in a series that combines the international socialist icons of hammer and sickle with the specifically Mexican symbols of *petate*, bandolier, guitar, and sombrero. Here, a modernist precision and simplicity of form is applied to manifestly political content that is at once local and international.

Modotti also shared the indigenists' interest in native people and cultures. Her photographs of popular arts and crafts illustrate Brenner's *Idols Behind Altars*. While some of these images picture objects in isolation—closer to the European modernists' appropriation of traditional artifacts—others show

FIGURE 15.1 Tina Modotti, *Woman from Tehuantepec Carrying Yecapixtle.*
Source: © The Museum of Modern Art / Licensed by SCALA / Art Resource, NY.

them in use, evidence of Modotti's concern with a living tradition situated within a larger social setting. Her photographs of Mexican Indians complement the themes of the muralists' paintings while placing particular emphasis on the activities of indigenous women. In Modotti's photographs, women engage in daily tasks of shopping, washing, and caring for children. They appear calm, untroubled, and directly connected to the products of their work, seeming to live out the socialist ideal of unalienated labor. Indeed, in some of these photographs, implements such as bowls, baskets, and jars appear as extensions of the human subject, their rounded surfaces echoing the contours of the female body.

As her political commitments deepened, Modotti documented the radicalization of the Mexican people in the years following the revolution. Her photographs of workers meeting, parading, and reading communist publications suggest their awakening connection to socialist struggles around the world. Modotti's iconic postrevolutionary subject is a politically conscious *mestiza*. One of her most famous photographs (figure 15.2) depicts a woman carrying an enormous red flag of communist solidarity. Her dark hair and skin bespeak indigenous ancestry; her actions identify her as a political comrade.

Modotti's photographs of *campesinos* reading the communist paper *El Machete* testify to the power of literacy to instill national and transnational political consciousness. The papers' headlines, which are clearly legible, address a combination of Mexican concerns (land redistribution) and international socialist causes (the war against Russia). Alluding to the device of modernist photomontage, these images derive their meaning from a combination of print and visual forms. Modotti would conduct a number of experiments that incorporated writing into her photographs. These include the bluntly political *Elegance and Poverty* (figure 15.3), where a man dressed in ragged clothing appears to sit beneath a billboard advertising an elegant clothier, although the two scenes actually come from different photographs artfully fused together. Here Modotti, like Porter, shows the failures of the postrevolutionary state to improve the lives of the people it claimed to champion. This image suggests that, for Modotti, photography was not simply illustration for written texts, as in the work of Porter and, in some cases, Brenner. The relationship could also be reversed so that words become a supplement to the photographic image. Words appear in Modotti's photographs in the form of slogans and headlines, which lack complexity but are capable of immediate and dramatic communication. Her work with photomontage responds to the problem of widespread illiteracy, which compelled socially conscious Mexican artists to seek forms

FIGURE 15.2 Tina Modotti, *Woman with Flag.*
Source: © The Museum of Modern Art / Licensed by SCALA / Art Resource, NY.

that could best reach untutored audiences. More than Porter or Brenner, Modotti aspired not only to represent the Mexican people but also to find ways to address them directly. In this sense, she would not simply mine Mexican indigenous and popular traditions—as was the case with so many forms of modernist primitivism—but rather engage with those for whom such traditions were still very much alive.

FIGURE 15.3 Tina Modotti, *Elegance and Poverty*.

Source: © The Museum of Modern Art / Licensed by SCALA / Art Resource, NY.

Modotti's departure from Mexico is a fitting place to end this reflection on modernism and tradition because it coincided with a waning of the Mexican renaissance, brought about by the growing conservatism of the government under President Portes Gil, the abandonment or dilution of revolutionary commitments, and the departure of many of Mexico's leading artists and intellectuals. Under these circumstances, the modernist embrace of indigenous forms begins to look like little more than an aesthetic exercise, shorn of its commitments to political representation and social justice. But as Michael Denning argues in *The Cultural Front*, political defeat is not an effective gauge for the cultural consequences of a revolution.[12] Like the U.S. Popular Front that is Denning's subject, the Mexican Revolution, whatever its many political failures, left an indelible imprint on North American modernist culture. For a brief period it gave rise to a Mexican bohemia where artistic creativity flourished, inspired by proximity to what were perceived as authentically American traditions and hopes for a new, more egalitarian social order that might incorporate the bearers of those traditions. The benefits of this heady moment were particularly significant for women. Due in large part to their efforts, it would subsequently be much more difficult for foreigners to view Mexico as left behind by modernity or its culture as slavishly indebted to European tradition. And Mexican culture, with its distinctive fusion of modern and traditional indigenous elements, would continue to exert a formative, if often unacknowledged, influence on the arts across North America.

Bringing the work of Porter, Brenner, and Modotti together and putting it in the context of a Euro-American artistic scene draws attention to the importance of Mexico on the map of international modernism. Not only does this altered perspective feature new personalities, but it brings into view a different set of aesthetic and political commitments than those associated with the more familiar transatlantic modernist cohorts. It prompts us to revise the more familiar story of modernism centered on Europe, in which "tradition" refers either to the cultures of outdated European ancestors or the aesthetics plundered from primitive regions of the world. Sharing an interest in formal innovation and the adoption of new or hybrid media, the Mexican modernists espoused a different relation to tradition as they aspired to produce an art that addressed the politics of revolution. This meant drawing from the rich legacy of Mexico's indigenous past but also seeking forms that could speak to audiences for whom that tradition was still very much alive. An awareness of their aspirations as well as their failures should be part of a more contextual and geographically specific understanding of tradition within global modernism.

NOTES

1. Virginia Woolf, "How It Strikes a Contemporary," *The Times Literary Supplement* (April 5, 1923), http://xroads.virginia.edu/~CLASS/workshop97/gribbin/contemporary.html.

2. James Joyce, *Ulysses*, http://www.gutenberg.org/files/4300/4300-h/4300-h.htm.

3. F. T. Marinetti, "The Manifesto of Futurism," in *Futurism: An Anthology*, ed. Christine Poggi and Laura Wittman (New Haven, Conn.: Yale University Press, 2009), 51. Theodor Adorno, "Philosophy of History and the New," in *Aesthetic* Theory, trans. C. Lenhardt (London: Routledge, 1984), 31; T. S. Eliot, "Tradition and the Individual Talent," in *The Sacred Wood*, http://www.bartleby.com/200/sw4.html.

4. Astradu Eysteinsson, *The Concept of Modernism* (Ithaca, N.Y.: Cornell University Press, 1992), 8, 52.

5. Laura Mulvey, with Peter Wollen, "Frida Kahlo and Tina Modotti," in *Visual and Other Pleasures* (Bloomington: Indiana University Press, 1989), 95, 96.

6. Cited in William L. Nance, "Katherine Anne Porter and Mexico," *Southwest Review* 15, no. 2 (Spring 1970): 145–146.

7. Roy Newquist, interview with Katherine Anne Porter, *McCall's* (August 1965): 142.

8. Katherine Anne Porter, "María Concepción," in *The Collected Essays and Occasional Writings of Katherine Anne Porter* (New York: Delacorte, 1970), 3.

9. Katherine Anne Porter, "Old Gods and New Messiahs" (review of *Idols Behind Altars* by Anita Brenner), in *"This Strange Old World" and Other Book Reviews by Katherine Anne Porter*, ed. Darlene Harbour Unrue (Athens: University of Georgia Press, 1991), 83, 88.

10. Anita Brenner, *Idols Behind Altars* (New York: Payson and Clark, 1929), 244.

11. Cited in Sarah M. Lowe, *Tina Modotti: Photographs* (New York: Abrams, 1995), 36.

12. Michael Denning, *The Cultural Front: The Laboring of American Culture in the Twentieth Century* (London: Verso, 1996).

16. TRANSLATION

GAYLE ROGERS

Anglophone modernism certainly was one of several hegemonic formations at the time, but how might we reposition it as a temporary stopping point, a transitory route through which many other modernist figures and texts briefly passed on the way to more substantive engagements? How might we treat the familiar and the unfamiliar in modernism in their dialogic development and see Euro-American languages and literary institutions as simultaneously enabling and disabling, major and minor, central and marginal?

In her influential book *The World Republic of Letters*, Pascale Casanova places Paris and the French language squarely at the center of the literary universe. Writers in other locales and languages only achieve international renown by having prestige conferred upon them by the Parisian literary system, a process for which Casanova takes the emergence of modernism as paradigmatic. While her schema is useful for examining cross-cultural dynamics and inequalities, it is limited for revising a field such as modernist studies—and when it is useful, it is double-edged. It implicitly encourages us to treat texts that originated in nondominant languages, but only insofar as they reached the Parisian bar. In Casanova's account, literary "revolts" come from the periphery and aim at the center, and translation is a silent, almost invisible mechanism for such action.[1] Thus, our studies first reinforce a preselected canon whose terms—from the ideals of literary autonomy and innovation to the elevation of formal experimentation over social realism—were created by select European modernists and their sympathetic critics. Then, as we import more non-Western materials into the metropole, we reinforce their exoticism, their unknowability in their source language, and that language's distance from our more familiar target languages.

Where Casanova's sociological-historical approach expands but essentially reifies the canonical map of modernism and the assumptions about originality, influence, and literary value that undergird it, much contemporary work on the topic of translation in world and comparative literary studies has productively unsettled these bearings. Such work prompts us to ask whether we must we begin or end our analyses of non-Anglophone literatures with their manifestations in a dominant tongue like French or with their lives in the Paris–London–New York–Berlin nexus that remains at the core of Anglophone-dominated scholarship on modernism. How do Anglophone scholars move beyond thinking about the English language, or about Anglophone modernists, as the only starting point, endpoint, or center of gravity for studies of translation in global modernisms? Anglophone modernism certainly was one of several hegemonic formations at the time, but how might we reposition it as a temporary stopping point, a transitory route through which many other modernist figures and texts briefly passed on the way to more substantive engagements? How might we treat the familiar and the unfamiliar in modernism in their dialogic development and see Euro-American languages and literary institutions as simultaneously enabling and disabling, major and minor, central and marginal?

This essay proposes thinking of the English language as an unstable medium, a fluctuating currency whose value was relative to specific collaborative transactions within disparate international economies of literature and translation. The cultural valence of translation varies radically, depending on spatiotemporal and geopolitical circumstances, and this variation opens up provocative questions about influence, dependency, canonicity, and the autonomy of minor-language texts. Thus, when framed through translation, the spheres of Anglophone modernism and its components (its authors, media, marketing, and more) appear to have numerous gates that open and close, often capriciously, along their borders. Writers from within and beyond these spheres negotiated those gates in ways that made Anglophone modernism both a field and a conductor between other fields in a network whose operations it did not control. Using translation as an organizing, constitutive concept for global modernist studies compels contemporary critics to resist the impulse simply to add more authors in translation to the existing canon or to emphasize diffusionist accounts of influence and technique. Translation and its mechanisms instead reveal both the connections and the fissures, gaps, ambivalences, and breaks—the inequalities that persist to the present— among the movements and figures that have been named "modernist."

I will consider here two paths into and through Anglophone modernism, paths that were interwoven yet had very different outcomes: those of Rabindranath Tagore and Juan Ramón Jiménez. They crossed briefly through translation in English, but their more substantive and long-lasting crossings were enabled by their overlap in their complex lives in translation as Tagore's work traveled from Bengali to Spanish. In a perhaps surprising textual journey, a writer from a colony (India) on the periphery of the Euro-American republic of letters became immensely popular and influential in a European country (Spain) that was on the margins of this same literary sphere. The contexts and results of this "minor-minor," Global South/European South journey from Kolkata to London to Madrid—a journey that both traced and deviated from familiar colonial routes—comprise but one slice of the intertwined histories of translation and modernism. We find that Tagore's flickering fame in English and his powerful legacy for over a century in Hispanophone literatures throw into relief some asymmetries that are unapparent until we use translation to hold dominant modernisms in a precarious, uneven balance.

Tagore, whose reputation in Bengali literature was already cemented by the early 1900s, translated his own works into English in complicated ways. His first major publication in English, *Gitanjali* (*Song Offerings*; 1912), was a mélange of previously published poems, excerpts from other texts, and standalone prose poems sewn together, in florid and often ornate language, with the appearance of narrative coherence. Tagore cut specific Indian and Bengali cultural references, toned down his anticolonialism, and amplified the mystical elements of his writing that appealed to the romanticized, exoticized desires of metropolitan audiences. He then fused pieces of poetry and prose to the point that the putative original fades almost completely out of view (see Chaudhuri, "The English Writings of Rabindranath Tagore"; Sengupta, "Translation, Colonialism and Poetics"). And though he saw the labor of translation as vital to a humanistic, universalizing reparation of the wounds of colonialism, Tagore was always uncomfortable with it; his formal studies of English were limited, and in his letters, he admitted serious doubts about his skill as a self-translator. He wrote that

> my English writing emerges out of my subconscious. . . . Once I mount the peak of conscious will all my wit and wisdom get muddled. That is why I cannot gird up my loins to do a translation. I can only set my boat adrift and not sit at the helm at all. Then, if and when I touch shore, I cannot quite understand myself how it all happened.
>
> (Qtd. in Gupta, *Rabindranath Tagore*, 59)

While he was aided in his self-translations by Anglophone writers and by his family, he nevertheless felt that he carried out a "gross injustice to my original productions partly owing to my own incompetence, partly to carelessness" (qtd. in Tiwari, "Rabindranath Tagore's Comparative World Literature," 46).[2] Aarthi Vadde notes, too, that Tagore's later poetry in Bengali *after* his translations into English shows evidence of his stylistic revisions based on his contacts with the English language (see Vadde, "Putting Foreignness to the Test").

Yet Tagore was—and still sometimes is—mistaken for a poet who composed originally in English, though he did so only once, with his later poem "The Child" (1930). Indeed, the *Daily Mail* declared of his *Gardener* (1913) that "one cannot tell what [the poems] have lost in the translation" (Briggs, "A Great Man from Bengal," 6). His works immediately resonated with Western readers, and he was successfully promoted as a new star on the Anglo-European modernist scene. His initial rise in status was remarkable: in 1912, the third issue of the new Chicago-based little magazine *Poetry*, which published dozens of leading modernist writers alongside extensive translations from a variety of languages, featured the first of its many translations of his prose poems. Tagore's appearance was accompanied by an essay by Pound, who claimed that this marked "an event in the history of English poetry and of world poetry" ("Tagore's Poems," 92). Several months later, when devoting an issue to Tagore, *Poetry*'s editor Harriet Monroe declared that "the serenely noble laureate of Bengal . . . [is] the ideal poet, the prophet aware of his world and now great-heartedly adopting ours; the Ambassador Extraordinary from East to West, bearing no passports from king to president, but speaking with supreme authority from race to race" ("Comments and Reviews," 102). (Five months in advance of the award, Monroe points, with her phrase "noble laureate," to the emergent campaign to make Tagore a "Nobel laureate.") In an article for the *Fortnightly Review*, Pound added that Tagore's poetry has "all the properties of action" that he and his imagist coterie desired at the moment, and he compared him to Dante. "We have found our new Greece," Pound affirmed, and Tagore steers us away from "the confusion of our Western life, in the racket of our cities, in the jabber of manufactured literature, in the vortex of advertisement" ("Rabindranath Tagore," 571, 576). Pound confessed to Yeats that Tagore was "greater than any of us," one of the greatest poets in the English language; Yeats concurred that "I know of no man in my time who has done anything in the English language to equal these lyrics" (qtd. in Longenbach, *Stone Cottage*, 23, 24). Yeats effused in his introduction to *Gitanjali* that the book "stirred my blood as nothing has for years. . . . A whole people, a whole civilization, immeasurably strange to us, seems to have been taken up into this imagination; and yet we are not moved because of its strangeness, but because we have met our own image" (xii).[3] André Gide translated Tagore into French, and other famed European writers could not stop praising him.

Tagore was awarded the Nobel Prize in 1913, becoming the first (and until 1945, the only) laureate from outside of Europe or the United States. Between 1913 and 1914, his works were translated into Swedish, Dutch, German, Danish, and Spanish, and he gave a lecture tour in the United States. By 1918, at least fifteen volumes of his poems and a handful of books of essays and autobiographical accounts had been published in English (Gupta, *Rabindranath Tagore*, 64). Prestige and acclaim flowed in both directions: by "discovering" Tagore, Pound, Yeats, Gide, Jiménez, and others were amplifying their own standing as kingmakers and arbiters of new trends in the literary world. Their often sensationalistic rhetoric regarding Tagore is replete with signs of colonialist appropriation, even while they emphasized that Tagore's English was his own. Pound called him "THE *Scoop*" and bragged that *Poetry* was "the only American magazine to print him, or even to know" of him (Letter to Monroe, 46; see also Saha, "Singing Bengal Into a Nation"). Robert Frost later contended that Tagore's "poetry overflowed national boundaries to reach us in his own English," and thus he "belongs little less to us than to his own country" ("Tagore's Poetry," 298). In its Nobel citation, the Swedish Academy remarked that Tagore "made his poetic thought, expressed in his own English words, a part of the literature of the West"—that is, his career as the de facto poet laureate of Bengal was pushed fully into the background. The British Empire knighted him in 1915, though he would renounce the honor in 1919 after the Jallianwala Bagh (Amritsar) massacre.

Tagore courted and accepted such a reception, but his writings speak to these ironic claims of authorial autonomy that greeted his "arrival" among European readers. One prose poem in *Crescent Moon* (1913) entitled "Authorship" has a boy complaining to his mother about his father, a writer who "plays at making" volumes of incomprehensible books. The boy wonders why his mother defends his father, tolerates his lack of communication and interaction, and takes out her frustrations with him on her children. In a moment that imitates Tagore's own self-reflexivity, the boy asks, "What's the fun of always writing and writing? / When I take up father's pen or pencil and write upon his book just as he does,—a, b, c, d, e, f, g, h, i,—why do you get cross with me, then, mother? / What do you think of father's spoiling sheets and

sheets of paper with black marks all over on both sides?" (49). The boy in
Tagore's text realizes that the difference between reproducing the alphabet
and "spoiling sheets and sheets of paper" with meaningless "black marks" is
purely a function of reception—and that reception can be fickle and without logic.

At almost precisely the same moment, Juan Ramón Jiménez, then the leading poet in Spain, began to focus increasingly on his own practices of translation, specifically on translating Anglophone American modernism. He found
himself "being reborn . . . and I felt this rebirth of American poetry as if it
were my own—much as I did the rebirth of Spanish poetry" (*Política*, 184).
This occurred as he read Robert Frost, Amy Lowell, Edna St. Vincent Millay,
and others, and he produced a number of poems that bear the influence of
and respond to these writers. Furthermore, Jiménez himself was entering this
same English-language world of letters when he traveled to the United States
in 1916 to wed the Spanish-born American Zenobia Camprubí: their honey-
moon was spent collecting and translating books and visiting the homes and
graves of famous U.S. writers. He writes of this in his six-part semiepic *Diary
of a Newlywed Poet* (*Diario de un poeta recién casado*, 1917), which he composed during his voyage. The book is an extended exercise in translation of
every type: there are traditional translations, such as his inclusion of complete
poems by Emily Dickinson and by Robert Browning; translations of phrases,
pamphlets, street signs, and conversations from his experiences in the United
States; and translations of forms such as the sonnet, the *modernista* poem
of anguish, and the aphoristic "one-image" poem of Pound's ideals. In one
prose poem, he takes up directly his own first appearance in English translation, when he criticizes the Hispanist James Fitzmaurice-Kelly's popular *Oxford Book of Spanish Verse* (1913) for its poor renditions of six of his poems.
(Four titles were liberally reworded, and one was changed without consulting
the author.) Fitzmaurice-Kelly, who was Britain's most important scholar of
Spanish letters, "baptized me in chromium blue," Jiménez writes, by reducing
his complex meditations on color and emotion to a ubiquitous, bland "blue"
at every turn, missing the nuances in his allusions to Rubén Darío's *Azul . . .*
(Azure . . . , or Blue . . . , 1888), the text that arguably launched the *modernismo*
movement (*Diary of a Newlywed Poet*, 290).

Jiménez found nothing on the order of the success and praise in Anglophone literary cultures that Tagore did. Instead, his journey into U.S. modernism took what might appear to be an unexpected turn to world literature. As
he devoured American literary periodicals, especially *Poetry*, and translated

figures ranging from Frost to Yeats to J. M. Synge, one writer captured his attention more than any other as an emblem of English-language modernism's capacities: Tagore. He and his collaborator Camprubí, who originally pointed him to Tagore's works, obtained permission from Tagore to become his exclusive, authorized Spanish translators for all Spanish-speaking territories.[4] Working from Tagore's English translations and consulting Gide's French versions, Jiménez and Camprubí produced an astounding fifteen volumes of Tagore in Spanish in three years and a total of twenty-two volumes between 1914 and 1922. Tagore was hardly known in Spain; indeed, potential readers were skeptical, if anything, because they believed Tagore had been awarded the Nobel unfairly over their countryman Benito Pérez Galdós in 1913. But Jiménez's 1914 translation of *La luna nueva* (*Crescent Moon*, 1913) was a runaway success: there were three printings in the first year alone, with over nine thousand copies sold, better sales than any Spanish-language poet saw at the same time. Jiménez also tried unsuccessfully to bring Tagore to Spain for a celebration of his works.

Jiménez's captivation was most similar to Yeats's. But where Yeats bestowed his "blessing" upon *Gitanjali* in his introduction, Jiménez coupled his name with Tagore's through translation. The translations themselves, despite the several hands involved, are mostly literal; they reproduce the exotic wonder imbued in Tagore's English versions and do not evince a great deal of creative license on Jiménez's part.[5] It is, rather, the *process* of translating and publishing, including the employment of paratexts, that Jiménez engages more robustly. He begins almost every volume of his and Camprubí's translations with a new poem or prose poem of his own, usually dedicated, like a literary benediction, to the narrative voice or protagonist of Tagore's text. He opens *La luna nueva*, for instance, with a note entitled "From the Spanish poet Juan Ramón Jiménez to the Indian boy of *Luna nueva*," asking the latter figure, "You are there, yes, we feel you with us . . . but where are you? . . . We have known you, yes; but are you aware of us?" He concludes that "it looks like the world, small as you see tangled in that tree, is your ball, and that as you play with that ball, you make what you wish of us" ("El poeta español," 10, 11). That is to say, the two worlds (East and West, children and adults) that seem separated are bridged not simply by a Western "discovery" of a childlike East but by a convergence initiated when an Eastern writer imagines and creates the West, just as Jiménez's European peers has posited.

Elsewhere in his Tagore translations, Jiménez opens the Spanish version of *Gitanjali* with a message to Tagore that fixates on their translational intercourse:

We [the translators] have aimed to give a new body to your great heart, to this book in which gathers your entire heart. Will your heart be moved by the book's blood and rhythm? Will your heart beat freely in our body? . . . Yes, your poems are going to be heard in our words by your God! . . . Can you speak to him with our Spanish voice—to this God of yours, close, visible, human, who hears beautiful words?

> ("Hemos intentado . . .")

Camprubí concludes the same collection with another note on *Gitanjali*'s various material sources and with a statement that "no work, much less if it is a translation, can have, while its author is living, anything more than a transitory value. In each new edition, this book has to undergo further stripping [*desnudando*] . . . until it reaches its permanent expression. Madrid: 1918" ("Nota"). Here, Camprubí invokes the term "*desnuda*" ("stripped," or "naked"), which became a keyword in Jiménez's own minimalist notion of *poesía desnuda*, or *poesiá pura*, and the title of one of his poems, as a conceit for the process of translating and revising Tagore that would occupy a middle part of his own career. Indeed, he first elaborated *poesía desnuda* in 1916, after reading Tagore, in his *Eternidades* (Eternities, 1918), and the mystical elements he saw in Tagore would surface in his poetry through the 1920s (see Johnson, "Juan Ramón Jiménez"). "Stripping" or "denuding," for Jiménez, blurs the boundary between the primary production of poetry and the secondary act of translation as both are conventionally conceived. Authentic poetic speech, Jiménez posits, was communal and universal, preexisting and belonging to no single author, and thus "there are things that" by their very form "appear not to have been said first by anyone," only discovered by the true poet (qtd. in Palau de Nemes, "Tagore and Jiménez," 191).

By 1918, thanks to Jiménez's translations, Tagore's work attracted commentary from José Ortega y Gasset, the philosopher, publisher, and culture broker who towered over Madrid's intellectual scene at the time. In a series of three articles in the literary section of the Madrid daily *El Sol*, Ortega greeted the Tagore translations with similar Orientalist exoticism, seeing in them a blend of Eastern mystical themes and Western individual poetic genius. But he appreciates most that Tagore can draw his poetry from the simplest of materials, from materials so familiar and collective in nature that every reader immediately recognizes them. Thus it is, as Ortega notes in a manner echoing Jiménez's own comments, that "every great poet . . . plagiarizes us" by appearing to channel our own experiences ("Un poeta indo," 5). Jiménez's translations of Tagore—several degrees removed from the "originals," if we can even call them that—helped canonize the Indian writer in the Hispanophone world and, as in the case of Pound and Yeats, elevated Jiménez's own standing as a cosmopolitan tastemaker. Tagore came to influence numerous Spanish writers, the future Chilean Nobel laureates Gabriela Mistral and Pablo Neruda (who sparked a small scandal by plagiarizing a Tagore poem), his own close friend Victoria Ocampo of Argentina, and many others. Indeed, Spain still awards a Tagore Prize for poetry, and, as Bhavya Tiwari notes, despite the resurgent interest in Tagore across contemporary India, "the number of translations of *Gitanjali* into Spanish surpasses those into Hindi" ("Rabindranath Tagore's Comparative World Literature," 47).

The connections in translation between Jiménez and Tagore were apparent to British reviewers, as was Camprubí's mediating role. In 1920, the critic and Spanish translator J. B. Trend wrote that

> by this time most of the works of [Tagore] have been translated into Spanish. They are rather a puzzle to Spanish readers, however. They have been so exquisitely and so naturally translated that they seem almost like original works of D. Juan Ramón Jiménez; and the fact that the translation has been made by Señora Camprubí de Jiménez seems to explain and perhaps justify the resemblance in style between Tagore in his Spanish dress and the poetry and prose of Sr. Jiménez. We are inclined to think that the resemblance in outlook is real. It is quite easy to imagine Tagore riding on an ass through Andalucía, and perhaps writing a book as good as *Platero y yo*.
>
> ("Window-Boxes from Madrid," 672)

This new imagined appropriation naturalizes an image of Tagore in southern Spain, in a province (Andalucía) that was on the margins of a country whose influence on the literary traditions of its former colonies was both fiercely contested and clearly dwindling. The title cited at the end is Jiménez's own landmark book of prose poems from 1914, which is similar to *Crescent Moon* in many ways. When *Platero*, in turn, was translated into Bengali, Jiménez wrote a preface for that edition in which he explained his theory of translation and its effect on his poetry.[6] His collaborations with his wife were not as simple and balanced as he often framed them, however; as Trend's note above alludes, it was Camprubí who rendered prose translations of Tagore's English into Spanish, then Jiménez who "poeticized" them. This process became a source of friction between them; Camprubí was initially eager to erase herself from the process since her husband was a well-known poet but later regretted her absence when Jiménez took most of the credit for the translations (see Palau de Nemes, "Tagore and Jiménez"). She claimed that she was "robbed" of her role and threatened to "tell the whole world" of Jiménez's secret, then alternatively wished "in the future, for us to unite with one another in our book. Thus we will live 'here' always" (*Monumento de amor*, 18). There are questions about the gendered dynamics of translation practices in history that cannot be explored here but that bear on lines such as Jiménez's declaration of the necessity for translation: "sometimes we read something in another language that feels so personal, so intimate to us that we mourn the fact that it was not our own expression. Then we give it—we must give it—its own form in our tongue, so that it might become ours, little by little. In this sense . . . translation is always a theft" (qtd. in Young, *The Line in the Margin*, xxi). This notion of theft, or what Ortega labeled plagiarism, was one that Eliot elevated in his writings on craft, too: a mode of *poeisis* in which ventriloquism, impersonation, and multiply layered translation are actually the poet's most authentic tools.

Against the familiar logic that nation-based literary studies have suggested, Jiménez saw his translations of Tagore as the culmination of his own "rebirth" in English-language American poetry—even more than translating Frost could have offered him. Thus, in his case and in Tagore's, tracing their lives in English-language modernism will yield an interesting though partial and incomplete story of their circulation and influence globally. For both Tagore and Jiménez, that is, their time in English was a necessary stage in the circuits that connected them, but it was also brief and somewhat strained. Jiménez did not gain international standing by publishing under the aegis of Pound, Yeats, and Monroe, and he remains unknown to most English-language critics despite having been addressed by contemporary scholars of modernism perhaps more than any other Indian writer except Mulk Raj Anand. Indeed, Tagore's star faded in Europe and England by 1920: the attacks on him had been vigorous for several years. D. H. Lawrence called him a "sheer fraud" and lamented the British "worship" of him in 1916 (Letter to Lady Ottoline Morrell). Pound became disaffected by Tagore's newer works and his celebrity, while Yeats insisted angrily that "Damn Tagore" produced only "sentimental rubbish" after his first few books; Yeats added that "Tagore does not know English, no Indian knows English" (qtd. in Chaudhuri, "The English Writings of Rabindranath Tagore," 112). Jiménez, too, regretted his connection to Tagore, wondering, "have I not invented in translation an An-dalusian Tagore, a Tagore who looks like me?" (qtd. in Young, "The Invention of an Andalusian Tagore," 49). The fact that Tagore's books sold better than those of many native Spanish poets was "galling" for Jiménez, who could not "accept the fact that his book collected dust on the shelves while Tagore's sold in the thousands," writes Howard Young (42–43).

The connections between Tagore and Jiménez also range from the generic (their use of the prose poem as a pliable, translatable form) to the lived (they both wrote and translated several of the texts I have discussed while sail-ing from their home countries to England or the United States). In fact, they crossed paths again through Anglophone modernist circuits, prompted and mediated this time through their readings of Eliot in the early 1930s. In 1931, Jiménez translated Eliot's "La Figlia Che Piange," "Marina," and the "Som de l'escalina" section of *Ash-Wednesday* (1927) for a Spanish periodical. But his relationship to Eliot's poetics and conservative politics became increasingly negative, even dismissive. In 1932, Tagore, writing in a Bengali magazine, re-jected Eliot's poetics and stirred a great debate among native writers about the merits of both Eliot and himself. Here again, two literary publications— one Spanish, one Bengali—that otherwise had little to no contact converged around a shared critique of Eliot. Following Jiménez and Tagore thus tells us something not only about a marginal, extracanonical circuit of exchange and influence but also about the global reception of a central modernist poet (Eliot) as his work continued to move well beyond his purview. The circle was nearly completed in 1953 when *Poetry*—the modernist magazine that introduced Tagore both to many Anglophone readers and to Jiménez in the 1910s—dedicated an issue to Jiménez. In 1956, the Spaniard was awarded the Nobel Prize, which poets and leftists in Spain quietly celebrated during the author's post–Spanish Civil War exile in the United States and Puerto Rico.

Across much broader swaths of literary historical space-time, translation has, to various degrees, fostered literary revolutions: the invention of blank verse in English, French Symbolism's emergence from translations of Poe, the Latin American Boom and translations of Faulkner—the list is extensive. Modernism is no exception. Pound wrote that "every allegedly great age" in literary history is "an age of translations," which seems to apply to the mod-ernist "age," in which nearly every writer was also a translator ("How to Read," 35). Pound himself initiated the pronounced break with Victorian notions of fidelity and accuracy in translation practices, and like countless writers around the world in the early twentieth century, he articulated myriad cultural, literary, and party politics through translation (see Venuti, *The Translator's Invisibility*, 187–224; Yao, *Translation and the Languages of Modernism*). But we must be careful not to read Pound's claim either as a directive that translation should enrich and renew domestic cultures and native languages alone or that Anglocentric modernist studies should profit from its imports. Indeed, one of the central tenets of the modernist reconceptualization of translation is that even foundational notions such as target and source are complicated by a number of factors, geopolitics among them. In addition to the meanings that exist at either pole of a translational exchange, the expansive and decentered practices that mediate translation itself, such as revision, distortion, politicization, and dissemination, require more scrutiny. If we examine the languages, practices, and objects of translation that have seemed marginal to modernism or to which modernism seemed marginal, we find new stories that, of course, were not always "new" to global critics. One of those stories would be the role of minor languages in casting Europe as paradoxically central and peripheral to literary transactions. Another would trace how dominant languages reconfigured the connections among lesser-known experimental texts and practices (as when the Japanese occupation of Korea inadvertently brought English-language texts into Korea for the first time) and vice versa.

That is to say, we can disorient and recast Anglo-European modernisms by understanding translation *within* them, but we can also understand their relative positioning on a global scale by seeing them as stages in the larger history of translation itself. Further scholarship on translation and foreign-language training clearly will be essential to reforming and rethinking the field of global modernist studies.[7] And, unlike a focus on certain formal aesthetics or a relationship to certain stages of capitalism or imperialism, translation studies are not and need not be grounded in Anglo-American or European histories. If we wish to disorient and defamiliarize—rather than simply expand—modernist studies in light of global conditions in the modernist era and in our own, the rhizomatic network of connections and aporias suggested by the still-unfolding story of translation is a starting point that is usefully unlocated.

NOTES

1. Casanova's *World Republic of Letters* appeared in French in 1999 and in English in 2004. More recently, Casanova has acknowledged overlooking translation in

World Republic and has attempted to address it; see Casanova, "What Is a Dominant Language?".

2. One of the writers who helped revise Tagore's translations into English was T. Sturge Moore, who nominated the Bengali poet for the Nobel Prize. Moore was a close friend of Yeats and the brother of the philosopher G. E. Moore; his wife, Marie Sturge Moore, translated Tagore into French.

3. For a brief overview of Tagore's translations and translators, see Radice, "Rabindranath Tagore." See also the many discussions of his translations in Tagore's letters with the painter William Rothenstein, who helped bring him to London audiences, in Rothenstein, and Tagore, *Imperfect Encounter*.

4. For a detailed documentation and bibliography of Tagore's translation and reception in Spain, which actually began a year earlier (1908) than in England, see Ganguly, "Spain and Latin America."

5. By speaking about the relative creativity or literalism of Jiménez's translations, I might appear to be making assumptions and judgments about Tagore's "originals"—a common practice in translation studies that Lawrence Venuti has often critiqued (see *Translation Changes Everything*). I am using these terms, however, as shorthand for pointing to the alternate reproduction of or deviation from established norms for translating in these specific cultural moments—even norms for translating Tagore specifically.

6. I have not been able to determine whether this translation into Bengali was made directly from the Spanish or through an intermediary English version. Continuing these interconnections, Trend translated Jiménez's *Fifty Spanish Poems* (1950), which helped disseminate Jiménez's work in the Anglophone world and contributed to his being nominated for, and eventually winning, the Nobel Prize.

7. My own limitations are evident in this essay, as I can address Spanish texts but not Bengali ones; a generous colleague has aided me.

WORKS CITED

Briggs, F. Ashworth. "A Great Man from Bengal." *Daily Mail* (October 29, 1913), 6.

Camprubí, Zenobia. "Nota de la traductora." In *Gitanjali (Ofrenda lírica)*, by Rabindranath Tagore, trans. Zenobia Camprubí with Juan Ramón Jiménez. Madrid: Tip. de Ángel Alcoy, 1918.

Casanova, Pascale. "What Is a Dominant Language? Giacomo Leopardi: Theoretician of Linguistic Inequality." Trans. Marlon Jones. *New Literary History* 44, no. 3 (Summer 2013): 379–99.

——. *The World Republic of Letters*. Trans. M. B. DeBevoise. Cambridge, Mass.: Harvard University Press, 2004.

Chaudhuri, Amit. "The English Writings of Rabindranath Tagore." In *The History of Indian Literature in English*, ed. Arvind Krishna Mehrotra, 103–115. New York: Columbia University Press, 2003.

Frost, Robert. "Tagore's Poetry Overflowed National Boundaries." In *Rabindranath Tagore, 1861–1941: A Centenary Volume*, 298. New Delhi: Sahitya Akadem, 1961.

Ganguly, Shyama Prasad. "Spain and Latin America." In *Rabindranath Tagore: One Hundred Years of Global Reception*, ed. Martin Kämpchen and Imre Bangha, 476–498. New Delhi: Orient BlackSwan, 2014.

Gupta, Uma Das. *Rabindranath Tagore: A Biography*. Delhi: Oxford University Press, 2004.

Infante, Ignacio. *After Translation: The Transfer and Circulation of Modern Poetics Across the Atlantic*. New York: Fordham University Press, 2013.

Jiménez, Juan Ramón. *Diary of a Newlywed Poet: A Bilingual Edition of* Diario de un poeta reciencasado. Ed. Michael Predmore. Selinsgrove, Penn.: Susquehanna University Press, 2004.

———. "Hemos intentado . . ." In *Gitanjali (Ofrenda lírica)*, by Rabindranath Tagore, trans. Zenobia Camprubí with Juan Ramón Jiménez. Madrid: Tip. de Ángel Alcoy, 1918.

———. "El poeta español Juan Ramón Jiménez . . ." In *La luna nueva: poemas de niños*, by Rabindranath Tagore, trans. Zenobia Camprubí with Juan Ramón Jiménez, 10–11. Madrid: Imprenta clásica española, 1915.

———. *Política poética*. Intro. Germán Bleiberg. Madrid: Alianza Editorial, 1982.

Johnson, Robert. "Juan Ramón Jiménez, Rabindranath Tagore, and 'la Poesía Desnuda.'" *Modern Language Review* 60, no. 4 (1965): 534–546.

Lawrence, D. H. Letter to Lady Ottoline Morrell, May 24, 1916. In *The Letters of D. H. Lawrence*, ed. George J. Zytaruk and James T. Boulton, 2:608–609. Cambridge: Cambridge University Press, 2002.

Longenbach, James. *Stone Cottage: Pound, Yeats, and Modernism*. New York: Oxford University Press, 1988.

Monroe, Harriet. "Comments and Reviews: Incarnations." *Poetry* 2, no. 3 (June 1913): 101–104.

Monumento de amor (cartas de Zenobia Camprubí y Juan Ramón Jiménez). Ed. and intro. Ricardo Gullón. San Juan: Ediciones de la Torre, 1959.

Ortega y Gasset, José. "Un poeta indo." *El Sol* (January 27, 1918), 5.

Palau de Nemes, Graciela. "Tagore and Jiménez: Poetic Coincidences." In *Rabindranath Tagore, 1861–1941: A Centenary Volume*, 187–197. New Delhi: Sahitya Akadem, 1961.

Pound, Ezra. "How to Read." In *Literary Essays of Ezra Pound*, ed. T. S. Eliot, 15–40. New York: New Directions, 1968.

———. Letter to Harriet Monroe, October 3, 1912. In *Dear Editor: A History of* Poetry *in Letters*, ed. Joseph Parisi and Stephen Young, 46–47. New York: Norton, 2002.

———. "Rabindranath Tagore." *Fortnightly Review* 99 (March 1913): 571–579.

———. "Tagore's Poems." *Poetry* 1, no. 3 (December 1912): 92–94.

Radice, William. "Rabindranath Tagore." In *Encyclopedia of Literary Translation Into English*, ed. Olive Classe, 2:1368–1371. London: Fitzroy Dearborn, 2000.

Rothenstein, William, and Rabindranath Tagore. *Imperfect Encounter: Letters of William Rothenstein and Rabindranath Tagore, 1911–1941*. Ed. Mary M. Lago. Cambridge, Mass.: Harvard University Press, 1972.

Saha, Poulomi. "Singing Bengal Into a Nation: Tagore, Nationalism, and Colonial Cosmopolitanism." *Journal of Modern Literature* 36, no. 2 (Winter 2014): 1–24.

Sengupta, Mahasweta. "Translation, Colonialism, and Poetics: Rabindranath Tagore in Two Worlds." In *Translation, History, and Culture*, ed. Susan Bassnett and André Lefevere, 56–63. London: Pinter, 1990.

Swedish Academy. "The Nobel Prize for Literature 1913." http://www.nobelprize.org /nobel_prizes/literature/laureates/1913/.

Tagore, Rabindranath. *Crescent Moon*. New Delhi: Rupa and Co., 2002.

Tiwari, Bhavya. "Rabindranath Tagore's Comparative World Literature." In *The Routledge Companion to World Literature*, ed. Theo D'haen, David Damrosch, and Djelal Kadir, 41–48. New York: Routledge, 2012.

Trend, J. B. "Window-Boxes from Madrid." *Athenaeum* 4724 (November 12, 1920): 672.

Vadde, Aarthi. "Putting Foreignness to the Test: Rabindranath Tagore's Babu English." *Comparative Literature* 65, no. 1 (Winter 2013): 15–25.

Venuti, Lawrence. *Translation Changes Everything: Theory and Practice*. New York: Routledge, 2012.

———. *The Translator's Invisibility: A History of Translation*. New York: Routledge, 1994.

Yao, Steven G. *Translation and the Languages of Modernism: Gender, Politics, Language*. New York: Palgrave, 2002.

Yeats, W. B. Introduction to *Gitanjali (Song Offerings)*, by Rabindranath Tagore, vii–xxii. New York: Macmillan, 1920.

Young, Howard. "The Invention of an Andalusian Tagore." *Comparative Literature* 47, no. 1 (Winter 1995): 42–52.

———. *The Line in the Margin: Juan Ramón Jiménez and His Readings in Blake, Shelley, and Yeats*. Madison: University of Wisconsin Press, 1980.

17. WAR

MARIANO SISKIND

What do we make of the privilege that the modernist critical tradition affords to British, French, German, and North American (and sometimes Italian) literature on war in general, and on the Great War in particular, in the face of the vast and unexplored Latin American, Asian, and African archives?

In *Una excursión a los indios ranqueles* (*A Visit to the Ranquel Indians*, 1870), Lucio V. Mansilla's fascinating and strangely rhizomatic narrative of his military expedition to meet Chief Mariano Rosas to negotiate a peace treaty between the Ranquel nation and the Argentine state, Mansilla invokes very recent memories of his days as a somewhat defiant captain in the Paraguayan War (1864–1870). In this bloody and ferocious conflict an alliance of the Argentine, Brazilian, and Uruguayan armies obliterated Paraguay, killing three hundred thousand men, which represented between 60 and 69 percent of the Paraguayan population, a proportional scale of death unknown in any other modern war (Whigham and Potthast, "The Paraguayan Rosetta Stone," 182). Mansilla's travel and autobiographical narratives challenged the formal and institutional boundaries of Argentine literature and abounded in decentering self-representations of his modern, ironic, and affected subjectivity. In that sense this narrative can be seen as a particular articulation of the global, asynchronous, transcultural drive to experiment with formal ways of destabilizing inherited traditions and institutions that the Anglophone critical tradition has narrowly called *modernism* and that volumes like this one decenter and deprovincialize. For Mansilla the Paraguayan war was an arsenal of narrative opportunities that he would exploit over the next four decades. In a martial *mise en abyme* of sorts, the narrator ("Mansilla") battles the tedium and fatigue of a long, delayed, and fruitless military expedition by telling stories of a previous war, with deliberate and mannered emphasis on moments of boredom during or between direct confrontations. One of the most remarkable of these moments is set right before the battle of Tuyutí in 1866:

> I shall tell you, friend Santiago, what I used to do in Paraguay when I got tired of seeing, from my redoubt in Tuyutí, the same thing everyday: the same Paraguayan trenches, the same woods, the same swamps, the same sentries—do you know what I used to do? I would climb up on the battery merlon, turn my back to the enemy, stand with legs apart, and bend down to look between them, and so spend a minute or so looking at things upside down. It is a most curious sight and a resource I recommend to you for when you are bored or tired of the sameness of life in that old Europe, which thinks itself young, which thinks itself progressive while it is actually sunk in ignorance.
>
> (*A Visit to the Ranquel Indians*, 46–47)

Mansilla's reduplicated inscription of war, of the memory of a war folded into a military campaign, evokes and undoes a world disrupted by warfare. The self-satisfied and overwhelmed representation of *war ennui* in this passage—an attempt to split open and displace the sense of a lifeworld fully totalized by war—serves as a good point of departure to reflect upon the tension that is central to the ways in which modernist literature processes the experience of war as a productive and traumatic form of displacement. On the one hand, this tension is expressed in the cosmopolitan drive inherent to modernism, a drive that reacts to war (as to other experiences of historical dislocation) by inscribing aesthetic agency within the imagined horizon of expanded transcultural communities, which are, for their part, bounded and unsettled by affective, moral, stylistic, tonal, and cultural-political practices and expectations. In turn, these cultural-political practices are the affective and epistemological frames that made possible the emergence of an asymmetric and uneven field of global modernist exchanges, attributions, translations, importations, appropriations, and misreadings (Berman, *Modernist Fiction*; Walkowitz, *Cosmopolitan Style*; Lyon, "Cosmopolitanism and Modernism"; Siskind, *Cosmopolitan Desires*). On the other hand, war threatens to dissolve this cosmopolitan spatialization of the world, which suggests a wide-open space of imagined universality, thus providing modernist artists from all over the globe with a horizon of experimentation that makes use of displaced materials, practices, and perspectives bearing the marks of violence as a way of processing a bellic interpellation that constitutes the specificity of what could be termed an ideology of modernist war-form.

I am interested in the different ways in which modernist aesthetic forms make themselves available to be shaped or shattered by an experience of war whose most evident trace in the arts is the disruption of the general order of signification. If Edward Said affirms that "the formal dislocations and displacements of modernist culture, and most strikingly its pervasive irony . . . include a response to the external pressures on culture from the *imperium*" (*Culture and Imperialism*, 188), the same can be suggested about the weight of the experience and imaginaries of war in their formal and tonal mediations. But the literary corpora within which modernist criticism is trapped is too narrow, particularly to understand the interactions between experimental literature and world wars. In this sense, in the second half of this essay, I will focus on World War I and attempt to deprovincialize the prevalently North Atlantic (mostly British) literary corpus through which the Anglophone critical tradition has reterritorialized the signifying potential of world wars.

The comparative perspective of global modernisms opens up the question of cultural difference, distance, and proximity between different sets of world war writings: what do we make of the privilege that the modernist critical tradition affords to British, French, German, and North American (and sometimes Italian) literature on the Great War, in the face of the vast and unexplored Latin American, Asian, and African archives? I argue that the canon's privileged status depends on a fiction of objective proximity to the corpses spread across the battlefields of Liege, Verdun, or Gallipoli (the naturalizing of Western European countries' contiguity to some original moment of war violence is reduplicated in the acritical assumption that their affective investment is nationally determined). Perhaps more important than the exclusion of new corpora of texts is that this critical hegemony overlooks the complex construction of affective proximity constitutive of war writings regardless of their geographical distance from, or national commitment to, the scene of death and suffering. This comparative approach traces new mappings of modernist engagements with the war, rearranged so that they are no longer nationally mediated but rather structured around a global economy of discourses and affects. That is, it is a geopolitical redistribution of the representation and feeling (signification and bodily experience) of distance and proximity to death in conflict, where metropolitan and marginal interventions are seen not through the hegemony of the canon but as differential responses to the universal interpellation posed by the Great War.

The making and unmaking of the modernist cosmopolitan world during war is prefigured by Mansilla in the battlefields of Paraguay. Composed as a letter addressed to his friend, the Chilean Santiago Arcos, who was residing in Paris at that time, Mansilla bridges the gap between France and Paraguay and reinscribes the ennui that Baudelaire had codified as a general modern condition in the context of the Paraguayan war. Mansilla's war ennui does not refer to the individual soldier's "pathological withdrawal caused by the repetitive shock of shells" that Carl Krockel wrote about in the context of World War I (*War Trauma and English Modernism*, 15) and that Siegfried Sassoon had thematized in his poem "Survivors" (1918). Instead his ennui points to Baudelaire's "The world, monotonous and small, today, / Yesterday, tomorrow, always, shows us our image: / An oasis of horror in a desert of ennui!" ("Le voyage," 291). Mansilla translates Baudelaire's meaning of ennui—a traumatized aesthetic relation to bourgeois urban modernization—into the grammar of the battlefield, where his contrived, artificial, and transgressive apathy rewrites the eventful exceptionality of war into a discourse on the same unbearable and repetitive nature of everyday life ("everyday the same thing") that can be read in Baudelaire's poem. These translations and resignifications are meaningful less as counterintuitive provocations than as the world-making and world-dislocating maneuvers constitutive of modernism's ambivalent discursive relation to social and political instrumentalizations of violence. And it is these kinds of uses of violence that gave rise to symbolic and imaginary condensations capable of producing both worlds and the conditions in which the signifying structures that give rise to them are threatened.

In the case of Mansilla, a world comes into being in the relation of contiguity he creates between the jaded feeling of annoyed weariness in the combat zone among trenches and enemies and the ennui he projects onto his friend Santiago Arcos in a Paris marked by bourgeois sameness and homogeneous mediocrity ("the sameness of life in that old Europe"). Paris, as the Argentine and Latin American master signifier of the dandy's ennui (via Baudelaire *and* Arcos), brings about a comparative and transcultural modernist estrangement of the Paraguayan war—not just a playful exercise in defamiliarization (as it has often been read) but the inscription of a local South American war and of Mansilla's own aestheticized subjectivity within a global field of modernist signification. As Mary A. Favret has suggested, epistemological uncertainty and instability constitute "the very texture of wartime mediation, of wartime *as* mediation" (*War at a Distance*, 5). Mansilla writes against the backdrop of the experience of war, which is always inscribed in the territorial and cultural particularity of the locales where its violence is felt most immediately as a concrete social relation. From his particular position on a battlefield in Tuyutí, he articulates a mediated world of modernist literary reappropriations structured around the internal geomodernist differences that prevent its totalization, where experimental literature continues to perform ethical and political tasks.

On the other hand, and working in the opposite direction, when Mansilla climbs a precarious battery merlon and looks at the war upside-down between his legs, he decomposes the unbearable order of a world at war, inverting the visual signifiers of the traumatic experience of proximity with the carnage taking place around him. And at the same time, he undermines the consistency of his own aestheticized self-representation as a disinterested dandy. If in a first maneuver Mansilla renders visible the effaced traces of a transatlantic network of modernist exchanges, the breakdown of the world provoked by its inversion is akin to the ways in which modernisms worked through the dislocation of the possibility of the world produced by the relatively immediate or highly mediated experience of war. With the concept of dislocation I intend to point to the impossibility, introduced by the traumatic eruption of war, of an experience of the world as a totality of meaning transparent to itself that can then be represented in discourse: "a social totality that lacks the mirror of its own representation is an incomplete social totality and, consequently, not a social totality at all" (Laclau, *Emancipations*, 85). War dislocates the order of representation that signifies the world as the categorical negotiation of local and distant, intimate and foreign effects of spatiality, temporality, and cultural content. And modernist discursive practices worked through the social and subjective meaning of the war's dislocation. This took place not only in the realm of modernist art but also in the discourse of psychoanalysis; in fact, Freud's 1915 essay "Thoughts on War and Death" deals entirely with the sense of social and subjective dislocation he was witnessing at the outset of World War I.

During the first two decades of the twentieth century, prolific in colonial wars across the globe, modernist and avant-garde war literature (a pleonasm of sorts because *avant-garde* is itself a military designation) registered this experience of dislocation and breakdown of the world both at the level of representation and in their self-reflective turn to the historicity and materiality of their own form, techniques, perspectives, and archives. In this context, modernist artists shattered and reinvented them against the euphoric or resigned backdrop of a generalized aesthetic drive to mourn the world that political and military violence was tearing apart or to reassemble it in opposition to the values of liberal/bourgeois cultural and aesthetic institutions while that very world was in the process of being demolished (Sherry, *The Great War and the Language of Modernism*).

Modernist and avant-garde experimentation and subversions tended to empty out the historical specificity of concrete suffering or nationalist ecstasy around particular wars and social upheaval, to turn them into a trope that indicated a desire for artistic revolution, breaking with the past, and calling for the violent destruction of the existing boundary between the aesthetic and extra-aesthetic spheres that the radical change of sensibility brought on by the war was rendering obsolete. F. T. Marinetti's 1909 "Futurist Manifesto" is perhaps the classical case of this kind of *euphoria belli*. He defines the group's program as an inversion of Clausewitz's famous dictum that "war is a continuation of politics by other means." For Marinetti, artistic practice is the continuation of war in the cultural realm: "We intend to exalt aggressive action . . . Poetry must be conceived as a violent attack on unknown forces . . . We will glorify war—the world's only hygiene . . . We will destroy the museums, libraries, academies of every kind, will fight moralism, feminism, every opportunistic or utilitarian cowardice" (251).

Blaise Cendrars's *La prose du transsibérien et de la petite Jehanne de France* (1913) (Trans-Siberian prose and of Little Jeanne of France) is a far cry from the exaltation of war as the master signifier of new aesthetic horizons in the futurist/avant-gardist fantasy (shared on the eve of the First World War by modernists such as Robert Musil, Thomas Mann, or Apollinaire, who soon after, by 1915, regretted their initial enthusiasm). In Cendrars's poem, published as a two-meter long, vertical, accordion-style, unfolding *antibook* (or "*livre* simultané," as he called it, referring to the interaction between his text and Sonia Delaunay-Terk's *pochoir* painterly interventions of the text), an adolescent "mauvais poète" travels from Moscow to Harbin in China through the devastated landscape of the Russo-Japanese War of 1904–1905—a transnational geography marked by the impact of war on the subjectivity of the migrant poetic I.

Cendrars's poem is structured around a constitutive formal tension that defines the experience of war that is central to the poem. On the one hand, the diachronic lineality is inscribed in the possibility of reading the poem without pause; its unfolded objectual materiality mimics the extension of the long, oppressive journey through a bloody Russian-Mongolian steppe. On the other, the folds of the accordion-like nonbook and the arbitrary changes in typography create a deliberate effect of dislocation, fragmentation, and discontinuity, an effect, in turn, exacerbated by the uneven rhythm of a poem continually interrupted by the unrelenting imagery of war, death, and suffering: "the artillery rumbled, it was war / Hunger cold plague cholera / And the muddy waters of the Amur carrying along millions of corpses." These violent disruptions in the linear temporality of the train's eastbound progress is reduplicated in the breakdown of language's poeticity into an affective babble that infantilizes the lover-companion: "Jeanne, Jeannette, Ninette, nini, nono, titty / Ma-mi my-me my poopoo my Peru / Dodo dolly dildo / Cuddle cunt / Mud pie sweet heart." The fragmentation of the trajectory and of the reading experience produces a dislocation of the poetic subject's self-representation, now lost in a universe suffocated by war, as well as of poetry's condition of possibility, now dislocated amid sick and starving bodies and corpses lined up by the side of the train tracks: "Overheated madness bellows in the locomotive / The plague cholera arises on our road like burning embers / We disappear in the war completely in a tunnel / Hunger, the whore, clings to the clouds as it spreads / And battle droppings are in rancid heaps of corpses." This is a discursive and formal interrogation of war as a dislocating experience that "anticipates the Great War in uncanny ways" (Perloff, "The Great War and the European Avant-Garde," 156).

Indeed, in spite of the many wars that were fought, written, and overwritten across the globe since the last quarter of the nineteenth century and until World War II, the critical tradition agrees that no conflict is as inextricably linked to the modernist aesthetic intervention as the First World War, which "scored a profound disruption into prevailing standards of value and so opened the space in cultural time in which radical artistic experimentation would be fostered" (Sherry, "The Great War and Literary Modernism," 113). The 1914–1918 Great War's difference as well as its preeminent place in the discourse of modernity—its being "phenomenologically and ontologically discontinuous with earlier modes of warfare" (Norris, *Writing War in the Twentieth Century*, 16)—have been explained through its traumatic social, technological, and discursive historical particularities: the sheer scale of death and suffering; the mobilization of entire economies in service of the war effort; the novel application of modern technology to mass killing (the submarine, the airplane, the tank, hand grenades, trench mortars, poison gas, military radios, range finders for artillery, the machine gun); and the discursive conceptualization of the conflict as a "total war," defined by its all-pervasiveness and the dissolution of the boundary between combatants and civilian populations to the point that no inhabitant of a warring nation lived or worked outside of the war effort (Mieszkowski, "Great War, Cold War, Total War," 213–214).

Regardless of whether these phenomena were truly new, and beyond the specifically Euro-colonial determinations of the actual conflict, the global nature of the event revealed itself in cultural fields across the world. The proliferation of markedly local engagements with the war were interconnected with local political and cultural contingencies (different in Latin America than, say, in India) while also articulating universalist imaginaries of a world-historical crisis of modernity. These articulated defensive universalist discourses clustered around a threat to the representation of "humanity at large." But in spite of a vast archive of global responses to the war that remains largely untapped, the modernist critical tradition, sustained by the majority of specialists in Anglophone literatures, continues to focus on the provincial North Atlantic specificity of this relation because "the specifically British record of the war remains the most popular, the most powerful and affective" (Sherry, "Introduction," 8).

When I describe this approach to the critical and literary interrogations of the First World War as *provincial*, I follow Dipesh Chakrabarty's concept and its attempt to undermine the assumed ontological privilege of hegemonic experiences of modernity (and, in this case, of world war modernism) in order to open the possibility of writing plural, *geomodernist* histories of the engagement with the war. The goal of this global approach is to undo the self-universalizing critical assumption of an organic relation between the ways in which these (British, French, German, and North American) modernist corpora process the symbolic dimensions of World War I and the homogeneously conceived national culture that constitutes the texts' first and most prevalent horizon of signification. The task then would be to deprovincialize the 1914–1918 Great War. We need to understand—beyond the localized immediacy of the incalculable sorrow over deaths and injuries nationally mourned—the worldliness of world wars as it is actualized in a global cultural field that becomes visible through worldwide, localized modernist reinscriptions, translations, and interventions of these wars' *civilizational* meaning, and we also need to understand that these displaced symbolic reappropriations are marked by differentiated affective representations of distance from and proximity to the dislocation of experience produced by conflict and by the disjointed temporalities that structure their global relations.

A global interrogation of the modernist experience of the First World War (along the lines of Santanu Das's *Race, Empire, and First World War Writing* but going beyond the still-narrow scope of European imperialism) demands opening new lines of collective research to unearth new bodies of modernist writings whose language, structure, and intent registered the radical dislocation of a war whose world-historical impact produced moral and aesthetic realignments across the globe. It is not a question of merely incorporating hitherto unknown texts by marginal modernist writers, texts that might run the risk of being seen merely as degraded imitations of their European counterparts because of their countries' supposed lack of immediate implication in the war and their affective distance from the tragedy of the war, thus fulfilling a supplemental logic (Derrida, *Of Grammatology*) that would reproduce the hegemony of a fossilized and restricted corpus of modernisms and avant-gardes, from Pound, Eliot, H.D., Ford, Woolf, D. H. Lawrence, and Wyndham Lewis to Apollinaire, Proust, Marinetti, D'Annunzio, Jünger, Mann, Zweig, E. E. Cummings, Hemingway, and Dos Passos, among others.

Unquestionably, the task of deprovincializing the experience of dislocation brought on by the war, of analyzing the ways in which modernists from different latitudes displaced and resignified the war, is a collective undertaking that could begin with an analysis of Liang Qichao and Shao Piaoping's reinvention in the vernacular of the generic protocols of journalism, poetic prose, and pamphletary agitation, to shed new light on the putative foreignness of the war and set it next to a vernacular demand for political and cultural reform in China. Alternatively, it could begin with the displaced representation of victory and defeat, militarism and liberal pacifism, through the migrations of Japanese characters in New York and Paris in the narratives of Shimazaki Tōson, Miyamoto Yuriko, and Natsume Sōseki, looking at their idiosyncratic appropriations of the modern European novel's formal traits. Or it could start with Rabindranath Tagore's astute ambivalence regarding the implications of the war for the Indian colonies, showing enthusiasm for Bengali youths taking part of the war as volunteers side by side British soldiers so that "we should at once become real to them, and claim fairness at their hands ever after" and simultaneously critiquing the war and anticipating the crisis of British imperialism (Featherstone, "Colonial Poetry of the First World War," 181).

With the exception of Tagore's essays on the war, which were written originally in English, none of the Chinese and Japanese texts have been translated, and the same goes for (paraphrasing Margaret Cohen) *the great world war unread* that scholars of global modernism will tap in the near future (Cohen, *The Sentimental Education of the Novel*, 23). Because of my area of expertise, I have identified a body of poems, novels, chronicles, essays, travelogues, and personal diaries of Latin American and Spanish modernist world war writings triggered by the desire to uphold the Allied cause (with special emphasis on France and French culture, for reasons I will analyze in relation to Vicente Huidobro's war poetry and that were largely shared in the wider Latin American literary field) and to cancel the geographical distance between their marginal subject positions and the cultures they saw under attack. This corpus includes poems and poetic prose by Rubén Darío, Ricardo Güiraldes, Vicente Huidobro, Ramón del Valle Inclán, and Salomón de la Selva; essays and chronicles by Amado Nervo, Enrique Gómez Carrillo, José Rodó, and the brothers Ventura and Francisco García Calderón; and fictional narratives by Vicente Blasco Ibáñez, Alejandro Sux, and Augusto D'Halmar.

The most obvious consequence of this deprovincializing gambit would be a rearrangement of the mandated canon of works that has become a staple of Anglophone scholarship on the war (poets of great national significance like Wilfred Owen, Isaac Rosenberg, and Siegfried Sassoon would perhaps seem less relevant in the context of a global proliferation of world war literature). But perhaps more meaningful is the fact that a comparative approach that analyzes the modernist responses to the global spread of differential experiences of the war presupposes a shift away from interpretations of crucial modernist works in rather unmediated relation to the ways in which a single privileged nation or cultural region (the English Channel and the North Sea) has worked through concrete public discourses on victimized or heroicized forms of identity. Especially if these particularized cultural identities are a result of a *world* war whose world-historical, opaque, and overwhelming eventfulness resides, for global modernisms precisely in its power to universalize the demand of aesthetic symbolizations across the planet and to render evident a wider map of affective relational positions, both distant and close by, vis-à-vis its traumatic nature.

For example, the very transcultural nature of modernist form (or, at least, of modernism understood as a global and disjoint drive toward formal and anti-institutional modes of experimentation) should invite us to avoid isolating the middle chapter of Woolf's *To the Lighthouse*, "Time Passes," with its dramatization of death and loss during the war (within and without battlefields), as a form of aesthetically mediated mourning that keeps the war at once close and far away from the Ramsay family household and from other modernist imaginings of the distant echoes of the war. I am proposing to read Woolf in relation to modes of aesthetic and affective distancing of marginal modernists who needed to negotiate, in their figurative language and generic inscriptions, their ambivalent place as non-Europeans within the dislocated global mappings of a war that rearranged the scales of affective distance and proximity from its traumatic core. The muffled symbolization of the impact of traumatic loss in the Ramsay household has led to apt and legitimate codifications of the mediated account of war in *To the Lighthouse*, in terms of its gendered specificity ("Woolf presents a unique feminist vision of the social context of war . . . her focus is not war action in itself but the war as felt and experienced at home"; Neimneh, "Literature of a Crisis," 126). But that same mournful distance and self-exclusion from the public ritualization of death in war that so much of World War I British poetry commodifies (Owen and Sassoon come to mind, among others) could be read in comparative contiguity with marginal modernist writers who perceive their unstable place to be closer or further away from the drama of war according to their identification with the cause of one faction or another or their estrangement from war itself.

In August 1914, while living in Buenos Aires and impeded from making another one of his regular pilgrimages to Paris, the Argentine Ricardo Güiraldes—notorious for having penned in 1926 the classic *Don Segundo Sombra* (Don Segundo Sombra: shadows on the Pampas), a postsymbolist novel that reworked the *gauchesque* tradition through a shadowy, imaginary character—decided to write a month-long poetic-prose diary of his experience from across the Atlantic of the eruption of the war in Europe, which he titled "Notas sobre la primera guerra europea" (Notes on the first European war). It was only published half a century after his death, and it remains entirely overlooked by a Latin American critical tradition that has also ignored the symbolic participation of Latin America in the global circulation of World War I literature. The diary begins on August 1 by taking stock of the affective register of the event and dating his intervention: "Immense meaning in the blood tableau . . . Never in the past has a cataclysm of equal planetary sorrow oppressed Man. Never have oppression and disgrace been so universal. To be of this century, to be in the moment and to be able to write on the very same day: August 1st 1914" (Güiraldes, *Guerra, violencia, dignidad*, 25). And every day during the next thirty days, the first month of the war, he writes his poetic prose on the events of the previous days, which he reads about in the local newspapers.

Woolf's *To the Lighthouse* alludes to the traumatic traces of war through its estranged dislocated grammar and the construction of emptiness in the Ramsey house, a narrative artifice that mediates the novel's construction of distanced proximity (or the other way around) from the war. From a markedly different politicocultural context, Güiraldes's diary delineates the contours of an affective closeness based on the slowed-down temporality of a day-by-day experience of war from afar. Güiraldes juxtaposes and interchanges yesterday's partial victory or defeat with occurrences in his everyday life in Buenos Aires, in which he wishes to be more useful to the cause of the allies and participates in gatherings downtown with fellow supporters of France and England. And most significantly, the diary constantly foregrounds the unsolved question of the obvious objective distance between Buenos Aires and the Western Front's trenches, in relation to the voluntaristic political and aesthetic construction of his affective proximity: "It's eleven at night in Buenos Aires. After the effervescence of cataclysms that has agitated her during the day, it quiets down darkly. Europe dawns over the mortal threat of armies" (26–27), and "I don't suffer from the indifference of the Pampas" (25).

Perhaps the most effective way of understanding the ways in which modernist war literature articulates its mediated proximity to war (by continually foregrounding the dislocated gap between discourse and the actual experience of violence) is by contrasting it with a highly visible subset of nonmodernist testimonial world war fiction. This war fiction is based on firsthand combat experience that authorizes its discursive stance through a binarist opposition of poet-soldiers versus civilian-writers—a differentiation that has become a common trope in the critical tradition (Cole, "People in War," 25). Modernist literature and what I will call testimonial moralist fiction present two strikingly different ways of conceiving the relation between language and literature, the traumatic exceptionality of the war, and the imaginary manners in which they articulate their symbolic proximity to or distance from the war.

Moralist testimonial fiction is inscribed within what Kate McLoughlin calls the "representational imperative" of war literature, marked by the need to understand; to record, memorialize, and achieve contingent political goals in relation to traumatized combatants and home audiences by methods such as catharsis and reparation; or to promote peace and, in more general terms, to restore meaning and reinstitute the order of general signification disrupted by war (*Authoring War*, 7). Underneath this representational imperative lies a moralist mandate to bear witness that depends on a manifest confidence in the capability of language to access and convey "a precise idea of the horror of these great massacres" (Barbusse, *Under Fire*, quoted in Winter's introduction, ix). No text fulfills this self-imposed duty like Henri Barbusse's *Le feu* (*Under Fire*), a fictionalization of the author's service on the Western Front from the beginning of the war until the end of 1915 when, sick and exhausted, he was discharged, condecorated, and reassigned to a desk job. There, during the first months of 1916, he wrote a novel that uncovered the subhuman life and death of common soldiers in the trenches with the deliberate intention of condemning the war as the cemetery of "thirty million slaves who have been thrown on top of one another by crime and error" (7). The narrator is a soldier recording his days in the festering mud of the trenches with a cast of French soldier-characters from different sociocultural backgrounds meant to represent the French People being sacrificed, something the novel achieves by emphasizing their different idiosyncratic sociolects and by repeating the slippage from a singular to a plural subject of enunciation, from "I" to "We." It is a narrative of populist realism organized around an aesthetic of testimonial denunciation invested in the rhetorical construction of an effect of immediacy. Many of the most notable texts in World War I literary anthologies fit well within this critical characterization of Barbusse's *Le feu*—from poetry by Owen, Sassoon, and Rosenberg; popular fiction like Vicente Blasco Ibáñez's *Los cuatro jinetes del apocalipsis* (The four horsemen of apocalypse); and even venerable modernists like Joseph Conrad, who wrote the rather simplistic short story "The Tale" (Cedric Watts calls it "morally affirmative and patriotically traditional"; "Joseph Conrad and World War I," 203), written to reinforce morale at the home front rather than opening a space of semantic ambivalence around the war, as his most remarkable novels had done with the colonial enterprise.

The opacity of modernist literary forms, on the other hand, presupposes an entirely different aesthetic manner of assimilating the dislocation of the order of signification at the heart of a world at war. And perhaps more significantly, they are marked by a lack of confidence in the possibility of literature, of discourse, to penetrate the traumatic core of the war and represent the undoing, by the technological organization of mass killing, of the belief in the civilizational values that once sustained the institution of literature. What is at stake in modernist forms is the ultimate impossibility of understanding war, of transcending it and gaining some knowledge from it that might be capitalized on in the achievement of progressive goals. Barbusse wrote his novel as an effective tool to attain specific ethical and political progressive goals, such as the end of hostilities and reparation for war victims (he created and donated the proceeds from sales to a veterans' organization, ARAC, Association Républicaine des Anciens Combattants). To the contrary, modernist war aesthetics lay bare the levels of mediation that underlie all representational forms and point to the immensity of the task of accounting for the traumatic kernel of loss and death on a scale unknown before 1914—a task that can only be tackled obliquely, disclosing its dislocating effects through the historicity of its form and materials.

The critical tradition has read this formal investment in terms of rupture, viewing dialectical overcoming and estranged newness as an immanent protest against "bourgeois ideals of rational progress and self-presence" (Nicholls, *Modernisms*, 98) or as an interruption of social modernization and rationalization "refusing to communicate according to established socioeconomic contracts" (Eysteinsson and Liska, "Introduction," 7). But war and social upheaval politicized modernist literature, inscribing in its form the elusive and traumatic experience of violence and loss. At the same time, the analysis of the ways in which a wide array of experimental aesthetic practices grapple with the traumatic core of war belies Peter Bürger's affirmation of an irreconcilable difference between modernism and the avant-garde based on the former's conservative fetishism of novelty as opposed to the latter's revolutionary purpose (Bürger, *Theory of the Avant-Garde*, 55): in the face of war, their historical and cultural differences are overshadowed by the relation of contiguity to the extreme experience of violence, an experience that turns them into the aesthetic grounds of an oblique and radical politicization of form.

This experimental production of texts is structured by the dislocating effects of war and articulated by a language that cannot derive moral certainties or historical truths out of the experience of radical violence because such certainties and truths can no longer be enunciated on solid epistemic ground. This dynamic can be read in two related series of poems by Guillaume Apollinaire and Vicente Huidobro, written from decidedly different positions of enunciation. In Apollinaire's *Calligrammes: poèmes de la paix et da la guerre, 1913–1916*, a voluminous book that gathers prewar poems presenting the most radical and well-known calligrammatic experiments (the "peace" section alluded in the title) as well as others written at the front in Champaign, where he was an infantryman until he suffered a head injury from an exploding shell in 1916. Almost every poem written after August 1914 deals with the war both as theme and affective background or as the traumatic trace that can be glimpsed in the cracks of their shattered form, typographical variations, and in the voids and sharp angles of verses violently, vertically, obliquely spread across the page, hand drawn, typed, and decentered.

In tension with the construction of a moralistic proximity to the scene of the war that is crucial to the testimonial function of world war literatures, Apollinaire's poems alternatively withdraw from the war and step into close affective contact with it. On the one hand, the figurative artifice of the calligrams in the collection produce a mode of distancing, sustained by the visual mimesis of words forming objects, as in "La mandoline, l'oeillet et le bamboo" (*Calligrammes*, 112–113), a poem whose words delineate the shape of the three objects alluded to in the title in order to refer to the trembling earth during battle that sounds "like a mandolin" and whose circularity suggests comparisons to the piercing sound of a bullet entering a human body but also to a statement of principles for art and love ("la verité car la raison c'est ton art femme [the truth for reason is your art woman]"), a normative dimension of avant-garde poetry that turns up again in the figuration of the carnage but now as an aesthetic "law of odors"; or in "2e Cannonier Conducteur" (124–125), where the militarily and sexually traumatic experience of "the whole artillery" is represented by the contours of a phallic rifle and where the nostalgic remembrance of Paris from the trenches draws the outline of an erect Eiffel Tower.

But before and after the calligrammatic imagination of the collection, where the figurative ambition is abandoned in favor of typographic, structural, and imagistic discontinuities, Apollinaire bridges the affective gap he deliberately opened by foregrounding the mimetic drive to outline the shape of exploding shells, represented by diagonal and upward disfigured verses, or of blind soldiers under the rain and "the liquid moon of Flanders," with its verses broken down into syllables arranged as streams of water ("Du coton dan les Oreilles," 288–289). Instead, the noncalligrammatic poems explore the possibilities of proximity as intimacy under war conditions or, rather, the potentiality of poetic language to address the dislocated affective state of frontline subjectivities, of subjects penetrated by the distressed and displaced factuality of war, rather than the moralistic interpellations it may bring about: "And their faces grew pale / And their sobs were broken / Like snow on pure petals / Or your hands on my kisses / Fell the autumn leaves" ("Le Départ," 300–301). Or the defamiliarization of war through protosurrealist imagery: "A bottle of champagne is artillery yes or no . . . Hello soldiers you bottles of champagne in which the blood ferments" ("Le vigneron champenois,"

302–303); and of the disrupted perception of temporal sequentiality: "bursting gunfire / Fades before it happens" ("Carte postale," 306–307); and the chaotic polyphony of the trenches, where fossilized military discourse ("Halt" or "Central combat sector / Contact by sound") is displaced when juxtaposed with images of a world colonized by war as symbolic totality ("Before the war we had only the surface / of the earth and the seas / After it we'll have the depths / Subterranean and aerial space" ["Guerre," 160–163]); and the introduction of pentagrams as graphical representations of the poetic musicality of war ("Venu de Dieuze," 198–201).

The formal experimentation around the war in the poems the Chilean Vicente Huidobro wrote between 1916 and 1917—between Santiago de Chile, Buenos Aires, and Paris—illuminates a different mode of articulating the distance from the war as an inescapable context of production and provides a counterpoint to think about war modernisms within comparative frames of signification. Until Huidobro's arrival in Paris in 1916, the only reference in his poetry to the war that had been going on for two years could be found in "Año nuevo" (New year), a poem he had included in *El espejo de agua* (The mirror of water), which was published only a few months before in Buenos Aires, where he had first articulated the aesthetic horizon of *creacionismo*'s notion of antimimetic autonomy. Very soon after his arrival in the French capital, Huidobro became close friends with the international community of avant-gardists in Paris (most especially with Picasso, Picabia, Miró, Ernst, Breton, Tzara, Cendrars, and Pound) and founded, together with Apollinaire, Pierre Reverdy, and Max Jacob, the influential Dadaist and cubist journal *Nord-Sud*. Simultaneously, he started rewriting in French many of the poems of *El espejo de agua* and began producing new ones in Spanish *and* French that would integrate the collection *Horizon carré / Horizonte cuadrado* (Square horizon), which he would publish there in December 1917.

In the new poems he wrote beginning in late 1916 in Spanish and French (with the help of the cubist painter Juan Gris; Huidobro admitted that his knowledge of French was ostensibly insufficient), the war is present as a haunting allusion to fear, death, tears, anguish, and things destroyed, dead airplanes—a military/technological image that became a topos of modernist literature (Schnapp, "Propeller Talk"; Saint-Amour, "Air War Prophecy and Interwar Modernism"): "El miedo se esparce por el aire / La peur se déroule dans l'aire" ("Medianoche / Minuit"); "Un poco de muerte tiembla en los rincones / Un peu de mort tremble dans tous les coins" ("El hombre triste / L'homme triste"); "Ahora ya no podrás llorar / Maintenant tu ne pourras pleurer" ("Otoño / Automne"); "De noche La alcoba se inunda UN GRITO LLENO DE ANGUSTIA / La nuit La chambre s'inonde UN CRI PLEIN D'ANGOISSE" ("Obscuridad / Noir"); "Pero los gritos que atraviesan los techos no son de rebeldía A pesar de los muros que sepultan LA CRUZ DEL SUR Es el único avión que subsiste / Mais les cris qui enfoncent les toits ne son pas de révolte Malgré les murs qui ensevelissent LA CROIX DU SUD Est le seul avion qui subsiste" ("Aeroplano / Aeroplane"). But of these signifiers of war-induced sorrow in *Horizon carré / Horizonte cuadrado* (some transposed and resignified from their previous monolingual iteration, some written into the self-translations/rewritings), the most remarkable is the radical transformation of the poem "Año Nuevo":

> Y las gentes que bajan a la tela
> Arrojaron su carne como un abrigo viejo.
> La película mil novecientos dieciséis
> Sale de una caja.
> La guerra europea.
> Llueve sobre los espectadores
> Y hay un ruido de temblores.
> Detrás de la sala
> Un viejo ha rodado al vacío

In this Spanish version, written in Buenos Aires and included in *El espejo de agua*, World War I is invoked from a distance as "La guerra europea": far from the immediate reality of death and destruction, the war is a film sent from Europe in a box, projected onto a screen for skinned spectators. Eduardo Mitre explains that the linearity of the poem establishes a relation of anecdotal causality between the movie's boxed provenance and its projection, which reinforces the sense of a removed exteriority regarding the conflict (*Vicente Huidobro*, 70). However, the most noteworthy marker of distance is the *europea* predicate pointing to the gap separating the poem from a war deliberately branded as foreign. When Huidobro reconceived the poem in Paris in 1917 and rewrote it both in Spanish and French as "Año nuevo / Nouvel an," its very shattered form recorded the new dislocating proximity with the war he had found in Europe (see figures 17.1 and 17.2).

In the recast poem, the war is no longer European; it is neither alien nor distant. The war is simply GUERRA (WAR), close by, imminent and massive, unavoidable and destabilizing: the diachronic temporal continuity expressed

NOUVEL AN

L'echelle de Jacob
            n'était pas un rêve

Un oeil s'ouvre devant la glace
Et les gens qui descendent
            sur l'écran

Ont déposé leur chair
            comme un vieux pardessus

LE FILM 1916   *GUERRE*

      SORT D'UNE BOITE

La pluie tombe devant les spectateurs

Derrière la salle

UN VIELLARD A ROULE DANS LE VIDE

FIGURE 17.1

AÑO NUEVO

La escala de Jacob
            no era un sueño

Un ojo se abre frente al espejo
Y las gentes que bajan
            a la pantalla

Dejaron su carne
            como un abrigo viejo

LA PELICULA 1916   *GUERRA*

      SALE DE UNA CAJA

La lluvia cae ante los espectadores

Detrás se la sala

UN VIEJO HA RODADO AL VACIO

FIGURE 17.2

in the verse's linearity of the previous version has been disrupted, dislocated. The oblique, destabilized, and destabilizing presence of the war now occupies an undecidable place in relation to the film: either the signifier WAR overflows and overwhelms the film and/or the box, falling over the spectators, or WAR is the cry of lacerated spectators that unsettles the year 1916—the cinematic experience of the year in which Huidobro arrived in Paris from across the Atlantic, unprepared to deal with the proximity of the war that the first version of the poem symbolized from a safe distance.

The strikingly different situations of a soldier-modernist like Apollinaire and a Latin American poet who responds to the interpellation of war from Paris is an invitation to interrogate the relation between modernist literature and world war within a comparative interpretative frame. Both of them explore the aesthetic productivity of short- and long-range accounts of the experience of war dislocation, of the thickened or slimmed-down effect of its traumatic shock. And so, what are the relational practices that mediate the economy of cultural differences capable of grounding a truly global field of modernist war literature in French, in Spanish, and in the ineffable gap between them? Unsurprisingly, the answer to this question is "translation": the mediating practice through which marginal writers produce their cosmopolitan subjectivities within such an interlingual space, strategically posed by voluntarist marginal artists as devoid of cultural particularisms and therefore open and welcoming of those who aspire to inscribe their aesthetic discourse in relation to the universalistic potential of modernism. Of course, this universalism is highly ideological and must be analyzed in light of its concrete, particular conditions of enunciation.

It has been argued that the specificity of Latin American avant-gardes and modernisms, given their international imagination and actual exchanges with European groups, resided not in *form qua form*, in formal experimentation and in the rupturist drive they shared—with expected variations among some forty groups that published manifestos since Huidobro's *creacionismo*—but in *form qua content*, form as the historical and geocultural particularity of their discursive materials and themes and the local cultural-political determinations that orient their polemical interventions (Schwartz, *Las vanguardias latinoamericanas*; Aguilar, *Poesia concreta brasileira*, 42; Balderston, "Avant-Garde in Latin America," 45; Rosenberg, *The Avant-Garde and Geopolitics*, 78–79). A hasty analysis of *Horizon carré / Horizonte cuadrado* (and of the war poems Huidobro wrote until 1918) could lead to an interpretation of his choice to write in French in terms of a mimetic inscription in the mappings of global modernism that would reproduce the ontological privilege of French culture in the discourse of aesthetic modernity and as an attempt to erase or at least suspend their Latin American or marginal (as in non-French) difference. I propose that the distance between Huidobro and Apollinaire, and thus the possibility of conceptualizing modernism as a global relation, can be seen precisely in the Chilean's turn to French as a process of self-translation that underscores the translational nature of Latin American and marginal modernisms: translation, once again, as a need to inscribe marginal aesthetic practices in a world literary field that, in the eyes of Latin American writers, was mediated by the global hegemony of French culture, whose particularity is represented as identical with the universalist premises of cosmopolitan modernism.

In the manifesto "Le créationnisme," published in 1925 in the Parisian *Revue Mondiale*, Huidobro explained that poetry should be translatable and universal: "If for creationist poets what matters is the presentation of new facts, creationist poetry is translatable and universal, since new facts are the same in all languages" (*Obra poética*, 1332). The affirmation of the transparent and therefore translatable universality of poetry should not be understood as a descriptive dictum; Huidobro's aesthetic and critical acumen as well as his personal experience of cultural unevenness should discount such a simplistic reading. Instead, I suggest that by transposing his declaration onto the specific historicity of the war, it could be read as the conviction of a marginal Latin American avant-garde writer whose language, his lack of combat exposure, and his condition as a foreigner in a belligerent nation place him outside of the French modernist scene where he wants to intervene. Once in Paris, in the context of a war he feels the need to respond to, he inscribes the experience of dislocating proximity to death and violence in the formal *transcreation* (to borrow the term from the concrete poet Augusto de Campos) of the poem he had first written in Chile.

Thinking about British romantic war poetry, Mary A. Favret writes about the always distant place of literature with regard to war, and she explains that for these British poets, "the task was to find sentient ground for what often appeared a free-floating, impersonal military operation removed from their immediate sensory perception" (*War at a Distance*, 9). I believe this idea can be used as a stepping stone for reflecting on the way modernisms from different regions of the world—regardless of their objective geographical, political, and cultural distance from the conflict—responded to a war that was perceived as the cause of a disruption of the general field of signification and, consequently, disarranged the experience and meaning of distance, understood as it is processed by literature: as an affective relation. The aesthetic production of a "sentient ground," of an affective mediation, is not significant simply because it is constitutive of the manner in which modernist war literature offers itself as a cultural site to work through the experience of dislocation. From a comparative perspective, it is relevant because in the unexplored archive of plural, asynchronous symbolizations of these investments one can read the making of a discrete global field of war modernisms beyond Britain and France—a global field made up of contingent assemblages of affective distance and proximity from a world-historical conflict that created the conditions for the modernist fantasy of universal belonging and intimacy.

WORKS CITED

Aguilar, Gonzalo M. *Poesia concreta brasileira: as vanguardas na encruzilhada modernista*. São Paulo: Editora da Universidade de São Paulo, 2005.

Apollinaire, Guillaume. *Calligrammes: Poems of Peace and War (1913–1916)*. Bilingual ed. Trans. Anne Hyde Greet. Intro. S. I. Lockerbie. Berkeley: University of California Press, 1980.

Balderston, Daniel. "Avant-Garde in Latin America." In *Encyclopedia of Latin American and Caribbean Literature, 1900–2003*, ed. Daniel Balderston and Mike González. London: Routledge, 2004.

Barbusse, Henri. *Under Fire*. Trans. Robin Buss. Intro. Jay Winter. London: Penguin, 2003.

Baudelaire, Charles. "Le voyage." In *The Flowers of Evil*, trans. James McGowan. London: Oxford University Press, 1993.

Berman, Jessica. *Modernist Fiction, Cosmopolitanism, and the Politics of Community*. Cambridge: Cambridge University Press, 2001.

Bürger, Peter. *Theory of the Avant-Garde*. Minneapolis: University of Minnesota Press, 1984.

Cendrars, Blaise. *La prose du transsibérien et de la petite Jehanne de France*. Paris: Editions des Hommes Nouveaux, 1913.

———. "The Prose of the TransSiberian and of Little Jeanne of France." In *Complete Poems*, ed. Rod Padgett and Jay Bochner. Berkeley: University of California Press, 1993.

Chakarabarty, Dipesh. *Provincializing Europe: Political Thought and Historical Difference*. Princeton, N.J.: Princeton University Press, 2008.

Cohen, Margaret. *The Sentimental Education of the Novel*. Princeton, N.J.: Princeton University Press, 1999.

Cole, Sarah. "People in War." In *The Cambridge Companion to World Writing*, ed. Kate McLoughlin, 25–37. Cambridge: Cambridge University Press, 2009.

Das, Santanu. *Race, Empire, and First World War Writing*. Cambridge: Cambridge University Press, 2011.

Derrida, Jacques. *Of Grammatology*. Trans. Gayatri Chakravorty Spivak. Baltimore, Md.: Johns Hopkins University, 1998.

Eksteins, Modris. *Rites of Spring: The Great War and the Birth of Modern Age*. Boston: Houghton Mifflin, 1989.

Eysteinsson, Astradur, and Liska, Vivian. "Introduction: Approaching Modernism." In *Modernism*, ed. Astradur Eysteinsson and Vivian Liska. Philadelphia: John Benjamins, 2007.

Favret, Mary. *War at a Distance: Romanticism and the Making of Modern Wartime*. Princeton, N.J.: Princeton University Press, 2010.

Featherstone, Simon. "Colonial Poetry of the First World War." In *The Cambridge Companion to the Poetry of the First World War*, ed. Santanu Das. Cambridge: Cambridge University Press, 2013.

Freud, Sigmund. "Thoughts for the Times on War and Death." In *The Standard Edition of the Complete Psychological Works of Sigmund Freud*, ed. James Strachey, 14:273–300. London: Hogarth, 1953–1974.

Güiraldes, Ricardo. *Guerra, violencia, dignidad*. Ed. Ramachandra Gowda. Buenos Aires: Editorial en Buen Romance, 1984.

Huidobro, Vicente. *Obra poética*. Paris: ALLCA XX, 2003.

Krockel, Carl. *War Trauma and English Modernism: T. S. Eliot and D. H. Lawrence*. London: Palgrave Macmillan, 2011.

Laclau, Ernesto. *Emancipations*. London: Verso, 1996.

Lyon, Janet. "Cosmopolitanism and Modernism." In *Oxford Handbook of Global Modernisms*, ed. Mark Wollaeger and Matt Eatough, 387–412. Oxford: Oxford University Press, 2012.

Mansilla, Lucio V. *A Visit to the Ranquel Indians*. Trans. Eva Gillies. Lincoln: University of Nebraska Press, 1997.

Marinetti, Filippo T. "Futurist Manifesto." In *Modernism: An Anthology*, ed. Lawrence Rainey. Malden, Mass.: Blackwell, 2005.

McLoughlin, Kate. *Authoring War: The Literary Representation of War from the* Iliad *to Iraq*. Cambridge: Cambridge University Press, 2011.

Mieszkowski, Jan. "Great War, Cold War, Total War." *Modernism/modernity* 16, no. 2 (2009): 211–228.

Mitre, Eduardo. *Vicente Huidobro: hambre de espacio y sed de cielo*. Caracas: Monte Ávila Editores, 1980.

Neimneh, Shadi. "Literature of a Crisis: The Great War in Anglo-American Modernism." *International Journal of Applied Linguistics and English Literature* 1, no. 6 (2012): 122–130.

Nicholls, Peter. *Modernisms: A Literary Guide*. Berkeley: University of California Press, 1995.

Norris, Margot. *Writing War in the Twentieth Century*. Charlottesville: University of Virginia Press, 2000.

Perloff, Marjorie. "The Great War and the European Avant-Garde." In *The Cambridge Companion to Literature of the First World War*, ed. Vincent Sherry, 141–165. Cambridge: Cambridge University Press, 2005.

Rosenberg, Fernando J. *The Avant-Garde and Geopolitics in Latin America*. Pittsburgh, Penn.: Pittsburgh University Press, 2006.

Said, Edward W. *Culture and Imperialism*. New York: Knopf, 1994.

Saint-Amour, Paul K. "Air War Prophecy and Interwar Modernism." *Comparative Literature Studies* 42, no. 2 (2005): 130–161.

Sassoon, Siegfried. "Survivors." In *The War Poems of Siegfried Sassoon*, ed. Rubert Hart-Davis, 83. London: Faber and Faber, 1983.

Schnapp, Jeffrey T. "Propeller Talk." *Modernism/modernity* 1, no. 3 (1994): 153–178.

Schwartz, Jorge. *Las vanguardias latinoamericanas: textos programáticos y críticos*. México: Fondo de Cultura Económica, 2002.

Sherry, Vincent. "The Great War and Literary Modernism in England." In *The Cambridge Companion to the Literature of the Great War*, ed. Vincent Sherry, 113–137. Cambridge: Cambridge University Press, 2005.

——. *The Great War and the Language of Modernism*. Oxford: Oxford University Press, 2003.

——. "Introduction." In *The Cambridge Companion to the Literature of the Great War*, ed. Vincent Sherry, 1–11. Cambridge: Cambridge University Press, 2005.

Siskind, Mariano. *Cosmopolitan Desires: Global Modernity and World Literature in Latin America*. Evanston, Ill.: Northwestern University Press, 2014.

Walkowitz, Rebecca L. *Cosmopolitan Style: Modernism Beyond the Nation*. New York: Columbia University Press, 2006.

Watts, Cedric. "Joseph Conrad and World War I." *Critical Survey* 2, no. 2 (1990): 203–207.

Whigham, Thomas L., and Barbara Potthast. "The Paraguayan Rosetta Stone: New Insights Into the Demographics of the Paraguay War, 1864–1870." *Latin American Research Review* 34, no.1 (1999): 174–186.

Winter, Jay. "Introduction: Henri Barbusse and the Birth of the Moral Witness." In *Under Fire*, by Henri Barbusse, trans. Robin Buss, intro. Jay Winter. London: Penguin, 2003.

Woolf, Virginia. *To the Lighthouse*. London: Routledge, 1995.

APPENDIX 1

MORE VOCABULARY

Autonomy	Laughter	Screen
Backwardness	Mask	Silence
Books	Memory	Skin
Censorship	Minor	Train
Collection	Minstrel	Transit
Content	Nature	Triumph
Data	Nonsense	Understanding
Energy	North	Ventriloquism
Folk	Occident	Vernacular
Fuel	Opportunism	West
Glass	Prestige	Xenophilia
House	Production	Yesterday
Information	Question	Zone
Justice	Readers	
Knowledge	Rural	

CONTRIBUTORS

RACHEL ADAMS is professor of English and director of the Center for the Study of Social Difference at Columbia University. She is the author of *Raising Henry: A Memoir of Motherhood, Disability, and Discovery*; *Continental Divides: Remapping the Cultures of North America*; and *Sideshow USA: Freaks and the American Cultural Imagination*. She is coeditor (with Benjamin Reiss and David Serlin) of *Keywords for Disability Studies*.

JUDITH BROWN is associate professor of English at Indiana University, Bloomington, and author of *Glamour in Six Dimensions: Modernism and the Radiance of Form* (Cornell University Press, 2009). She is working on a new project called *Passive States: Style and Global Modernism*.

CHRISTOPHER BUSH is associate professor of French and comparative literary studies at Northwestern University and coeditor of the journal *Modernism/modernity*. His research and teaching focus on comparative and interdisciplinary approaches to literary modernisms, especially the interactions between European and East Asian aesthetic theory, avant-gardes, and media. His publications include *Ideographic Modernism: China, Writing, Media* (Oxford University Press, 2010) and *The Floating World: Japoniste Aesthetics and Global Modernity* (forthcoming from Columbia University Press).

DAVID DAMROSCH is Ernest Bernbaum Professor of Comparative Literature at Harvard University. A past president of the American Comparative Literature Association, David Damrosch has written widely on comparative and world literature from antiquity to the present. His books include *The Narrative Covenant: Transformations of Genre in the Growth of Biblical Literature* (1987), *We Scholars: Changing the Culture of the University* (1995), *What Is World Literature?* (2003), *The Buried Book: The Loss and Rediscovery of the Great Epic of Gilgamesh* (2007), and *How to Read World Literature* (2008). He is the founding general editor of the six-volume *Longman Anthology of World Literature* (2004), the editor of *Teaching World Literature* (2009), and the coeditor of *The Princeton Sourcebook in Comparative Literature* (2009), *The Routledge Companion to World Literature* (2011), and *Xin fangxiang: bijiao wenxue yu shijie wenxue duben* (New directions: a reader of comparative and world literature; Peking University Press, 2010). He is presently completing a book entitled *Comparing the Literatures: What Every Comparatist Needs to Know* and starting a book on the role of global scripts in the formation of national literatures.

JACOB EDMOND is associate professor of English at the University of Otago, New Zealand. He is the author of *A Common Strangeness: Contemporary Poetry, Cross-Cultural Encounter, Comparative Literature* (Fordham University Press, 2012; honorable mention for the ACLA Harry Levin Prize and ASAP book prize) and has published essays in such journals as *Comparative Literature, Contemporary Literature, Poetics Today*, and *China Quarterly*. He is currently completing a book manuscript on the poetics of iteration.

MARK GOBLE received his Ph.D. from Stanford University and has taught at the University of California, Irvine, and the University of California, Berkeley, where he is currently associate professor of English. He is the author of *Beautiful Circuits: Modernism and the Mediated Life* (Columbia University Press, 2010) and has published essays in such journals as *American Literature, Modern Fiction Studies, ELH, MLQ, ELN*, and in collections on Alfred Hitchcock and Henry James.

ERIC HAYOT is Distinguished Professor of Comparative Literature and Asian Studies at the Pennsylvania State University. He is the author of *Chinese Dreams* (2004), *The Hypothetical Mandarin* (2009), *On Literary Worlds* (2012), and *The Elements of Academic Style* (2014).

TSITSI JAJI is associate professor of English and African and African American studies at Duke University. She is the author of *Africa in Stereo: Modernism, Music, and Pan-African Solidarity* (2014), which received the African Literature Association's First Book Award and honorable mentions from ACLA and SEM, as well as a chapbook of poems *Carnaval*, featured in *Seven New Generation African Poets* (2014).

B. VENKAT MANI is Professor of German at the University of Wisconsin–Madison. He is the author of *Cosmopolitical Claims: Turkish-German Literatures from Nadolny to Pamuk* (University of Iowa Press, 2007) and *Recoding World Literature: Libraries, Print-Culture, and Germany's Pact with Books* (Fordham University Press, 2016); coeditor of three special issues, "Cosmopolitical and Transnational Approaches to German Studies" (*Transit* 2011), "What Counts as World Literature?" (*Modern Language Quarterly* 2013), and "Measuring the World" (*Monatshefte* 2016); and coeditor of Wiley-Blackwell's forthcoming *Companion to World Literature*. He has published numerous articles on cosmopolitanism, world literature, and postcoloniality. He is founder and codirector of UW-Madison's World Literature Research Workshop (2007–2014) and is codirector of the project Bibliomigrancy: World Literature in the Public Sphere (2014–2016), a Mellon Sawyer Seminar in Comparative Cultural Studies. He was Alexander von Humboldt Senior Scholar at the Institut für Buchwissenschaft, University of Leipzig and the German National Library (2011–2012).

MONICA L. MILLER is associate professor of English at Barnard College, Columbia University, in New York. She is the author of *Slaves to Fashion: Black Dandyism and the Styling of Black Diasporic Identity* (2009), which won the 2010 William Sanders Scarborough Prize for the best book in African American literature and culture from the Modern Language Association and was shortlisted for the 2010 Modernist Studies Association Book Prize. She is currently at work on two book projects: *Affirmative Actions: How to Define Black Culture in the Twenty-First Century*, which examines very contemporary black literature and culture to assess the consequences of thinking of black identity as "postblack" or "postracial," and *Blackness, Swedish Style: Race, Diaspora, and Belonging in Contemporary Sweden*, a multigenre investigation of multiculturalism, integration, and black Europeanness/Afro-Swedishness in relation to theories of diaspora and diasporic belonging.

DAVID L. PIKE is professor of literature at American University. His books include *Passage Through Hell: Modernist Descents, Medieval Underworlds* (1997), *Subterranean Cities: The World Beneath Paris and London, 1800–1945* (2005), *Metropolis on the Styx: The Underworlds of Modern Urban Culture, 1800–2001* (2007), and *Canadian Cinema Since the 1980s: At the Heart of the World* (2012). He is coauthor of *Literature: A World of Writing* (Pearson, 2012) and coeditor of the *Longman Anthology of World Literature*, and he has published widely on nineteenth- and twentieth-century urban literature, culture, and film. Current book projects include the nineteenth-century city after the nineteenth century and "Slum Lore: The Imagination of Poverty."

MARTIN PUCHNER is the Byron and Anita Wien Professor of Drama and of English and Comparative Literature at Harvard University. He is the author of *The Drama of Ideas: Platonic Provocations in Theater and Philosophy* (Oxford University Press, 2010; winner of the Joe A. Callaway Award), *Poetry of the Revolution: Marx, Manifestos, and the Avant-Gardes* (Princeton University Press, 2006; winner of the MLA's James Russell Lowell Award), and *Stage Fright: Modernism, Anti-Theatricality, and Drama* (Johns Hopkins University Press, 2002; 2011), as well as of numerous edited volumes and sourcebooks, including *Karl Marx and Friedrich Engels:* The Communist Manifesto *and Other Writings* (2005). He is the general editor of the *Norton Anthology of World Literature* and the *Norton Anthology of Western Literature*. He also writes for the *London Review of Books, Raritan, Bookforum, n+1, Public Books,* and *Inside Higher Ed.*

JAHAN RAMAZANI is University Professor and Edgar F. Shannon Professor of English at the University of Virginia. He is the author of five books: *Poetry and Its Others: News, Prayer, Song, and the Dialogue of Genres* (2013); *A Transnational Poetics* (2009), winner of the 2011 Harry Levin Prize of the American Comparative Literature Association, awarded for the best book in comparative literary history published in the years 2008 to 2010; *The Hybrid Muse: Postcolonial Poetry in English* (2001); *Poetry of Mourning: The Modern Elegy from Hardy to Heaney* (1994), a finalist for the National Book Critics Circle Award; and *Yeats and the Poetry of Death: Elegy, Self-Elegy, and the Sublime* (1990). He edited the most recent edition of the *Norton Anthology of Modern and Contemporary Poetry* (2003) and, with Jon Stallworthy, "The Twentieth Century and After" in the *Norton Anthology of English Literature* (2006, 2012). He is also an associate editor of the *Princeton Encyclopedia of Poetry and Poetics* (2012).

CHRISTOPHER REED is professor of English and visual culture at the Pennsylvania State University. His recent books include *Art and Homosexuality: A History of Ideas* (2011), the coauthored *If Memory Serves: Gay Men, AIDS, and the Promise of the Queer Past* (2012), and *The Chrysanthème Papers: The Pink Notebook of Madame Chrysanthème and Other Documents of French Japonisme*, a translation and critical introduction of a novella by Félix Régamey (2010). He has also published widely on the Bloomsbury group. A new book, *Bachelor Japanists: Japanese Aesthetics and Western*

Masculinities, is forthcoming in the Modernist Latitudes series of Columbia University Press.

EFTHYMIA RENTZOU is associate professor of French literature in the Department of French and Italian at Princeton University. She studies avant-garde and modernist literature and art, particularly poetics; the relation between image and text; social analysis of literature; politics and literature; and the internationalization of the avant-garde. Her first book, *Littérature malgré elle. Le surréalisme et la transformation du littéraire* (2010), examines the construction of literary phenomena in the production of an antiliterary movement, surrealism. She is currently working on a second book, *Concepts of the World: The Avant-Garde and the Idea of the International*, that explores the conceptualization of the "world" in the work and activities of writers and artists within and around historical avant-garde movements—futurism, dada, and surrealism—during the period 1900 through 1940.

GAYLE ROGERS is associate professor of English at the University of Pittsburgh. He is the author of *Modernism and the New Spain: Britain, Cosmopolitan Europe, and Literary History* (Oxford, 2012) and, with Sean Latham, *Modernism: Evolution of an Idea* (Bloomsbury Academic, 2015). His work has appeared in *PMLA*, *Modernism/modernity*, *Comparative Literature*, *Novel*, *Journal of Modern Literature*, *James Joyce Quarterly*, and *Revista de Estudios Orteguianos*, and in volumes including the *Oxford Handbook of Global Modernisms* (2012) and the *Cambridge Companion to the American Modernist Novel* (2015). His book *Incomparable Empires: Modernism and the Translation of Spanish and American Literature* will be published by Columbia University Press in 2016.

MARIANO SISKIND is professor of Romance languages and literatures at Harvard University. He teaches nineteenth- and twentieth-century Latin American literature with an emphasis on its world-literary relations as well as the production of cosmopolitan discourses and processes of aesthetic globalization. He is the author of over two dozen academic essays and of *Cosmopolitan Desires: Global Modernity and World Literature in Latin America* (Northwestern University Press, 2014). He has edited Homi Bhabha's *Nuevas minorías, nuevos derechos. Notas sobre cosmopolitimos vernáculos* (2013) and *Poéticas de la distancia. Adentro y afuera de la literatura argentina* (Norma, 2006) (together with Sylvia Molloy). His monograph *Latin American Literature and the Great War: On the Globality of World War I* will be published in 2017.

REBECCA L. WALKOWITZ is professor and director of graduate studies in the English Department and affiliate faculty in the Comparative Literature Program at Rutgers University. She is past president of the Modernist Studies Association and, with David James and Matthew Hart, coeditor of the book series Literature Now, published by Columbia University Press. She is the author of *Born Translated: The Contemporary Novel in the Age of World Literature* (2015) and *Cosmopolitan Style: Modernism Beyond the Nation* (2006) and the editor or coeditor of seven books, including, with Douglas Mao, *Bad Modernisms* (2006).

INDEX